Scripture People

On 9/11, many Americans were introduced to an Islamic movement called Salafism, the theological strand that includes Al Qaeda. Since then, Salafism, an important and popular movement in global Islam, has frequently been disparaged as "Radical Islam" or "Islamic fundamentalism." *Scripture People* is the first book-length study of the embattled American Salafi movement and the challenges it has faced post-9/11. Matthew D. Taylor recounts how these so-called Radical Muslims have adopted deeply rooted American forms of religious belonging and values. Through comparison with American Evangelical Christianity, informed by his own Evangelical background and studies, Taylor explores the parallel impulses, convergent identities, and even surprising friendships that have emerged between Salafis and Evangelicals in America. Offering an entry point for understanding the dynamics and disagreements among American Muslims, Taylor's volume upends narratives about "Radical Islam" by demonstrating how Salafi Muslims have flexibly adapted to American religious patterns in the twenty-first century.

MATTHEW D. TAYLOR is a scholar at the Institute for Islamic, Christian, and Jewish Studies in Baltimore. He has served on the faculty of Georgetown University and George Washington University. He holds a PhD in Religious Studies and Muslim–Christian Relations from Georgetown University and an MA in Theology from Fuller Theological Seminary.

Scripture People

Salafi Muslims in Evangelical Christians' America

MATTHEW D. TAYLOR

Institute for Islamic, Christian, and Jewish Studies

FOREWORD BY AMIR HUSSAIN

Loyola Marymount University

CAMBRIDGE
UNIVERSITY PRESS

CAMBRIDGE
UNIVERSITY PRESS

Shaftesbury Road, Cambridge CB2 8EA, United Kingdom

One Liberty Plaza, 20th Floor, New York, NY 10006, USA

477 Williamstown Road, Port Melbourne, VIC 3207, Australia

314–321, 3rd Floor, Plot 3, Splendor Forum, Jasola District Centre, New Delhi – 110025, India

103 Penang Road, #05–06/07, Visioncrest Commercial, Singapore 238467

Cambridge University Press is part of Cambridge University Press & Assessment, a department of the University of Cambridge.

We share the University's mission to contribute to society through the pursuit of education, learning and research at the highest international levels of excellence.

www.cambridge.org
Information on this title: www.cambridge.org/9781009352741

DOI: 10.1017/9781009352727

First published 2023
First paperback edition 2025

A catalogue record for this publication is available from the British Library

Library of Congress Cataloging-in-Publication data
Names: Taylor, Matthew D., 1980- author. | Hussain, Amir, 1965- writer of
    foreword.
Title: Scripture people : Salafi Muslims in Evangelical Christians' America /
    Matthew D. Taylor ; foreword by Amir Hussain.
Description: 1. | New York : Cambridge University Press, 2023. | Includes
    bibliographical references and index.
Identifiers: LCCN 2022062320 (print) | LCCN 2022062321 (ebook) |
    ISBN 9781009352765 (hardback) | ISBN 9781009352741 (paperback) |
    ISBN 9781009352727 (epub)
Subjects: LCSH: Salafῑyah–United States. | Islamic fundamentalism–United States.
Classification: LCC BP195.S18 T39 2023 (print) | LCC BP195.S18 (ebook) |
    DDC 297.8/3–dc23/eng/20230119
LC record available at https://lccn.loc.gov/2022062320
LC ebook record available at https://lccn.loc.gov/2022062321

ISBN   978-1-009-35276-5   Hardback
ISBN   978-1-009-35274-1   Paperback

*For Lyndsay, Hazel, and Abraham – my writing partners
and my life*

Contents

Foreword

At the close of the last century, I did my graduate work at the University of Toronto on Christianity and Islam, with a dissertation on Muslim communities in Toronto. Those were the heady, early days of work on the relationships between Muslims and Christians in North America. It has been a delight to see the work that has developed in that area in the first decades of this century. With this book, Dr. Matthew Taylor provides a magisterial addition to the scholarly literature, and to a better understanding of our fellow citizens. I first became aware of his work when he was a doctoral student at Georgetown University, as I had been invited to speak there about my own work, and more broadly about best practices for scholarship in the study of religion. It is a privilege to be asked to provide this brief introduction to his book.

Dr. Taylor was born into an American Evangelical family, and so is a "native informant" about those communities. His deep knowledge of Evangelical traditions, both from personal experience and scholarly study is evident in the book. This is one of the reasons why the book is so rich, because the author has such a deep understanding of the peoples that he writes about. It was, as he describes, the "scripturalism" of Evangelicals, notably their fidelity to the Bible, that drew him to another scriptural people, Salafi Muslims in America.

Both groups, Salafis and Evangelicals, are subject to broad misunderstandings within North American society, and also among their own respective traditions of Islam and Christianity. As someone who is neither an Evangelical nor a Salafi, I nonetheless understand how these groups are caricaturized and misrepresented by others. In this way, they may have more in common with each other than one might otherwise suspect. I mention this to return to the authority with which Dr. Taylor writes. He *knows* these religious traditions, knows them intimately and deeply. He is no outsider with scant knowledge, seeking to make his own point and using other people to further his own aims. As he writes in his introduction, "This book is an exercise in bridgebuilding and border-dwelling where Islam meets Christianity in America". This is an extraordinary book, and Dr. Taylor is an extraordinary scholar.

Amir Hussain
Chair and Professor of Theological Studies,
Loyola Marymount University
President, American Academy of Religion

Acknowledgments

The Georgetown University Department of Theology and Religious Studies was the uniquely interreligious setting where many of the ideas of this book were hashed out with faculty mentors, classmates, interlocutors, and friends. I am especially grateful to Paul Heck, an intrepid interreligious mentor and a good friend. Erin Cline, John O. Voll, Julia Lamm, Michael Slater, Peter Phan, Dan Madigan, Felicitas Opwis, Francisca Cho, and Yvonne Haddad all contributed to my thinking in ways that are overt and also subtle. George Marsden had been a professor and a thoughtful reader who has helpfully refined my paradigms of Evangelicalism.

My colleagues at the Institute for Islamic, Christian, and Jewish Studies have supportively stood with me in this endeavor. Their feedback, proofreading, and challenging questions have made me a better scholar and a better writer.

I am also deeply grateful to Cambridge University Press and Beatrice Rehl for believing in this project and shepherding it through all the processes of publication. I received invaluable feedback while presenting portions of this research at conferences for the American Academy of Religion, the British International Studies Association, the North American Association of Islamic and Muslim Studies, and the Christian–Muslim Studies Network.

When I was muddling through my first career as an Evangelical minister and seminary student and as I started reading and studying Salafi Muslims and finding deep affinities with them, many of my friends and Evangelical compatriots had some qualms. But through the whole crazy journey of moving cross-country, earning a PhD, raising young children, and writing this book, my wife Lyndsay has been my companion in adventure, my encouragement, and my closest ally. She deserves much of the credit for whatever is good in these pages.

Introduction

I am sitting in a large lecture hall at a local public university listening to a dynamic speaker. It's a Sunday evening, not a typical time for class, but the hall is filled. I'm surrounded by eager students, and I am awash with déjà vu.

The students are here to learn about scripture. Having paid good money to come to the weekend conference, they lean forward in their chairs, taking notes, attentively listening to the preacher/teacher who lectures from the front. He has a smoothly integrated PowerPoint presentation – he's clearly done this before. He speaks deftly, authoritatively, quoting a scripture passage to back up every point. There's a branded hashtag written on the classroom whiteboards, so participants can share about their experiences and promote the event on social media. The premise of the whole weekend is simple and graspable: Scripture gives meaning to our lives; it's connectable, applicable to our every circumstance. The whole gathering is both an educational and a devotional exercise, mixing dense intellectual engagement with ancient texts and personal spirituality and morality.

Sitting there in the audience, my brain toggles back and forth from memory to the present. In my memories, *I'm* the preacher/teacher, an Evangelical campus minister extolling and distilling straightforward lessons from the Bible for the audience of college students. In that not-so-distant past, I work for a college ministry, a nondenominational organization dedicated to gathering and empowering Evangelical young people. I'm the one with the savvy PowerPoint, exhorting about the clear and practical lessons from the Bible. It was a previous life, a previous career, a previous worldview, but it's not so long ago that I can't surface the memories in an instant.

Returning to the present, I'm reminded that, for all their familiarity, the people in this lecture hall aren't Christians. They're Muslims, who have enrolled in this weekend seminar with AlMaghrib Institute, a diffuse educational organization that conducts seminars like this all over the USA and around the world. Unlike at an Evangelical gathering, almost all of the female participants, who make up about half of the audience, wear hijabs, and they sit across the aisle from the male students out of propriety. The crowd is a diverse cross section of American youth – South Asian- and Middle Eastern-American Muslims sit alongside African American Muslims. There are a few white faces like mine, but this gathering reflects the vibrant mélange of cultures and ethnic backgrounds that make up the American Muslim community as a whole.

The lecturer/preacher at this event is something of a celebrity: Yasir Qadhi, an erudite and eloquent Pakistani American and one of the leading figures in discussions about Salafi Islam in America. He's humorous, confident – he speaks about common sense and the plain meaning of the Qur'an and the Hadith (collected memories of the sayings and deeds of the Prophet Muhammad). In the world of American Islam, Qadhi helped make AlMaghrib Institute a popular brand, a go-to establishment for religious education.

This is a book about AlMaghrib Institute, about Qadhi and his fellow instructors, about the American students who devote their weekends and free time to studying Islamic scripture. On a deeper level, this is a book about Salafism, an amorphous global movement of scripture-based reform and devotional invigoration that is the backdrop of AlMaghrib. This is a book about 9/11 and the impact it had on the American Muslim community. But it's also a book about Evangelicalism and my own religious background, the echoes I hear when I listen to Salafi preaching and discussions about scripture. I am convinced, counterintuitive as it may seem, that one of the major clues to understanding Salafism in America starts with the role Evangelicalism has played in American culture. So how did I, a former Evangelical minister, end up in Yasir Qadhi's class?

FROM EVANGELICAL MINISTRY TO
INTERRELIGIOUS SCHOLARSHIP

When I left my first career in Evangelical ministry, I found myself with more questions than answers. The theological frameworks and plain truths I'd received in my Evangelical seminary education didn't suffice anymore. I was curious about other traditions, other ways of being religious that were not Evangelical, and over time I found that I was supremely curious about Islam. I wasn't so much keen on conversion as on conversation. I was so interested, in fact, that I went and got a PhD in Islamic studies and Muslim-Christian relations.

According to the Pew Research Center, given current demographic trends, by sometime around the year 2070, the world population will be one-third Christian, one-third Muslim, and one-third everyone else.[1] Put simply, Muslim-Christian relations is a topic that pertains to a supermajority of humanity. That means that one of the most important global interreligious projects of the twenty-first century is furthering Muslim-Christian understanding. How do we help facilitate moments of recognition, of bridge-building, of sympathy, of dialogue, and of neighborliness among Christians and Muslims? That's what I primarily work on and research.

It's in that context of interfaith peacebuilding and mutuality that Salafis and Evangelicals are often presented as problems: Evangelicals are the famously sharp-elbowed American Protestants, whose populist appeals to the Bible exert great influence on American culture and politics. In the liberal interfaith spaces I inhabit now, Evangelicals (which includes most of my family and many of my oldest friends) are largely disdained as uncouth, aggressive, and politically beyond the pale. Similarly, Salafism is often cast – including by some Muslims – as the most troublesome, most fundamentalist, most rancorous form of Islam. And in Europe and the USA, where Islam is always under arduous scrutiny, Salafism is presented as the most foreign and most scary part of Islam. For example, right-wing French politicians, when they have recently sought to soften the edges of their anti-Islam bashing, will sometimes say that their goal is not to outlaw Islam but rather to "outlaw Salafism."[2]

In the USA, the public reception history of Salafism is more complicated for reasons I will explore below. "Salafism," as such, is not often discussed or recognized in the America, outside of intra-Muslim discussions and among a small range of counterterrorism and security-focused think tanks and scholars. Instead, the concept of Salafism has been translated into an assortment of more descriptive, pejorative euphemisms in American political and popular discourse: Radical Islam, Islamic fundamentalism, Saudi-exported Wahhabism – all of these are meant to signal to people like me (i.e., Americans, Western Christians) that Salafism is something strange and distant.

But what I experience when I listen to Salafis talk is ... familiar. It has a certain hard-to-explain element of homecoming for me. As I pursued my research about contemporary Islam, something about the Salafi Muslim authors and preachers I was reading and hearing felt peculiarly resonant. These flashes of familiarity only increased in tenor and frequency when I looked more closely into the Salafi discourse in America. Intrigued, I began to immerse myself in American Salafi conversations – attending that weekend conference with AlMaghrib Institute and Yasir Qadhi, listening to Salafi sermons and lectures, delving into the massive online discussions among Salafis on message boards and YouTube, interviewing Salafi leaders – and I was continually catching those resonances and echoes from my previous life as a fervent Evangelical leader.

Jonathan Z. Smith has wisely observed that scholarly projects of comparative religion typically arise "as if unbidden, as a sort of déjà vu, the scholar remembers that he [or she] has seen 'it' or 'something like it' before ... It is a process of moving from a psychological association to an historical one."[3] In other words, we scholars can spiff up our research projects and highbrow comparisons between religious traditions in neutral, objective language, but many times those very projects begin in flashes of intuition, in unexpected affinities, and in our own autobiographies. Everyone, even us scholars, comes from somewhere and brings a perspective to her or his analysis. This means that the scholar who wants to compare two religious traditions cannot simply sit in some neutral third position, some Archimedean point from which she or he can dispassionately compare bracketed entities. Even though I wouldn't call myself Evangelical anymore, the reverberations that echo in the chambers of my mind from Salafis' scriptural conversations do so in a mind deeply shaped by that Evangelical upbringing and experience.[4] My own identity and backstory are wrapped around the data of this study.

But I'm not the only one who thinks there's some resemblance between Evangelical Protestants and Salafis. For instance, the afore-mentioned seminar leader, Yasir Qadhi, a bona fide expert on Salafism both by experience and study, analogizes,

> Salafis are the Protestant Reformation of Sunni Islam . . . The Salafis view themselves as the Protestant Reformation. They're purifying the syncretic practices that crept into the faith over the centuries in the exact same manner that Martin Luther viewed himself as purifying a cultural, corrupted Christianity . . . Salafis want to get rid of all of that baggage and return to the original pristine Islam as practiced by the first three generations of Islam.[5]

Likewise in the entry on "Salafi Muslims" in the *Encyclopedia of Muslim-American History*, we find that, "On account of Salafism's literalist, populist approach to scripture and its conservative social ethos, Western scholars often draw analogies between Salafism and American Christianity, describing the movement in such terms as 'the Protestant reformers of Islam,' 'Puritan Islam,' 'Evangelical,' and 'neo-Fundamentalist.'"[6] At a recent lecture I offered about Evangelicals to a group of Jews and Muslims, I started by asking them to just shout out the first thing that came to mind when I said the phrase "Evangelical Christians;" a Muslim woman in the group shouted "Salafi Christians." I'm not the only one with a sense of déjà vu.

So whence comes this resemblance between Salafis and Evangelicals, particularly in America? How did Salafis in the USA come to mirror, in form and rhetoric, many of the tropes of American Evangelicalism? These are the underlying questions of this book, but, in order to search out answers to these questions, we need to understand the pervasive influence of the 9/11 attacks on twenty-first-century America and the environmental pressures it created for American Salafism.

Most Americans who have heard of Salafism probably heard about it in connection with terrorism and 9/11. Al Qaeda (and, its patricidal offshoot, ISIS) was and is a "jihadi-Salafi" international terrorist network, and the terrorists who attacked the USA on 9/11, by and large, identified with a Salafi-style of Islamic theology. This was, to be sure, an inauspicious American introduction to the global Salafi movement, which is much broader and more multi-faceted than just Al Qaeda. The events of 9/11 cast a harsh spotlight on the American Muslim community as a whole and especially on the fledgling American Salafi movement that had developed in the 1990s. So, to fathom what is described and analyzed in this book, the transformations and adaptations of American Salafism, we must understand the metanarratives that came to the fore for explaining 9/11 and created the environment where an organization like AlMaghrib Institute would emerge.

THE POST-9/11 AMERICAN NARRATIVES ABOUT ISLAM AND SALAFISM

Within hours of the terrorist attacks on the morning of September 11, 2001, Americans began casting about for how to understand what had befallen the decimated Twin Towers, the damaged Pentagon, and Flight 93 that crashed in Western Pennsylvania. Why was America attacked? Who attacked it? What motivated them? What eventually took hold were three different deep-rooted, interlocking American narratives about Islam. These narratives certainly predated 9/11, but afterward they became the dominant interpretations and set the paths for the various American perceptions of Salafism. The narratives are, namely: (1) America is a Christian or a Judeo-Christian nation at odds with Islam; (2) Islam is prone to religious fundamentalism; and (3) Salafism – or "Radical Islam" as some persist in calling it – intrinsically poses a threat to the United States. As I briefly survey the foundations of these narratives, some readers may find one or more of them will seem natural or prosaic, to the point of being matter-of-fact, because these narratives govern and undergird our very contemporary vocabulary. Prevalent terms like "Judeo-Christian," "civilizations," "the West," "fundamentalist," "radical," "moderate," and "American," have been imbued with derived meanings in our current lexicon, but I hope that the following chapters will aid in generatively disrupting these seemingly clear categories.

Narrative 1: "A Judeo-Christian Nation"

Our first narrative finds its roots in a deep ambiguity at the founding of the United States. On the one hand, the vast, vast majority of citizens in early America identified with one of the European Protestant sects or denominations that had come across the Atlantic during the colonial era: Pennsylvania Quakers and Amish and Mennonites, Scottish Presbyterians, Rhode Island Baptists, New England Puritans and Congregationalists, French Calvinist Huguenots, Church of England Episcopalians, and Scandinavian, Dutch, and German Lutherans. On the other hand, because of the cultural and theological and ethnic divergences among these Protestantisms, no one Protestant sect was so federally dominant as to be a natural choice as *the* national American Christian sect. (Incidentally, as I will explore in Chapter 1, the effort to bridge across such intra-Protestant denominational divisions was one of the major forces that gave rise to American Evangelicalism.) So one central question that faced the founding generation of American politicians was how or whether to reflect the religious character of the new nation within the various levels of American government. The famous American arrangement of disestablishing religion (the First

Amendment) and the notional separation of church and state may have been the eventual legal consensus, but the founding generation of Americans, and every generation of Americans since, has been quite divided over whether the USA was a) truly secular, b) tacitly Christian, or c) verging on officially Christian.

To illustrate with one pertinent episode: A potent threat to the stability of the early USA came in the form of piracy committed against US shipping and travel by the Barbary States in North Africa, which were largely populated by Muslims. The US Navy was initially created in 1794 by George Washington to fight back this threat all the way "to the shores of Tripoli" (i.e., modern Libya).[7] In 1796, the US government signed a treaty with the Bey (ruler) of Tripoli of Barbary, widely known as the Treaty of Tripoli, which includes the declaration: "As the government of the United States of America is not in any sense founded on the Christian religion, as it has in itself no character of enmity against the laws, religion or tranquility of Musselmen [Muslims] ... no pretext arising from religious opinions shall ever produce an interruption of the harmony existing between the two countries."[8] The text of this treaty was presented before the US Senate in 1797 where it was unanimously approved without objection and then signed by President John Adams.

This incident would seem like proof positive that the founding generation of Americans did not regard the USA as a Christian nation, except ... the Treaty of Tripoli did not work. Relations between the USA and the North African rulers broke down shortly after its ratification, and the USA would fight its first overseas war against the Barbary States (often titled the Barbary Wars) well into the nineteenth century. Moreover, as much as the text of the Treaty of the Tripoli is often cited by proponents of early American secularism, it certainly did not reflect the consensus view among Americans at the time. Within a few years we have an exchange between two of President Adams' cabinet members corresponding about that very treaty, with James McHenry (of Fort McHenry fame) writing to Oliver Wolcott, Jr., "The Senate ... ought never to have ratified the treaty alluded to, with the declaration that 'the government of the United States, is not, *in any sense*, founded on the Christian religion.' What else is it founded on? This act always appeared to me like *trampling upon the cross.*"[9] Indeed, many Americans "viewed the struggle between the United States and the Barbary nations ... as a kind of holy war" – Christian America versus the barbarous Muslims.[10]

I bring up this particular incident inasmuch as it bears upon a crucial question throughout American history: What is the status of Muslims and Islam vis-à-vis American society? Is the USA neutral and secular or do its supposed Christian nature and Christian foundations imply a certain set of Christian values and a corresponding animosity toward Islam and Muslims? McHenry's general sentiment lingers today with one national survey finding that the statement, "The Federal Government should declare the United States a Christian nation," was endorsed by 29 percent of Americans in 2017 and 22 percent in 2021.[11] To be sure, this is not a majority, but neither is it a rounding error. Fully one-fifth of Americans today are on board with tossing out the Disestablishment Clause of the First Amendment and instantiating Christianity as the national religion. Relatedly, another 2021 survey discovered that 50 percent of Americans (74 percent of Republicans and 35 percent of Democrats) agree with the statement "The values of Islam are at odds with American values and ways of life."[12] Caught in the Treaty of Tripoli episode and in these contemporary statistics are two correlated American sensibilities: The more the United States is imagined as a Christian country, the less room that leaves for religious others, particularly Islam and Muslims. In other words, since very early in US history right up to the present, the more America's purported Christianness is emphasized and embraced the less open America is to Islam and Muslims.

This same sentiment does not necessarily extend to all other religions. In fact, in the early twentieth century, this narrative of America as "a Christian nation" underwent a slight modification in some corners as more and more Jews escaped rising antisemitic persecution in Eastern Europe through emigration to the USA and more and more Catholics from Europe likewise sought opportunity in the United States. American Protestant hegemony and collective Protestantism's sense of demographic power were threatened. A new approach arose in some circles to update and expand – while also limiting – America's religious inclusion. According to this reframing of American history, the USA became not merely a Christian nation but the inheritor of the "Judeo-Christian tradition."[13] The coining of this term "Judeo-Christian" as a sort of coalitional religious identity reframed the USA as not purely a Protestant nation, but as a big-tent, civic religious space where Jews, Catholics, and Protestants alike could find belonging.[14]

This expanded "Judeo-Christian" identification of America was not without its incongruities. Despite Christianity finding its roots in the Hebrew Bible and the Jewishness of Jesus and his original followers, the religious identities of "Christian" and "Jew" have congealed over the ensuing centuries in complicated polemics and potent separation, particularly driven by Christian persecution of Jews continuing even into the twentieth century when the "Judeo-Christian" concept was trying to bind them together. There is ongoing debate among scholars of Judaism as to whether Jews and Jewish perspectives were ever really incorporated into the "Judeo-Christian" frame or whether it was always a supersessionist Christian embrace.[15] Nonetheless, in some circles, "America as Judeo-Christian nation" came to operate alongside "America as Christian nation" as twin narrations of America's unsecular nature. Notably excluded from the "Judeo-Christian America" frame is the third sibling in the Abrahamic religions family: Islam (not to mention atheism, Buddhism, Hinduism, etc.). Today, about 2 percent of the US population is Jewish, and, depending on the estimate, roughly 1 percent of the population is Muslim. But the number of American Muslims is growing and is estimated to surpass the number of Jews by 2040 or 2050 to become the largest American religious minority.[16] Can America ever be an "Abrahamic nation" or a "Judeo-Christian-Islamic" nation, and, if not, what is it about Islam that would create that line of separation?[17]

This inherited narrative of America's fundamental "Christian" or "Judeo-Christian" (and, thus, non-Islamic) character reached its most sweeping expression in Bernard Lewis and Samuel Huntington's 1990s predictions of the impending "Clash of Civilizations" between Islam and the Judeo-Christian United States. Lewis originated the "Clash of Civilizations" phrase in a 1990 *Atlantic* article that oxymoronically attributed "The Roots of Muslim Rage" against the USA to "the perhaps irrational but surely historic reaction of an ancient rival against our Judeo-Christian heritage, our secular present, and the worldwide expansion of both."[18] Put differently, America's global promotion of secularity and its globally thriving "Judeo-Christian heritage" had awakened a primal animosity for "the Muslim." In such broad-brush terms, Lewis warns of "the danger of a new era of religious wars."

Huntington took up Lewis' "Clash of Civilizations" phrasing a few years later to paint a post–Cold War picture of a world that was reverting from a bipolar (Soviet Union vs. United States) ideological conflict between communism and capitalistic democracy to a multipolar one where "[t]he great divisions among humankind and the dominating source of conflict will be cultural."[19] Huntington takes Lewis' blithe generalizations about the essential qualities of religions and civilizations and enlarges them into a theory of global politics, where the geographical fault lines between ancient civilizations (highly correlated to the footprint of world religious traditions) will form the boundaries of geopolitical conflict, and the West is defined by its vaguely Christian or Judeo-Christian heritage.[20] The West-vs.-Islam theme also carries over, with Huntington's famously pointed phrasing that, "Islam's borders *are* bloody, and so are its innards," and:

> The causes of this ongoing pattern of conflict [between Islam and the West] lie not in transitory phenomena such as twelfth-century Christian passion [i.e., the Crusades] or twentieth-century Muslim

> fundamentalism. They flow from the nature of the two religions
> and the civilizations based on them.[21]

Library shelves of justified criticism have been leveled against Huntington (and, at a distance, Lewis) over this still alarmingly popular thesis, but I would like to narrow the focus to just observe its effect on American Muslims.[22]

Eleven years after Lewis' original article and five years after Huntington's book was published, as Americans and others grasped for explanations for the tragedy and brutality of 9/11, many implicitly and explicitly latched onto this narrative: The USA was attacked not merely by audacious terrorists, madmen, or Salafi-jihadi ideologues, but by *Islam*.[23] In this interpretation, 9/11 was not a singular, devastating day, but one more chapter in an ongoing battle between Judeo-Christian civilization (personified in the USA) and Islam. Hence, Al Qaeda was no outlier but the tip of the bloody Islamic spear. Part of what this book tracks is the immensely difficult position this interpretation placed American Muslims in – Muslims who, prior to 9/11, felt quite at home in the USA, but who after 9/11 were forced to position themselves vis-à-vis not only actual Al Qaeda but also vis-à-vis the constructed American enemies of "Radical Islam," "Islamic fundamentalism," and Islamic civilization.

Narrative 2: "Islamic Fundamentalism"

Speaking of fundamentalism, have you ever paused to consider how the term "fundamentalism" came to be so closely associated in the modern mind with Islam? As with the "Judeo-Christian tradition" and the "Clash of Civilizations," the concept of "Islamic fundamentalism" is not some medieval holdover or organic category within Islam but arises from another American vocabulary innovation that occurred in the twentieth century, out of which our second narrative materializes. If the first narrative above posits a profound dissimilarity between an aggressive Islam, on one side, and Western Judaism and Christianity (or Judeo-Christianity), on the other, this second

narrative assumes a certain modern similarity among religious traditions: the impulse among some religious communities toward
"fundamentalism."

"Fundamentalist" was a positive identity coined by evangelical
American Protestants in 1920 to capture an inter-denominational
reactive tendency against the modernizing and liberalizing of
Christianity, a desire to get back to the fundamentals of the faith.
As I develop further in Chapter 2, "Fundamentalist" and
"Evangelical" operated for the remainder of the twentieth century as
correlated synonyms in American vocabulary, with Fundamentalism
being the more belligerent, rigorist wing of broader Evangelicalism.
Indeed, in the conservative Evangelical world I was raised in in the
1980s, Fundamentalist wasn't necessarily an insult, but more a signal
of a person's vigor and vexation. As late-twentieth-century
Fundamentalist political crusader par excellence Jerry Falwell used
to joke, "A fundamentalist is only an evangelical who is mad about
something."[24]

Then, through the 1980s and 1990s the word "fundamentalism"
underwent a major connotative shift: It was universalized. Triggered
by the mostly unrelated Islamic revolution in Iran in 1979 and the so-
called Reagan Revolution (fueled by the consolidation of Evangelical
and Fundamentalist voters) in 1980, journalists, politicians, and religion scholars began labeling any global religious movement that they
saw as too political, too literalist, too opposed to Western hegemony,
too outside the norms defined by liberal Christianity as "fundamentalist."[25] We see in those two decades and well into the new millennium an explosion of publishing – hundreds of books, thousands of
academic articles, and dozens of collaborative projects – all aimed at
categorizing and castigating a now generic "religious fundamentalism." In the 1990s, the Library of Congress actually created a new
subject heading BL 238 Religious Fundamentalism (leaving intact the
historic BT 82.2 for the topic of Protestant Fundamentalism) to contain this massive corpus.[26] The intra-Protestant feuds and archetypes
of America were foisted onto all of the religions of the world: Buddhist

fundamentalists, Jewish fundamentalists, Hindu fundamentalists, and, most conspicuously, Islamic fundamentalists.[27]

When you dig deeply into this comparative fundamentalism library, you see at least two dominant themes. First, virtually no one – scholar, journalist, or other – has anything very nice to say about the so-called fundamentalists. They are treated throughout as a nuisance or a menace: to secularism, modernity, rationality, liberalism, pluralism, academia, etc. For the theologians and religious studies scholars who analyzed them, the fundamentalists were *other*: objects of study, ideological foes, and almost never fellow travelers, conversation partners, or friends. The religious fundamentalist, within this frame, is not an identity to be inhabited but almost a bogeyman and certainly a problem to be solved.[28] Over the past forty years, fundamentalism became a synonym for bad religion, a pejorative that almost no one (including its native Evangelical Christians) self applies today.

The second theme that emerges from a thorough review of this comparative fundamentalism literature is its utter fixation with Islam. Consider Illustration I.1 which shows how frequently the phrases "Islamic fundamentalism" or "Islamic fundamentalist" occur compared to "Christian fundamentalism" or "fundamentalist Christian" in all Google-cataloged English-language books from 1970 to 2019.[29]

We see a remarkable inversion at work at the end of the twentieth century. A word that was coined less than a century before as an affirmative identity for assertive Protestants has migrated over to become primarily a term for scolding Muslims and Islam. Well before 9/11, the concept of "Islamic fundamentalism" had become deepseated in the American imagination.

So what is an "Islamic fundamentalist?" That has always been an open question. The term has been extensively applied to different Muslim communities – from anti-colonial Shi'ite revolutionaries in Iran who supported Ayatollah Khomeini to Islamist Muslim Brotherhood supporters who have sought to build a grassroots, anti-

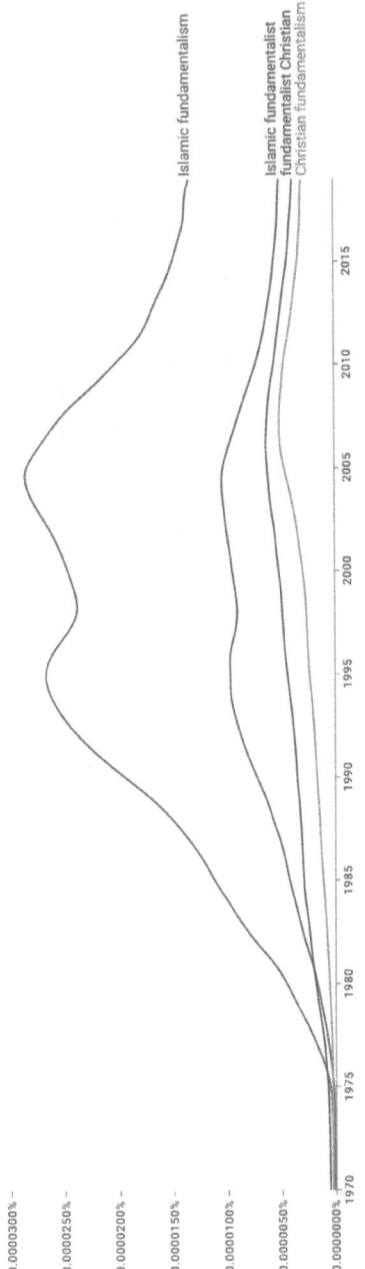

ILLUSTRATION 1.1 Usage of Islamic fundamentalism vs. Christian fundamentalism

secularist reform program from Sunni Islam; from Saudi Wahhabi hardliners who use state power to police top-down, strict rules on society to Hamas radicals who wage an insurgent war against Israel; from out-and-out terrorists and suicide bombers to pious scholars who take a (by some inscrutable measure) too literalist approach to the Qur'an and Hadith.[30] Unlike the original, self-declared American Protestant Fundamentalists who, despite shadings and disagreements among themselves, had a fairly clear shared agenda and worldview, "Islamic fundamentalist" is an aspersion, not adopted positively by Muslim groups but generically leveled against any Muslims who seemed out of step with liberal sensibilities.

So, if the "Judeo-Christian America" and "Clash of Civilizations" narrative led people to draw the conclusion that Islam itself was essentially behind the 9/11 attacks, this seemingly more nuanced and high-minded narrative said: "The USA was not attacked by Islam, but by the bad Muslims – the Islamic fundamentalists."[31] Al Qaeda, Salafism in general, and anything associated with it were all lumped together, once again, under the broad heading of "Islamic fundamentalism." The fact that this was an American Protestant category clumsily transposed onto Islam did not appear to trouble (or, perhaps, even occur to) anyone at the time. The 9/11 Commission Report, the most definitive US government document to analyze the attacks, quotes this comparative fundamentalism literature calling the 9/11 terrorists "fundamentalists" – "for want of a better term."[32]

So, given the general fervor around the "Clash of Civilizations" concept and the fact that George W. Bush, the American President on 9/11, identified as an Evangelical and had been elected, in large part, by a coalition of Protestant Evangelicals and Fundamentalists, this second narrative coalesced around a different interpretation of the attacks and their aftermath. Watching the post-9/11 ramp-up of combative rhetoric between Bush and his American Evangelical supporters on the one hand, and the raging Al Qaeda jihadist propaganda on the other, some liberal Americans and others around the globe began to speak of – in what they seemingly believed was a more polished riff on Huntington – a "Clash of Fundamentalisms."[33] It appeared to them that the most obnoxious parts of Western Christendom were en route to battle ideologically and geopolitically against the most hostile parts of Sunni Islam – American Evangelicals versus Islamic fundamentalism on a global stage. Or as Nicholas Kristof put it, "Militant Christianity rises to confront Militant Islam."[34]

To be clear, many Muslims both in the USA and abroad have also participated in this "Islamic fundamentalism" rhetoric. In an effort to define the boundaries of a normal Islam that would exclude Al Qaeda, a lot of Muslims appeared only too eager to separate themselves from the bad Muslims, the fundamentalists, whether that included terrorists, Islamists, Salafis, or all of the above. Even within many American Muslim circles, as the coming chapters will demonstrate, "Salafi" has become a byword, an epithet, a part of the Muslim community that is discussed, if at all, in hushed or angry tones.

This book offers a set of deep case studies at the heart of this supposed "Clash of Fundamentalisms:" What happened to the Salafi Muslims at home in the United States who experienced an – I think undue and unfair – clampdown by the American government and its security forces, and who were pressed, in the aftermath of the attacks, to reinvent themselves and build organizations like AlMaghrib Institute? Taking seriously the widely acknowledged similarities between Salafis and Evangelicals (and, yes, though the term has become hackneyed, Fundamentalists), I try to find new ways to think about this analogy not in abstraction or solely relying on Protestant frames but dialogically, within the shared horizons of American culture. How did Salafis weave their thread into the tapestry of American religious pluralism? How did they come to share some striking affinities and even friendships with the very Evangelicals with whom they were purportedly locked in a global confrontation?

Narrative 3: The Threat of "Radical Islam"

Our third narrative arises at the juncture of the first two. It stands to reason that if Islam itself (Narrative 1) or "Islamic fundamentalism" (Narrative 2) poses a potent threat to Western/American interests, then those threats should be carefully studied and addressed. Throughout the late 1990s, the US government recognized – albeit insufficiently – the growing peril of Al Qaeda terrorism, so it created structures and policies to attempt to reckon with that threat. The two Federal Bureau of Investigation units that processed some of the pre-9/11 intelligence that might have averted the attacks were actually titled the "Radical Fundamentalism Unit" (created in 1994) and the "Usama bin Laden Unit" (created in 1999 as a sub-focus of the "Radical Fundamentalism Unit"), demonstrating that the transposed phraseology among academics and media around "fundamentalism" from reactionary Protestants to militant Muslims had reached into the realm of government policy well before the 9/11 attacks.[35] The FBI certainly was not devoting man-hours to tracking down Bible-thumping, politically mobilized American Evangelicals (i.e., George W. Bush voters) in the late 1990s and early 2000s! After 9/11, counter-fundamentalism intelligence analysis and strategy continued developing within the government, and the academic field of Security Studies, which specializes in such threat assessment and policy responses, pivoted and advised the US government's counterterrorism and "Global War on Terror" work through think tanks, white papers, and academic publishing. It's worth noting that the field of Security Studies had first emerged in the Cold War era and was primarily concerned with state actors prior to 9/11, so the post-9/11 shift of some Security Studies scholars to thinking about non-state actors (i.e., Al Qaeda) and terrorism was itself a metamorphosis for the field.[36]

Unlike the unwieldy and broad ("civilizations") and inescapably vague ("Islamic fundamentalism") framings of the first two narratives, this third Security Studies narrative was comparatively precise and conscientious, particularly in the wake of 9/11, in zeroing in on how Al Qaeda actually understood and positioned itself within the landscape of Islamic theology, jurisprudence, and practice. Security Studies analysts and scholars accurately discerned that Al Qaeda was a jihadi-Salafi, transnational terrorist network, which had grown out of the 1980s insurgency against the Soviets in Afghanistan and which was intellectually and financially backstopped by strong anti-Western and anti-American sentiments among Wahhabis, Salafis, and others in Saudi Arabia and other majority-Muslim countries.[37] The analysis that emerged within these post-9/11 Security Studies reports and articles offered a far more textured and sharp understanding of the contours of global Salafism – its internal political arguments, Salafi debates about violence and its permissibility, and the relationship between Saudi Arabia and Salafism – than had ever obtained within the previous generalities about Islamic fundamentalism, much less the impressionistic "Clash of Civilizations" literature.

The vast, vast majority that has been written about Salafism in the USA since 9/11 comes from this Security Studies genre of threat assessment, counterterrorism strategy, political analysis, and policy response recommendations, and I draw selectively from this literature for this book.[38] Additionally, there is an ever-growing body of excellent scholarship on global Salafism, and even Salafism in Europe – perhaps because it is a more openly debated and widely recognized phenomenon there – has begun to receive more careful, ethnographic, and nuanced academic analysis.[39] Yet, in the USA, Security Studies remains the dominant paradigm for understanding and analyzing Salafism.

There are two core deficiencies in this Security Studies mode of analysis that, instead of just offering solid analysis and interpretation, transmuted it into another stereotyped American narrative about Islam and Salafism. First was a communications disconnect: All of the Security Studies technical jargon and precision about Salafism has evidently proven difficult to translate into popular American parlance or understanding. A handful of notable US news articles and editorials have ventured to explore Salafism in the USA, but American public discourse has proven allergic to this clear terminology.[40] So while there are dozens of academic and counterterrorism books by American authors analyzing the different shadings of Salafism, Wahhabism, international jihadism, etc., and offering careful delineations between jihadi-Salafis, say, and politico-Salafis on their reasoning around violence or between standard Islamists and quietist Salafis in their view of political participation (topics I take up in Chapter 5), these tomes and peer-reviewed articles remain at a distance from American media and popular discourse.

Hence, instead of American politicians and policy wonks publicly debating straightforwardly how to fine-tune counterterrorism strategies to protect against militant terror attacks, the American public gets euphemistic commentary about the threat of "Islamic extremism" or "Radical Islam" (phrases that often parallel, in their grim murkiness, "Islamic fundamentalism") and arguments about whether political leaders should say "Radical Islamic Terrorism," as urged by Republicans in the 2016 US presidential campaign, or the more finely parsed "Radical Islamism," as preferred by the Hillary Clinton campaign.[41] What exactly "Radical Islam(ism)" is or what its relationship to non-Radical Islam may be is simply elided in the gulf between Security Studies scholarship and the American political to and fro.

The second, and more grievous, distortion brought about by the Security Studies lens dominating studies of Salafism in the USA is that the entire field is designed to ask a defensive, threat-oriented set of analytical questions: "Does person X or group X pose a peril to US interests? How does ideology Y undergird such a potential threat? How would policy Z intercept such a threat?" These are not bad questions if one's objective is to prevent kinetic terror attacks or identify the seedlings of terrorist ideologies, but, if they are the only questions asked, they have a highly prejudicial and warping effect on the identity of a religious community. In short, the securitization of studies of Salafism in the USA has contributed directly to the securitization of Salafism itself, framing the entire movement around questions of violence, terrorism, political ideology, and foreignness to Western sensibilities, instead of asking the questions about Salafi identity that Salafis themselves ask. Surveying this Security Studies literature while getting to know actual Salafis in the USA, the main complaint I have about this literature is that the information is fairly accurate, but it doesn't *feel* right. Most of the notes are on the page, but the melody is missing.

This book endeavors to find the melody of American Salafism by asking a different set of questions. Namely, how do Salafis understand themselves and where do they anchor their own identities? I begin with Salafis' distinctive educational forms, their scriptural popularization, and their suspicion of the authority of tradition as such, the places where they locate their own standpoint within Islam. Through a series of interviews with American Salafi thought leaders – my guides in this study – I strive to have them speak for themselves, to introduce Salafism as they see it.

SCRIPTURE PEOPLE AND CONVERGENT EVOLUTION

This book invites a reconsideration of Salafism through the prism of Salafis' post-9/11 American experience. As I have tried to show above, the narratives that have taken hold about Islam and Salafism before and after 9/11 – from "Judeo-Christian America" to the "Clash of Civilizations," from "Islamic fundamentalism" to the securitization of Salafism and "Radical Islam" – have created neuralgic responses that lead to general ignorance of Salafism and caricatured imaginings of the threat of the Salafi strand of Islam in America. Moreover, as the following chapters will set forth, the Salafi experience in the USA has actually played out in a way that is distinct among all the different forms of Salafism that are extant today and it doesn't neatly fit into any of these prescribed narratives. If the caricature of Salafism is that it is rigid, insular, illiberal, and susceptible to violence, AlMaghrib Institute and the form of Salafism it has incubated has proven the opposite of all such stereotypes. I theorize that this distinctively American form of Salafism emerges not only from the pressures of the post-9/11 American security state but also, unexpectedly, from Salafism coming to inhabit the same cultural space as American Evangelicalism.

What I offer is not a dispassionate side-by-side analysis of Evangelicalism and Salafism in America but an, at times personal, interreligious exploration. I draw heavily on my own background within and study of Evangelicalism to probe the affinities between Evangelicals and Salafis. This book is an exercise in bridge-building and border-dwelling where Islam meets Christianity in America. I have incorporated elements of ethnography, comparative religion, comparative theology, and spiritual biography to present a sympathetic (as in, dialogical and interested in Salafis' own self-narrations) introduction to American Salafism.[42]

Let me, then, briefly sketch the argument of the following chapters. On a surface level, there is a pretty good reason that people are constantly observing correlations between Salafism and Evangelicalism – both are revivalist and reform movements that try to reinvigorate their respective Sunni and Protestant traditions through theological originalism and an appeal to scripture. This tendency, which I call *scripturalism*, ties individual and communal identities to direct access to scripture, so that Evangelicals often call themselves "Bible-believing Christians" and Salafis will often identify as "Ahl al-Hadith" (the People of the Hadith), or, to paraphrase both: Scripture People.[43] Both communities attempt to distinguish themselves from their co-religionists by invoking their fidelity to, pedagogy around, literal reading of, and primal connection with scripture, tapping into the wellsprings of the Sunni and Protestant traditions.

Yet, for all these similarities, I contend that Salafism and Evangelicalism are really quite different under the surface, even as Islam and Christianity have very different conceptions of scripture, distinctive modes of interpretation, and divergent underlying questions. To use a zoological analogy, Salafism and Evangelicalism have somewhat similar traits (or phenotypes) but quite distinctive evolutionary histories and native ecosystems. Evolutionary biologists call this *convergent evolution*. Birds and bats both evolved light bones and wings to be able to fly, but they do not even belong to the same class of animals – birds are technically reptiles, whereas bats are mammals. These similarities can emerge over time from a shared environment or from parallel needs in different environments. As George McGhee puts it, "Natural selection has a limited repertoire of potential forms from which to choose, and convergent evolution is the result."[44]

Within their native locales: American Evangelicalism is an outgrowth of Protestantism's prioritization of scripture as the primary source of authority. It has had three centuries of development in the USA, binding together an experiential spirituality, revivalist tendencies, and direct-to-the-Bible appeals that have become entwined with the American nation and identity as a whole. Evangelicalism is, I argue, a distinctively energetic and populist form of religion, that through globalization and efficient missionary work, spread around the globe. Salafism, on the other hand, has deep roots in the Hanbali strand of Sunni Islam, where generation after generation of scriptural interpreters and scholars hewed toward straightaway appeals to the Qur'an and the Hadith. The movement we call Salafism today emerged in the early twentieth century, amid a crisis of authority in the Sunni world during the crack-up of the Ottoman- and Western-colonial order, as different Muslim communities in the Middle East, North Africa, and South Asia sought to recover what they thought to be the pristine qualities of early Islam. Through accidents of history (i.e., oil discoveries) and proactive institution building, Salafism's many local variants came to flow through Saudi Arabia, and especially through the educational networks and universities the Saudis created to harness the energy of Salafi-reinterpretation within Sunnism.

Starting in the 1980s and 1990s – the very timeframe where scholars and journalists were turning their gaze to the putative rising tide of global religious fundamentalisms, and the FBI began keeping a wary eye on Al Qaeda, a.k.a.,"Islamic fundamentalism" – a nascent, mostly unnoticed community of Salafis began forming within American Islam. American Muslims (many of them African

American but also some, like Yasir Qadhi, first- or second-generation immigrants to America) began to accept scholarships to study at the Saudi Salafi universities, bringing back scriptural knowledge, preaching and teaching skills, and Salafi pedagogies to build a numerically small but robust Salafi movement in the USA. Many of these early American Salafis were converts to Islam who were searching for the authentic religion through their Arabian sojourns in the very heart of Islamic geography.

This pre-9/11 American Salafi movement feels like an artifact of a bygone era now, hard to access except through autobiographical recounting. When 9/11 befell them, the combined ignominy among their fellow Muslims of being theologically akin to Al Qaeda and the overreaching American security state dismantled most of the pre-9/11 Salafi infrastructure and institutions. It looked, for a moment, like American Salafism might come to naught.

But then something unusual happened. As we shall see in the voices and experiences of the American Salafi thought leaders of this book and through the institutional prism of AlMaghrib Institute, 9/11 had a host of different effects on American Muslims, but for many American Salafis, it created what we might call an accelerated evolutionary shift. Pushed by the American security state and pulled by the competitive American religious marketplace, Salafi shaykhs (leaders/teachers) and students reinvented Salafism for a post-9/11 world. They built nondenominational, Salafi-style institutions like AlMaghrib, and leaders like Yasir Qadhi demonstrated how fluid and agile the supposedly uncompromising and dogmatic Salafi strand of Islam could be. And, in this process of adaptation to a new environment under threatening conditions, in the shared American pluralistic religious milieu, Sunni Islamic scripturalism has settled into an ecological niche carved out over centuries by the homegrown Protestant Christian scripturalists, adapting many of the same styles and mannerisms as American Evangelicals.[45] Today, Salafism – whether it calls itself that or not, and it often does not – is an accessible and vibrant strand of Islam in America.

Any good comparative study should scramble our assumptions and prior knowledge a little – make what seemed familiar unfamiliar, and what was previously strange more understandable. My hope is that, whether you, the reader, start with a dense knowledge (and maybe experience) of Evangelicalism or Salafism or only the vaguest impressions of both, whether you have partaken of the "Clash of Civilizations" or comparative fundamentalism or Security Studies literature or not, you'll leave this book thinking differently and maybe a little more creatively and sympathetically about that imperative project of our time: Muslim-Christian understanding. So come reconsider Salafism in America with me, building not upon the toxic foundations of the "Clash of Civilizations" narrative but upon the similarities and convergences that can occur in a shared cultural environment. I contend that Salafis and Evangelicals are not inexorably destined to be locked in a "Clash of Fundamentalisms" but instead may discover deep affinities and kindred spiritualities around devotion to scripture. And I offer a redescription of Salafism (and, to some extent, Evangelicalism) that begins not in terror and animosity but in déjà vu and dialogue.[46]

I The Evolution of Two American Species of Scripture People

Oh, give me a home where the Buffalo roam
Where the Deer and the Antelope play;
Where seldom is heard a discouraging word,
And the sky is not cloudy all day.
"Home on the Range," American folk song

The Kansas state song and unofficial anthem of the American West contains a zoological and taxonomic error: There are no antelope in North America, except in zoos or exotic game habitats. "Antelope" is a broad term encompassing a number of species from the family Bovidae (think: sheep and goats) native to Africa and Eurasia. What North America has is the pronghorn – an animal that looks remarkably like the antelope but belongs to the family Antilocapridae. The pronghorn is an evolutionary orphan, the last remaining member of the Antilocapridaes that flourished in the North American continent a million years ago.

While the various types of antelope (Illustration 1.1) and the pronghorn (Illustration 1.2) are distantly related (both are cloven-hooved mammals), their evolutionary and genetic development has occurred in thoroughly separate ecosystems over many millennia. The pronghorn is actually more closely related to modern giraffes than to their distant antelope cousins. Yet the two species have evolved in parallel to occupy similar niches in different ecologies: antelope in what zoologists still call the contiguous "Old World" (Africa, Asia, Europe), pronghorns in the ocean-bounded "New World." Both may be horned, fleet-footed, plant-eating herd mammals, but when you peek under the evolutionary hood, they are quite different genetically.

ILLUSTRATION 1.1 Antelope (Namibia)

ILLUSTRATION 1.2 North American pronghorn

This raises some interesting questions: What if actual antelope came to live in North America alongside the pronghorn? What happens when convergently evolved species occupy the same ecosystem? Or, to drop the metaphor for a moment, what happens when a religious movement – like Salafism – that evolved to fit a scripturalist niche in the majority-Muslim world comes to inhabit the same eco-system as American Evangelicalism, an outwardly similar movement which evolved natively in North America?

At an elementary level, Salafism and Evangelicalism share some clear resemblances. Both are scripture-based, popular, global, modern, revivalist movements that make normative claims within their respect-ive Sunni Muslim and Western Christian traditions. They are largely non-hierarchical and diffuse, with no single central religious figure or theological authority structure. And they are both, as a rule, proselytiz-ing movements that seek to win over fellow Muslims and Christians, not to mention non-Muslims and non-Christians, to their understanding of religion. Simple enough – but when we peek under the hood at these movements, which emerged in very different scriptural, cultural, and religious contexts, we see that Islam and Christianity may share words and concepts, like "scripture," "revival," "reform," and "tradition," but these ideas function and interplay very differently in each religion.

So while most of this book dwells on the intriguing similarities and convergences I see between Evangelicals and Salafis in the USA, this more technical and historical chapter will introduce both move-ments with attention to difference: differences between Islam and Christianity, different bodies of scripture, different traditions of inter-pretation, and the different avenues Evangelicalism and Salafism have traveled to arrive in twenty-first-century America. Rightly done, com-parison always entails a basic recognition of difference (if two things are the same, there is no need for comparison) and then "a playing across the 'gap' in the service of some useful end."[1] As I retell here the stories of how Evangelicalism and Salafism arrived in their present forms in America, I will highlight facets of their evolutionary histories where similarity or difference are more evident. After establishing the taxonomy and evolutionary history of the homegrown American pronghorn (Evangelicalism), the rest of this chapter will trace the migratory path of how the more recently imported species of antelope (Salafism) entered the American ecology.

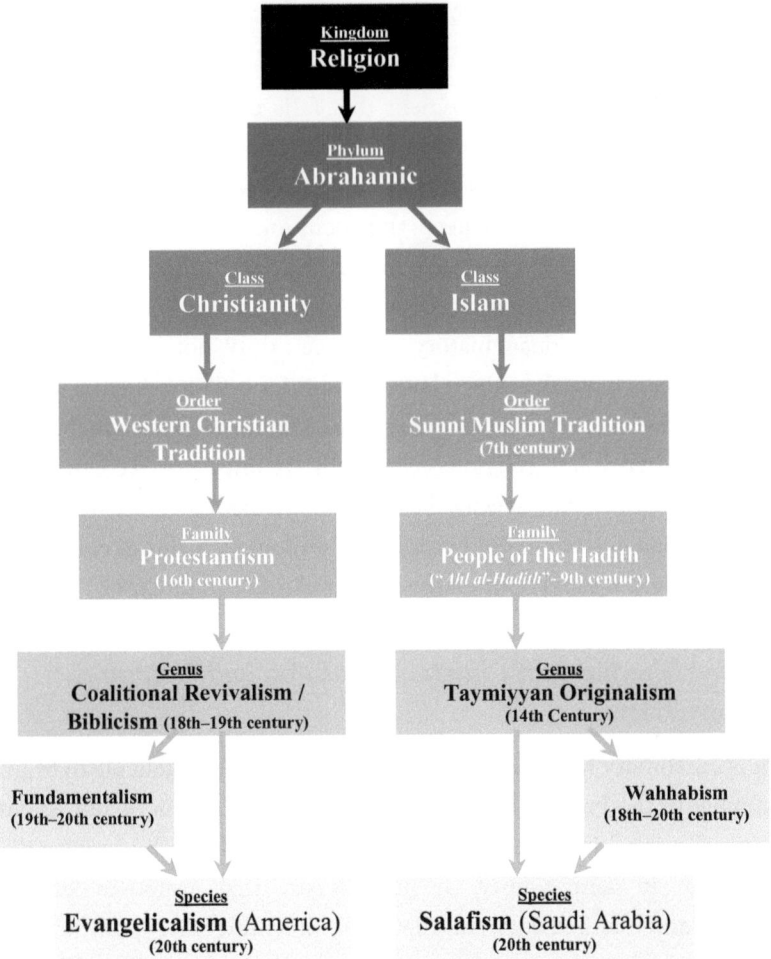

ILLUSTRATION 1.3 Evolutionary taxonomy: Evangelicalism and Salafism

Let me offer a diagram (Illustration 1.3) that I will unpack for the remainder of this chapter. Readers may want to return to this page for reference at different stages reading the chapter. In keeping with the evolutionary metaphor, I have playfully adopted the analogy of scientific classification – kingdom, phylum, class, order, family, genus, species – as a way to quickly situate each movement and see their parallel (and sometimes divergent) evolutions.

EVANGELICALISM: AMERICA'S HOMEGROWN SCRIPTURE PEOPLE

As with Salafism, the movement that falls under the contemporary title of Evangelicalism is a massive, multifarious global phenomenon. I have purposely subtitled this book "Salafi Muslims in Evangelical Christians' America" to keep the focus on the distinct dynamics among Salafis and Evangelicals in the USA and to signal how much Evangelicalism and its antecedents have been influential in and interwoven with American history. I am certainly not suggesting that Evangelicals have any more claim to America or being American than anyone else, but in order to understand Salafis' adaptive inhabitation of the United States' religious ecosystem, we must first recognize how a cognate Christian species has already shaped that ecosystem for generations. So where did Evangelicalism (our pronghorn) come from and how did it emerge interwoven with American culture?

Order: The Western Christian Tradition and Scriptural Primitivism

It is customary to narrate the history of modern Evangelicalism beginning with the Protestant Reformation, and we'll get there, but, evolutionarily speaking, the heredity of what I am calling the scripturalist impulse in Christianity, a primitivism that espouses original Christianity and the direct appeal to the Bible over traditional or hierarchical authority, goes back much further. The Western Christian Tradition (which was originally simply Roman Catholicism and later came to include Protestantism and its derivatives) officially split with the Eastern Orthodox Church in the eleventh century, but shortly thereafter we see in this tradition a recurring tendency among some toward scripture-based renewal.

The twelfth-century Waldensians in the Lyon region of eastern France sought to "return to the life they believed the apostles had lived," encouraging educated lay people to read the Bible and challenging the authority of the official preachers of the Catholic Church.[2]

These were followed by the English supporters of Oxford don John Wycliffe (the so-called Wycliffites or Lollards) in the fourteenth century. The Lollards typified a tendency in some corners of late-medieval Christendom toward vernacular translations of scripture that made the text of the Bible available to literate people who did not have formal training in the official Latin of the church and who could then check the teachings of the church against the text. The Catholic authorities in England responded by banning the translation of the Bible or other unauthorized theology books into English. In the early fifteenth century, the Hussites of Bohemia, inspired by Wycliffe's program, joined their eponymous leader, Jan Hus, dean of philosophy at Prague University, in similar reforms, translating and popularizing the Bible. Hus was burned at the stake after being condemned at a church council in 1415.

These movements, which well predate the more famous Protestant Reformation, signal how deep-seated the scriptural-as-source-of-reform tendency is within Christianity. In the toolbox of renewal within Christianity, no instrument is quite as popular or as powerful as Bible access and fresh biblical interpretation. For reform movements who aim to counter what they see as ossified traditions or entrenched hierarchies, expanding access to and widespread utilization of scripture has a proven track record of success – or, at least, invigoration.

Family: Protestant ("Evangelical") Christianity

Against this backdrop, the theological departures of the Protestant Reformations from magisterial Catholicism are evidently less a set of innovative ideas that happened to occur to Martin Luther, John Calvin, or Huldrych Zwingli in the early sixteenth century and more continuations of a persistent propensity toward scriptural primitivism.[3] It is during the Reformation that the adjective "evangelical" (German: *evangelisch*) came into usage. Luther, Calvin, and the other Reformers did not actually call themselves "Protestants" – then a political designation for princes who took Luther's side against the Holy Roman Emperor – but in their self-identification, they were evangelical Christians, derived from the New Testament Greek term *euaggelion*, which means "good news" or "gospel."[4] What connected these disparate evangelical reform movements across Europe was the belief that they were recovering the good news of the Christian message from what they saw as the corruption and deformity of the late-medieval Catholic church.[5] They were also united in the assumption that through a realignment around the Bible as the preeminent authority for all Christian belief and practice (hence, *sola Scriptura*) they could return the church to its original vision.[6]

Yet even the common practice to speak of Protestantism as a movement or a branch of Christianity must be tempered with a recognition of the deep fissures that separated these different "evangelical" movements or confessions. While they might have all agreed on the supremacy of the Bible's authority, the early Protestant family fought incessantly about the actual interpretation of the Bible; how and where to trust the authority of the Christian tradition; which conventional Catholic practices to maintain (i.e., eucharistic theology, children's baptism, etc.); and how the newly forming "evangelical" churches ought to be governed. Early on, these different strands of interpretation coalesced into the four major currents of Protestantism: the Anglicans (Church of England), the Reformed/Calvinists, the Lutherans, and the more radical Anabaptists. But beneath that echelon of identifiable Protestant currents arose countless other subdivisions, breakaway churches, internal arguments, and political divides. The gushing forth of this fissiparous Protestant energy combined with the breakup of the Holy Roman Empire and the emergence of modern nation states splintered Europe and occasioned a century of chaotic wars, culminating in the Thirty Years War, as savage and frantic an era as any time in European history prior to the World Wars.[7]

All this intra-Protestant ferment and sectarianism made its way across the Atlantic into the European colonies in North America. Different confessions, European-nation aligned churches, nonconforming movements, pacifist sects, and minority groups (not to mention a contingent of Catholics and some small communities of Jews) sought opportunity and refuge in the various colonies. The resulting potpourri of Protestantisms – Quakers, Presbyterians, Congregationalists, Dutch Reformed, Lutherans, Lutheran pietists, Anglicans, Puritans, Amish, Mennonites, Baptists, Moravians, etc. – was one major dimension of the diversity that imbued early America. What the New World represented to many of these sectarian communities was a chance to start over and get away from the by-then entrenched post-Reformation religious hierarchies and established churches of Europe.

Genus: Coalitional American Revivalism and Biblicism

If the Protestant Reformers and the proto-Protestant movements of scriptural renewal were the distant ancestors of contemporary Evangelicals, their more intermediate forebears emerged in the revivalist upsurges of the eighteenth and nineteenth centuries in England and the American colonies. Fiery revivalist preachers – Jonathan Edwards, John Wesley, George Whitefield – stirred up what historians call the First Great Awakening, an outpouring of passion for a shared piety among colonial churches. This "evangelical" (still in adjectival form) revival movement was, from the start, an exercise to counter the denominational cul-de-sac tendencies of Protestantism, to unite theologically disparate believers around shared experiences of conviction and conversion and being "born again."

A paradigmatic episode from the 1739 colonies-wide preaching tour of the inimitable British revivalist George Whitefield captures this dynamic well. While he was frequently opposed or snubbed by institutional clergy or denominational leaders in cities like Philadelphia, Whitefield found great favor in the small settlement of Germantown, a few miles outside the city, where he preached to eager crowds of 6,000 people. Whitefield took a particular liking to Germantown, because the mass audiences there roused to his emotive preaching, but also "because the town had so many Protestant refugees of one sort or another from the Continent. He thought that at least fifteen denominations were represented there, and yet to Whitefield they seemed remarkably cooperative and committed to true Christianity."[8] Here is a quintessential scene of the Awakening that would become part of the evangelical DNA: a transdenominational multitude drawn to populist revival preaching and a sense of pious kinship.

History textbook-style summaries of the colonial Great Awakening sometimes miss that this newly activated religious passion was not only for personal responsibility, enthusiastic worship and prayer, or being "born again," but it was also a passion for and fixation with the Bible and the empowerment of everywoman and everyman to read, study, and apply the Bible to their own lives. Consider these exhortations from one of Jonathan Edwards's less literarily famous sermons,

> Content not yourselves with this, that you have been taught your catechism in your childhood, and that you know as much of the principles of religion as is necessary for your salvation ... God hath spoke to you in the Scriptures; labour to understand as much of what he saith as you can. God hath made you all reasonable creatures; therefore let not the noble faculty of reason or understanding lie neglected.[9]

Like so many other Awakening sermons, Edwards's words bristle with republican sentiment, suspicion of self-satisfied denominationalism, egalitarian Bible popularization, and Enlightenment optimism: You, the everyday human being, are rational, so don't leave religion to the specialists – pursue knowledge, and, for God's sake, study your Bible!

The Awakening fomented a revolutionary spirit in the colonies, as it "marked a transition from clerical to lay religion, from the minister as an inherited authority figure to self-empowering mobilizer."[10] Across the spectrum of the different Protestant denominations, the revival experiences created networks of activated church members and moral agents, who would, in a matter of decades, become activated citizens of the nascent American republic. In fact, the debates among the American colonists about whether and how to declare a bloody independence from England took up the biblicist rhetorical stylings of the Awakening and centered on direct references to the Bible to make the case for and against revolution.[11]

As I briefly highlighted in the Introduction, the intra-Protestant conflicts also contributed to the famous American separation of church and state in two ways: First, no Protestant sect or denomination was so geographically predominant throughout the newly formed United States as to be a natural choice as the national religion. Second, the experience of Europe's religious wars and persecution of sectarian and non-Christian minorities by established churches left many in the founding generation hoping for a more laissez-faire religious culture.

What the First Amendment and the disestablishment of religion, in turn, created was one of the great democratic experiments of early America: a religious marketplace where Christian churches, leaders, sects, and even other religions would compete for attention, passion, and members. It was an ecosystem ready-made for "religious entrepreneurs ... [and] no group has functioned more effectively in this marketplace than evangelicals themselves."[12] One central mode of this entrepreneurial, republican, populist appeal was an empowering biblical primitivism – getting back to the ethos and practices of the New Testament church through a commonsense reading of scripture.[13]

The revivalist and biblicist ethos that was inaugurated in the colonial Great Awakening became engrafted into the American character through wave upon wave of Protestant revitalizations from the 1820s to the 1840s, often called the Second Great Awakening. As Jill Lepore has noted, the antebellum Awakening entrenched evangelical and Protestant devotion as the principal segment of America's collective religious identity: "Before the revival began, a scant one in ten Americans were church members; by the time it ended, that ratio had risen to eight in ten."[14]

In the religious free marketplace, not everyone flourished. The "upstart sects" – e.g., agile, revivalist, biblical-populist Methodists and Baptists – fared far better than the more staid and elite Congregationalists, Presbyterians, and Episcopalians (Anglicans).[15] Uncouth Baptist pastors built upstart churches where they expounded theatrically on the plain sense of the Bible, and Methodist circuit-riding preachers led iconic revival camp meetings on the American frontier. These upstart denominations had few educational standards for clergy, but that meant that their pastors' rhetorical appeals were low-to-the-ground and fit the democratic spirit of the era.[16] It was also remarkably expansive. For instance, in 1776, there were a meager sixty-five Methodist churches spread throughout the colonies. By 1850, there were more than 13,000 Methodist churches with more than 2.6 million members, making Methodism the largest denomination in the country by far with 34 percent of all religious adherents.[17] Not coincidentally, this was the era of that champion of the "common man" Andrew Jackson, president from 1829 to 1837 – scriptural populism and political populism grew up together, twin saplings in the fertile, democratic American soil.

While the word "evangelical" was certainly in wide usage in nineteenth-century America, I would hesitate to label anyone in that century with the noun "Evangelical" or any movement as part of the species "Evangelicalism." Indeed, "evangelical" is difficult to define in the nineteenth century, as its claimants could be liberal or conservative, Northern or Southern, theologically explorative or restrictively orthodox. When someone described themselves as "evangelical" in nineteenth-century America (as opposed to holding up a denominational identity or generic Protestant claim), it usually carried a connotation of "activist." They were the busybodies of the American religious scene: defending slavery in the South or passionately promoting abolition in the North; creating temperance societies and Bible distribution schemes; campaigning for or against the death penalty; sending steady streams of missionaries overseas for the sake of world evangelization. In 1830, the combined budgets of the major evangelical voluntary societies (The American Board of Commissioners for Foreign Missions, the American Education Society, the American Bible Society, etc.) was greater than the budget of the US federal government.[18]

What connected all these efforts with the adjective "evangelical"? What tied together all of these disparate causes from education to temperance to abolition? For self-affirming evangelical Christians, the answer was simple: the Bible. As one mid-nineteenth-century chronicler of the movement put it, "evangelical Protestant churches [are those] churches whose religion is the Bible, the whole Bible, and nothing but the Bible."[19]

The Fundamentalist Disruption

If the Second Great Awakening and antebellum America pulsed with the energy and idealism of this evangelical culture, the late nineteenth century saw its gradual deflation. The Civil War cleaved the movement, like the country, in two, and the evangelical believers who joined the Union and Confederate armies both claimed that the plain sense of the Bible vindicated their diametric causes.[20] In the aftermath of the war, many activist evangelical Christians became more pessimistic about reforming American society and building the Kingdom of God on earth.[21]

Beyond these cultural forces, evangelical Christians' straightforward, commonsense approach to the Bible was under increasing intellectual challenge in the late nineteenth century. Darwin's Theory of Evolution, while embraced by some progressive evangelical interpreters, left many believers feeling an increasing tension between the emergent scientific consensus and their own plain sense reading of the book of Genesis. So-called Higher Criticism (or historical criticism) of the Bible slowly migrated from German universities into American academia in the late nineteenth century, similarly calling into question the integrity and facticity of how most evangelical Protestants perceived their scriptures. And new strands of liberal Protestant theology, responsive to Darwinian science and critical views of the Bible, threatened to undermine orthodox evangelical confidence and missionary zeal.[22] The response for theologically and socially conventional evangelical Protestants, as they observed these looming perils and saw many of their fellow activism-oriented, ostensibly evangelical Christians embrace or accommodate such modern departures, was to reiterate and reclaim the basics, the fundamentals of Christianity.

These efforts to circle the wagons around indispensable Protestant doctrines proved to be a galvanizing and a divisive force in many denominations. People on both sides of these debates (liberal/ modernist and conservative/fundamental) thought of themselves and their churches as "evangelical," and, amid these intra-evangelical rhetorical volleys, a new word was coined in 1920 to describe the reactionary camp: Fundamentalists. The term caught on quickly as it denoted, for the self-ascribing Fundamentalists, their single-minded commitment to the core tenets of the Christian faith. If "evangelical" was an amorphous adjective, "Fundamentalist" was an unequivocal noun. It drew a line in the sand.

One of the defining sermons of that era, preached in 1922 by the liberal lion Harry Emerson Fosdick titled "Shall the Fundamentalists Win?" captures the intra-evangelical feud:

> Already all of us must have heard about the people who call
> themselves the Fundamentalists. Their apparent intention is to
> drive out of the evangelical churches men and women of liberal
> opinions ... If they had their way, within the church, they would set
> up in Protestantism a doctrinal tribunal more rigid than the pope's.[23]

For their opponents, like Fosdick, the epithet Fundamentalist summed up the doctrinaire and oppositional attitude that they found so distasteful in the group.[24]

Fundamentalism had several overlapping proclivities: an apocalyptic ideology bolstered by the earth-shaking climate of two world wars; an interdenominational effort to build a Christian counterculture; and a reaction against the rapid scientific and technological change of the early twentieth century. But at its core, Fundamentalism was about the Bible – defending the Bible; vindicating the Bible; relying on the Bible as the apex of truth. In point of fact, for all their rumored anti-intellectualism, Fundamentalists were practically obsessed with knowledge and education, though their pedagogical interests remained narrowly attached to the Bible. Consonant with their sense of cultural alienation, the Fundamentalists create a massive, alternative infrastructure of educational institutions – Bible colleges, Bible institutes, Fundamentalist universities – where they could send young devotees "to fortify them against secular ideologies and lifestyles."[25]

And yet, for all the Fundamentalists' impassioned safeguarding of the "literal truth" of the Bible, Fundamentalism intensified the already schismatic temper of Protestantism. Because the Fundamentalists put supreme importance on protecting the "fundamentals" of Christianity *but*, apart from the ardent defense of the truth of the Bible, there was never a fixed and agreed-upon set of clearly articulated fundamentals, the movement fractured in acrimonious disputes and theological eddies.

I have designated Fundamentalism (and, as we shall see, Wahhabism in the Salafi family tree) as an evolutionary disruption, in that it seemed for a few decades that the strong "evangelical" chord in the American symphony had fallen into disharmony.[26] Unlike the culturally confident evangelical Christians of the nineteenth century, the Fundamentalists took an antagonistic and militant stance toward an American culture they thought had turned against God. Where the coalitional, activist evangelical churches of the nineteenth century had defined the energetic Protestant mainstream, Fundamentalism was an enclave-building, culturally suspicious, and more bellicose variant that, for a while, dominated the evangelical landscape.

In reality, Fundamentalism and its ideological battle with more liberal forms of Protestantism (what Fundamentalists derisively called "modernism") produced two major evolutionary shifts that marked the landscape of American Protestantism. First, in the eyes of many early twentieth-century Protestants, including people like Fosdick who were still calling themselves "evangelical," Fundamentalism was beyond the pale – a backward, intellectually bereft, head-in-the-sand avoidance of modern science and historical consciousness. These liberal Protestants would band together in an ecumenical coalition of their own, bent on recapturing the American Protestant mainstream. They would, eventually, come to call themselves Mainline Protestants, a cadre of genteel and old-school denominations that would confidently claim the American public religious sphere that Fundamentalists had abandoned throughout the mid-twentieth century.[27]

Mainline Protestantism was the ideological foil to Fundamentalism, but Fundamentalism's more potent competition would come from within. Starting in the 1940s, a group of disillusioned and ambitious Fundamentalists began repurposing the term Evangelical, now situated as a noun to stake out their own identity in between what they saw as the toxic rigors of Fundamentalism and the loosey-goosey ecumenism of the Mainline Protestants. It was from within and in reaction to this Fundamentalist impulse that contemporary American Evangelicalism was born, so we cannot understand the modern Evangelical movement without recognizing its parentage that comes both from the earlier optimistic nineteenth-century biblicist revivalism and the more culturally alienated, hard-nosed Fundamentalism of the early twentieth century.

Species: Evangelicalism in America

In our taxonomic history of Evangelicalism, we have finally arrived at the species that would define the scripturalist terrain of modern America. The early Evangelical leaders – they sometimes called themselves "Neo-evangelicals" in recognition of the earlier connotations of the term – in the 1940s centered on the rising star evangelist Billy Graham.[28] They founded the National Association of Evangelicals; they created *Christianity Today* as the premier Evangelical magazine; and they sloughed off the culturally disreputable and internally fraught identity of "Fundamentalist" in favor of a more positive culture-facing affect (see Illustration 1.4).

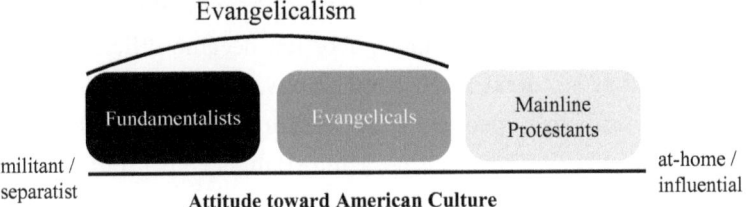

ILLUSTRATION 1.4 Spectrum of coalitions of twentieth-century American Protestantism

Recognizing the power and potential of Fundamentalist educational networks, the Evangelicals built Bible schools and universities of their own, including Fuller Seminary in California, my alma mater, where arguably this new Evangelical identity first took root.[29] Evangelicalism sought to be more big-tent, erudite, and inclusive than Fundamentalism, welcoming anyone who could affirm their biblicist values and intention to proclaim the gospel to the whole world.[30] As I show in greater detail in Chapter 2, the tensions and affinities that remained between Fundamentalists and Evangelicals left the two movements locked in a complicated dance – less "competing species" and more "two varieties of the species" Evangelicalism for the remainder of the twentieth century, until 9/11 brought an end to self-affirming Fundamentalism.[31]

This mid-century, organically American, culturally adroit, Bible-claiming, mission-focused coalition of theologically conservative Protestants (with some pugnacious Fundamentalists in the mix) is more or less the Evangelical movement as it exists today. But the movement underwent one more infamous shift in the second half of the 1970s and 1980s that is essential for understanding its current orientation and outlook. Like the social and theological ferment at the end of the nineteenth century that left the eventual "Fundamentalists" feeling dispossessed and combative, the Civil Rights Movement, sexual revolution, and cultural liberalization that occurred in the 1960s and 1970s caused a good deal of heartburn in Evangelical and Fundamentalist communities. Conservative White

Protestantism was losing its cultural power: Prayer and Bible reading were removed from public schools; abortion became officially legal and protected at a federal level; pornography seemed ascendant and unchecked; and gay people were beginning to step forward unashamedly to experience the same rights and privileges as everyone else.[32]

The majority of Evangelicals and Fundamentalists perceived all of these atmospheric changes as a threat to their biblical interpretations and cultural power, and the movement did something that had not happened before in American evangelical history: They coalesced around one political party. The consolidation of the Evangelical/ Fundamentalist bloc of voters in favor of Ronald Reagan and the Republican Party, first in 1980 and iteratively in each election thereafter, has made the Evangelical movement polarizing in a different way.[33] If the evangelical Protestants of the nineteenth century were the religious busybodies of that era, their busybody-ness was omnidirectional. Since 1980, Evangelical activism (with a few notable exceptions) has mostly aligned with Republican politics, and the name Evangelical has taken on political and partisan connotations.

This was the context of my upbringing. I was born in 1980, a few months before Reagan won the election. I attended Evangelical churches and Evangelical schools where to be anything other than a Republican loyalist or conservative independent voter was anathema. The Bible, as preached and taught, seemed to make the Republican policy platform obvious. Even living in the otherwise culturally liberal and diverse world of Southern California, I was in high school before I met someone who was (I suspected) a Democrat, and it took me a while to trust him.

To sum up: Evangelicalism is a modern, energetic, global – though America-inflected – fashion of scriptural piety. It is other things as well: an emotive spirituality that appeals to transformative experiences for life change; a political force and demographic bloc in America and elsewhere; an adaptive, missionizing movement; a marketable, consumeristic form of religion. But when you live among the

Evangelicals, when you listen to how they describe and orient themselves, what is unmistakable is their avowed fidelity to the Bible. As Stanley Grenz summarizes, "[E]vangelical self-consciousness embodies two central principles: the concern to be a 'gospel people' and the concern to be a 'Scripture people.'"[34]

Evangelicalism is like the pronghorn: a long-situated native of the American religious ecosystem. Though American Evangelicalism's distant roots may go back to even before Old World Protestantism, its identity and genetic structure has been thoroughly formed in the New World. It grew up adjusting itself to the environmental transmutations and peculiarities of American culture but always with a fixation on the Bible as the communal lodestar. There are Protestants and churches who still name themselves "evangelical" in Europe, linking back to the old use of the word from the Protestant Reformations, but when they encounter the North American Evangelicals they tend to be struck by how eccentric the Americans are. They puzzle over how these distant cousins in the Protestant family tree read and claim the Bible and construe a form of Christianity that is simultaneously partisan, consumeristic, egalitarian, transdenominational, and unmoored from the past.[35] Evangelicalism evolved to fill and, indeed, define the scripturalist niche of American culture, but we turn now to another scripturalist species from distant lands.

SALAFI SCRIPTURALISM: FROM MEDIEVAL HADITH PEOPLE TO AMERICAN SHORES

As with the deep roots of scripturalism in Western Christianity, the Sunni scripturalist tendency goes back a long way. "Scripture" for Muslims, of course, refers primarily to the Qur'an. The Qur'an (Arabic for "recitation") is not simply a parallel sacred text for Muslims to what the Bible is for Christians. For Muslims, the Qur'an is the directly revealed word of God, the divine communication preserved in book form. While certainly held as sacred, the Bible has almost universally been understood by Christians to have a human element – multiple human authors in different eras have shaped the text with their personalities and perspectives. Not so the Qur'an – according to the Islamic tradition, the Qur'an is *through* Muhammad, not *by* Muhammad. Muhammad recites; it is God who speaks in the Qur'an. Thus the role of the Qur'an in Islam might more adequately be compared to the role Jesus plays in Christianity: directly exhibiting the divine message and divine character.[36]

The challenge with interpreting the Qur'an is that most Muslims view it as simultaneously an eternal, heavenly corpus of divine communications and a text that was revealed in history to the early Muslim community during the life of the Prophet Muhammad. So from the earliest moments of Muslim reflection, the original context of the Qur'an was supremely important for understanding its meaning.

The Prophet Muhammad is, naturally, also very important in this interpretive endeavor as the one who received the Qur'anic revelation and as the revered leader of the early Muslim community. The Prophet was and is seen as the normative interpreter of the Qur'an and the one who knew best how to apply the principles and lessons of the revelation to everyday life, which brings us to the second body of literature that may be called "scripture" in Islam: the Hadith.

Order: The Sunni Muslim Tradition and the Sunna

The Hadith (Arabic for "stories," "narrations," or "traditions") are the remembered sayings and deeds of the Prophet Muhammad and his early community. They were originally oral traditions, memories from the first Muslims passed down generation to generation. Some hadiths are simple sayings, for instance:

> The Prophet (ﷺ) said, "A woman entered Hell because of a cat which she had tied [up], neither giving it food nor setting it free to eat from the vermin of the earth."[37]

The Prophet famously liked cats. Other hadiths are short little stories that set a scene, like:

> A funeral procession passed in front of us and the Prophet (ﷺ) stood up and we too stood up. We said, "O Allah's Messenger (ﷺ)! This is the funeral procession of a Jew." He said, "Whenever you see a funeral procession, you should stand up."[38]

By putting all of these flickering images together, you get a sense of the personality of Muhammad – his principles, his community, his lifestyle, his interspecies and interreligious instincts. As a whole, this Muhammadan model – the right way to live as a Muslim – is called the Sunna ("path" or "way") from which Sunni Muslims get their name. Accordingly, this Hadith literature surrounds the Qur'an, offering context, explications, and practical applications of the Qur'an's more exhortative style, all filtered through the prism of the life of the Prophet and his model community. The Hadith include tens of thousands of narrations treasured by the early Muslim community, remembering the smallest details and profoundest insights of the Prophet and his Companions. Jonathan Brown observes that, by the logic of the early Sunni tradition, "The Qur'an and Sunna functioned in tandem. Like a locked door without a key, the Qur'an could not be accessed without the Sunna."[39] When talking about "scripture" in Islam, one must be careful to always note what sort of scripture is in view: the essential divine revelation in the Qur'an or the far more malleable and diverse Hadith.

Indeed, if we are looking for a somewhat parallel text to the Bible in the Islamic tradition, I would argue that the Hadith are more akin to the Christian Bible than the Qur'an is.[40] Unlike the Bible, the Qur'an was codified and collected into its present form relatively quickly – within a generation after the death of Muhammad. But, similar to the Bible, the Hadith had a more complex transmission history, only being written down and collected into their present form more than a century later. Like the Christian Bible, the Hadith entail a composite, multi-perspectival, multi-genre corpus of reflections and remembrances. This analogy, like every analogy, is not perfect, but it does help us keep in mind the asymmetries that occur in putting two different religions into conversation.

Muslims in general rely on both the Qur'an and the Hadith. But there is one family in the order of Sunni Islam that attaches itself first and foremost to rigorous, direct Hadith interpretation that will eventually lead to the species Salafism.[41] This family of scripturalists actually began to emerge in Sunni Islam in the ninth century (in the Christian calendar), right around the same time as the Hadith were being codified and organized into their present form.

Before we proceed though, it's important to make note of another structural difference between the Islamic and Christian traditions that will pop up repeatedly throughout this book. Christianity is primarily a theological religious tradition, and the lines that divide different sects and denominations of Christians are historical, practical, cultural, ecclesiastical (i.e., arguments about how to govern the church), etc. but almost always also at some ground level *theological*. Islam certainly has theological debates about the nature of God, predestination, etc., but the primary concerns and central discourse of Islam are, like Judaism, *jurisprudential*. In other words, arguments among Christians tend to boil down to "What do you believe?" whereas disagreements among Muslims tend to boil down to "What should we do and how should we do it?"[42] If we imagine the different traditions as meals, the main course of the Christian tradition is theology (creeds, statements of faith, biblical exegesis, confessions, etc.), and there are side-dish accompaniments of ethics, practical theology, canon law, political theology, etc.

The main course of the Islamic tradition is jurisprudence and the pragmatics of applying the teaching of the Qur'an and Hadith. The integral Islamic jurisprudential endeavor ("What should Muslims do according to the Qur'an and the precedents of the Prophet?") is what goes by the title of the Shari'a, the effort to discern and apply the will of God to everyday life.[43] The majority of Shari'a reasoning is rooted in the Hadith, brimming as they are with practical examples and clear precedents from the life of the Prophet. While Christians and Muslims both have scripture, the clusters of questions adherents bring to those scriptures differ widely. This can sometimes be simplistically phrased as: Christianity is an *orthodoxic* religion (focused on right belief), whereas Islam is an *orthopraxic* religion (focused on right practice). It's more complicated than that, but as a shorthand, this distinction can help us understand the different core concerns each tradition brings to scriptural interpretation. Now let us trace the evolutionary family tree that leads to Salafis arriving in America.

Family: People of the Hadith

The two centuries after the death of the Prophet were filled with energy and expansion for the Muslim community. Within decades after Muhammad's death, Muslim armies had conquered most of the Middle East, toward the Indian subcontinent, across North Africa, and up into the Iberian Peninsula on the doorstep of Europe. This was the era, according to later Sunnism, of the Salaf (the "righteous ancestors," the first three generations of Muslims) held in high esteem for their proximity to the Prophet and his Companions. Jurisprudential and theological reasoning in this era was more ad hoc. Everyone was in agreement that the Qur'an and the Sunna (the example of Muhammad) were definitive for what it meant to be a Muslim, but the Hadith were still mostly an oral body of knowledge, hundreds of thousands of stories and morsels – some of questionable provenance – from the Prophet's life being passed from generation to generation, from scholar to scholar by memory.

Two major camps of legal scholars emerged in the late eighth century of the Christian Era. One group called themselves the *Ahl al-Ra'y* (the people of rational discretion), and they mostly accepted the reliability of the Hadith as a guide, but they were also pragmatic jurists, who thought the guidance of the Prophet was not only contained in the Hadith texts but also in the practical wisdom and legal methodologies of the scholars. Where the Hadith accounts were indeterminate or chaotic, these jurists saw it as their job to iron things out.[44]

The other camp in this debate established itself as the hardline defenders of the Hadith. They even called themselves the "people of the Hadith" (*Ahl al-Hadith*). These were, by and large, Hadith special-ists, who spent their time memorizing and correlating and sifting and sorting individual hadiths.[45] For the Hadith People, the authority question was straightforward: *If you have access to the mind and the practice of the Prophet in the form of Hadith* – jumbled and multivalent though they may be – *how dare you elevate your prag-matic logic over scripture?*

The intellectual champion of the Hadith People in the ninth century was a jurist and Hadith scholar named Ahmad ibn Hanbal. Ibn Hanbal was a ram-rod straight sort of fellow. In one of the key theo-logical debates of early Islam on whether the Qur'an was created in time or eternal, he took the unyielding position that the Qur'an was uncreated and eternal, and when three successive Caliphs took the other position, Ibn Hanbal endured repeated physical torture rather than even pretend to change his view. Given this firm conviction – and the fact that his view won out and became standard in the Islamic tradition as a whole – Imam Ahmad, as he's popularly referred to, has since been upheld as a heroic and exemplary thought leader in early Islam.

Ibn Hanbal was one of the first to create a written Hadith collection, and the two greatest Hadith collectors of all time, al-Bukhari and Muslim, were Ibn Hanbal's younger disciples. His stu-dents remembered him as having an encyclopedic knowledge of Hadith, claiming that he had personally memorized and could recite *one million* hadiths.[46] This might sound far-fetched, but multiple of Ibn Hanbal's disciples and his own son attest to his remarkable powers of retention, and he would play a key role in culling the disparate oral Hadith corpus into its more manageable, canonical form.

Imam Ahmad and his followers argued for the primacy and interrelatedness of the Qur'an and the Hadith. Authority and right practice were secured by these memories from the early Muslims and their pristine practice of Islam, and any departure from that model, any unprecedented human invention in the realm of religion was labeled by the Hadith People with a dirty word: innovation (bid'a). An anecdote from Imam Ahmad's life helps capture this worldview. One of his disciples remembered: "I asked Aḥmad ibn Ḥanbal about what Abū Thawr [another respected scholar] had written, and he said: 'It's a work where he comes up with bad novelties!' He didn't approve of writing books. 'Stick to Hadith!' he said."[47] To be clear, Ibn Hanbal was one of the most learned and literate people of his time. Books aren't the problem in his evaluation; "bad novelties" in books are. For the Hadith People, there were sharp gradations of knowledge with revelation serving as the only firm basis for action. Since the teaching of the Qur'an was embodied in the life and practice of the Prophet, the Hadith took on a revelatory status as well. The Qur'an inscribes the will of God, and the Sunna/Hadith enacts it. Muslims didn't need to innovate away from the precedent of the Prophet or appeal to abstract human reason or to philosophically grounded theology – we have the text; let's stick to the text.

Ibn Hanbal and the Hadith People managed to mostly win this authority debate according to the mainstream Sunni tradition, and everyone came to agree that the Hadith were central to Islamic theology and practice. But that did not mean that all hadiths were equal. An entire field of medieval Islamic literary science evolved and matured among Hadith scholars in the ninth and tenth centuries, sorting and sifting the amazing variety of hadiths, organizing them thematically, and even tossing out, on the basis of correspondence and reliability of transmission, those that seemed to have been fabricated.[48]

According to the Sunni consensus that emerged from this process (Illustration 1.5), the Hadith might be thought of as a scriptural canon with a clearly defined core and fuzzy edges. Certain hadiths are considered unshakably reliable – sahih (verified sound / authentic) – and beyond that there are various gradations of reliability (ḥasan – good, ḍaʿīf – weak, mawḍūʿ – fabricated). There are six canonical Hadith collections, with two occupying preeminent status: the books of only sahih hadiths edited by those two disciples of Ibn

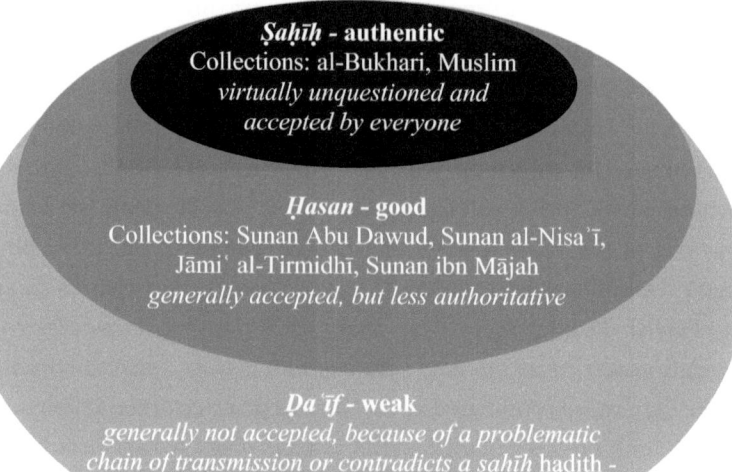

Ṣaḥīḥ **- authentic**
Collections: al-Bukhari, Muslim
virtually unquestioned and
accepted by everyone

Ḥasan **- good**
Collections: Sunan Abu Dawud, Sunan al-Nisaʾī,
Jāmiʿ al-Tirmidhī, Sunan ibn Mājah
generally accepted, but less authoritative

Ḍaʿīf **- weak**
generally not accepted, because of a problematic
chain of transmission or contradicts a ṣaḥīḥ hadith -
but might be edifying

Mawḍūʿ **- fabricated**

ILLUSTRATION 1.5 Authority/authenticity of Hadith collections

Hanbal – al-Bukhari and Muslim. If one imagines concentric circles of traditional Hadith authority, the sahih collections by Muslim and al-Bukhari are the innermost core, the other four canonical collections are the next (reliable, but not absolute) circle, and further lower levels of gradation expand out from there.

In this same era that the Hadith were becoming more canonically coherent and fixed, Sunni jurists and theologians were also becoming more systematic in how they organized themselves. Different regional or methodological *madhhab*s, or schools of jurisprudence, coalesced, each of them nominally attached to a great scholar from late in the Salaf period. There were a number of these schools early on, but ultimately four of them consolidated and became definitional for Sunnism: Hanafis, Malikis, Shafiʿis, and, last but not least, Hanbalis (after Imam Ahmad). These *madhhab*s are the prime carriers of Islamic tradition, the vehicles of normative scriptural interpretation.

As with any legal tradition, each of the Islamic traditions includes a mix of jurists consulting the source texts – Qur'an and Hadith – then looking at legal precedents and the consensus of past scholars, applying their own reason and methods, and finally advising Muslims on how to live. The four *madhhab*s are not really sects, in the sense of competing with each other to be the *real* Islam; they, as a rule, recognize each other as valid ways of being Sunni. But true to Ibn Hanbal's "Stick to Hadith!" admonition, among the *madhhab*s, the Hanbali scholars have been the most scripture-bound, choosing to rely more upon direct appeal to the Hadith rather than allowing traditions of interpretation or legal precedents to create hard-and-fast intellectual superstructures around the scriptures.[49]

This led to an interesting identification quandary: Yes, the followers of the *madhhab* or methodology of Ahmad ibn Hanbal admired his thought and approach to Islam, but in naming themselves "Hanbalis" weren't they doing the very thing that he had counseled against, that is, lifting the view of Imam Ahmad above that of the text? Starting a few centuries after his death, we can see some Hanbali scholars beginning to use a new adjective for themselves in their theological texts: *salafi* (following the Salaf).[50] For the Hadith People, the Salaf were the *ur*-Muslims, who had access to unspoiled Islam flowing from the fountainhead of the Qur'anic revelation and wisdom of the Prophet. This new coinage was a means of solving the conundrum: We aren't following Ahmad ibn Hanbal; we are following the Prophet and his Companions. We aren't "Hanbali" in our theology, per se; we are "salafi."[51]

Genus: Ibn Taymiyya's Theological Originalism

The figure who most typifies this commingling between being juridically Hanbali and drawing his theological inspiration directly from the Salaf is an iconoclast polymath scholar of the fourteenth century named Ibn Taymiyya. Born into a respected family of Hanbali scholars, he began to learn Hadith interpretation and jurisprudence when today's children would be in elementary school. He quickly gained a reputation as a brilliant scholar and a thorn in the side of the authorities.

The medieval Islamic world which Ibn Taymiyya inhabited was relatively religiously tolerant: The four official legal *madhhab*s accepted each other's different approaches; Sunnis and Shi'ites could usually coexist peacefully; all manner of orders of mystics and popular devotion flourished around the Sufi saints; various philosophers, inspired especially by Aristotle, brought older Greek ideas into conversation with Islam; whatever the official strictures of Islamic law, some Muslims casually visited brothels and wine shops. All of these trends were extremely troubling to Ibn Taymiyya. He was not interested in civil coexistence but in True Islam – capital T, capital I. And he wasn't bashful about his opinions.

Multiple times Ibn Taymiyya faced legal trials and imprisonment for outspokenly making his ideas known. "He was a relentless activist who engaged in social reform, even vigilante dispensation of justice and moral policing, which he did with his group of devoted fellow scholars and students."[52] He stringently opposed those he called People of Innovation (*Ahl al-Bid'a*) who deviated from original Islam. He condemned the Sufis for venerating the graves of their saints (*bid'a!*). He wrote long treatises deconstructing Aristotle and upbraiding any Muslim foolish enough to incorporate Greek philosophical logic into their religion (*bid'a!*).[53] He was famous in Damascus for encouraging his followers to storm wine shops, break the bottles, and pour the wine on the floor.[54]

In 1299, Ibn Taymiyya published a theological treatise that contained a creed he urged all Muslims to adopt. Typical of strict salafi theology, Ibn Taymiyya's creed hewed closely to the literal text of the Qur'an, condemning the various philosophical innovations and newer ideas that had entered into the Islamic discourse of his time. He stressed the utmost importance of *tawhid*, the unity and uniqueness of God. This simple creed prompted his theological opponents to put Ibn Taymiyya on trial, accusing him of heresy and anthropomorphism. The Qur'an and some hadiths describe God with physical language, e.g., sitting on a throne, and most Muslim thinkers argued this is purely symbolic because God is not corporeal. Ibn Taymiyya rejoindered, who are you to question the revelation of God? If the text says God sits on a throne, then God sits on a throne. Maybe you don't and can't understand what the Qur'an means by that, but you're in no position to overrule the text.

After several months and several rounds of one of these trials, everyone except Ibn Taymiyya tired of the dispute, and his opponents offered him a compromise: They said, "you have compiled the creed of Imam Aḥmad; shall we just say, then, that this is the creed of Aḥmad? I mean, the man has merely compiled [a creed] according to his school (madhhab); he should not be molested for this. For this [Hanbali] school is a recognized school." Ibn Taymiyya's response was potent: "I have simply compiled the creed of all the Pious Ancestors as a whole; Imam Aḥmad has no special claim to this. Imam Aḥmad simply communicates whatever knowledge comes to him on the authority of the Prophet ... Indeed, this creed is the creed of Muhammad, God's blessings and salutations be upon him!"[55] He spent several months in jail after that, one of several such stints throughout his theologically controversial life.

In Ibn Taymiyya's time, the Mongol armies were advancing south, gradually conquering more and more of the lands that the Arabs had themselves conquered six centuries earlier in the initial spread of Islam. In 1258, just a few years before his birth, the Mongols sacked Baghdad, the intellectual capital of Islam at the time, largely bringing to an end the era that scholars today call Classical Islam. The aggressive Mongol rulers (the grandchildren and great-grandchildren of Genghis Khan) had found a convenient hack in mainstream Sunni jurisprudence: The consensus among scholars of the different madhhabs was that Muslims should not declare war (jihad) or take up arms against a Muslim ruler. The Mongols outwardly declared themselves to be Muslims, hence any aggression against their encroaching armies was deemed impermissible by most jurists.

Ibn Taymiyya became famous, and quite popular with the common people, for bucking this consensus. He issued several *fatwas* (the learned opinions of a Muslim jurist scholar) sanctioning war against the Mongols on the basis, not of the scholarly discussions of his day, but on the precedent of the Salaf. He reasoned that the Mongols were not true Muslims in their behavior and, based on the precedent of the early Caliphs, therefore jihad against them was not only fair game, it was an obligation on all true Muslims.[56] Ibn Taymiyya put his money where his mouth was, joining a number of battles and skirmishes against the Mongols – a warrior jurist.

One of the most striking things about contemporary Salafi discourse is just how much they make reference to Ibn Taymiyya, this relatively obscure late-medieval, hard-minded scripturalist. For a religious movement that, like the medieval Hanbali theologians, eschews attributing their approach to any teacher other than the Prophet and the Salaf, the modern Salafis are constantly citing and referencing and drawing upon the thought of Ibn Taymiyya. He is for them a near irrefutable guide, an anchor point, a precedent from the past to validate the practices of the present – "Look, we didn't make this up. We're just doing Islam in our time the way Ibn Taymiyya did it in his time, and the Salaf did it in their time." The fact that he was popular with the people but not his fellow scholars bolsters contemporary Salafis' confidence in the face of disdain from many learned Muslims. The fact that Ibn Taymiyya was a political lightning rod vindicates Salafis' own politically fraught presence in many Muslim societies. Put differently, to live by the way of the Salaf is to court controversy, whether in the fourteenth or the twenty-first century.

The Wahhabi Disruption

We have one more historic evolutionary waypoint to consider on our way to American Salafism, and it arose in a Sunni revival in the very decades that the preachers of the First Great Awakening were spreading evangelical zeal around the American colonies. Its leader was Muhammad ibn 'Abd al-Wahhab, an über-Hanbali who lived in

Arabia. Like Ibn Taymiyya before him, Muhammad ibn 'Abd al-Wahhab centered his theology and his jurisprudence on the principle of *tawhid*, the unity of God, but this simple point of departure had grave consequences in his construction.

For Ibn 'Abd al-Wahhab, *tawhid* flowed incontrovertibly out of the divine realm and into the human one: If there is only one God, then God has only one will and directive. Ergo, there is only one right way of worshipping and obeying God, only one societal model that is acceptable, and all other ways of worshipping or organizing society are therefore deviant, idolatrous, and in need of reprimand.[57] This meant, in his mind, that the righteous community of true monotheists – the *muwahhidun*, the proclaimers of divine unity – was justified in declaring war upon any other community (including self-ascribing Muslims) who did not fulfill "true" monotheism. Punishable idolatry could be anything from belief in magic to befriending unbelievers, from praying to saints to wearing a magical amulet.[58] Any departure from the model of the Salaf – according to Ibn 'Abd al-Wahhab's understanding of it – justified the prosecution of jihad against any community or society, including fellow Muslims, who refused to repent. You can imagine that, unlike Ibn Taymiyya, who endorsed jihad against the malignant Mongols, Muhammad ibn 'Abd al-Wahhab, who endorsed jihad against anyone who substantially disagreed with him, was not very popular in his time.

Paradoxically, given the radical, globally ambitious nature of Ibn 'Abd al-Wahhab's theological vision, he was relatively apolitical and even quietist when it came to governing. He believed that society should have a single, male, divinely sanctioned, political, and military ruler. As long as that ruler was theologically orthodox, he was exempt from criticism for injustice or even tyranny. Indeed, while Muhammad ibn 'Abd al-Wahhab pitched himself as an reformer and re-interpreter of contemporary Islam by way of the Salaf, à la Ibn Taymiyya, he did not really depart much from conventional Hanbali thought and jurisprudence on most questions.[59] In 1744, he formed an alliance with a local tribal leader named Muhammad ibn Sa'ud, the progenitor of the Saudi royal family; both swore loyalty to each other, and Ibn ʿAbd al-Wahhab deemed Ibn Saʿud the governing protector of *tawhid* – and more practically, the political and military guarantor against interference with the Wahhabis' domineering religious reform program.

To call the Wahhabi-Saudi alliance a "theocracy" is not entirely accurate, given that the political realm remained mainly untrammeled by the reformer's theological idealism.[60] So long as he and his followers had dictatorial power over peoples' religion and outward morality, Ibn ʿAbd al-Wahhab didn't care much about the political machinations that externally guided society. He sanctioned Ibn Saʿud's wars of expansion to spread the alliance's realm of authority and the message of uncompromising *tawhid*.[61]

Wahhabism was an effort to imperiously de-localize Islam, to strip away the corruptions, accretions, syncretisms, and appendices – the *bidʿa* – of local cultures over the centuries, to return to the simplicity of *tawhid*, which the Wahhabis imagined guided the original Muslims. Their presence in Arabia, the locale of the Prophet's paradigmatic emergence and conquests, only increased their confidence that they could recreate the polity and practice of the Salaf in Arabia. The political alignment between Ibn ʿAbd al-Wahhab and Ibn Saʿud allowed the movement to grow locally through proclamation (*daʿwa*) and warfare. In the first years of the nineteenth century, after Ibn ʿAbd al-Wahhab's death, they even captured Mecca and Medina from the local Ottoman-backed rulers, and the Wahhabis quickly began imposing their decidedly anti-pluralist views at the heart of Muslim spiritual geography.

This was not a sustainable arrangement. The Ottoman Empire, which ostensibly retained its claim to power over the Arabian Peninsula, could not allow an upstart, rigorist reform movement to control the holy cities, particularly Mecca, the locus of the annual *hajj* pilgrimage. After a mere fifteen years of Saudi-Wahhabi rule, in 1818 the Ottoman armies pushed the movement out of Mecca and Medina and into the backwaters of the Arabian Desert – into the Najd region, Ibn 'Abd al-Wahhab's birthplace.[62] The Saudi-Wahhabi alliance would remain there in relative obscurity, ruling over a small swath of desert for a century.

But Wahhabism did not stay forever in the Najd hinterlands. For the remainder of the nineteenth century after their defeat by the Ottomans, the grandsons and great-grandsons of Muhammad ibn Sa'ud managed to maintain control over Najd by not further provoking the Ottoman sultans in distant Istanbul. Then in the 1920s, 'Abd al-'Aziz ibn Sa'ud, a fifth-generation member of the dynasty, took advantage of the dissolution of the Ottoman Empire and began a campaign of military expansion in imitation of his great-great-grand-father. He eventually conquered most of the Arabian Peninsula and established the present day Kingdom of Saudi Arabia, the third instantiation of the Saudi-Wahhabi religio-political alliance.[63] This new, twentieth-century monarchial nation-state gave the Wahhabi clerics a larger platform for instituting their societal vision than they had ever had before. What's more, with the discovery of massive deposits of oil under the Arabian desert early in the century, the Kingdom had the wealth and influence to become an international Islamic power center and build institutions and universities to export Wahhabi theology to the global Sunni community by the mid-century period. I explore in greater depth in Chapter 3 how these very institutions would become the locus of modern Salafism.

As we saw with Fundamentalism, I would characterize Wahhabism as a sort of evolutionary disruption that is simultaneously discordant with and also integral to later Salafism. This is not to simplistically equate Fundamentalism and Wahhabism, as so many proponents of "Islamic fundamentalism" have done explicitly and implicitly. The cultural contexts of twentieth-century American denominational struggles is a far cry from eighteenth- or nineteenth-century Arabian religio-tribal warfare. Protestant Fundamentalists may have been theologically militant within their denominations and had an austere morality, but the Fundamentalists weren't waging literal wars with their enemies. No, the similarity lies in the relationship between Fundamentalism and Evangelicalism: Wahhabism was a harsh predecessor that became a subspecies of Salafism.[64] Today, Salafism is a Hadith-renewalist reform movement, intellectually anchored in the Saudi Arabia that Wahhabis built, and some contemporary Salafis speak of Ibn 'Abd al-Wahhab as a theological forebear and ideological hero. On the other hand, Salafism is a "global intellectual current," many sub-movements of which operate with little reference to or, as we shall see, stark critiques of the Saudi-Wahhabi religious establishment.[65] Wahhabism is but one influential faction among the many forms of Salafism today. One thing that can be said: Were it not for the eighteenth-century austerity and exclusivism of the Wahhabis, Salafism would be a very different phenomenon today.

Species: Saudi Salafism Comes to America

In 1994, at the eighth annual conference of the Qur'an and Sunnah Society (QSS), one of the first major American Salafi organizations, Abu Muslimah, an African American Salafi who had discovered Islam first through the Nation of Islam and then studied in Saudi Arabia at the Islamic University of Medina, got up to give an exhortative lecture. Consider this short excerpt:

> The Messenger of Allah said, in a hadith collected by Muslim and al-Bukhari, that "The best of humanity is my generation, and the generation that followed them, and the generation that followed them." This is what Allah – *subhanahu wata'ala* [glorious and exalted is He] – is referring to when He says, "the path of the believers," (Q 4:115) the believers that actually lived and understood properly the Book of Allah [the Qur'an] and the *Sunna* of his Messenger – *salla-llahu 'alayhi wa-'alihi wa-sallam* [God bless him and his family and grant him peace] – and not just any Muslim ... We are to take into consideration [those first three generations of Muslims] ... on that practical application of the Qur'an and the *Sunna* to the Day of Resurrection.[66]

Take away some of the English phrasing, and this statement could have easily come out of the mouth of Ibn Taymiyya seven centuries earlier. Abu Muslimah goes on to criticize those "deviant groups who have left Islam . . . who still claim to be Muslim" including the Nation of Islam ("deviant" here is a translation of *bid'a*). In the lecture, he fluidly moves back and forth from Arabic to English, quoting the Qur'an and Hadith, and then explicating the text to his English-speaking audience.

What is most fascinating to me about this scene is how enmeshed and integrated and unexceptional it is. Abu Muslimah was just one of many American Salafi lecturers that day at the QSS conference with the others offering similar messages and idiomatic exhortations. By the mid-1990s, there were thousands if not tens of thousands of African American Salafis, not to mention a multitude of other converts and Muslim immigrants to the United States who identified as Salafis.[67] They built institutions like QSS, hosted annual conferences, circulated tape cassettes of favorite preachers' sermons like this one by Abu Muslimah, and networked mosques across different cities with lecturers going on speaking circuits from city to city. How do you get to this point nearly two centuries after the Wahhabi revivals in Arabia? How did the approach of Ibn Hanbal and rhetoric of Ibn Taymiyya reach American shores and become ingrained among distant American Muslim communities?

While scholarship on global Salafism is advancing rapidly, the full-fledged history of this American Salafi community has yet to be written. What is available in contemporary sources are oral histories, autobiographies, and discrete, intriguing data points.[68] There are at least two major twentieth-century shifts that converged to produce someone like Abu Muslimah and the American Salafi community of which he is emblematic: one a terminological shift, the other an American policy change.

First, a change in terminology. We have noted the perennial difficulty in naming this scripturalist strand of Islam. A tendency that started with the ninth-century Hadith People and Ibn Hanbal didn't necessarily want to call itself Hanbali, because their point of reference was the original Muslims. So, by the time of Ibn Taymiyya, the adjective *salafi* had come into vogue to describe a type of theological primitivism that roots itself not in intervening tradition but in earliest Muslim practice (as mediated by the Hadith).[69]

In the early twentieth century, a series of societal and identity crises gripped majority-Muslim nations. Many nations were transitioning from colonies of Europe or vassal states of the Ottoman Empire into modern countries. In 1924, the abolition of the Ottoman Caliphate, the nominal leader and point of unity for all Sunni Muslims, brought to the surface deep disharmonies and diverging interpretations of Sunnism and of that historic moment. It is not surprising then that there emerged in that period a welter of geographically diverse, radical and reformist movements seeking to rethink and reconfigure Islamic societies.[70] It is also in the same period that several of these revivalist movements embraced the noun Salafism (*Salafiyya*) to characterize their projects. As I show in greater depth in Chapter 3, suddenly you had multiple movements – all of them vaguely Taymiyyan, some progressive and modernist, some conventional and Hadith-centric – naming themselves *Salafis*. The word was vague enough in meaning and reference that different groups could adopt it to diverse ends.[71] Like the various Protestantisms that arose in sixteenth-century Europe, all claiming to recover the primitive and true ethos of Christianity, many laid claim to the free-radical term Salafi in the early twentieth century.

This rise of a diverse spectrum of "Salafi" movements and the aforementioned instantiation of an affluent Saudi-Wahhabi theological kingdom flowed together and merged in curious ways. The ridiculously wealthy Saudi state soon realized that it could spread its purist and politically quietist vision of Islam (and its own international influence) through educational and international institutions. And the intellectual and physical descendants of Ibn 'Abd al-Wahhab happily adopted the Salafi moniker as they had always objected to being called Wahhabis (i.e., followers of a controversial eighteenth-century reformer as opposed to restorers of original, pristine Islam).

The Saudi royals created and sponsored the Islamic University of Medina (1961), the World Muslim League (1962), and the World Assembly of Muslim Youth (1972) to promote Wahhabi values internationally, form sponsorship alliances with like-minded groups, train Wahhabi missionaries, and engender Saudi-friendly, Wahhabi sentiment in other communities.[72] Salafi-identifying scholars from around the world were funded and welcomed into the Kingdom. Sympathetic young Muslim men hailing from everywhere from Nigeria to the United States to Malaysia were given full scholarships to study Hadith, theology, jurisprudence, and da'wa (proclamation/missionizing) at the Islamic University of Medina and other Saudi schools.[73] For Salafis in particular, who were so focused on the earliest Muslim experiences and ideas, the inherent authenticity of the holy homeland of the Prophet was magnetic.

But the enactment of this grand Saudi strategy also subversively redefined Salafism: By making itself the intellectual nexus for all of these culturally diverse Salafi identities, the Saudi state diluted the cohesion and internal influence of Wahhabism. As Chapter 3 will demonstrate through the life of one paradigmatic Salafi scholar, the conformist and quietist scholars, who continued – in the vein of Ibn 'Abd al-Wahhab – supporting the Saudi royal family and never entering into political activism, were suddenly studying alongside more politically oriented Salafis and iconoclastic scholars who had Hadith interpretations that made old-school Wahhabis shudder.[74] Non-Saudi Salafi thinkers, who had no deep attachment to established Wahhabi jurisprudential mindsets, brought new ideas and questions into the very schools and institutions that were created by the Saudis to inculcate the Wahhabi perspective.[75] Salafi scholars with very different interpretations of the Hadith even came and taught at the ostensibly Wahhabi schools, creating controversies and developing student disciples, who, in turn, brought those ideas back to their global homelands.[76] The unitive alignment of Wahhabism (tawhid, the requisite siloing of political and theological authorities, the demand for unanimity) was fractured and unintentionally pluralized through Saudi internationalism.

The second shift is one that is specific to American immigration policy. In 1965, the US Congress passed and Lyndon Johnson signed the Hart-Celler Immigration and Nationality Act, which removed the National Origins Formula that had privileged northern Europeans (i.e., white people) immigrating to America since the 1920s. The 1965 act made immigration to the United States far more possible and attainable for people from parts of the world, especially Asia and Africa, that had previously been seriously restricted. And many of the Asians and Africans and Middle Easterners who established themselves as Americans after 1965 were Muslims. Due to the separation of church and state, the US Census and immigration officials do not ask about religion, but we know that "[f]rom 1966 to 1997, approximately 2,780,000 people immigrated to the US from areas of the world with significant Muslim populations."[77] Today somewhere between 3.5 and 4 million Americans are Muslim (about 1.1 percent of the US population) with 76 percent identifying as either immigrants themselves or the children of immigrants.[78] It is very difficult to count the number of Salafis among these first- and second-generation immigrant communities in the USA (for reasons, I will unpack in the next chapter), but they easily number in the tens or hundreds of thousands.

All of these historical forces – the scripturalist DNA of the medieval Ahl al-Hadith, the non-conformist and originalist ideas of Ibn Taymiyya, the exacting monotheism of the Wahhabis – have fed into what we today call Salafism, a twentieth-century, worldwide, Hadith-revival movement in Sunni Islam, centered in Saudi Arabia. And it has arrived in America in the past fifty years with all of its global complexity in tow. Global Salafism today is an adaptive scriptural discourse that draws together Wahhabism and many other streams of thought. At the intersection of these new Muslim immigrant communities and the Saudi scholarship incentives for American

Muslims, the international currents of ideas and Hadith-centric Islam that flowed through Saudi Arabia also flowed into the United States.[79]

To return to our evolutionary analogy, Salafism is like the antelope: an umbrella term for a diverse collection of identities that congealed in the twentieth century in various societies and nationalities. Salafism is native to Syria, Lebanon, Jordan, North Africa, Sub-Saharan Africa, South Asia, the United Arab Emirates, Egypt, and, archetypically, Saudi Arabia. Through government-sponsored Saudi missionary endeavors and American immigration policy, these global Salafis have come to reside in the USA. For all their diversity, there are certain features that unite all these "Old World" Salafis, most prominently a scripturalist, direct-to-the-source attachment to the Hadith, a close affinity with Ibn Taymiyya, and a quest to recapture the energy and vision of original, authentic Islam.

CONCLUSION

What would happen if the antelope came to reside in the native lands of the pronghorn? If Evangelicalism evolved and emerged in concert with American history, Salafism evolved and emerged across many centuries and in many different historical and intellectual biomes. Clearly American Evangelicalism has gone through many phases and permutations, but those different strata of evangelical history have been coordinated in subtle and obvious ways with American cultural and political shifts. Like the pronghorn, Evangelicals have developed over the past three centuries to fill a niche in the American ecology: the fleet-footed, populist, revivalist brand of American Protestantism, proclaiming the veracity and clarity of the Bible, an innovative and adaptive form of modern religion whose impulse toward activism has recently adjoined the movement to the Republican Party to create a powerful political bloc.

As these two side-by-side evolutionary histories make visible, Salafism is something quite different, proceeding organically from various originalist, Taymiyyan, Hadith-focused, theological and social currents in Sunni Islamic history. The Salafi relationship with the

Qur'an and Hadith resembles the Evangelical relationship to the Bible, but there are many eye-catching differences: The Hadith canon remains enormous and layered and complex; the Qur'an is a scripture without parallel in Christianity; and the orthopraxic, jurisprudential orientation of the Islamic tradition as a whole means that, naturally, the questions Salafis ask of their scriptures will be more focused on action and details of behavior than on abstract theological arguments (though Salafis have plenty of those too).

While Evangelicals may respect and sometimes quote figures like Martin Luther or Jonathan Edwards, there is no correspondent historical thought leader in Evangelicalism who holds a position of primacy like Ibn Taymiyya does for Salafis. The different strands of twentieth-century Salafism have emerged within a diverse array of majority-Muslim, post-colonial political orders all undergoing upheaval, but few of them are what we might conventionally call "liberal" or "democratic," and virtually none of them are religiously pluralistic (at least not in the American sense of separation of religion and state). And even at a very practical level of American reality: Most Evangelicals in America are white, with all the attendant privileges, security, and freedoms that white Christianity brings. Most Salafis in America, like most Muslims in America, belong to African American or first- or second- generation immigrant communities, and their experience of America is affected by racism, xenophobia, Islamophobia, and other forms of cultural alienation, often coming from Evangelicals and other white Christians.

In the post-9/11 American imagination, Salafism was depicted as something foreign, wild, and rigid – a Wahhabi-inspired, Saudi-exported Islamic animus that was medieval-minded and retrograde. Consider this passage from the 9/11 Commission Report:

> Usama Bin Ladin and other Islamist terrorist leaders draw on a long
> tradition of extreme intolerance within one stream of Islam (a
> minority tradition), from at least Ibn Taimiyyah, through the
> founders of Wahhabism ... That stream is motivated by religion

and does not distinguish politics from religion, thus distorting both ... Bin Ladin and Islamist terrorists mean exactly what they say: To them America is the font of all evil, the 'head of the snake,' and it must be converted or destroyed.

It is not a position with which Americans can bargain or negotiate. With it there is no common ground – not even respect for life – on which to begin a dialogue. It can only be destroyed or utterly isolated.[80]

After 9/11, Salafis who were in America, of both the African American and the immigrant variety, whether they were sympathetic to Bin Laden's sentiments about America or not, were designated as an invasive foreign species – ideological interlopers, exponents of an arcane and dangerous religious fundamentalism.

It's true that Salafism *is* native to many different locales, mostly spread throughout the Middle Eastern, African, and South and Southeast Asian lands where Islam has flourished. Yet, despite the divergence between the hereditary and cultural and racial experiences of Evangelicals and Salafis in America, the fact is that Salafis have managed in the last forty years to make a home for themselves in American society. Doing so, they have instinctively grabbed hold of many of the localisms and styles that Evangelicalism has long exhibited, in order to inhabit an often-hostile cultural milieu in which Salafism did not organically emerge. As we shall see in the coming chapters, this acculturation of a mature, diverse, and fluidly American community of Salafis bespeaks the profound flexibility and adaptability of Salafism.

2 What Is a Salafi or an Evangelical Anyway?

Once upon a time there were real-life Fundamentalists. They roamed America, proud to bear that title. They banded together in cities and rural locales. They hosted conventions and built Bible colleges. They fought against teaching evolution in public schools and strove for what they saw as the defense of American Christianity from the slow creep of secularism and modernism. They battled the sexual revolution and mobilized a political bloc to be reckoned with. Then, in the early twenty-first century, the Fundamentalists disappeared . . .

A TALE OF TWO "FUNDAMENTALISMS"

When the term "Fundamentalist" was conceived in 1920 and embraced by an interdenominational coalition of theologically uncompromising American Protestants, it was meant to signal their Christian backbone. They championed what they believed were the *fundamentals* of Christianity: the utter reliability of the Bible, the reality of miracles, the need for sins to be atoned through the cross of Christ, and so on. The Fundamentalists declared the Bible to be a clear, factual document, invulnerable to the scrutiny of modern historical criticism or science. In a previous generation they might have called themselves orthodox Protestants or theologically conservative evangelical believers, but they felt that those older terms were too weak-kneed, too corrupted by invasive, new *liberal* theologies. The Fundamentalists affirmed the truth of Christian dogma in the face of disintegrating faith. They stood athwart the accelerating cultural change of their time and shouted, "No."

This identity marker "Fundamentalist" existed for the rest of the twentieth century in creative tension with the identity marker "Evangelical." They were two ideological and identity poles of the same movement, often with "Evangelical"/"Evangelicalism" serving as the broader, umbrella term for the movement as a whole. Fundamentalism was the stringent, belligerent, hard-line wing of Evangelicalism's more moderate, inclusive, culture-facing ethos. Fundamentalists and Evangelicals mobilized together in the 1980s and 1990s to support Ronald Reagan, then George H. W. Bush, and, finally, his son George W. Bush, consolidating a voting bloc that exercised immense power in the Republican Party.

This was the world in which I was raised. The church where my father worked as a pastor would have not shied away from calling itself Fundamentalist. In the virtual enclave of Evangelical and Fundamentalist Christians in which I grew up in Southern California (homeschooling, private Christian schools, theologically adamant churches, little contact with non-Christians), there wasn't much differentiation between the two. "Fundamentalist" wasn't a bad word but an ambivalent shading of vigor and antagonism.

But then self-described Fundamentalists began to vanish. No single survey was consistently structured in such a way to precisely track this demographic nosedive, but over the course of several religion polls from the 1990s to the 2010s, we see the numbers of self-identifying Fundamentalists melt away.

As shown in Illustration 2.1, two surveys conducted in 1996 found that somewhere between 10 and 13 percent of all Americans identified as "Fundamentalist Christians," as compared with the larger group (23 percent) of "Evangelicals" or "white Evangelicals."[1] A Pew Center study administered in March 2001 found roughly the same: 11 percent of all Americans were continuing to use the Fundamentalist descriptor for themselves.[2] Three years later, a Public Broadcasting Service Religion and Ethics Newsweekly poll registered that while the number of white Evangelicals had stayed steady at 23 percent of the American population, only 24 percent of those white Evangelicals (i.e., 5.5 percent of all Americans) identified as Fundamentalists.[3] In just three short years, the number of self-described Fundamentalists in America had evidently shrunk by half.

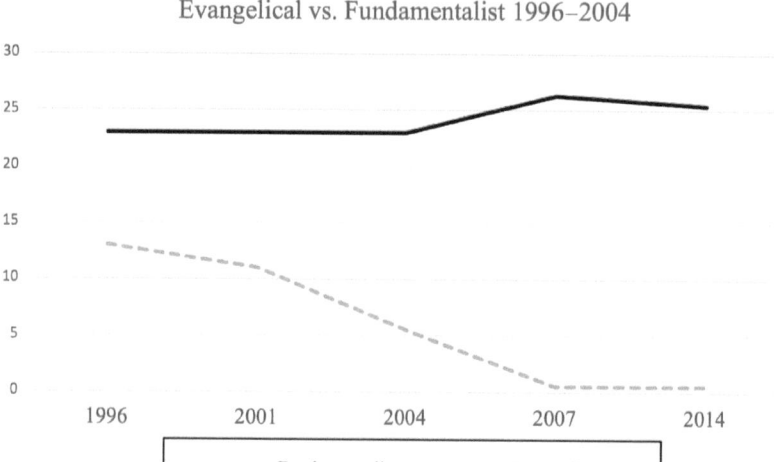

ILLUSTRATION 2.1 Declining use of the identity "Fundamentalist"

By 2007, when Pew Research published the first round of its preeminent US Religious Landscape survey, Fundamentalists had seemingly dissolved into oblivion. Just six years from the previous Pew study that showed 11 percent of Americans being Fundamentalists, Pew was now pegging them (or, at least, those who called their churches "Fundamentalist") at under 0.5 percent of the US population.[4] When Pew revisited the same survey in 2014, the results were basically the same.[5] In less than two decades, Fundamentalism had gone from stably encompassing one in every ten Americans to incorporating only one in every two hundred Americans. Today you may find tiny pockets of people who might still proudly call themselves Fundamentalists, but they are a marginal phenomenon, vanishingly rare even as about one in every four Americans declares herself or himself an Evangelical. Less than a century after the confident and assertive identity "Fundamentalist" was born, it has more or less died.

What happened to all the Fundamentalists?

The fairly obvious answer we find in these data is that nearly all of them simply began calling themselves Evangelicals.[6] They didn't necessarily start believing anything different or even leave their churches – they just adopted another moniker.[7] The more complicated question is: Why? Why do we see this consolidation among theologically and socially right-wing Christians around the term "Evangelical" in the early 2000s?

One theory might be that this terminological and identificational shift had to do with the presidency of George W. Bush. Unlike Ronald Reagan and the first President Bush, George W. Bush appealed directly to Evangelical voters by describing himself as an Evangelical Christian, narrating his own "born-again" experience, and speaking in the Evangelical idiom. Perhaps he shifted the preferred nomenclature.[8] Perhaps ... but it is worth pointing out that these two identities and the two interwoven tendencies they described had had a relatively stable coexistence in distinction for the better part of a century before the self-affirming Fundamentalists suddenly dissipated.

I would point to a different factor. It is striking that the 2001 Pew study referenced above – the last survey I can find where a significant fraction (11 percent) of Americans used the term Fundamentalist to describe themselves – was conducted in March of that year. Just six months later, the American populace would come face to face with members of another religious movement, namely Salafi Muslims, who were also widely dubbed "fundamentalists."

The American media and the public at large cast about for how to understand the motives and identities of the al-Qaeda terrorists after 9/11. As I surveyed in the Introduction, for some commentators the terrorists were simply *Muslims*. For these Americans, 9/11 represented another stage in an imminent "Clash of Civilizations" pitting Christians against Muslims, or Islam against "the Judeo-Christian West." In their view, *Islam itself* provided all the explanation needed for such brutal attacks. At the opposite end of the analytical spectrum, experts in Islamic Studies and Security Studies accurately categorized al-Qaeda as a jihadi Salafi organization, that is, a militant subtype of the otherwise stringent but largely nonviolent Salafi–Wahhabi strand of Sunni Islam. That, at least, was how the members of al-Qaeda understood themselves and their intellectual genealogy.

But the term that stuck to al-Qaeda in the post-9/11 American conversation, particularly in those early months and years after the attacks, was "Islamic fundamentalists." This phrase was not plucked out of nowhere. For decades up until that point, various scholars and pundits had been drawing analogies from the original Protestant Fundamentalist movement and its famous theological retrenchment to describe what they thought were parallel developments in non-Christian religious traditions, especially in Islam.[9] For a good number of American commentators, "Islamic fundamentalism" became the way to split the difference between broad-brush castigating all Muslims and getting lost in the technical distinctions among different substrates of Wahhabism, Salafism, Islamism, and so on.[10] The devastation of 9/11 seared pitiless images of terrorist violence into the American psyche, and in the process, it put a new face and an even greater stigma on the phrase Islamic fundamentalism.

Is it any wonder then that after 9/11, as the conversation in the American public square shifted to the War on Terrorism and battling Islamic fundamentalism, Christian Fundamentalists in America slowly oozed away from their old identity and rebranded themselves as Evangelicals? This process didn't even have to happen at a conscious, individual level. As vocabulary shifts in meaning, as the parlance of our time morphs beneath our feet, our own identities and self-articulations shift in relation to it. Fundamentalism as an affirmative branch and movement of American Protestantism died after 9/11, but the patchwork that had long existed of different Protestants calling themselves "Evangelical" absorbed (or reabsorbed) the Fundamentalists with little notice.[11] Meanwhile, the term "Islamic fundamentalist" became the de rigueur title appended to all Salafis and any other Muslims who were deemed bad or at odds with modern America.

The identity shift of 9/11 was not merely felt in the terminological realignment it produced in the American Protestant community. In the same period that the Fundamentalists were fading into the Evangelical backdrop, the American Muslim community experienced a severe backlash as they were stereotyped into the same contempt as was directed at the Al Qaeda attackers. More particularly, as we saw in the last chapter, a sizable and diverse self-affirming Salafi Muslim community had emerged in America in the 1980s and 1990s. Tens of thousands of African American Muslims identified as Salafis, and many children of immigrant Muslim communities were attracted to Salafi practices and theology. Dozens of Americans received scholarships to travel to Saudi Arabia in the 1990s to study under the most acclaimed Salafi scholars and then came back to become Salafi preachers and shaykhs in America.

Before 9/11 these Salafi shaykhs had built an educational infrastructure with organizations like the Qur'an and Sunnah Society (QSS) and the Islamic Assembly of North America (IANA) and were quite prominently promoting Salafism among their fellow Muslims and welcoming a host of converts to the movement. After 9/11, as public attention and the security apparatus of the American government shifted to rooting out Al Qaeda and anyone sympathetic to it, like the word fundamentalist, "Salafi" became a bad label to have draped around your neck.

In one illustrative incident in 2006, a *Washington Post* reporter, who had extensive reporting experience in the Middle East, profiled a mosque in College Park, Maryland, outside of DC, named Dar-us-Salaam, and she accurately categorized it as a Salafi-leaning mosque. She also quoted an Islamic Studies professor who explicitly drew a comparison with Fundamentalist Christians and asserted that "Salafis are the fundamentalists of the Muslim world."[12] These characterizations frustrated many of the Dar-us-Salaam members, and they wrote a series of public letters challenging her depiction of their religious orientation. As one Dar-us-Salaam board member put it,

> The piece talked about "Salafism," "Wahabism," and
> "Conservative" Islam. We never ever use labels on ourselves or

others ... we say we follow the Qur'an and Sunnah and that's it.
The average American equates [the terms] she used with
terrorism ... and now might think of us as having terrorist leanings,
which is a smear on our organization.[13]

As with Christian Fundamentalist identification, just five years after
9/11, the labels "Salafi" and "Wahhabi" had become widely known
enough and freighted with negative connotations as to be toxic and
avoided, at least to public audiences.

In his autobiographical account of living through this convul-
sion in the American Salafi movement, Umar Lee sums up the community's experience of the post-9/11 period:

Salafis became pariahs and were falsely accused of supporting
terrorism, and many moderate speakers were thrown in jail. After
this upheaval, other speakers took themselves off the circuit [of
Salafi conferences and local gatherings]. This killed off
organizations like IANA almost overnight and other activities
stopped.[14]

In this environment of heightened awareness and unsympathetic
scrutiny, many people who previously identified as Salafis began to
craft new identities – as "orthodox Muslims," "conservative
Muslims," or just "Muslims" – that were not burdened with the
Salafi designation. Yes, there are still small communities, especially
of African American Muslims who will proudly call themselves
Salafis (for reasons I'll examine in Chapter 5), but the vibrant, public
American Salafism of the 1990s has evaporated in the present. As
mosques like Dar-us-Salaam and their members distanced themselves
from the Salafi label, the movement became almost impossible to
track demographically in America.

In 2002, a new educational organization grew up out of the
ashes of IANA, convened by many of the same shaykhs who used to
lead that now-defunct, explicitly Salafi organization. They called it
AlMaghrib Institute. It was actually founded out of educational

programs at Dar-us-Salaam, the very College Park mosque that was itself trying to pivot away from the Salafi epithet.[15] Anyone navigating the world of Islamic education in the United States in the twenty-first century knows that AlMaghrib is a powerhouse, offering unaccredited weekend courses to over 120,000 unique students, in dozens of cities across the United States and around the world. As Zareena Grewal has put it, AlMaghrib "has almost single-handedly revived the Salafi movement in the US among Sunni American Muslim college students."[16] Yet, unlike IANA, AlMaghrib does not describe itself as Salafi anywhere in its promotional or public-facing materials. Most of the AlMaghrib shaykhs and instructors studied in Salafi institutions, some even will call themselves Salafis (often adding a "Reformist" or "Progressive" adjective to soften the harsh post-9/11 inference), but AlMaghrib is ostensibly not a Salafi organization.[17] Like the Christian Fundamentalists of the twentieth century, after 9/11, many Salafis in America rebranded, jettisoned old titles, and found more purchase in the American religious marketplace under various different monikers.

When people use the terms Salafism or Evangelicalism in America, they seem to believe that these words describe something concrete, identifiable, and quantifiable. Clearly there are people who call themselves Evangelicals and Salafis in America – do those people who self-identify with the terms constitute the whole of Evangelicalism or Salafism? What about theology? Are there definitive theological criteria that distinguish Salafis or Evangelicals from their coreligionists? What about people like the AlMaghrib instructors and students who hover on the edges of Salafism but consciously avoid the title? What about the numerous Americans who say "I'm just a born-again Christian"? Are most demographers correct in classifying those people as Evangelicals, even if the surveyed people don't employ that word? What happens when big identity categories, like Fundamentalism and Evangelicalism, covertly merge or when a movement like Salafism quickly rebrands and reformulates its public identity? Put simply, *what is an Evangelical or Salafi today anyway?*

THE MAP IS NOT THE TERRITORY

There are two prevalent routes to answering these questions. Demographers and sociologists, like those at the Pew Research Center and others who were witnessing – if not necessarily noticing – the numerical disappearance of Fundamentalism, tend to take a "belonging" approach to defining these religious movements: does a person self-identify as an Evangelical or belong to a community that is explicitly Salafi in its orientation? Alternatively, historians, theologians, and other religion scholars are more interested in the ideas that generate these identities. They tend to search for thematic theological or ideological commonalities that unite all Salafis or Evangelicals across time, such that "believing" those ideas links a person or community to the movement and makes them distinguishable from other Muslim or Christian movements. Both of these methods have their merits and their drawbacks, but both produce comparatively stable maps that tell us who is a Salafi or an Evangelical. The problem is that both of these sets of maps, while capturing *something* about Evangelicalism and Salafism, fail to reflect the complex and roiling realities on the ground in and around these movements. The map is not the territory, as they say. But are there other ways of describing the territory that might complement the work of our sociologist and historian cartographers?

In this chapter, after highlighting the problems inherent in the *belonging* and *believing* approaches to answering this foundational Salafi and Evangelical identity question, I suggest a third complementary approach to thinking about the boundaries of Evangelicalism and Salafism. It is a proposal that attends to how Salafis and Evangelicals themselves parse their identities, and it is sensitive to the moving-target nomenclature that real-life religious actors themselves soundlessly and expressly use to locate themselves. When asked how they understand themselves, Evangelicals and Salafis tend to offer answers that intermingle believing and belonging – "I belong to an Evangelical church" or "I believe in the authority of the Salaf" – but they also

constantly uphold a different criterion for how to distinguish themselves. It is a criterion that is rooted more in "behaving," particularly
how one behaves toward and relates to scripture. I will unpack all of
this in a moment, but let me first examine briefly the advantages and
problems attached to the other two major methods of answering these
questions: capturing religious identity through *belonging* or through
believing.

Demographers of religion are given a straightforward, albeit
difficult, task: find the number of people who identify themselves
with a religious tradition or movement. So, in Pew's aforementioned
archetypal Religious Landscape survey, researchers determined that,
in 2014, just over a quarter (25.4 percent) of the US population was
Evangelical Protestant. That was a slight decrease from the
2007 number (26.3 percent), but was much more durable than the
rapidly declining Mainline Protestant and Catholic populations,
which indicated sharp numerical drop-offs in those two faith traditions in America in the space of seven years (Mainline Protestants
from 18.1 to 14.7 percent; Catholics from 23.9 to 20.8 percent).[18]
There it is, in plain numbers: Evangelicalism is the statistically dominant Christian faith tradition of America, holding more or less steady
even as other strands of American Christianity dwindle apace. So read
the religion headlines in various media sources that week. Religion
enumerated!

Yet, when one digs into the data that Pew is gathering and
analyzing, those solid, factual numbers get more murky. First, denominational affiliation was the primary criterion the demographers chose
to employ to sort out the dog's breakfast of different movements of
Protestantism in America. The researchers labeled each Protestant
denomination as belonging to one (and only one) of three distinct
traditions: Evangelical Protestant, Mainline Protestant, and
Historically Black Protestant. Consequently, the demographers would
ask a Protestant respondent which denomination she or he belonged
to, plug that into their matrix, and determine which of the three
buckets the person belonged in.

This method of sorting created attendant problems however. What about American Christians who say they are "nondenominational" or "just Christian," as in, they transcend the sectarian distinctions Pew researchers want to use to categorize them? For the full 38 percent of Protestants who said they were nondenominational (or gave only a vague "I'm just a Methodist" or "I'm just a Christian" type of response), Pew researchers had to find other sifting criteria. What they decided was that if the nondenominational or ambiguously denominational respondent was black, then she or he belonged to the Historically Black Protestant category. If she or he was not black, then the researcher asked: "Do you identify as 'born again'?" – an expression that has classically been central to Evangelical narratives of personal redemption. If the white or Asian American or Latino/a American respondents understood themselves as "born again," they were determined by Pew to be Evangelical; if not, they were Mainline Protestants.[19]

All of these sorting decisions seem sensible and rational if our goal is to arrive at a quantifiable statistic of how many Evangelicals are in America today. To its credit, Pew Research Center has been largely consistent in its methodology across these surveys, so one can compare the numbers in useful ways. But any experience in the kaleidoscopic world of American Protestantism belies the straightforwardness of Pew's numbers. Let me list just a few of the questions and challenges a skeptic like me might pose to the accuracy of Pew's tallies:

- Many black Protestant churches and denominations are akin to (and often forthrightly identify as) being Evangelical in their theology and orientation. Does the firm division between Historically Black Protestant denominations and Evangelical Protestant denominations really hold up on a theological or social level?
- Relatedly, the phrase "born again" and even the self-descriptor "Evangelical" is not, by any means, exclusive to non-black Evangelical Protestants. In fact, a parallel survey by Gallup in 2005 showed that 70 percent of black Christians say that they are Evangelical or born again,

and 19 percent of American Catholics say the same.[20] By its methodology, the Pew study would not count any of these Catholics or most of these black Christians in the terms they choose for themselves.

- Many of the people Pew puts in the Evangelical bucket would not call themselves Evangelical. They might say they are Baptists or Mennonites or just Christians. Do the Pew researchers' sortings reflect the reality of their belonging to the category of Evangelical or does the survey (and others like it) shape that reality?

- I have met a conspicuous number of self-affirming Evangelicals who belong to Mainline Protestant denominations. I have met people who are more theologically aligned with Mainline Protestants but prefer participating in the liturgical styles (or lack thereof) in Evangelical churches. Are these people outliers or occupants of the blurred borders among different strands of Protestant belonging?

The Pew numbers – indeed, all such demographic studies – make for good newspaper headlines, quick snapshot insights into the American population. Demographers have a task: to put a number to something that is almost definitionally unquantifiable. And they do that adequately. However, the facts on the ground are far more multifarious. The working definition of "Evangelical" *belonging* that the demographers use inevitably fashions and constrains the numbers they come up with.

Though Salafis comprise a far smaller community and are far less studied by the demographer class, Salafism in America is similarly bewildering to systematically measure. Depending on the survey, Muslims overall in America are approximately 1.1 percent of the population (3.5 million people).[21] Because this number is already such a small fraction of American society, few demographers bother to tailor questions or subdivide American Muslims further, though, those who do find some similar dynamics around identity among American Sunnis with other American religious groups. For instance, about 20 percent of American Muslims identify as either Shi'ite (16 percent) or "Other" (4 percent – "Other" can include the Nation of Islam or controversial sects such as the Ahmadiyya). So that means that the remaining 80 percent of American Muslims are Sunnis, right?

Not exactly. Actually 55 percent of American Muslims identify as Sunni, leaving 14 percent who identify simply as Muslim, and another 10 percent who said they did not know or refused to answer the question.[22] Given that around 85 percent of all Muslims globally are Sunni, and there are many subtraditions within Sunnism, even to call yourself Sunni does not have the specificity of a denominational identity. It seems that among Sunnis, as among Protestants or other Americans, there's a certain pull toward having a nondenominational or nonsectarian, "I'm just a Muslim" or "I'm just a Sunni" identity.

But what about numbers on Salafis? Very few surveys of American Muslims even ask about Salafi identification. In fact, the only nationwide study I have unearthed quantifying Salafis is a 2012 survey of American mosques by the Council on American-Islamic Relations (CAIR). It found that only 1 percent of respondent mosque leaders identified that they "Follow the Salafi *minhaj* [methodology]," and about 3 percent of mosques overall identified as Salafi. The report also notes that "[a]lthough salafi mosques are few, most salafi mosques are African American."[23] If the CAIR survey numbers are accurate, then the American Salafi community might be in the neighborhood of 30,000–100,000 people (1–3 percent of the 1 percent of the American population who are Muslim). But, as with Evangelicals, simple numerical reckonings of American Salafis can be profoundly deceptive.

I described above the bind that many Salafi-oriented Muslims and mosques – like the suburban DC mosque Dar-us-Salaam that was written about in the *Washington Post* – find themselves in in contemporary America. In the popular lexicon, to the degree that the average American even knows the word, "Salafi" is freighted with connotations of terrorism, foreignness, fundamentalism, and retrograde religious tendencies. Hence, many American Muslims, who in other parts of the world might call themselves Salafis, search for other descriptors. This does not mean that Salafi ideas or Salafi approaches to Islam have disappeared from the American scene.

In fact, Umar Lee, whose autobiography I quoted earlier, in an interview with me estimated that as many as one-third of the mosques in America are influenced by Salafi thought, theology, and prayer practices.[24] To be sure, this was a back-of-the-napkin opinion offered by one (former) American Salafi, but he is also one of the few participant-chroniclers of the movement to date. After long observation of American Islam as practiced and after numerous conversations with American Muslims on this topic, I would hazard that his estimate is closer to the demographic reality than the CAIR survey of mosques would indicate. Michael Muhammad Knight, like Lee an American "revert" to Islam (a term some Muslims use for a convert, i.e., someone who has "reverted" to their original state of Islam and submission to God), describes his own experience in entering various American Muslim communities:

> Ideas and practices can dig tunnels under the borders, and not every Sunnī who expresses a Salafi-influenced thought would necessarily identify that thought (or herself/himself) as "Salafi" ... Because the books and pamphlets that fell into my hands did not clearly mark themselves as Salafi, and the well-intentioned mosque uncles who shared stories and advice with this young revert did not present their own views as Salafi, it can sometimes become hard to say where Salafism begins and ends, or whether Salafism is even a useful term to explain anything.[25]

Clearly, the boundaries of the influence of American Salafism do not correlate perfectly with the self-ascribed identity "Salafi."

In summary, movements like Salafism and Evangelicalism do not lend themselves easily to straightforward counting. Demographers, almost inevitably, default to external **belonging** factors: Does a person describe her/himself with X term? Does a person attend a mosque or denominational church that identifies with Y tradition? Does a person use a synonymous identifier (i.e., "born again") that is historically linked with Z identity? Even if these numbers were refined through qualitative interviews and careful, theologically conversant person-to-person interactions, they would still fall short, in large part because Evangelicalism and Salafism are made up of magnetic ideas and theological hues and tints, personal affinities and subtle influences that do not always take on the title of Evangelical or Salafi.

All of which points to the advantage of the other dominant academic way of defining participation in these movements: by the content of Salafis' and Evangelicals' **believing**. Historians and theologians have sought to distill distinctive Evangelical and Salafi beliefs down to sets of core affirmations or tenets, so that, while the numerical precision of the demographers may recede into the background, one is left with a clear impression of what it means to view the world as a Salafi or an Evangelical. These theological, or perhaps ideological, definitions of Salafism and Evangelicalism abound and are widely used in historical scholarship to capture the essence or the core of these movements.

Historian David Bebbington has developed the most widely accepted definition of Evangelicalism based on four characteristics, or, in Bebbington's phrase, "a quadrilateral of priorities." They are, namely, "conversionism, the belief that lives need to be changed; activism, the expression of the gospel in effort; biblicism, a particular regard for the Bible; and what may be termed crucicentrism, a stress on the sacrifice of Christ on the cross."[26] Bebbington is correct that most historically evangelical and conscious expressions of Evangelicalism have foregrounded these priorities as markers of the movement for the past 300 years. The great advantage of this ideological prioritization approach to understanding Evangelicalism is that it offers a concentrated set of qualitative criteria against which one can appraise an individual or a community to determine whether they are, broadly speaking, Evangelical. And Pew and other demography firms inevitably rely on these studies to determine which denominations fit under the Evangelical umbrella.

On the other hand, the hindrances of Bebbington's (and others') ideological definition are evident from one survey conducted in

December 2017. LifeWay Research, an Evangelical polling firm, found that roughly one in four Americans described themselves as Evangelicals, appearing to confirm Pew's basic numbers with a different methodology. But the LifeWay researchers added a qualitative dimension into the mix, asking if the respondents "strongly agreed" with four statements that correlated with Bebbington's set of theological priorities. The results were illuminating: "Fewer than half of those who identify as evangelicals (45 percent) strongly agree with core evangelical beliefs ... [and] [o]nly two-thirds (69 percent) of evangelicals by belief self-identify as evangelicals."[27] In other words, the majority of self-described American Evangelicals did not strongly prioritize Bebbington's constellation of ideological markers, and nearly a third of the American Christians who did prioritize those beliefs *did not call themselves* Evangelical. Can we really say that these theological indicators are the essential characteristics of Evangelical believing if they correspond so poorly with Evangelical identity on the ground?

What emerges from the collision of Bebbington's astute historical observations and surveys like the LifeWay one is a paradox. Evangelicalism is a religious movement with some brightly identifiable themes and porous, nebulous borders.[28] It is an ideology whose adherents are often ignorant of its central features. It is a worldview that is so fuzzy at the edges that the center may be impossible to find.

Similarly, American Salafism – and Salafism in general – can be defined theologically as a type of Muslim **believing**. Historian Bernard Haykel has written most prominently in this mode of identifying Salafism as "a group that defines its reformist project first and foremost through creedal tenets (i.e., a theology)."[29] Like Bebbington's schema, Haykel offers a six-fold delineation of distinctive Salafi theological principles:

1. A return to the authentic beliefs and practices of the first three "generations" of Muslims – the Salaf al-Salih ("pious ancestors");
2. An emphasis on a particular understanding of *tawhid* (God's oneness);

3. Making certain that unbelief is fought, especially all forms of associating other beings with God (*shirk*);

4. Claiming that the only valid sources of authority are the Qur'an and the Sunna of the Prophet Muhammad (the latter is equated with the canonical Sunni *hadith* collections) and the consensus of the Prophet's companions;

5. Ridding Muslims of the reprehensible innovations (*bida'*, sing. *bid'a*) in belief and practice that they have wittingly, or unwittingly, adopted;

6. Arguing that a strict constructionist interpretation of the Qur'an and Sunna is sufficient to guide Muslims for all time and through all contingencies, and that these sources are perspicuous.[30]

Haykel goes on to add one point of connection that is quasi-theological and also unites all Salafis: an abiding respect for the teachings of that fourteenth-century jurist and theologian Ibn Taymiyya. Like Bebbington's quadrilateral, Haykel's theological description of Salafi ideology is perfectly serviceable in capturing the basic orientation that unites Salafis.

Except, what happens when Salafism doesn't call itself Salafism anymore, as is the case with so many Muslims in America who are canny about the post-9/11 stereotypes of the term? What happens when Salafi ideas and theologies burrow into and bleed and blend with other strands of Islamic thought as Michael Muhammad Knight poignantly describes? What do we make of cases like the AlMaghrib Institute shaykhs, who hold to many of the markers of Salafi theology, but who are purposely repackaging and reformulating (and, in the process, transforming) those ideas to speak to non-Salafis? The crystalline theological definitions that Bebbington or Haykel offer become much more amorphous in the world of practice and presentation.

To be clear, I am not arguing that demographic studies like those conducted by Pew or CAIR or the thematic studies of historians like Bebbington or Haykel are *wrong*. Salafism and Evangelicalism have unquestionably vital dimensions of **believing** and **belonging**. But what is missing if we rely wholly on these definitions are the ways that identities shift and morph, the hybrids that form at the unpoliced boundaries of religious movements, and the people whose habits of mind and way of being in the world have been ineradicably shaped by Salafism and Evangelicalism, even if they sidestep that title.

HADITH PEOPLE AND BIBLE BELIEVERS

In the face of this thorny problem of determining who precisely is a Salafi or an Evangelical or what exactly Salafis and Evangelicals believe, I would like to suggest a different approach at characterization, one that begins where many Salafis and Evangelicals themselves begin. As Haykel's theological outline of Salafi belief and Bebbington's fourfold list of prime Evangelical priorities attest, scripture and the distinctive Evangelical and Salafi approaches to scripture are at the molten core of the movements' self-understandings. If we are going to appreciate lived Salafism and lived Evangelicalism in America, we must go beyond the level of theological affirmations or credos to experience the ethos and substance of daily participation in these movements. It is difficult to overstate the importance of the Hadith/Qur'an for all Salafi and the Bible for all Evangelical expressions.

A recent study of Salafism argues that "to be a Salafi is not merely to hold specific theological or legal commitments but also to engage in particular visible practices."[31] My contention here is that the very mode of Salafi engagement with the Qur'an and Hadith, both in style and substance, is itself a key specimen of those "visible practices." Salafi preaching, social media, and conversations are littered with references to individual hadiths, with Qur'an verses, and with exhortations to study and read the source texts for oneself. American Salafis can log onto Internet sites like Quran.com and Sunnah.com and cross-reference individual hadiths and their translations in English (and Urdu for those of South Asian descent).[32] Indeed, the Internet has thrown this self-taught, direct-access dimension of Salafism into hyperdrive, with neophyte students of scripture able to bypass the 'ulama' (conventionally trained scholars and clerics) and traditional modes of Islamic learning by consulting "Shaykh Google" and crowdsourcing networks of peers through online message boards.[33] One cannot browse, even at a superficial level, American Muslim discussion boards or YouTube channels and not encounter Salafi ideas, Salafi Hadith-reasoning, and Saudi-trained Salafi preachers, though whether they overtly identify as Salafis is an open question. American mosques are filled with books and pamphlets, like those Michael Muhammad Knight encountered, that are either printed in Saudi Arabia or derived from Salafi sources.

Certainly, other American Muslim teachers reference the Hadith and, of course, the Qur'an. What distinguishes Salafi appeals to the sacred texts is a matter of volume and of style. As Yasir Qadhi put it to me, "I challenge you to listen to any Salafi lecture except that it's peppered with Qur'an and Hadith directly. Whereas non-Salafis wouldn't be as peppered, let's say, with as many obvious quotations."[34] Both the *direct* manner of the references and the overall *infusing* of the exhortations with scripture quotations are important here. Combined they convey a pair of core values of the Salafi ethos: Scripture should be accessible to and understood by all, and scripture is an indispensable guide in every aspect of life. In fact, some Salafis continue to nickname their movement with a reference to the ninth-century movement of Ahmad ibn Hanbal: *Ahl al-Hadith* (Hadith People).[35] In both the day-to-day experience of Salafism and in the resultant identities of Salafis, scripture is the anchor, the axis around which all conversations turn. They are, foundationally, Scripture People.

Similarly, anyone who has spent time with many Evangelical Christians might be forgiven for describing them as being preoccupied with the Bible. Evangelical biblicism (à la Bebbington) has saturated American society with Bible references, bumper stickers, t-shirts, websites, and Evangelical preaching on the radio and television that is littered with commonsense Bible reasoning. There is a paradigmatic episode that occurred at the establishment of the contemporary Evangelical movement. The National Association of Evangelicals (NAE), the leading organization of Evangelical institutions, was founded in 1942. At the first meeting of the NAE, the founding president, Harold Ockenga told the assembly, "The division is no longer between the denominations; the division is between those who believe in Christ and the Bible, and those who reject Christ – the Christ of the cross and the Bible."[36] Ockenga's formulation captures a conceit that many Evangelical Christians have used in the decades before and since: Christians can be sorted into devout Bible believers and others, Scripture People and non-real Christians. Denominational identities recede before this Bible-ensconced identity. Many Evangelical churches (including ones under the NAE umbrella) will eschew the word Evangelical to simply name themselves "Bible" churches or their members "biblical" or "Bible believing" Christians.

Naturally, other Christians, particularly non-Evangelical Protestants, also feel comfortable quoting the Bible. It is by no means an exclusive domain of Evangelicals. But Evangelicals tie their personal and communal identities to the Bible in a manner that is simply not reflected in other strands of American Christianity. Like the Salafi manner of referencing the Qur'an and the Hadith, Evangelical Bible citations are distinct both in quantity and in their colloquialism.

In the Evangelical imagination the Bible (a library of sixty-six books, in two asynchronous testaments, with dozens of authors) has a singular meaning that is evident, clear, obvious to the well-intentioned reader: "The Bible says …." Hence, Evangelical pastors and popular speakers admonish their audiences to read the Bible devotionally, study the Bible personally, and divine the message of the Bible for their every question and circumstance. Like Salafis, Evangelicals invite and even expect rank-and-file believers to have direct contact with the texts, democratizing and popularizing the scriptural interpretive endeavor. The Bible becomes for them an existential foundation for confidence in the world. As one popular Evangelical bumper sticker pithily outlines: "The Bible said it, I believe it, that settles it."

There is a technical term for all of this. In addition to being demographic and theological movements, Salafism and Evangelicalism are, *discourses about scripture*. A discourse is an embodied communal conversation. As Robert Wuthnow writes:

> Discourse subsumes the written as well as the verbal, the formal as well as the informal, the gestural or ritual as well as the conceptual. It occurs, however, within communities in the broadest sense of the word: communities of competing producers, of interpreters and critics, of audiences and consumers, of patrons and other significant actors who become the subjects of discourse itself. It is only in these concrete living and breathing communities that discourse becomes meaningful.[37]

A *scriptural* discourse, then, is an embodied communal conversation that centers on scripture – a conversation that has certain habits and conventions, folkways and grammars, colloquial markers and rhetorical styles. I contend that being Salafi or Evangelical definitely entails core beliefs and forms of belonging, but it is also *behavioral*, enacted by the individual's participation in a distinctive communal conversation about scripture.[38] Salafism and Evangelicalism are, among other things, discursive styles, methods of appeal to scripture, that result in distinct-but-overlapping discourses with Protestantism and Sunnism writ large. They are communal and individual interdependencies with the Hadith/Qur'an and the Bible that are personal, democratic, pedagogical, and epistemically grounding. The distinctive scripturalist existential attachment to scripture is what creates this field of discourse: If the individual and the community's identity is tied to scripture, then the communal idiom of scriptural knowledge and inhabitation becomes integral.

This terminology of "discourse" is more native to Salafism, where you will find American Salafis themselves referring to "the discourse," as in, the natural back-and-forth of legitimate debates about theology and jurisprudence and interpretive questions. But I want to be clear that, while my definition of discourse includes that intellectual and deliberative element, it also wraps in dimensions that are more palpable and wordless. Discourse encompasses theology, ideology, and communal belonging, without being synonymous with any one of them.[39] Discourse lives in customs, mannerisms, styles, rhetorical modes, and viral values. It shows up in communal shibboleths like saying one is "born again" or deferentially quoting Ibn Taymiyya. Discourse does not have an essence, because it is performative. Put evolutionarily, participation in a discourse is phenotypical; it is observable rather than ontological. It is the learned conventions from within a community, a dance whose moves are familiar to the initiated.

Most extant demographic and theological definitions of Evangelicalism and Salafism are muddled by the identity dynamics at play at the borders of these movements, particularly in an environment like America. We tend to assume that people are one thing religiously or that they easily fit into one identity bucket. To think of Salafism and Evangelicalism as discourses about scripture is to move away from precise human boundary definition and to focus more on styles and idioms that create a distinctive field of conversations about and interactions with sacred texts.[40] Aligned with Michael Muhammad Knight's observation about ideas and practices, discourse and its idiom burrow under the borders between denominations and other identities, so that you can find people who appear and sound Evangelical in communities that would forswear that name and skew demographers' questions. They might just name themselves as Bible Christians or Christians without any modifiers. You can find people who are behaviorally, attitudinally, and ideologically Salafi, by most definitions, but who evade that label.

Unlike theology, a discourse is not necessarily discriminative, because it is not propositional. A theologian or a statement of belief usually poses confessional assertions so that one is required to either affirm or reject that formulation. But peoples' identities do not work that way in real life. The Gallup poll I referenced above found a demographically troubling anomaly: In addition to 19 percent of

American Catholics describing themselves as "born again or evangel-ical," there was a statistically not insignificant number of respondents to the survey who said they were not Christian or did not state any religious preference, "but who agree with the 'born again or evangel-ical' criterion."[41] Pause for a moment to consider that. Evangelical non-Christians. The Gallup researchers, naturally, lopped off those respondents, along with the self-identifying Evangelical Catholics, from their count of Evangelicals, as would nearly any self-respecting theologian or historian of Evangelicalism. By almost any existing definition, a secular or non-religious Evangelical is a contradiction in terms. Yet when we think in terms of discourse and behavior, it is actually easy to imagine people who have been so deeply shaped by Evangelicalism that they are idiomatically Evangelical and have habits of mind stamped by that ethos. They may have had that "born-again" moment, even if they have now abandoned that iden-tity. They might still be religious, or not. They might still quote the Bible in customarily Evangelical tones. I have met many such people. I might well be one of them. Discourse, as a learned behavior, can persist even where institutional affiliation, belief, or communal belonging has evaporated.

"IS YASIR QADHI A SALAFI?"

As I close this chapter, let me illustrate the new light this discursive definition of Evangelicalism and Salafism sheds on the ways real people sort and think of themselves in America. Yasir Qadhi, whose seminar I began this book with, is a respected and popular, if contro-versial, Muslim shaykh in America. The child of Pakistani immi-grants, Qadhi grew up going back and forth between Houston and Jedda, Saudi Arabia, where his father taught medicine. As a college student at the University of Houston, Qadhi became fascinated with Salafism and the Salafi mode of learning and interpreting scripture. He became involved with QSS and IANA, the two major pre-9/11 American Salafi networks, and then he enrolled in a master's program at the Islamic University of Medina in 1996, where he studied under some of the most revered Salafi teachers of the late twentieth century.[42]

When he moved back to the USA in 2001, Qadhi made a name for himself as a zealous, fire-eating Salafi missionary preacher (*dā'ī*) of the first order, denouncing Zionism, homosexuality, and the cultural decay of the West. In the space of a few years, he became a popular, lightning-rod figure of the post-9/11 Salafi movement in America: young, brash, whip smart, eloquent, and able to cite a Hadith reference for every confident assertion of Salafi theology and jurisprudence. In 2006, Qadhi joined and quickly became one of the most popular shaykhs at AlMaghrib Institute.

But Yasir's intellectual and academic career took an unusual turn: He enrolled in a PhD program in Islamic Studies at Yale University in 2004. For almost the whole time at Yale, Qadhi was simultaneously learning Western academic approaches to understanding Islam and leading weekend seminars for hundreds and thousands of eager young American Muslims, encouraging their devotional development and scriptural learning. His dissertation project was an analysis of the intertwined roles of reason and revelation in the thought of Ibn Taymiyya.[43] He eventually moved to Memphis to begin teaching at Rhodes College, a historically Presbyterian school, all while maintaining his role as Academic Dean of AlMaghrib. And slowly along the way, he began distancing himself from the Salafi trademark. For more than a decade Qadhi lived between two worlds: one his academic life as a religion scholar at Yale and Rhodes, and one as a popular Muslim preacher and shaykh.

Is Yasir Qadhi a Salafi? One can hardly pretend that he is ill-informed about the meaning of the term or what identification with it implies. He is currently writing a book about Salafism and the complex inner contours of the movement. Terminologically, he has cast about for a new term to describe himself. Many of his followers (especially those who live abroad) would happily identify as Salafis, and many of his American AlMaghrib students would, like Qadhi, conscientiously avoid that label. He has attempted using the

formulation that he is an "orthodox with a capital O" Muslim, arguing that "Jews, especially Orthodox Jews, are the closest religious
group to Muslims in terms of practice and legal code."[44]

When I tried, in an interview, to locate Yasir in the world of
Salafism, he bristled, offering several cautions, "I would be more left-
wing progressive, and I'd definitely be somebody who, even if you
wanted to consider me a Salafi, you'd have to give some caveats, you
know, 'reformist' or 'thinking,' or whatever …."[45] Yasir Qadhi the
professor has worked hard to leave behind the hard-line preacher he
was when he returned from Medina. But every time he pops up in the
news or strikes out in some new direction, Islamophobic websites,
which delight in "exposing" American Salafis' "deception," will rapidly link to his most controversial early comments and video clips,
unwilling to imagine that he could change.[46]

In his believing, Qadhi is mostly Salafi, affirming the fine points
of Salafi theology while challenging certain mainstream Salafi practices, especially the way many Salafis treat outsiders and women and
their tendency to denounce non-Salafis as un-Islamic.[47] In his
belonging, Qadhi is on the bubble of Salafism. He still quotes Ibn
Taymiyya attentively. He still trades on his Salafi credentials and
his education in Medina. When he was asked at a Salafi conference
in Norway in 2014 about whether he had "left the way of the Salaf?" –
he responded,

> I, *astaghfirullah* [expression of disgust, but, literally, "I ask Allah's
> forgiveness"], never said that I left the way of the Salaf … The way
> of the Salaf is the most orthodox and the best way of understanding
> Islam. Our Prophet (*salla llahu 'alay-hi wa-sallam*) has praised the
> three generations [i.e., the first three generations of Muslims] …
> I disagree with some of the methodological practices of the *current*
> Salafi movement, not the theoretical Salaf understanding of
> Islam.[48]

He goes on in those same comments to mention 9/11, his own location in the USA, and the connotations of terrorism that have come to

be associated with the word Salafi in America. He also narrates how one of his Saudi shaykhs, one of the most esteemed Salafi scholars named Ibn Uthaymeen, encouraged Qadhi and other Medina students to leave behind the Salafi label when it became burdensome.

All of this might seem like identity gymnastics or distinctions without a difference: He doesn't call himself a Salafi anymore because his Salafi mentor recommended that? To Qadhi's Salafi critics, he is mincing words for the sake of respectability: One either is a Salafi or is not. To the Islamophobia-website writers Qadhi is two-faced, playing the popular, crypto-Salafi cleric to some audiences and the evolved academic to others. I can sympathize with him though, having been in a number of circumstances where someone still labeled me an Evangelical, and I wanted to offer a lengthy clarification about my complicated evolution within and then away from that identity while still being honest about my years as an Evangelical minister and how Evangelicalism shaped me.

In 2019, Yasir left Rhodes College, claiming that he had been professionally discriminated against for his socially conservative views, especially around homosexuality, writing to colleagues that "in academia, my very public life as a cleric has (quite drastically) impacted my academic life, to the extent that I now feel it's best for me to withdraw from academia to a great extent."[49] He also left AlMaghrib to serve as founding dean of The Islamic Seminary of America, whose institutional theological orientation is still yet to be determined.

Who knows what a demographer would make of Qadhi? When I speak to them about my research, I find that his fellow American Muslim scholars across the theological and ideological spectrum remain perturbed about what to call him, so public has been his evolution and so lingering the stylistic markings of Salafism in his self-presentation.

I do not aim to accuse Yasir of duplicity or disingenuousness, but merely to observe the deficiencies of believing and belonging for categorically defining the boundaries of an uncircumscribed discourse. Identity is not an on/off switch – Salafi or not, Evangelical or not. With a discursive lens, we can see that Yasir's theological approach, social identity, preaching style, orientation to the Qur'an and Hadith, and religious authority proceed from his grounding and formation in Salafism. While he can identify his own form of Islam however he pleases, I think it is most analytically clear-cut to call Qadhi "post-Salafi," even as I could justly be labeled "post-Evangelical."[50] Salafism has, perhaps ineradicably, imprinted Qadhi, so that the habits, idioms, concerns, and locution of Salafism remain, even if he has publicly moved on. What differentiates Yasir from me is that I am one in an anonymous legion of American Ex-vangelicals, whereas he has remained a superstar religious leader with tens of thousands (maybe hundreds of thousands) of young Muslims in America tracking his identity shifts, following his lead, and walking with him and the other AlMaghrib shaykhs into a still-vaguely-Salafi, nondenominational future.

CONCLUSION

Historians and theologians have long sought to thematize and title and organize the Evangelical and Salafi movements around a core set of theological or ideological beliefs, to make sense of the amorphous interpretive chaos they manifest in real life. And with the rise of modern demographic surveys, statisticians and pollsters have come alongside the historians and theologians to add a numerical definitiveness to what was previously more ethereal: 25.4 percent of Americans are Evangelical Protestants. Period.

What I have taken pains to disentangle (or, perhaps, re-entangle) in this chapter is how the stable theological demarcations proffered by the historians and the comforting precision provided by the demographers can only capture fleeting images of these burbling scriptural discourses. When marketplace pressures increase and terminological tides turn, scripturalists change their names – Fundamentalists become Evangelicals; Evangelicals become "just Christians;" Salafis become orthodox Muslims – because these identities are organized not by titles or denominational bodies or long-reaching traditions but by alignment around and behavior toward texts. The very characteristics that have made these scriptural piety tendencies thrive (agility, decentralization, commonsensical rhetorical styles, lack of ties to traditional naming conventions) also make them tiresome to enumerate and to define squarely who is in and who is out.

While Bebbington's quadrilateral of priorities or Haykel's outline of Salafi theology are more or less faithful renderings of what many or most Evangelicals and Salafis believe, they chart an inadequate map of the movements and expressions that exist within those discursive coalitions. I am not arguing that there's no such thing as Evangelical or Salafi theology – of course there is. Many books have been written by Evangelicals and Salafis themselves to pin down exactly what the content of those theologies is. To put a finer point on it: Evangelical and Salafi theologies are contested and evolving, part and parcel of the discursive ferment, rather than static and unifying.

If we are to locate Salafism and Evangelicalism (much less post-Salafis and morphing Evangelicals) in their real-world manifestations and communities of conversation, I would contend that the focus should be on how they write and speak about, directly invoke, and appeal to scripture as their source not only of authority and knowledge but of identity itself. Religious actors and religious communities can moor their sense of themselves to any number of berths and docks along the religious shore: mystical experience, ritual, tradition, distinctive practices and laws, sophisticated theological and philosophical systems, etc. Evangelicals and Salafis in America have affixed themselves primarily and behaviorally to scripture as their source of belief and religious belonging. They are first and foremost Scripture People. It is out of these parallel primary attachments that their most interesting similarities flow.

3 Splitting the Atom of Text and Tradition

Saad Tasleem is a charismatic, suave, thirty-something American Muslim preacher. Raised in a nominally Muslim family in the Washington, DC suburbs, he was not very interested in his faith as a younger man. He was the lead singer in a local punk rock band in high school. Then he had a reawakening of faith in college. He became a passionate seeker of religious knowledge, and he discovered AlMaghrib Institute, which had only recently been founded in nearby College Park, Maryland in 2002. He eagerly took every course he could on weekends, and he would devour any recordings of lectures from the AlMaghrib shaykhs he could find. Eventually, like most of his shaykhs, he spent seven years studying at the Islamic University of Medina, the premier center of Salafi learning and missionary training in the world.[1]

Now he is himself a popular lecturer and shaykh with AlMaghrib. He teaches courses on Islamic jurisprudence about culture, identity, fashion, and recreation. He curates his own website, social media profiles, and YouTube channel where he posts deftly edited short motivational religious videos. He has 340,000 followers on Facebook and 39,000 subscribers on YouTube. He also promotes his own boutique, religiously inflected clothing line. Young, stylish, entrepreneurial, technologically savvy – Tasleem epitomizes a substrate of American religion that is accessible, appealing, marketable, and chic. Toggle a few variables, and Tasleem is a mirror image of what some have called Evangelical "Hipster Christianity."[2] He embodies a flexible, adaptive, popular American religious ethos. But Tasleem is more than a brand or a self-promoter. He is a through-and-through scripturalist.

In a recent lecture-sermon delivered at AlMaghrib's IlmFest Conference ('ilm is Arabic for knowledge, especially of jurisprudence and theology) titled "My iPath," Tasleem aims to bridge "the Qur'an and how it relates to today's youth."[3] He describes the frequent occurrence of young Muslim women and men coming to him and complaining that they feel like they have lost "that spark, that feeling, that *īmān* [faith] rush," a waning invigoration in their personal devotion. This is Tasleem's response:

> You know one of the first questions that I ask this person is "Brother or Sister, what is the status of your relationship with the Book of Allah – *ʿazza wa-jalla* [The Mighty and Sublime]? What is the status of your relationship with the Book of Allah – *ʿazza wa-jalla*? When was the last time you picked up the Qur'an and you read it?" Not: "Yeah, I listened to the Qur'an on the way to work and, you know, it was nice and this and that, and it was soothing ...." No! I mean a relationship with the Qur'an! Where you picked up the Qur'an, you read it. You understood its meanings. You read the *tafsīr* [exegetical commentaries], and you related the Qur'an to your everyday life.[4]

Several elements are worth highlighting here. First, scripture (here the Qur'an, but similar admonitions from Tasleem and other shaykhs frequently accompany the Hadith) has taken on a personal status, so that the individual must maintain a quality relationship with it. Second, that relationship has a strong intellectual component. Merely passively taking the Qur'an in through soothing recitation recordings "on the way to work" is not enough – it must be intellectually engaged with, relying on the *tafsīr* commentaries and Hadith to supplement the individual's reading. Third, the onus of personal application and relating the text to the person's everyday life is firmly with each individual. Implied but not entirely articulated in Tasleem's exhortation is that we are living in the Internet age, where the Qur'an, Hadith, and *tafsīr* commentaries are merely a click away in easy-to-access online English translations for his Anglophone audience.

Tasleem ends his sermon with an autobiographical testimonial:

> The first time I read *tafsīr* from cover to cover, or I read the Qur'an from cover to cover, and I went through the Qur'an, and I realized

that Allah – 'azza wa-jalla – is making the world relevant for me.
This book that was written fourteen, fifteen hundred years ago, now
in this day and age, makes my life, makes things make sense. All of
a sudden I look at world issues and world problems, and inner
struggles and outer struggles, and I look at everything, and I realize:
These things now make sense! And that is what the Qur'an can do
for us.[5]

There is a profound empowerment that comes through direct access
to and engagement with the ancient text. The fourteen or fifteen
hundred years of Islamic history are flattened and removed from view,
so that Tasleem and his audience can experience the exhilaration that
comes with a personal relationship with scripture. In Tasleem's
experience, the Qur'an and its Hadith-based commentaries become
an existential keystone, a paradigm-setting vision of the world and his
place in it.

To anyone familiar with American Evangelical preaching, there
is probably something intensely resonant in Saad Tasleem's message
and framing: Scripture offers approachable, practicable, ancient
wisdom to everywoman and everyman. Personal testimony reinforces
theological exhortation. Individuals are admonished to renew their
faith through intimate engagement with and disciplined piety toward
the sacred text. There are even echoes of Evangelicals' notorious
"personal relationship with Jesus" language in Tasleem's "What is
the status of your relationship with the Qur'an?" phrasing. For
Tasleem and his ilk, religion is vigorous, personal, immediately
applicable, grounded in an intuitive connection to scripture, and readily adaptable to new circumstances.

WHAT DO YOU CALL THEM?

Our popular lexicon around religion is impoverished with terms to
categorize entrepreneurial scripturalist figures like Tasleem and his
Evangelical counterparts. Words like "conservative" or even "ultraconservative" are sometimes thrown around to describe Evangelicals

and Salafis, and, to a degree, it's true: The scripturalists tend to hold fast to conventional or conservative social attitudes (e.g., customary gender roles and sexual ethics, family values, the importance of public morality informed by religion). But "conservative" has connotations of conserving and upholding the past order in the present, an aversion to change or innovation. That hardly characterizes the adaptive and inventive style of religion Tasleem is propagating.

"Traditional" or "traditionalists" are, likewise, words that are sometimes deployed to position the scripturalists as awkward outliers in the shifting landscape of modern culture. "Traditional" carries connotations of looking to the past to rectify the present, anchoring oneself in older wisdom and practices that might seem fuddy-duddy in the face of modernity's forward-looking demands. And, to an extent, that is true of the Evangelicals and Salafis: They *are* looking to ancient scriptures and early communities of Christians and Muslims to inspire their religious inhabitation of the present. Yet Tasleem's slick, leading-edge handling of technology and the Internet, his marketing techniques, individualistic rhetorical flourishes, egalitarian admonitions toward scriptural engagement, and his general fashionability are not "traditional" in any standard use of the word. Like hipster Evangelical preachers with their own stylized YouTube videos and conspicuously *relevant* religious ideas, Tasleem is a comfortable and highly flexible creature of modernity.

These words – traditional, conservative, traditionalist – that are at hand in the religious vocabulary of our times capture elements of but also miss the mark significantly when it comes to the scripturalists. In the free-ranging religious marketplace of America, Salafis and Evangelicals are anything but staid traditionalists or conservators of the recent past.[6] They are innovators, casting off hidebound liturgical and interpretive traditions for the sake of making scripture and religion applicable now. They are scriptural *radicals* (in the sense of grasping the roots), who downplay the intervening centuries of interpretive custom in favor of getting straight to the "authentic" meaning of the text.

The contemporaneity, the technological mastery, the habitual adjustability of these movements combined with their seemingly fixed and scripturally rooted orientation leave analysts casting about for new terms: emergent, revivalist, neo-fundamentalist.[7] And all of these labels are functional – more suitable, indeed, than "conservative" or "traditionalist" – because they highlight the scripturalists' idiosyncratic and often misinterpreted relationships to history and to scripture. On the one hand, the scripturalists are voracious consumers of books and written texts: Bible study guides, commentaries like the *tafsir* literature Tasleem references, historical studies of the original scriptural era, be it the eastern Mediterranean of the first century or the Arabian peninsula of the seventh. It is a misconstrual to call the scripturalists anti-intellectual or ahistorical. They seek to investigate every possible detail of the scriptural context and glean every insight available from those ancient moments. This dynamic is exemplified in a saying from a famous evangelical preacher of the nineteenth century, Dwight L. Moody, "I have one rule about books. I do not read any book, unless it will help me to understand *the* book."[8] Hence also, the Salafi fixation with the Hadith literature; it gives thousands of access points to the life of the Prophet Muhammad and the early Muslim community that was receiving the Qur'an. On the other hand, the intervening centuries – the eras in which the Christian and Muslim traditions were developing and growing into their present forms, the contingent decisions and events that created the present order – are of far less interest to the Scripture People. Their steady historical gaze leapfrogs from the present straight back to the first or the seventh century.

Sacred texts, in most religious expressions and communities, do not exist on their own: They are surrounded by history, by layers of interpretation, application, ideas, and expositive frameworks that get attached to the texts. The nickname we give to all these layers and histories of interpretive effort is "tradition." It can be formal and dogmatic or informative and atmospheric. Most strands of Islam and Christianity give top billing to *tradition* as the sinews that tie believers to the past, the fathomless centuries of resources and rituals for connecting scripture to the present. But Salafis and Evangelicals downplay and demote the role of tradition. They, at least rhetorically, snip the sinews to lay hold of the thing itself: scripture. Consider how Alister McGrath, in a tongue-in-cheek passage, channels what many Evangelicals think about tradition:

> [T]here is a concern that tradition can be seen as a human invention or fabrication, in opposition to the word of God ... [T]radition carries with it the sense of "traditionalist" – the dead hand of previous generations, which demands that we continue to think and act in precisely the same manner as earlier generations, thus locking evangelicalism into a sixteenth-, eighteenth-, or nineteenth-century worldview. To give authority of any kind to this "tradition" might therefore seem to run the risk of condemning evangelicalism to sleepwalking with the dead ... Tradition is thus directly opposed to contemporanity[sic].[9]

With some adjustments to terminology, similar sentiments often circulate in Salafi conversations: Tradition or inherited interpretations are set in opposition to scripture instead of being a complement to scripture.

This apparent separation of sacred text from tradition is scandalous to many of the Salafis' and Evangelicals' coreligionists; indeed, it is one of the most substantial and sustained lines of criticism leveled against the scripturalists. In their critics' eyes, this traditionlessness is naive presentism, sawing off the very religious tree limb that the scripturalists aim to stand on. But what these critics often miss is that this overt traditionlessness is the source of the very energy and verve that makes the scripturalists popular and exciting. They have split the atom of text and tradition, unleashing waves of inventive new interpretations, thrilling applications of scripture, and personalized attachments like the experience to which Tasleem is inviting his audience.

Let me illustrate the fission, the dynamism, and the new possibilities, that emerge through the splitting apart of sacred text and interpretive tradition by way of two paradigmatic, historical scriptur-alist figures: Charles Grandison Finney and Nasir al-Din al-Albani. Both of them are, in different ways, antecedents and forebears of the style of religion that Tasleem is inhabiting, whether or not he would recognize them as such.

CHARLES GRANDISON FINNEY:
REVIVALIST EXTRAORDINAIRE

There is a region of upstate New York that historians call the Burned-Over District. It is so named, because, in the first half of the nine-teenth century, the spiritual flames of Second Great Awakening revivals burned through the area in wave after wave like forest fires. The Burned-Over District was a sort of religious laboratory or forge, shaping numerous idiosyncratic American religious movements. Joseph Smith and the Mormons, the short-lived utopian Oneida Society, contemporary Jehovah's Witnesses and Adventists, and the séance-holding Spiritualists all trace their roots back to that wild and woolly era and region. But there is arguably no other proselyte or preacher of the Burned-Over District who exerted such a great influ-ence over American religion as Charles Grandison Finney.[10]

By his own account, Finney grew up in a veritable spiritual wilderness in upstate New York that was without "religious privil-eges," that is, easy access to any established churches or regular preachers. Instead, he experienced the subpar itinerant sermonizers of the frontier and, occasionally, "some miserable holding forth of an ignorant preacher who would sometimes be found in that country."[11] The son of farmers, Finney did not go to college, but instead appren-ticed himself to a local lawyer. As a young adult, he half-heartedly joined a hum-drum Presbyterian church, but his real conversion occurred through an overwhelming experience of God's presence and his own sin and need for repentance one evening on a walk through the woods.[12] That was 1821, just two years before Joseph Smith would testify to his first encounter with the angel Moroni in nearby Palmyra.

Baptized by fire, Finney almost immediately began preaching wherever he could. At 6' 3" with piercing eyes, he was a compelling and eminently watchable figure, and within a year of his conversion experience he became a candidate for ministry in the Presbyterian church. He was invited to attend Princeton, the foremost Presbyterian seminary in the country, but he demurred. When his pastor friends urged him, even offering a full scholarship, he "plainly told them that I would not put myself under such an influence as they had been under, that I was confident they had been wrongly educated, and they were not ministers that met my ideal of what a minister of Christ should be."[13] Even at such an unformed and early stage, his instinct was drawn toward a more rough-and-tumble style of religious work.

He also found himself scandalized by the predominant placid Calvinism rampant among his Presbyterian and Baptist peers. According to the 1647 Westminster Confession, the guiding creed of the Presbyterian Church, "By the decree of God, for the manifestation of His glory, some men and angels are predestinated unto everlasting life, and others fore-ordained to everlasting death." This seemed to foreclose the possibility of human choosing or agency – the chosen Christians were predestined by God and saved by no power or effort of their own, and everyone else was damned by no special fault or agency of their own. Though he was ordained as a Presbyterian minister, Finney saw no logic in this traditional Calvinist view of salvation, worrying that it led only to complacent and self-satisfied pew-sitters. He was fond of quoting the anti-Calvinist jingle composed by his fellow evangelist, Lorenzo Dow:

> You can and you can't
> You will and you won't
> You'll be damned if you do
> You'll be damned if you don't.[14]

Finney openly defied the creed of his own church, recounting a debate he had with his "thoroughly Calvinistic" early mentor:

> I had read nothing on the subject except my Bible; and what I had
> there found upon the subject, I had interpreted as I would have

understood the same or like passages in a law book. I thought he
had evidently interpreted those texts in conformity with an
established theory of [salvation].[15]

This would, indeed, be a trope of Finney's life, perpetually contrasting
his own untutored, plain-sense reading of the Bible against the
inherited wisdom and elaborate traditional formulations of
Presbyterian (or other) dogma – "I had no where to go but directly to
the Bible, and to the philosophy or workings of my own mind, as
revealed in consciousness."[16] He downplayed all denominational dis-
tinctives and elitist forms of knowledge in favor of a direct, egalitarian, biblical, experiential spirituality. This might seem like an
inconsequential debate about calibrating the free-will fineries of
Protestant theology, but it was the germ of Finney synthesizing a
vigorous form of Protestantism that we today call Evangelicalism.[17]

Finney's preaching was bold and energetic, filled with fire and
brimstone yet also with a sympathetic tenderness and heart-
wrenching emotional appeals. He spoke, as he put it, "the *language
of common life*," disdaining the fancy theological language and elitist
hermeneutical flourishes that filled many church sermons.[18] He drew
upon what he knew: "I was bred a lawyer. I came right forth from a
law office to the pulpit, and talked to the people as I would have
talked to a jury."[19] He reasoned persuasively with the crowds and
offered a gospel message that blended the sour anthropology of
Calvinism (all people are sinners condemned to hell) with an
empowering message of hope and agency (God summons all to choose
repentance, rejecting no one, because Christ died for all).

Within a few years, he became nationally recognizable, touring
New York and Boston, stirring up revival meetings and ruffling
feathers in the established congregations. By 1827, a scant six years
after his conversion experience, he was the most sought-after preacher
in the country. While many evangelists fanned the flames of the
Second Great Awakening, none did more than Finney to encourage
and instantiate the revivals.

Charles Finney was an evangelism and proselytism technologist. He helped design what was probably the world's first megachurch, the Brooklyn Tabernacle, which followed a theater-in-the-round arrangement and could seat 3,000 people.[20] He experimented with different types of appeal, using empirical methods of assessing what worked and what didn't. Confident that a simple decision was all that kept a nonbeliever from becoming a saved one, he was famous for advocating "New Measures" that seemed to foster greater audience responses and repentance: bold and theatrical preaching to capture peoples' minds with images of impending hell; allowing women and not just men to testify to their conversion experiences; extended revivals with protracted meetings; an "anxious bench" where the affected audience members could come forward to be counseled and furthered toward conversion by a group of volunteer prayer partners; advertising campaigns in advance of meetings; musical performances and congregational singing of hymns that would get people in mind of conversion. In Nathan Hatch's insightful phrasing, "Finney called for a Copernican revolution to make religious life audience-centered."[21]

Finney's license to experiment and scientific-formula approach arose, again, out of his disdain for tradition, be it liturgical or theological, and his artless reading of the Bible. "It is," he wrote,

> absolutely fanatical, for the Presbyterian church, or any other church, to be sticklish in her particular forms, and to act as if *they* were established by divine authority. The fact is, that God has established, in no church, any particular *form*, or manner of worship, for promoting the interests of religion. The scriptures are entirely silent on these subjects, under the gospel dispensation, and the church is left to exercise her own discretion in relation to all such matters.[22]

In his mind, the urgent business of the church was the harvesting of souls, and if farmers could use empirical observation and experimentation to improve their crop yield, so could preachers. Finney gathered all of this research and development, his alchemy of souls and observable proselytizing success, and wrote an instruction manual (perhaps the first in the evangelical how-to genre) drawing together a method of revival preaching. "And in an age of nascent industrialization and one increasingly enamored of technology, Finney's formulaic approach to revival matched the cultural moment."[23] He set the model – countless others from country preachers to notables like Dwight L. Moody, Billy Sunday, and Billy Graham would follow Finney's paradigm.

Finney was also a social instigator of the first order. His revival-minded, commonsense reading of the Bible led him not to political complacency but to applying the same boundary-breaking energy of his revivals outward to society in general. Filled with the triumphalistic optimism that fueled nineteenth-century evangelical activism, he asserted:

> Now the great business of the church is to reform the world – to put away every kind of sin. The church of Christ was originally organized to be a body of reformers. The very profession of Christianity implies the profession and virtually an oath to do all that can be done for the universal reformation of the world. The Christian church was designed to make aggressive movement in every direction ... to reform individuals, communities, and governments ... until every form of iniquity shall be driven from the earth.[24]

To wit, while he believed evangelism to be his life's work, Finney preached against the social iniquities he saw in American society around him: the hypocrisy of slavery; "the outrageous injustice with which this nation has treated the aborigines of this country;" "the national love of money;" "the legal sanctioning of duels;" and "the desecration of the Sabbath 'especially by the Post Office Department.'"[25]

To call Finney an intellectual lightweight or merely a savvy, intuitive preacher would be to mistake the sea change he represented. He traveled in the same lofty social realms as his more traditional interlocutors. From 1835 until his death, the self-taught Finney served as a professor of theology and then president of Oberlin College. He wrote a two-volume work on systematic theology, which he would proudly send to his traditional critics to see if they could find any fault in his reasoning from the Bible.[26] When his elite pastoral interlocutors would mock his repetitive, plain-spoken style and aver that he could not hold their "educated" audiences, Finney rejoindered, "facts soon silenced them on this point. They found that, under my preaching, judges, and lawyers, and educated men were converted by scores."[27]

In his landmark *Anti-intellectualism in American Life*, Richard Hofstadter profiles Finney, offering a very mixed verdict: on the one hand acknowledging that "he must be reckoned one of our great men," while at the same time noting of Finney and his revivalist ilk that "their culture was exceptionally narrow; their view of learning was exceptionally instrumental."[28] Reading Finney's *Autobiography*, one gets the sense that his heart might have swelled to Hofstadter's backhanded compliment, because for him everything was instrumental – preaching, revivals, methods, learning, books – all cannon fodder in the great war to win souls and reform the world.

As we saw in Chapter 1, no one person built the edifice and style of modern American Evangelicalism, but many contributed. If evangelical piety was conceived as a nascent personalized biblical spirituality in the colonial First Awakening, Charles Finney served as the midwife to bring evangelical revivalism and biblicism into the world as a sustained, untraditional, innovative, activist, always-reviving religious movement through the Second Awakening. He cared less for denominational territorialism than measurable success. He was a social engineer of souls, formulating an ethos of revivalism that branded the young American nation with a "born-again" veneer that remains to this day. His empirical methods were adopted by generation after generation of American preacher, right up to the present, even if many of them never knew their intellectual progenitor. He pioneered a form of religion whose "What works?" impulse was tempered only by a direct appeal to the Bible as touchstone.

NASIR AL-DIN AL-ALBANI'S HADITH UPHEAVAL

Muhammad Nasir al-Din al-Albani might be the most important religious figure of the twentieth century that you've never heard of. As I outlined in Chapter 1, Sunni scripturalism has historically been advanced by pivotal, prototypical figures – Ibn Hanbal, Ibn Taymiyya, Ibn 'Abd al-Wahhab – who crystallize an approach to scripture and reform in their time that winds up setting the tone for their era in the movement. I would hazard that Albani is that sort of figure for twentieth-century Salafism. But in order to recognize his peculiar contribution and impact, we must first sketch the world he inhabited.

Born in Albania in 1914 (hence his affectionate honorific "Albani" – the Albanian), he spent almost all of his life outside of his homeland. When he was a child, Albani's family migrated to Damascus because his father, a trained Muslim scholar, did not want to live under the secular regime that was established in Albania in 1923 as the Ottoman Empire disintegrated. That imperial disintegration marked an epochal shift in modern Islam: For many Muslims who had lived under Ottoman rule and elsewhere in majority-Muslim lands, there was a sense of staleness in authority, of defunct and rigid old systems, and there was a longing for new ideas that would galvanize a Muslim world that was on its back foot. Most Sunnis live according to one of the *madhhab*s, the four major traditions of jurisprudence. In post-Ottoman Syria, where Albani would spend his early life, the Hanafi school of jurisprudence – the Ottomans' preferred *madhhab* – was still dominant, so that Hanafi-trained scholars and clerics had the plum judicial and academic jobs and held sway through their ability "to interpret scripture and to define the religious outlook of society."[29]

Similarly, in the newly founded Saudi Arabia, where Albani would sojourn briefly but impactfully, the Wahhabi leadership "had been monopolized by a small religious aristocracy from Najd, first centered around Muhammad ibn 'Abd al-Wahhab and his descendants (known as the Al al-Shaykh) before opening up to a small number of other families."[30] This Wahhabi system of theological maintenance and authority lionized Ibn ʿAbd al-Wahhab as its architect and the Salaf as its inspiration, but it also perpetuated a facade: The Wahhabis, going back to Ibn ʿAbd al-Wahhab himself, cast themselves as a revolutionary theological and jurisprudential reform movement, forsaking the authority of Islamic traditions and appealing directly to the Salaf. In the realm of theology, of *tawhid* and fixating unswervingly on the utter uniqueness of God, they had some claim to this primal connection. But in the realm of jurisprudence – the lived reality of their system and application to daily life –they were more or less following the conventions of the Hanbali *madhhab*, relying on intervening centuries of tradition, precedents, and interpretations, hardly the radical reformation that was promised.[31]

Contrastingly, there were two major movements at the time offering pan-Islamic programs of renewal. The first was an intellectual and philosophical project of forward-thinking, reformist Muslim scholars who had adopted for themselves the title "Salafi." These modernist Salafis, students of the Egyptian reformer Muhammad ʿAbduh and his disciple Rashid Rida, were watching the disarray in the Islamic world after the collapse of the Ottoman Empire and seeking to develop a version of Islam that was intellectually agile and rationally calibrated for the modern world. They admired the intelligence and iconoclastic approach of Ibn Taymiyya, but they had a more ambivalent relationship with the Hadith –many modernists felt that while some hadiths could be upheld as reliable, the Hadith canon as a whole needed to be approached critically and judiciously, not unlike the way modern Western historical critical scholars had taken to scrutinizing the Bible.[32] The other major renewal effort was a cluster of movements that all come under the heading of Islamism, or political Islam. Centered, most prominently, on the Muslim Brotherhood movement in Egypt founded in 1928, these efforts aimed at invigorating Muslims to look to the Qurʾan and to the Shariʿa (broadly defined) to reconstitute Islamic civilization within modern national political orders. Driving all these post-colonial, post-imperial rethinks, retrenchments, and reformulations was not merely a sense of malaise but also a recurring question: What is authentic Islam, and how do we get access to it now?

Floating amid all these currents of turbulence and reform was the young Albanian in Damascus. Albani's father himself was one of the class of privileged, post-Ottoman Hanafi scholars, and he instructed his young son in some of the basics of Islamic law. But Albani was an intellectual nonconformist from a very early age, and would later characterize this period – both in his home life and in Damascene society – as living in "a fanatical Ḥanafī atmosphere," where scholars were expected to abide with "unquestioning submission" by the past rulings of Hanafi scholars.[33]

What singled Albani out was his love for reading and his proximity to the first public library established in Syria. His professional training and first career was as a watchmaker, but he spent all his free time reading voraciously through the Islamic tradition, especially in the scholarship of the Hadith, eventually gaining a self-taught encyclopedic knowledge of that labyrinthine literature. He had a falling out with his father, because, as he compared the Hanafi jurisprudence he was being taught against the Hadith, he couldn't reconcile the two. He fought with his father over specific prayer practices and particular Hanafi rulings, but their disagreement was more fundamentally about authority and authenticity: Albani could not understand why his father would follow the arcane traditions of Hanafi interpretation instead of going directly to consult the Hadith.[34]

He began teaching classes on Hadith, at first, to small study groups in the back of his watch shop and eventually at Damascus University. In a striking parallel to Charles Finney, who a century earlier became an Oberlin College professor of theology without any formal training, by the age of forty, this watchmaker and anomalous auto-didactic expert on Islamic law and Hadith was teaching university classes, without having any *ijazas*, certificates of learning under a master scholar.[35]

In Syria, Albani avidly read and studied, among other things, the writings of the modernist Salafis. He frequented the Damascus salons of the modernists and even took to calling himself a Salafi as inspired by Rashid Rida's use of the term. Like Ibn Taymiyya, Albani was gravitationally drawn to root his theology and his understanding of the Hadith back in the earliest sources. With the hubris of a self-taught genius who has no attachment to traditional authority, when he came across an article by Rida arguing that the whole Hadith endeavor needed a modern critical reappraisal, Albani took it upon himself to singlehandedly do this reappraising of the entire Hadith corpus.[36]

Instead of adopting some modern or rationalist criteria for assessing the Hadith, as Rida and others were suggesting, Albani decided to reboot the entire Hadith science going back to before the ninth-century work of Ahmad ibn Hanbal and the Hadith People. Agreeing with Ibn Hanbal and against the modernists, he argued that "the use of reason must at all costs be banned from the juridical process."[37] In other words, scripture is scripture, whether it accords neatly with our finite rationality or not. Nonetheless Albani slightly recalibrated the criteria that medieval sifters of the Hadith had used to create the ranked Hadith canon, prioritizing the character and morality of the early transmitters over how widely attested or otherwise aligned a hadith account might be.[38] This may seem like tinkering around the edges, but Albani was bucking the entirety of the Islamic tradition in a fundamental way.

The whole of the Islamic jurisprudential and theological tradition is built upon a foundation of Qur'an and Hadith interpretation with all of the madhhabs and scholars and reasoning through the centuries constructing structures on top of that scriptural base. As we've seen, many scripturalists in the Taymiyyan-Wahhabi strand would argue they were drawing directly on the wisdom of the Salaf, while still conforming to the traditional Hanbali style of legal reasoning, but Albani's comprehensive distrust of tradition led him to outright reject the authority of all of the madhhabs, including the

Hanbali one, as post-Salaf innovations (*bid'a*).[39] He said, "The founders of the four Sunni *madhhabs* were also part of the *Salaf*, and they
relied directly on the Qur'an and the Sunna, so we should do the
same!"[40] He wanted Muslims to get back to the fundament of Islam,
"bypassing centuries of consensus-building among scholars and
instead [approach] the Quran and hadiths anew."[41]

Armed with his new criteria of Hadith sifting and his encyclopedic knowledge, Albani was also chiseling at and adding to these
very foundations of Islamic knowledge. He began validating as *ṣaḥīḥ*
(sound, reliable) some Hadith accounts that had been deemed
unsound or weakly attested in the classical collections and invalidating others that had the imprimatur of even Muslim and al-
Bukhari.[42] In effect, Albani took what had been assumed to be a
traditionally settled canon of scripture and reshuffled it – he was, in
the middle of the twentieth century, *canonizing new Islamic scrip-*
ture and invalidating pieces of the received canon.

Now all of this –Albani's profound anti-traditionalism, his off-
the-beaten-path approach to Hadith re-certification – might have
remained an obscure footnote on the radical new ideas arising among
Muslim scholars in the twentieth century had he remained in
Damascus as a marginal teacher of informal Salafi study groups. But
Albani was growing increasingly popular in Syria and well-known
abroad, and his immense knowledge of Hadith and original application of Hadith-reasoning were starting to attract attention. Though
Albani was avowedly apolitical, highly critical of the Muslim
Brotherhood and preferring Hadith scholarship over meddling in the
political hustle and bustle, the government of Syria put him under
surveillance, sensibly fearing what unruliness might arise from a
popular cleric who was offering refractory new interpretations of
scripture.[43] It was in that moment that Shaykh 'Abd al-Aziz bin Baz,
a friend and admirer of Albani and vice chancellor of the newly formed
Islamic University of Medina, invited Albani to teach Hadith at the
soon-to-be-premier Saudi school. Momentously, this brilliant
autodidact who was undertaking a total reworking of the Hadith

corpus was being brought into the heart of the new Saudi-Wahhabi effort to spread their version of Islam around the world.[44] There is even credible conjecture that Albani was the one who brought the noun and identity "Salafi" from the salons of the modernists squarely into the Wahhabi discourse.[45]

When he came to Medina to teach in 1961, Nasir al-Din al-Albani landed in the nascent Wahhabi educational system like a ton of bricks. He was immediately beloved by the international cohorts of students who had come to the newly formed university to learn true Islam in the Prophet's city.[46] Albani did not carry himself like the established Wahhabi shaykhs and teachers who felt entitled to the students' respect by dint of their credentials and aristocratic pedigree. He did not have any pedigree or formal training, but he scratched that supreme itch of his era: authenticity. As he would later reflect upon his time in Medina, "I was with the students as if I were one of them."[47] After his classes, students would follow him into the courtyard, and he would hold impromptu group office hours, with students from other classes coming to learn meritocratically from this approachable genius professor. Counter to the – what I think can justly be labeled – Wahhabi indoctrination agenda that created the Saudi universities, Albani was making a pitch for, in both pedagogy and content, a version of Salafism that amounted to a sort of "'do-it-yourself' Islam."[48] His model called for a vital and elemental connection between his shaykhs-in-training and the Hadith, not allowing any tradition or reigning consensus to dictate the scriptural interpretive process.

While he was all the rage with the student body, Albani had a knack for provoking his Wahhabi colleagues. Shortly after arriving in Medina, he began overtly criticizing Muhammad ibn 'Abd al-Wahhab! While Albani could affirm and agree with the eighteenth-century reformer for his *tawhid* theology, the untraditionalist criticized the Wahhabis' founder and exposed the contradiction at the heart of Wahhabi scholarship: They were functionally just traditional Hanbalis when it came to jurisprudence and not the radical proponents of the Salaf they claimed to be. Albani dug the dagger in deeper by pointing out that Ibn ʿAbd al-Wahhab had once, in a letter, cited a weak hadith as evidence, which Albani found utterly unacceptable, and held up as proof that Ibn ʿAbd al-Wahhab was not knowledgeable in the field of Hadith.[49] This was, to put it mildly, a frontal assault on the Wahhabi authority structure by a foreign scholar with no formal training, who had been invited to teach at what would become their flagship school.

The Wahhabi establishment was deeply disturbed by the upstart Albani, but his popularity with the students gave them pause, and because his theology – if not his jurisprudence or his quirky approach to the Hadith – impeccably aligned with theirs, they couldn't find any way to label him a heretic. After a couple of years, the Wahhabis found a pretext to get rid of him: When Albani decertified some previously unquestioned hadiths, he issued a *fatwa* (a scholarly jurisprudential opinion) that women should not have to cover their faces in public.[50] This flew in the face not only of Wahhabi jurisprudence but contradicted long-established social practice in Saudi Arabia. In 1963, Albani's teaching contract was not renewed, and he was sent back to Syria.

Though he had only taught in Medina for a couple of years – and, despite his friend Bin Baz's many efforts, the Wahhabi establishment never allowed him to teach there again – the seeds of Albani's Hadith upheaval had already taken root in Saudi Salafism. Someone who was present in the Salafi schools, observing the residual reverberations after the Albanian's departure, summarized:

> The *hadith* had become a virtual dictatorship. When in a sermon or a conference an ʿalim [scholar] cited a *hadith*, he could be interrupted at any moment by one of his students asking him: "Has that *hadith* been authenticated? Has al-Albani authenticated it?["] That could hardly fail to reinforce the mistrust felt by the ʿulama [scholars] belonging to the religious institution toward al-Albani.[51]

The traditional deference and hierarchy of the Wahhabi establishment was suddenly answering to the now-absent Albani's erudition and having to justify their opinions in his terms.

The Albanian shaykh wrote a small book titled *The Characteristics of the Prophet's Prayer*, where, using his recertified hadiths, he reconstructed the Prophet Muhammad's prayer practices with a precision that challenged the established practices all of the *madhhab*s. He determined, for example, that all other Muslims were holding their hands improperly during prayer and that it was perfectly acceptable for Muslims to keep their shoes on during prayer.[52] These might seem like negligible details, but imagine the disturbances that can emerge when a contingent of participants in collective daily prayer change the script *in Arabia*, at the notional heart of Islam. Now imagine those same proponents arguing that their modifications are the *authentic Sunna of the Prophet* and everyone else has been doing it wrong for centuries. Religion and identity and friction often live in these practiced details, much more than in high-minded debates about ideas.

Albani's students and disciples usually do not identify as Wahhabis. They obviously don't belong to one of the *madhhab*s, and since, in the wake of Albani's short-lived and disruptive tenure in Medina, everyone, Wahhabis included, took to calling themselves Salafis, Albani's people resurrected an old title for themselves: *Ahl al-Hadith*, the Hadith People.[53] Some of these Albani students remained in Saudi Arabia, with many going on to become shaykhs and teachers in Salafi schools themselves. But, by virtue of the intentionally international and globalizing project of Saudi policy in creating the Wahhabi universities in the first place, many, many more of the devotees of Albani have spread around the globe with his rethought Hadith program. They landed in Egypt and Yemen and Jordan and Britain and the United States and countless other places. Richard Gauvain found in his ethnographic study among Salafis in Cairo that Salafis there are fiercely loyal to the point of deeming the Albanian shaykh "incapable of error." In Gauvain's summation, "particularly within the ritual sphere, Albani provides most of the ideological foundations upon which the edifice of Egyptian Salafism now stands."[54]

For his part, Albani returned to Syria in 1963 only to be imprisoned by the government in 1967 when the socialist Ba'ath party took power. Though he had maintained his stringent apolitical stance, there was hearsay evidence presented that he did not support the new "regime because it did not govern according to Islam." He was, ironically, charged with "promoting the 'Wahhabi da'wa [invitation/proclamation].'"[55] Some of his students invited him to move to Jordan, where he would be more protected, and he spent the remainder of his days there. Students from around the world would now journey to Jordan to study with the great Hadith scholar, creating an alternate, though not necessarily rival, power center in late twentieth-century Salafism.[56] He continued issuing controversial *fatwas* based upon his recertified Hadith canon until his death.

When he died in 1999, Salafi newspapers and publications around the world heralded Albani, the idiosyncratic watchmaker, as the *muhaddith al-'asr* – the greatest Hadith scholar of his generation.[57] While his particular jurisprudential interpretations might only hold sway for a portion of global Salafis today, no one could dispute that, on Hadith matters, Albani had reset the table. Today if you look up a hadith in online Salafi databases, you will find it thoroughly cross-referenced to the ninth-century Hadith collections of the classical canon, but you'll find another notation as well: How did Albani grade this one?[58]

As with Evangelicalism, no one person inspired or made Salafism from whole cloth – it was the collective work of hundreds and thousands of scholars and shaykhs and millions of global "students of knowledge," as Salafis-in-training like to title themselves. Likewise you can pin the founding of Salafism to any number of historical moments – Ibn Taymiyya's pioneering late medieval ideas, the Wahhabi revolution of the eighteenth century, the founding of the modern kingdom of Saudi Arabia – but I would like to suggest that Salafism as we know it today came into view with the shockwave that Albani made in his two years in Medina. In Gauvain's words, "because of al-Albani, traditional Saudi-Wahhabi realities imploded."[59] What Albani did was not merely reshuffle the Hadith corpus; he blew out the boundaries of what Salafism could be. The Albanian shoved the Islamic tradition so far to the margins that direct Hadith interpretation opened up a thousand new (and often disruptive) possibilities.

CONCLUSION

Returning to the contemporary hipster preacher, Saad Tasleem, with whom we began this chapter – I doubt that he has ever heard of Charles Grandison Finney and he does not identify with Albani's strand of Salafism, but both are intellectual ancestors of the genre of religion that Tasleem is propagating. Finney was the nineteenth-century perfecter of this style of experiential, adaptive, egalitarian, "straight talk from scripture" preaching that Tasleem now takes up to spread his AlMaghrib-style, post-Salafi message. In its emotive testimonial appeal, its vesting of agency for religious transformation in the individual audience member, its call to commitment to a life-changing relationship (with the Qur'an, instead of Jesus), Tasleem's preaching idiom is Finneyite, whether he recognizes it or not. How he arrived at this convergence with Evangelical revivalist rhetoric – whether he is gamely imitating American Evangelical preachers, has independently landed on a similar style, or has picked up on Evangelical vernacular that is simply in the ether in America – is a question I will take up in depth in Chapter 6. For now, we can observe that he is pitching his "what works," technologically savvy, direct-to-scripture style of religion to an American Muslim audience whose Christian analogue Charles Finney deciphered two centuries ago.

Tasleem's easy-access scripturalism is also recognizably a paraphrasing of the modern Salafism which Albani helped to create. As with the relationship between Finney and Evangelicalism, not all Salafis or Salafi-influenced Muslims have even heard of Albani, and many Salafis do not agree with his sweeping rejection of the *madhhabs*, but Albani's impact cannot be overstated. By challenging all of the layers of tradition, all of the formalities and scaffolding of *madhhabs* and elite knowledge hierarchies, by kicking the feet out from under the Wahhabi authority strictures that might have kept Saudi Salafi knowledge pinned down, Albani set in motion a global Salafism that was light-footed and egalitarian. Tasleem attended the Islamic University of Medina more than forty years after Albani's tenure there, and I see no direct connection between them.[60] But I would submit that the dynamism, the adaptiveness, the personalization we see in Tasleem's preaching is downstream of Albani's Hadith recanonization and the room it created for wholesale rethinking and reformulating in Salafi Islam. Tasleem's existential, "you should cultivate a personal, intellectual relationship with the Qur'an and its commentaries" exhortations to young American Muslims have the untraditionalist earmarks of the heart-grabbing, scriptural authenticity that Albani offered his Medina students: Do-It-Yourself.

In this chapter, I have tried to present these scripturalist paragons the way they see themselves – demoting and depreciating tradition, facilitating energetic new modes and methods of religious communication, empowering everywoman and everyman with an experiential attachment to textual religion. I have sought, in other words, to capture the potency, the gravitational pull of text without tradition, that attaches modern people so easily to these movements. I would like to end with two serious caveats.

First, for all their free-wheeling inventiveness and inveighing against the dead authority of tradition, for all their attempts at grabbing hold of the unmediated text, the authority of tradition prowls in the shadows of Salafis' and Evangelicals' theological affirmations and ways of being in the world. The voice of tradition is never fully silenced, and tradition comes, for both movements, to exert a subterranean influence on their presuppositions, beliefs, and views on a host of issues. As much as Finney might project an attitude of "just my consciousness and the Bible" in constructing his theology and in his elastic revival methods, he could only succeed in his time because he was squarely within the four corners of the Protestant Christian tradition. His systematic theology volumes make it clear that he was more of a careful and well-read theologian than his "I'm just a simple lawyer" affect would lead one to think.

Likewise, even as Albani is riding roughshod over the *madhhab*s and selectively reaccrediting the entire Hadith corpus, he is still more or less playing by the rules of the classical Islamic tradition and just tweaking a few Hadith criteria. What Rashid Rida had suggested – a modernist, rationalist, historical critical reappraisal of the Hadith – was not the path that Albani chose. While claiming to principally follow the Salaf, the Salafis are constantly depending on texts and methods transmitted to them by the intervening generations and the *madhhab*s.[61] Even the Salafi reliance on Ibn Taymiyya as a near incontrovertible guide speaks to the longing for some linchpin, some precedent from the past to validate the practices of the present. Like the Hanbali revivalists of old and like the original Wahhabis at the doorstep of modernity, the Salafis fall within a long line of Sunni retrievalists, playing text off tradition, while being governed by habits of thought long-established by tradition. For both movements, traditions patrol the ancestral borders of what scripture is and which scriptural interpretations are permissible in ways that are acknowledged and unacknowledged. The Scripture People are "traditionless," not traditionless.

Second, what is lost when tradition is rhetorically jettisoned? Tradition carries within it the accumulated maturity and wisdom and lived experiences of innumerable thinkers and communities through the centuries. The Christian traditions and Islamic traditions of interpretation, if they have any coherence, have discerned over time the unscrupulous means and violent ends to which unmitigated, self-confident scriptural discourse can lead. The "dead hand of previous generations," to use McGrath's vivid phrase, has learned how to steer the ship of interpretation through the narrows. In other words, traditions impose safety rails on sacred texts: You can read it this way, but don't read it that way, since dangerous outcomes lie down that road. By conspicuously stripping away the authority of tradition, new readings become permissible, new aggressions become vindicated, new abusive misdeeds seem evidently "scriptural."

Many preachers through the decades since Charles Finney have used his affective revival strategies and straight-to-the-Bible reasoning quite coercively and, I think, unethically. If you've ever found yourself emotionally swept up in the midst of an evangelistic event (and I have been in more than a few) by a charismatic preacher who knows every trick in the book for eliciting a reaction or commitment (or donation!) from you, you might well be experiencing, at three or four orders removed, the pragmatic emotional engineering of Charles Finney.[62] I've met many people whose first and lasting impression of Evangelical Christianity came from emotional appeals that they found disrespectful, manipulative, and dislocating.

Moreover, while it is not original or exclusive to him, Finney's "directly to the Bible, and to the philosophy or workings of my own mind" approach to interpretation and theology has been replicated by many Evangelicals since to justify their injustices, iffy voting choices, ethical lapses, and methods of coercion.[63] Some self-conscious Evangelicals even have a pejorative phrase for this self-persuasive interpreting: "playing flex-y-Bible." Finney is certainly not the only origin point of this tendency, but, in the broad Bible-only penchant of which he is a key part, the text detached from tradition can, in the creative and autonomous reasoning of everywoman and everyman, say and vindicate almost anything. To the motivated interpreter, just about anything can be "biblical."

Similarly, Albani's Hadith revolution has opened up new wounds and contradictions within the Salafi community. While the Albanian shaykh maintained a principled distance from national and international politics, not all of his students and disciples have done the same.[64] Some of his followers, led by an Albani acolyte and Islamic University of Medina professor named Rabi' al-Madkhali, have become fierce loyalists to the Saudi royal family and vehement critics of anyone who disagrees with their totalizing politics. They have toned down Albani's criticisms of the Wahhabis and fastidiously avoided censuring the Saudi royals, including for their glaring human rights abuses and corruption.[65] In a deep irony, one of the legacies of the disruptive and nonconforming Albanian shaykh is a movement of Salafis who are as conformist and protective of the Saudi establishment as they come. Many American students studied under Rabiʿ al-Madkhali in the 1990s, and they returned to America as hard-line and zealous defenders of true (a.k.a., Madkhali) Salafism, denouncing anyone who does not perfectly align with their understanding, all while quoting Albani and his recertified hadiths in hushed and reverent tones. We will further encounter these Madkhali polemicists and see their impact on America in Chapter 5.

But that's not the limit of Albani's influence: In November 1979, a heavily armed group of 300 rebels led by a charismatic but largely uneducated Saudi man named Juhayman al-ʿUtaybi stormed the Grand Mosque in Mecca, which contains the Kaʿaba, the devotional nucleus of Islam, the place to which hajj pilgrims venture and toward which Muslims point in prayer. Precedents, going back to the time of the Prophet, forbid the use of weapons in the Grand Mosque, but Juhayman was willing to override these injunctions because he had recently divined that one of his companions was the Mahdi, an apocalyptic messianic figure described in many hadiths. The rebels had chosen that timing because it was the first day of the year 1400 in the Islamic (Hijri) calendar and because there is a hadith that predicts that a "renewer of Islam" will appear at the turn of every century.[66] Juhayman and his followers hoped to consecrate their Mahdi at the Kaʿaba, in accordance with some hadith predictions.[67] The rebels took hostage thousands of worshippers and pilgrims who were present in the mosque, and they held off for two weeks against a siege by the Saudi military and police forces. Finally, the Saudi authorities recaptured the mosque, but not without more than 250 deaths (a mix of pilgrims, rebels, and Saudi military) and hundreds more injured.[68]

In the aftermath of the Grand Mosque siege, the stunned Saudi regime and Wahhabi establishment tried to reconstruct where Juhayman and his group had come from. Subsequent investigations revealed that the rebel movement had its origins in Medina in the mid-1960s from a group inspired by Albani and his new approach to

Hadith. These Albani followers were vigilant in rejecting all connections to tradition or precedent, including going so far as to deny the authority of Ibn Hanbal, Ibn Taymiyya, and Ibn ʿAbd al-Wahhab, but they continued to revere Albani. The Juhayman group had been rigorously following Albani's *Characteristics of the Prophet's Prayer* book, and their practice of wearing sandals while they prayed had caused confrontations at the iconic Prophet's Mosque in Medina, leading them to form their own small mosque community.[69] They had become increasingly isolated and alienated from the rest of Saudi society, breaking ties with their teachers and shaykhs, and forming an apocalyptic cult of personality around Juhayman al-ʿUtaybi. Before the attack, Juhayman had declared for his followers that even the institution of the Saudi government was illegitimate and inauthentic because it did not govern according to the Qurʾan and Sunna.[70] The attack on the Grand Mosque was, for many Saudi and Wahhabi leaders, the first sign that their whole international Wahhabi propagation scheme might have unleashed some forces they did not understand and were not prepared for.

It would be patently unjust to lay all the responsibility for the Juhayman al-ʿUtaybi incident and its ensuing violence at Albani's feet, as some of Albani's critics at the time sought to do. As with America's own religiously propelled mass casualty events (Jonestown, Branch Davidians, etc.), the Juhayman disaster unfolded in a layered cultural, governmental, sociohistorical, and interpersonal context. But there *is* a connection between the cleaving of the Hadith from their traditional interpretive scaffolding and the 1979 attack. Albani took the guard rails off the Hadith discourse – not that those guard rails were perfect or always kept wild interpretations in check, but they did draw upon the wisdom of many generations to constrain the possibilities of going awry. The atom-splitting fission from the breakup of text and tradition that scripturalists harness to produce their dynamism and horsepower can just as easily become a weapon.

Salafis and Evangelicals are not unaware of these risks and pitfalls. A significant part of their scriptural discourses involves noticing, remarking upon, and rebuking outlier interpretations and absurd scriptural citations for positions they find indefensible. So how do these decentralized, "traditionless" movements work to keep the Juhaymans of the world and the beckoning interpretive chaos in check while still democratizing the scriptural interpretive process? Their corresponding answer is fairly simple and also prefigured in the careers of Tasleem and Finney and Albani: Educate the masses.

4 Education and the Democratization of Scripture

As a child in elementary school, my parents wanted to help my brother and me gain more Bible knowledge. To be sure, it was not as if we were remotely deprived on that front: Attending a private, Evangelical school, we had daily Bible classes on near equal footing with our reading, writing, and arithmetic. Every Sunday we were in Sunday school at church, learning our Bible lessons. Nonetheless, it seemed important to fill the scriptural reservoir in our young minds to the brim. So once a week we would go to AWANA.

AWANA is shorthand for an organization cumbersomely titled "Approved Workmen Are Not Ashamed," a name that, for the life of me, I cannot see what it had to do with the organizational mission, except that it was a Bible quote (2 Timothy 2:15) and gave you an easily pronounceable acronym.[1] AWANA specializes in child and youth Bible memorization. It is what Evangelicals call a "parachurch" organization. These nondenominational outfits do not aim to replace churches but operate alongside them to augment some essential function, often some form of scriptural education. The program was not hosted by our church but by another community church where some friends attended. Every week, on a weeknight, about 100 kids would be dropped off by their parents for an evening of games, competitions, and memorizing Bible verses.

As with so many Evangelical institutions operating in the deep soul-engineering furrows carved by Charles Finney and his inheritors, AWANA has spent decades empirically discovering the key to unlocking a child's mind: It is candy, lots of candy. For each Bible verse I memorized and accurately recited to one of the adult volunteer "Listeners," I would receive a piece of candy. Longer passages would even earn me an actual candy bar.

You might think that passages of text, memorized amid a sugar fix for a purely short-term motive, would evaporate from memory quickly, but you would be wrong. I still have verses from AWANA kicking around my head from the New International Version (NIV) translation of the Bible, AWANA's preferred translation. Today, when listening to a sermon or Bible lecture my old AWANA conditioning will switch on, and I can often complete the Bible verse in my head before the pastor or lecturer will finish reading it.

I somewhat regularly have occasion to mentally contrast my childhood with my own children's experience: We attend a progressive, Mainline Protestant church where the sermons might start with the Bible as a point of departure ... maybe. Every week, our church switches up the beginning of the Lord's Prayer so as not to privilege one gendered understanding of God: Our Father ... Our Mother ... Our Creator. My children will probably not even have the iconic phrasing of the Lord's Prayer stably locked in their memories.

My son and daughter attend a slightly wishy-washy Mainline Protestant preschool where each class, once a month, has a short chat session with the pastor of the church where the preschool is housed. That's about as biblical or religious as it gets. I recall our initial meeting with the preschool director, who, not knowing our religious affiliation or lack thereof, assured us that the preschool focuses on Christian values, which are really universal values. Every time I drop my son off at preschool and see that the Christian value of the month is "friendship" or "kindness;" every time one of our pastors offers a children's lesson that barely touches on the Bible; every time my daughter brings home a Sunday school coloring project that could come from any generic, irreligious coloring book, there's a voice hidden deep in the Evangelical recesses of my psyche that blows raspberries mockingly.

I have to remind myself that my wife and I have *chosen* all of this for our children. We could enroll our kids in an AWANA program – there are five chapters within ten miles of our home, according to their website – but we haven't even seriously considered that. My wife and I did not really want to replicate the provincial and Bible-soaked parts of our own Evangelical upbringings for our kids. But I'm not sure we ever truly leave behind how we were raised, the values and verses that were inscribed upon our memories, in the grooves and synapses of our brains.

At any rate, this snarl of memory and emotion all comes to mind when I'm perusing a copy of *al-Minhaj*, an American Salafi magazine, and I come across an advertisement:

UMMIE'S [Mommy's]
kiddie kottage
LEARNING CENTER
cultivating the minds of future generations

Servicing 4 wks through-school age …
Onsite Homeschooling Program …
• Structured Curriculum • Islamic Studies •
• Math - Science - Reading - Writing •
Quran Recitation • Hadith memorization • Arabic[2]

From a young age, Scripture People are primed to be sacred text handlers, to gain facility with ancient tomes, to take on the guardianship of scripture.

In the previous chapter, I illustrated the energy that comes with the scripturalist impulse to lay hold of the sacred text without the layers and centuries of tradition. Especially in a religious marketplace environment like America that rewards freshness, adaptation, and marketable repackaging, interpreting scripture afresh means that scripturalist communities are teeming with new ideas, excited converts, and devoted participants who are drawn toward a personal, subjectively buttressing attachment to the text. Instead of scriptural interpretation being in the hands of an elite hierarchy of well-trained scholars, clerics, and clergy, the exertion of textual engagement among the scripturalists is dispersed, enlisting all in the tasks of study and accumulating knowledge – a sort of hermeneutic egalitarianism. This creates problems.

Consider, for instance, an exhortation from another charismatic American Muslim leader and frequent Salafi critic, Shaykh Hamza Yusuf. He challenges the Salafis' democratic scriptural impulse without naming them:

> One of the problems among modern Muslims is that they read Hadith and they're not trained to read Hadith. The collections of Hadith were written for scholars, they weren't written for common people, and many of those hadiths have no application [i.e., they're not utilized in traditional jurisprudence]. They weren't meant to be implemented ... That's why it's very important to learn a *madhhab*, because the 'ulama' [scholars] – that's what they did: They looked at all these Hadith ... Now you've got people buying the Ṣaḥīḥ [Hadith Collection] of al-Bukhari and getting confused and, "Whoa, why does it say that ..." This is for the 'ulama', this isn't for common people ... People read these things and they think they know Arabic.[3]

Hamza Yusuf is not wrong: The scriptural texts being handled *are* old and complicated. While certainly all Muslims are encouraged to recite and appreciate and even memorize portions of the Qur'an, the Hadith have always been the realm of experts. With their layers of gradation of authority, different versions in different collections, and imposing number (thousands upon thousands of memories of the Prophet and his community), Hadith collections aren't formatted to be readable narratives.[4] They are arranged and sorted by esoteric topics designed for quick reference on medieval jurisprudential questions. Take, for example, some of the section headings from al-Bukhari's collection: Prayers, Virtues of Medina, Agriculture, Menstrual Periods, Mortgaging, Apostates, Sales in which a Price is Paid for Goods to be Delivered Later, Invoking Allah for Rain, Penalty of Hunting while on Pilgrimage. "Whoa, why does it say that ..." indeed.

Similarly, while Christians often talk colloquially about "the Bible" as though it was some single, uncluttered book, the Christian scriptures are anything but simple or straightforward. The Christian

Bible is really made up of two different libraries: one a set of Hebrew texts compiled by the Jews in the aftermath of the Babylonian exile, the other a jumble of Greek texts cherished by the early Christian church. Historically, Christians have theologically smushed those two libraries (testaments) together into one big book by putting Jesus, the Jewish Messiah and God Incarnate according to Christian theology, at the center. And that's not even getting into the apocryphal texts that are included in some Christians' Bibles but not others. Any practiced Christian exegete will tell you that understanding the Bible – its warring internal voices, its different contexts of composition, its sundry genres, and its dueling Jewish and Christian reception histories – is no walk in the park.

A second order of problems that Yusuf identifies, at least in the American context: These scriptures are not originally English texts. The majority of Muslims around the world and in America do not speak Arabic, and those who do speak Modern Standard Arabic fluently likely do not speak Classical Arabic, the ancient language of the Qur'an and the Hadith. Just as we would not expect the average English speaker to pick up *The Canterbury Tales* and easily decipher its arcane fourteenth-century Middle English, the Qur'an and the Hadith are texts that require a high level of technical and linguistic mastery.

Likewise, the Christian Bible is linguistically inaccessible in both of its original languages (Hebrew and Greek) to the vast majority of Christians. Most Christian seminarians are expected to spend several semesters acquiring the biblical languages, and even then, many seminary professors will privately acknowledge that most seminary graduates are far from proficient in Greek and Hebrew and should probably stick with the existing English translations of the Bible. But at least Christian pastors and priests have the ability to look up the linguistic considerations around a verse or a phrase; at least they can pull off the shelf and read the heavy, technical biblical commentaries that spend paragraphs laboring over one Hebrew or Greek word. That is a far cry from some neophyte picking up an English Bible and pretending that she or he knows exactly what it means. To paraphrase Hamza Yusuf, "These texts are the domain of experts and scholars and trained exegetes; this isn't for common people."

The caution and challenge leveled by Hamza Yusuf against the Salafis' popularization of the Hadith above – and the similar cautions leveled by Mainline Protestants and Catholics against Evangelicals' easy access biblicism – are not lost on the scripturalists. How do Evangelical and the Salafi scholars and experts square the circle of inviting amateurs to invade their realm? How do they move forward their scriptural popularization and democratization schemes that empower "common people" to have direct access to scripture when working with such complex, ancient texts? Amid the rambling, bountiful proliferation of scriptural explicators, how do the Scripture People prevent anarchy from taking over? How do they weed out bad interpretations that might harm their communities?

One of the main things that differentiates Salafi and Evangelical communities from those of their coreligionists is the culture of education that permeates every square inch of the scripturalist endeavor. Of course, non-Salafi Muslims and non-Evangelical Christians care about education, but it is difficult to exaggerate the centrality of *scriptural* education – educational institutions, informal scripture study groups, enriching reading, learning facilitated by Internet platforms, etc. – for the scripturalists. Children, youth, young adults, older adults: All are encouraged to maximize their scripture knowledge, to directly engage scriptural texts, and to become, to the degree possible, scripturally proficient. Not every Salafi, not every Evangelical is going to have the education, technical vocabulary, or linguistic know-how to study and engage in elite theological and jurisprudential discourse about ancient and composite texts. But, if scripture intends to speak to everyman and everywoman (as most Salafis and Evangelicals would affirm), then the scripturalist scholars cannot bar their untrained confederates from the text. What emerges in both movements are thinly demarcated, porous interchanges between scholarly and more popular discourses of scriptural interpretation. The democratization of scripture comes about, not haphazardly, but through the massive infrastructure of scripturalist education and a rejection of Hamza Yusuf's strict partition between scholars and common people. In this chapter I will juxtapose what are arguably the two foremost American Muslim educational institutions, one built by Salafi scripturalists and the other by Hamza Yusuf himself, to surface what is distinct about scripturalist pedagogy and culture.

ZAYTUNA COLLEGE VS. ALMAGHRIB INSTITUTE

In 1977, Mark Hanson, a teenager in California, was in a near-death car accident. This precipitated an existential crisis for him, ultimately leading to him reading the Qur'an and converting ("reverting," as some Muslims say) from Christianity to Islam. The young convert went in search of real and true Islamic knowledge, which, in most American Muslims' view at the time, meant going abroad. There were simply no reputable institutions of formal Islamic learning in America.

Leaving the USA in 1979, he did not go to Saudi Arabia to study at the Salafi institutions; instead, he studied with British and Mauritanian Sufi shaykhs and with traditional scholars in Morocco and the United Arab Emirates. Since medieval times, Muslim scholars ('ulama') have been trained in a direct teacher-to-student model where the student sits at the feet of the mentor scholar, learning for as long as is needed not only sacred texts but scholarly etiquette and how to read and interpret the texts aligned with a *maddhab* tradition. When the student has attained a sufficient mastery of the material, he or she is given an *ijaza* or a certificate from the teacher accrediting their ability to teach others. In these traditional learning circles, a scholar-in-training would never approach the Qur'an or the Hadith directly but only under the tutelage of the master. *Ijaza*s, at least in their premodern ideal form, show a chain of instructors and mentors running all the way back to the Prophet Muhammad and the Salaf itself, making the student "a trustee in his [or her] generation as part of the long tradition of Islamic learning handed down from the past."[5]

When he returned to America after ten years of study abroad, Hanson had taken the name Hamza Yusuf and inhabited a vaguely non-sectarian Sufi identity combined with his own panache of "signature turbans and robes."[6] *Ijazas* in hand, he exuded a passion for preaching the virtues of the Islamic tradition. With his movie-star good looks, his California accent, and his flowing robes, the young Yusuf was slightly reminiscent of an actor in a bad Hollywood adaptation of *One Thousand and One Nights*. But he quickly demonstrated the range of his intellect, his deep knowledge of the classical Islamic sciences, his impeccable Arabic skills, and his charismatic ability to enrapture audiences with his enlightening applications of medieval knowledge to present-day life. His return to America coincided with the 1990s surge in American Salafism, and the sagacious Yusuf cast himself as the Sufi-inspired, *madhhab*-praising, traditionally trained antidote to the spread of Salafi "fundamentalism."[7] Today he is among the most prominent Muslim scholars, and probably the most prominent Muslim convert, in the United States.

Hamza Yusuf is an avatar for a movement in contemporary Western Islam that likes to call itself "Traditional Islam."[8] Like Mainline Protestantism counterpoised against Evangelicalism, Traditional Islam is a trans-denominational alliance among different Sunni strands and sectarian identities designed to push back against the ambitious claims of the Salafi scripturalists to definitively speak for true Islam in America and other Anglophone countries. If Salafism eschews and downplays the layers of accumulated Islamic tradition in favor of disintermediated Qur'an and Hadith, Traditional Islam glories in the plurality and complexity of the Sunni interpretive tradition. Self-described "Traditional Muslims" like to think of themselves as big-tent, inclusive types. Inspired by the mutual tolerance exhibited in the classical Islamic era by different jurisprudential *madhhab*s and different Sufi communities, the various leaders of the Traditional Islam network have generally agreed to accept their many differences and banded together to resist the Salafization of Islam in America and Europe.[9]

Yusuf and his rebranded traditionalism were catapulted to national and international prominence when, after 9/11, he was invited to advise President Bush on Islam. For a time he laid aside his trademark "robes and turbans for two-piece suits in media appearances."[10] He eventually grew disillusioned with Bush's unwillingness to follow his advice regarding the ramp up to wars in Afghanistan and Iraq, but the exposure to national fame has made Yusuf a respected Muslim public intellectual and resulted in an abundance of glowing media portrayals over the past two decades proffering Yusuf as a model for a pluralistic, "moderate" Islam acculturated to the American milieu.[11]

In 1996, Yusuf founded Zaytuna Institute in the San Francisco Bay Area to promote this renaissance of classical Islamic learning. It offered evening and weekend courses, drawing together the diverse voices that had inspired Yusuf's own intellectual formation. In 2004, Imam Zaid Shakir, an African American convert to Islam and a renowned preacher, joined the staff of Zaytuna. As a young man, Shakir, like many other ambitious African American Muslim leaders-in-training in the late twentieth century, had dabbled in Salafism and even applied to the Saudi Salafi schools, but "a letter admitting him to the Islamic University of Medina arrived too late for him to accept" because he was already studying Arabic in Egypt.[12] Ultimately, through his own learning abroad, he came around to Yusuf's neo-Traditionalist style of Islam.

The meeting of the minds between Yusuf and Shakir birthed an ambitious new idea: an accredited liberal arts *madrasa* (traditional Islamic school) in America that would bring together the pedagogical styles of classical Islamic learning with American higher education. The shaykh and the imam launched an experimental Islamic seminary program in 2004, that eventually morphed and consolidated into a traditional four-year liberal arts college. They aimed to "revive Islam's mystical tradition of Sufism and its pedagogical model of initiatic transmission, specifically the *ijaza* system that formed the basis for the transmission of the religious disciplines within Sunni Islam."[13]

After years of planning and experimenting and fundraising, Zaytuna College was launched in 2009 as the first Muslim liberal arts college in America.

In Arabic, *zaytuna* means olive tree, and the arboreal image is an apt one for the college. With metaphorical roots running deep into the diversity of Islamic learning – Sufism, different Sunni *madhhabs*, Islamic philosophy – the college has its literal roots sunk into a postage-stamp sized campus in Berkeley, California.[14] Zaytuna has taken root in a neighborhood affectionately known as "Holy Hill," because of all the seminaries and affiliates of the Graduate Theological Union, now including Zaytuna, that reside there. Like a recently planted sapling, growth at Zaytuna is slow-going. The inaugural freshman class in the fall of 2010 started with only fifteen students and five dropped out before the year's end.[15] By 2015, Zaytuna was up to fifty students, all undergraduates, and was only offering one degree: a Bachelor of Arts in Islamic Law and Theology.[16] The school has a vanguard model of social change: Instead of sending the American Muslim community's best and brightest like Yusuf and Shakir overseas to gain Islamic knowledge, they can study domestically with "scholars trained in our tradition who can also speak to the reality here in America."[17] In so many ways, Zaytuna College is a transplant, an olive tree of knowledge and shaykh-to-student pedagogy long cultivated in Islamic lands, now stretching its young limbs on Holy Hill.

AlMaghrib Institute is a near-perfect scripturalist antithesis to Zaytuna College. Founded in 2002 by an enterprising Islamic University of Medina graduate named Shaykh Muhammad Alshareef, "it wouldn't be a stretch to say [AlMaghrib] has probably educated more English-speaking Muslims about their religion than any other institute in the world right now."[18] The institute is now ostensibly headquartered in Houston, TX. Though if you go looking for some august and secluded academic atmosphere, you won't find it at AlMaghrib's headquarters; the nondescript Houston office is in a strip mall next to a Chinese restaurant and a grocery store. Holy Hill it is not.[19] Unlike Zaytuna, which is trying to import knowledge and learning models from centers of Islamic culture into America, AlMaghrib is a pedagogical exporter, with regional headquarters (one might call them franchises) in Malaysia, Singapore, Australia, Canada, the United Kingdom, Denmark, Sweden, and Ireland.

As I explored in Chapter 2, AlMaghrib's colorable non-denominational identity is tied up with the freighted reception history of the identity "Salafi" in the post-9/11 Western world. As internal politics roiled Muslim communities and the scrutiny of the American security apparatus zeroed in on rooting out Islamic fundamentalism and Wahhabi Salafism (if the two were even distinguished in the agita after 9/11), the fledgling infrastructure that supported the American Salafi movement of the 1990s crumbled. AlMaghrib was what rose from the rubble, with many of the Salafi shaykhs and Saudi-trained preachers rebranding themselves and coalescing around the institute. Like the Magic Eye 3D posters that were still popular when AlMaghrib was founded, to those who know how to adjust their eyes properly, the Salafi intellectual underpinnings of the institute emerge with clarity, but you would be hard-pressed to find the word Salafi anywhere in its promotional literature or marketing.[20]

What distinguished AlMaghrib from earlier Salafi institutions was not merely its eschewal of the Salafi label. It also had an inclusive, coalitional mentality that was willing to enlist non-Salafi and even Sufi-leaning volunteers and other types of Muslims that many Salafis avoid. In fact, when a long-form *New York Times Magazine* profile was published about Yasir Qadhi and AlMaghrib in 2011 that explored his and the institute's knotty relationship with Salafism, "former AlMaghrib students expressed surprise and regret that they had taken classes at a Salafi institute without realizing it."[21]

If Zaytuna is arboreal, AlMaghrib is rhizomatic; its grass-like growth has popped up in patches, with chapters centered in nearly every American city or region with a significant Muslim population: suburban DC, San Francisco, Chicago, Dallas, New York,

Los Angeles, Detroit, etc. Indeed, while the institute is physically headquartered in Houston, only a small fraction of its seminars and courses occur there. Like Zaytuna, what draws students to AlMaghrib is its collection of shaykhs and teachers (ustadhs).[22] But the AlMaghrib instructors are itinerant, taking their intensive long-weekend seminars from city to city.

If Zaytuna College's alumni number in the dozens, AlMaghrib's participants number in the tens of thousands.[23] The architecture of AlMaghrib is local leadership groups called "qabeelas" (Arabic for "tribe"), usually anchored in a city or metropolitan area. The qabeelas, which are overseen by a pair of male (ameer) and female (ameerah) volunteer leaders, host and take care of all the legwork for AlMaghrib's seminars; they "are encouraged to outdo one another in advertising, Web site construction, exam results, and other areas of healthy competition."[24] If Zaytuna's model is to form an indigenous vanguard of American Muslim scholars, AlMaghrib aims to invigorate and educate the grassroots.

Zaytuna's course catalog is a mash-up of classical Islamic learning and your standard liberal arts curriculum structure. Freshmen students take courses in "Hanafi Fiqh" (jurisprudence), "Maliki Fiqh," and "Shafi'i Fiqh," three of the four classical madhhabs. Notably absent – in fact, evidently elided in the entire Zaytuna program of studies – is the fourth classical madhhab: Hanbalism. The scripturalist strand of Islam is extracted with almost surgical precision in the otherwise exhaustive curriculum, signaling the ideological orientation that bristles underneath Zaytuna's inclusive exterior. Which is not to say that Zaytuna's students do not study Islamic scripture – threaded into the curriculum are courses like "Introduction to the Qur'an," "Qur'anic Sciences," and "Prophetic Tradition" (i.e., Hadith) where they even occasionally "interact with excerpts from original Arabic hadith canons."[25] But the balance of the classes skews heavily toward understanding the polyvalent world of medieval Islam and the evolution from there to modernity. Scripture, at Zaytuna, is couched within, fenced in by, insulated with tradition.[26] All of this is complemented with your classic liberal arts fare to flesh out the residential college learning experience: "Politics," "Economics," "Philosophy," and "Principles of Democracy."

By comparison, the AlMaghrib seminars crackle with relevance and low-to-the-ground approachability: "All Around Us: Signs of the Last Day," "Deception: Study of Shayṭān [Satan]," "Collector's Edition: An Introduction to the Sahih of Imam al-Bukhari," "Fiqh of Love: Marriage in Islam," or "Trends: Culture, Identity, Fashion."[27] Every seminar has a short accompanying video preview on the AlMaghrib website, edited with the pizzazz and aesthetic of a movie trailer. If the straight-laced Zaytuna course catalog is designed to reassure Muslim parents that it is worth sending (and likely helping finance) their teenager to a residential, liberal arts college, the AlMaghrib promotions appeal directly to the students.

AlMaghrib's shaykhs and ustadhs take pains to make the Hadith and the Qur'an get-at-able and usable, not walled off behind formalities and medieval Islamic technicalities. Consider a short clip, posted on AlMaghrib's YouTube channel, with Ustadha Yasmin Mogahed to promote her "Transformed: Principles of Spiritual Development" seminar. She begins with the question: "Does making the Hereafter our primary concern mean losing out on this life?"[28] Looking directly into the camera with an earnest expression, she segues from the question directly to a hadith in which the Prophet Muhammad describes "two worldviews" and the "consequences that go along with them." She recites the hadith pausing to linger over interesting words or phrases that might be confusing to a non-Arabic speaker. She is not dumbing down the hadith, so much as unpacking it and making its message clear. She concludes, "This whole hadith is teaching us, if we want success and happiness in this life, if we want contentment in this life, we actually need to chase the next life. If you benefited from this reminder, join me for my next class ...." This hermeneutical pirouette (introduction, exegesis, application, exhortation, invitation) is accomplished in the space of three and a half minutes. A tiny morsel of scriptural knowledge to whet your appetite for her seminar. Mogahed, who holds a bachelor's in Psychology and a Master's in Journalism and Mass Communication, does not possess the credentials in Islamic Studies or Hadith to be able to teach at a place like Zaytuna College, but in the more exhortative and devotionally bolstering atmosphere of AlMaghrib, she serves as the institute's first female instructor.

In the mid-2000s, when Zaytuna was still Zaytuna Institute, with Shaykh Hamza and Imam Zaid conducting seminars all over the country, and AlMaghrib was a scrappy, quasi-Salafi entrant into the American Muslim educational landscape, there were real tensions between the two in competing for broader audiences. As one Midwestern AlMaghrib qabeela leader from that era recalls, "In my experience as a volunteer back in the day, we were all pretty hard-line pro-Salafi, anti-Sufi. The rhetoric was there, in our volunteer camps ... Zaytuna would come up, you know, Zaytuna Institute, with Shaykh Hamza Yusuf and Imam Zaid, and brothers would basically say that, 'Yeah, Zaytuna's a poison.' And everyone was cool with it."[29] This rivalry is replicated in many Muslim communities around the globe: populist, informally credentialed Salafi student movements versus neo-Traditionalist/Sufi-aligned scholars ('ulama') with both scornfully claiming they hold authentic Islam and rightful interpretation of the text.[30] But in 2007 the shaykhs intervened, with Yusuf and Zaid and the AlMaghrib leaders (Qadhi, Muhammad Alshareef, and Waleed Basyouni) signing a "Pledge of Mutual Respect and Collaboration" along with dozens of other Western Sunni leaders to quell "the specter of sectarianism" that was portending.[31] You can still find "Traditional Islam" proponents and AlMaghrib aficionados trading barbed comments online, but, at least in the AlMaghrib sphere of influence, the resentful Sufi-Salafi ruckus in America has largely simmered down.[32]

In truth, today, given the gulf between their approaches, the new incarnation of Zaytuna College and AlMaghrib are not practical competitors in any discernible way. Both are catering to the immigrant Muslim communities who make up the majority of America's

Muslims, but their constituencies likely do not overlap much. Zaytuna's learning is largely reserved for its select body of Traditionalist students. AlMaghrib's competition now is YouTube and Salafi-adjacent social media networks, downloadable lectures that put access to scriptural knowledge on a young person's smart phone and don't require a weekend's dedication. As we saw with Albani, Salafi learning is largely unregulated and authority is meritocratic, built upon charisma and facility with the sacred texts. Without traditional-*ijaza* boundaries on knowledge or any agreed-upon level of educational attainment for becoming a shaykh (including among the AlMaghrib instructors), the Internet abounds with Salafi-esque teachers demonstrating their interpretive skills with or without credentials.

That's why, forthrightly on AlMaghrib's website, the question is posed: "Why then, would you sacrifice your time and money to attend a weekend course onsite with an instructor and a room full of students?" and the answer is readily at hand:

> Simple. Because knowledge needs to be lived and experienced firsthand, as opposed to just reading about it on the side. We guarantee you our unique, trademark style of mind-blowing academics, pure spirituality, and lively classroom interactions. It's addictive, it's enlightening, it's real brotherhood and sisterhood. It will leave you crying one moment and laughing the next, and it is potentially life-changing. We apologize in advance, but you will experience withdrawal symptoms after you complete a course, long until the next one comes along![33]

Like so many weekend Bible conferences I attended as an Evangelical high school and college student, the scriptural content and knowledge, while supremely important, isn't what gets you in the car or on the bus bound for the conference center. It's the promise of a life-changing experience, of real community, of personal transformation.

The lasting image I have of Zaytuna comes from a classroom moment described in *Light Without Fire: The Making of America's*

First Muslim College, where Scott Korb chronicles the first year at Zaytuna. The class is taught by Hamza Yusuf, and beyond the dozen Zaytuna students, the small room is packed with Zaytuna staff who have taken the opportunity to audit the class and sit at the feet of Yusuf. Though it is a couple months into the fall semester, "[m]any of the students still actually seemed a little stunned, or starstruck."

> While Muslims around the world often gather in the thousands and tens of thousands for the sheikh's keynote lectures, Zaytuna's students have this front-row seat each week, which has made them the envy of their friends and families back home. Their Facebook profiles explode with quotations from their classes and videos of Sheikh Hamza – followed with comments: "Just looking at his luminous face made me smile:) May Allah (SWT [*Subhanahu wa ta'ala* – "may He be glorified and exalted"]) preserve him!"[34]

To anyone familiar with the authority and devotional dynamics within Sufism, this scene aptly recreates classical Sufi learning circles, the students – in Arabic, *murīd*, "one who seeks" – arrayed around the extraordinary shaykh, basking in his wisdom and other-worldliness. "Shaykh" for Sufis can take on the connotation of "saint." It is striking how often the comments section on Yusuf's videos online call attention to his physical looks, the blessing they are from God, how his attractiveness somehow amplifies his insight. I'm not the first to remark upon it – and I write this as a white man myself and as someone who admires Yusuf's intellect – there's something unsettling about the icon of a white shaykh wielding this sort of authority and even a physical spell over audiences of predominantly immigrant Muslims.[35] Scott Korb, the observer of this scene, does not describe Yusuf's garb, but I can conjecture from other videos of his teaching at Zaytuna that he is probably arrayed in his robes and *kufi* (a turban-like cap). He's the literal sage on the stage, recreating ancient hierarchies of knowledge on Berkeley's Holy Hill.

Juxtapose that scene with the one that I witnessed in Yasir Qadhi's AlMaghrib seminar with which I began this book. We're in

College Park, Maryland, AlMaghrib's original stomping grounds. Hundreds of college-age young folks fill the university lecture hall, with its amphitheater style of seating. Yasir is authoritative, commanding the attention of the classroom, but he's also colloquial and sometimes self-deprecating. He moves fluidly from Hadith to Qur'an to common sense to anecdote, all while guiding students through his well-crafted PowerPoint presentation. He is dressed in a simple tailored *kurta*, a knee-length, collar-less tunic common among South Asians. It covers his stout frame. He's not unhandsome, but no one comes to these seminars to luxuriate in the AlMaghrib instructors' physicality – with the possible exception of Saad Tasleem, the most dapper of the AlMaghrib teachers. They are there for the shaykhs' knowledge.

Qadhi is respected; he is not revered. His words are not gospel. Salafi-friendly online message boards and Yasir's social media mentions erupt every time he makes a controversial statement or an identity pivot – "I agree with him on X, but Y is beyond the pale." For instance, when he and the other AlMaghrib shaykhs signed that 2007 de-escalation pledge with the Zaytuna leaders, the comments section of Qadhi's blog post about the pledge filled up with provocations and queries from his students and colleagues demanding that he justify his actions.[36] Part of the empowerment of scripturalist education is the maturing capacity to evaluate the scholars for oneself, to become a skilled and principled discerner of good interpretations.

On a break in the session, I strike up a conversation with a young man next to me. He is excited to learn that I am not a Muslim but am interested in his shaykhs, an opportunity for *da'wa* (inviting me to Islam) perhaps flashes across his mind. He begins recommending other shaykhs and AlMaghrib instructors he thinks are top-notch: Saad Tasleem, Waleed Basyouni, Omar Suleiman, Yasmin Mogahed. Each has her or his strengths. Each has something to teach us.

In the audience around me, most of the women and men are paying rapt attention, as well they should – Qadhi is a skilled and riveting presenter. But there are exceptions. Behind me a couple of guys are joking and snickering. A young man in front of me is playing a boxing game on his phone. Someone is asleep. It is asking a lot for teenagers and twentysomethings to commit to receiving twenty hours of instruction over the course of one weekend, and it's Sunday evening, and people are understandably flagging. The dual challenges with educating the masses are keeping their attention and quality control.

I go out to dinner with Qadhi after the session, or rather, I and thirty local AlMaghrib insiders and qabeela leaders go out to dinner with Qadhi after the session. They rearrange the halal Thai food restaurant so that everyone can hear and see what the shaykh is saying. The other folks there aren't groupies exactly; they want to keep learning, to squeeze every last drop out of their instructor before he leaves town. Qadhi for his part, after eight hours of lecturing that day and twenty hours of lecturing that weekend, is still buzzing with energy. He spares me ten minutes to talk about AlMaghrib. "This is the real movement of American Salafis today," he tells me, "the inheritors of the 1980s and 1990s Salafism." I point out that I've seen some Salafis online criticizing AlMaghrib, saying that it has sold out and watered-down Salafism. Qadhi ripostes, "They are tens; we are tens of thousands."[37]

THE DEMOCRATIZATION OF SCRIPTURE

This contrast between Zaytuna and AlMaghrib captures, for me, some of the texture and experience of scripturalism that might be perplexing to outsiders. I think that for most people who have never been inside the scripturalist persuasion, Hamza Yusuf's scholastic approach to scripture makes intuitive sense: There is obviously a lot at stake in how Christians and Muslims interpret their scriptures. Wouldn't we want elite scholars who are trained in the original languages, informed by and embedded within centuries of hermeneutical traditions to be the ones who shape our understanding of these sacred texts? What I have ventured to draw out in the Zaytuna and

AlMaghrib comparison is that the Traditional Islam vs. Salafi instincts when it comes to scripture – similar to the dynamics between Catholics and Mainline Protestants vs. Evangelicals – hinge on different presuppositions about authority and pedagogy.

Hamza Yusuf and Zaytuna think of the landscape of American Islamic knowledge, indeed of Islamic knowledge in general, as having two tiers: the scholars (*'ulama'*) and the common people. Hamza Yusuf *is* an educator, but through Zaytuna he aims to reify the boundary line between the scholar caste and the everyday Muslim. In fact, in some of Zaytuna's promotional literature, it affirms, "Islam has never become rooted in a particular land until that land began producing its own religious scholars."[38] Zaytuna exists to build up American Muslim scholars and traditional thought leaders, to make more Hamza Yusufs and Zaid Shakirs. On that account, in 2018, the college launched a two-year Master of Arts program, calling back to the earlier idea of creating an Islamic seminary in America. Now advanced students can earn a master's degree in Islamic Texts, "with higher-level access to the Islamic tradition through a guided course of study in Islam's primary sources."[39] Likewise, Mainline Protestant and Catholic seminaries exist to train hermeneutical experts, skilled scripture handlers who will do the work of propagating learned interpretations.

But in the age of the Internet, of translated texts, of globalized knowledge flows and social media, the Hadith and Islamic knowledge are no longer enclosed in traditional learning spaces like Zaytuna. As we saw with the case of Albani in the previous chapter, Salafism has been both a reaction to and a vehicle for the palpable accessibility of religious knowledge, including knowledge about Muslim scripture. If Yusuf wants to maintain the hierarchical learning and traditional custodianship that surrounded classical Islamic scripture interpretation, Albani and his Salafi and post-Salafi heirs have embraced the meritocratic, do-it-yourself, free marketization of Islamic knowledge.

Accordingly, AlMaghrib's quasi-Salafi or post-Salafi approach to authority and knowledge-transmission is much more manifold. Some of the senior AlMaghrib shaykhs are Salafi or Salafi-adjacent *scholars*, like Yasir Qadhi, who are every bit as methodologically sophisticated and well-versed as other Islamic scholars. But what about the AlMaghrib shaykhs and instructors like Saad Tasleem, who holds simply a bachelor's from the Islamic University of Medina, or Yasmin Mogahed, who has no formal, credentialed Islamic schooling to speak of? They are definitively not scholars, but they *are* transmitters of Islamic learning, charismatic, devotional mentors. What of the AlMaghrib students who devote long weekends to bolstering their nascent scriptural knowledge, most of whom will never become shaykhs much less scholars? Are they what Yusuf calls "common people" when it comes to scripture? Not exactly. The vast majority of what goes on in AlMaghrib seminars does not fit neatly into Yusuf's two-tiered universe. Learning and knowledge in Salafism has some structure but is largely unregulated and informal, creating a middle class of Islamic learners. Salafis call these people "students of knowledge," amateurs who are in it for the love of scriptural learning, devout acolytes. It is here in this middle tier of part-time, enthusiast learning where the real action of scripturalism is.

Studying and immersing myself in American Salafism has many times caused me to think in new terms about my own Evangelical experience. In my first career as a college campus minister, I held no formal credentials. I had become involved with an Evangelical parachurch organization called InterVarsity Christian Fellowship when I was a college student, and I was mentored and trained in leadership by recently graduated InterVarsity campus ministers just a few years older than me who were similarly unaccredited but passionate. When I graduated and became an InterVarsity employee, I was, functionally, a missionary to the college campus, present to continue facilitating the energetic apprenticeship of scripture. I was trained on the job to lead enlivened Bible studies, to develop the next generation of student leaders, to preach compellingly, to facilitate scriptural knowledge. I was, mutatis mutandis, like the AlMaghrib shaykhs: an informally schooled specialist in devotional education mentoring other amateurs in self-motivated scriptural apprehension. To borrow the Salafis apt phrase, my InterVarsity mentors, the students I mentored, and I myself were all "students of knowledge," in it for love of the Bible, caring little for formalistic religious degrees. Sure, I eventually enlisted in an Evangelical seminary as I continued this work, because credentials are nice, but that was icing on the cake. The fuel that fires the scripturalist educational machine is not accreditation in interpretation but attachment to the text.

Despite accusations that such plebeian scripturalism is intellectually bereft or hermeneutically naive, actual Salafi scholars and Evangelical Bible scholars are, as a rule, just as educated and equipped in interpreting scripture as their Traditional Islam and Mainline Protestant and Roman Catholic counterparts. Evangelical Bible scholars who teach in Evangelical colleges and seminaries or write Evangelical Bible commentaries almost universally have their doctorates in Hebrew Bible or the New Testament, often from the same elite institutions from which other Bible scholars got their degrees. While they might differ theologically from their more tradition-guided Catholic and Mainline colleagues, Evangelical Bible scholars quite robustly populate the ranks of the Society for Biblical Literature in America, "the oldest and largest learned society devoted to the critical investigation of the Bible from a variety of academic disciplines."[40] I've been to the annual SBL meetings, and seen the Evangelical scholars – many of them my old seminary professors and cohort – mixing it up, proving their adroitness in critical scholarship, engaging in the topflight discourse of biblical hermeneutics in the United States. Similarly, there are Salafi scholars (many of them still clustered in Saudi Arabia, but, increasingly with the accelerating global decentralization of Salafism, situated locally around the world) who are as intelligent and knowledgeable as anyone in the world of Islamic learning. Yasir Qadhi is every bit as much of a Muslim intellectual as Hamza Yusuf. The upper echelons of the elite scripturalist discourse are as robust, as academically informed, as intellectually engaged as any other in their respective Protestant and Sunni traditions.

In fact, the mid-tier infrastructure of scripturalist discourse feeds off the elite scripturalist discourse without ever becoming equivalent to it. For all their anti-clericalism and leeriness about human hierarchies, Salafis constantly speak glowingly about their shaykhs and scholars, their access points into Islamic knowledge. And while lay Evangelicals might be skeptical of historical critical Bible scholarship in general, they have entire publishing houses dedicated to disseminating academically robust Evangelical biblical scholarship. More advanced students of knowledge, like Yasmin Mogahed or my younger self, break down the bookish insights of distinguished scholars, translating them into bite-sized devotional morsels for less advanced students of knowledge. Once I started on my seminary degree, I was weekly taking my classroom learning and transmuting it into material for my Bible studies and exhortative lectures with college students – a gray market of scriptural knowledge. This also helps explain why the Saudis structured the Islamic University of Medina (IUM) not so much as an elite university to comprehensively train up scholars (*'ulama'*) but instead to build up an international corps of Wahhabi-Salafi missionaries and preachers (*du'āt*).[41] The IUM graduates, including many of the AlMaghrib instructors, were trained to return to their home countries to pedagogically spread the message. This mix of formal and colloquial, of official and bootlegged learning demarcates scripturalist communities from their traditional coreligionists by the enfranchisement of the hoi polloi. Anyone who desires to can become a student of knowledge in their free time.

So while the Scripture People may have adopted the democratizing rhetoric of scriptural populism, inviting everywoman and everyman to directly interface with scripture and occasioning the ire of the Hamza Yusufs of the world, the reality of it, the warp and woof of American scripturalism is something more cautious. It speaks the language of populism, but, concretely, it is more like republicanism. The popular discourse of Evangelical and Salafi "common people" is substantively superintended by scholars and specialists, who train the students of knowledge and guide interpretation on behalf of and with the consent of the scripturalist governed.[42] Authority flows upward from the students of knowledge in the form of support and followership of the scholars, and authority flows downward from the scholars in the form of practical know-how and scriptural intelligence.

To take another telling instance, contrast the curricular requirements of Biola University, an Evangelical school, and California Lutheran University, a Mainline Lutheran school, both in the Los Angeles suburbs. Cal Lutheran, despite its name, makes every effort to tone down the particularities of the Lutheran tradition and to present itself as a generic liberal arts school where "The Lutheran Experience" boils down to: "We believe that understanding our purpose as individuals will help us make our best possible contribution to the world."[43] (Cue the blowing of raspberries in the Evangelical recesses of my mind.) The promotional materials make it clear that you do not need to be Lutheran or Christian or remotely interested in religion to attend. All undergraduates at Cal Lutheran are required to take "Religion 100: Religion, Identity, Vocation" as a head nod to the school's history and identity. They must take one more religion course to fill out their humanities requirement: be it "Exploring the Qur'an," "Liberation and Theology," "Cooperation in Modern India," etc.[44] Maybe the Cal Lutheran students, at least those who do not choose to be religion majors, encounter something of the Christian Bible somewhere in their undergraduate education, but it is an aside, a throat-clearing, before the largely secular work of the university may ensue.

Biola, which is now a proper name, but was originally an acronym for the Fundamentalist-founded Bible Institute of Los Angeles, is a different kettle of fish. First, Biola University makes clear that as part of its admission process: "The student must be a believer in the Christian faith (the applicant's statement of faith will be articulated in the personal essay section of the application)."[45] Biola exists for Christian students, and that segues into how Biola implements its curriculum. Among the university's three articulated learning outcomes for all academic programs is: "All students will be equipped with patterns of thought that are rigorous, intellectually coherent and thoroughly biblical."[46] Every Biola undergraduate, like undergraduates everywhere, chooses a major field of study, and they must complete thirty credits of study to fulfill the requirements for that major, but at Biola every undergraduate must also complete thirty credits of Bible in order to graduate. Functionally, whether it says it on their transcript or diploma or not, every student at Biola is a Bible major. Both Cal Lutheran and Biola are Christian colleges in the same metropolitan area, accredited by the same association of schools, but Biola's explicit Evangelical mission is to stamp every undergraduate with a knowledge of and some intermediate expertise in the Bible. The Scripture Peoples' claim to scriptural fidelity, to be Bible Christians and Hadith people, is not a nonchalant identity assertion, but a hard-fought, ongoing attainment.

From this pedagogical angle, it is evident that a substantial proportion (perhaps a majority) of Salafi and Evangelical institutions exist to facilitate or support this middle-tier scriptural enfranchisement, the transfer of interpretive knowledge and skills from experts to students of knowledge. Evangelical churches and Salafi mosques not only offer sermons and *khutba*s (preaching at a Friday prayer service) from – hopefully learned – pastors and imams who exhort from scripture; they also offer Sunday school classes, *halaqa*s (Qur'anic study circles), Bible studies, lectures, etc. Evangelical and Salafi publishers and magazines and websites disseminate scriptural knowledge and commentary and application, often written by clerics and scholars, but aimed at popular audiences. AWANA programs and Ummie's Kiddie Kottage and countless other youth programs prepare the young for lives of scriptural enrichment. Bible conferences and AlMaghrib seminars endow, iteratively, people whose minds are just a little more informed about the texts, a little more equipped with scriptural confidence. If Salafism and Evangelicalism are scriptural discourses, education is the fecund soil of those discourses, cultivated and nurtured on some level by scholars, but sowed, tended, and made verdant by the thousands and millions of non-expert participants.

This helps to make sense of a phenomenon in both the Salafi and the Evangelical movements that is otherwise puzzling to many people: the celebrity preacher or celebrity shaykh. These are people – usually men, given the gendered notions of authority that still leaven both discourses, but not always – who build up a popular audience based on their ability to communicate about scripture. Celebrity shaykhs and preachers come in different flavors, some more home-spun and exhortative imams and pastors, some more lettered and studious shaykhs and Bible expositors, but they all are purveyors of scriptural knowledge. I am thinking here less of the televangelists or prosperity preachers, religious celebrities whose popularity is obvi-ously premised on their ear-tickling messages and probable grift. I have in mind more the AlMaghrib shaykhs and ustadhas, the John Stotts, the Tim Kellers, the Beth Moores, the Francis Chans – people who, whether formally credentialed like Qadhi or auto-didacts in the vein of Albani, have fostered groundswell audiences of eager students. They are occupants of that permeable space between scholarship and religious pop culture. They draw their authority not only from scrip-ture and their adroit handling of it, but also from the unquenchable appetite for Evangelical and Salafi learning.

While, as many have noted, Zaytuna College and AlMaghrib Institute do illustrate global intra-Sunni debates between Sufi-aligned Traditional Islam and energetic Salafi education networks, both insti-tutions also show the Muslim adoption of different models of American education. It is unsurprising that Yusuf's Traditional Islam, with its reverence for high-minded scholarship, has institution-ally blended a classical *ijaza*, madrasa system with an American liberal arts college model. Liberal arts colleges, after all, have long served as walled gardens for the close-quartered conveyance of know-ledge, authority, and prestige. But how would we describe the come-as-you-may, Salafi-inspired model of AlMaghrib? Whether its leaders are conscious of it or not, AlMaghrib has adopted an organizational structure that looks a lot like an Evangelical parachurch organization. As someone who has spent decades participating in, working for, and observing these parachurch organizations, there's something decidedly paramosque-y about AlMaghrib: its nondenominational character, its use of secular and functional spaces, its no-nonsense offices and decentralized structure, its sometimes-credentialed-but-always-charismatic instructors, its narrow focus on crafting "addict-ive" and "enlightening" scriptural educational experiences.[47] AlMaghrib is less higher education than a mission-driven, devotional teaching organization, and in its own way, AlMaghrib has adopted in form and function a mode of doing scriptural education that has a proven purchase with American audiences.

CONCLUSION

As I close this chapter, we should widen the aperture a little and take note of the broader post-9/11 American environment in which Zaytuna and AlMaghrib have grown up. At stake in the divergence between Yusuf and Zaytuna on the one hand and Qadhi and AlMaghrib on the other are not merely educational approaches but also larger acculturation and integration questions. Well before 9/11 and continuing with even greater intensity in the securitized atmos-phere since, debates have raged within the American Muslim com-munity about what it means to be American and Muslim simultaneously. I am not the first to juxtapose Zaytuna and AlMaghrib or Yusuf and Qadhi in these respects, for they are two of the most prominent American Muslim institutions and two of the most prominent teachers in the American Muslim community.

For instance, in Scott Korb's *Light without Fire*, he not only narrates the story of the first-year experience at Zaytuna College, he also argues the college is building an "indigenous" form of American Islam in contrast with "culturally predatory ... ideologies includ[ing] more literalist and ultraconservative approaches like Salafism and Wahhabism, brands of Islam known for the militant minorities within them."[48] Korb is up front with the fact that he does not know very much about Islam, so he relies heavily on the Zaytunies, as he calls the students, and on the vision of Islam presented by Zaid Shakir and Hamza Yusuf.[49] In Zaytuna's merging of traditional Islamic learning, Sufism, and the American liberal arts college model, Korb extols what he sees as the leading edge in the development of an Islam that is habituated, acclimated, and suitable for modern America.

For Hamza Yusuf, in Scott Korb's telling, inhabiting Americanness is not merely about building American-style institutions. It is something more civic, more attitudinal, more spiritual. Korb summarizes Yusuf's thinking on these matters: "Believers who cannot find it in their hearts to love the ideals of the country or whose Islamic legal reasoning prevents them from developing allegiances to America, these Muslims ought to have no place in American public life."[50] Yusuf's own civic and allegiance behavior is instructive to understand what he means here.

One might surmise, based on the parallels I've drawn between Mainline Protestantism and Traditional Islam and the conventionally liberalizing culture of liberal arts education, that Yusuf's politics would skew toward the progressive and liberal views common among the Mainliners. Quite to the contrary – Yusuf is in many ways a very right-wing figure in American life. Not only did he align himself with George W. Bush as an adviser after 9/11, but more recently he has sought political alliances with Evangelical and conservative Catholic leaders, so long as they are also people who have a history of calling out Christian Islamophobia. "Specific domestic issues Yusuf and his Christian allies have discussed or addressed jointly include pornography, pro-life issues, traditional marriage, transgenderism, homosexuality, the free exercise of religious conscience in higher education settings, and exempting employers from providing benefits for employees if it substantially violates religious conscience."[51] On that front, in 2019 Yusuf was invited by Secretary of State Mike Pompeo, a prominent Evangelical, to join a Commission on Unalienable Rights sponsored by the Trump administration. Yusuf's participation in the Commission frustrated many American Muslims who saw it as unacceptable to collaborate with the Islamophobic and abusive Trump administration. Moreover, the Commission itself drew sharp criticism from scores of human rights groups who saw its creation and its eventual report as an effort to "open[] the door to any number of problematic actions by governments that seek to undermine their human rights obligations and violate individual liberties," particularly those of LGBTQ individuals.[52] And, in the wake of the Arab Spring, based upon his undergirding theology about authority and the role of scholars, Yusuf has endorsed and defended repressive and autocratic regimes in the majority Muslim world, in Syria, in Turkey, and in the UAE, because "our ʿulamāʾ [scholars] traditionally were opposed to revolution."[53] This is all included in what Yusuf understands as the task of Americanizing Islam – building allegiances around shared religious concerns, diving into the turbulence of national politics and foreign policy, carving out a Muslim niche in the public sphere, articulating Islamic morality with an American intonation.

In March 2011, toward the end of Scott Korb's year spent chronicling the opening of Zaytuna College, he describes a back-and-forth with Hamza Yusuf while driving him to the San Francisco airport. The exchange takes place on the same day that the long-form profile of Yasir Qadhi and AlMaghrib was published in *The New York Times Magazine*, and Yusuf and Korb compare notes about the article, Qadhi, and AlMaghrib as they drive. They home in on a topic that comes up in the article and is a big part of the global Salafi discourse and debate: Should Muslims maintain loyalty only to fellow Muslims or is love and friendship with non-Muslims (and loyalty to non-Muslim governments) permissible? As is his wont, Qadhi has carved out a nuanced position on this question that is progressive compared to many global Salafis': American Muslims' primary allegiance is to God and their fellow Muslims around the world, but they should also be conscientious American citizens and create friendships with agreeable non-Muslims neighbors, all while maintaining the capacity to criticize and vehemently advocate against American policies that are harmful to fellow Muslims.[54]

Here is Korb's recreation of that conversation with his own commentary embedded:

> Qadhi simply doesn't strike Sheikh Hamza as a particularly American Muslim, and for the *ummah* [the Muslim community], whatever anxiety Qadhi inspires in his followers over this question of love and enmity [toward non-Muslims] represents "a real calamity and a crisis ..."

> ... while [Qadhi], like Hamza, calls America home, there seems to exist no comfortable way for Qadhi and his Orthodox Muslims to "balance our loyalties between the requirements of faith and those that are increasingly imposed on us by our country." Not to put too fine a point on it, but Qadhi's Muslims are simply – perhaps even unfortunately – "in America"; Hamza's Muslims are American.

> As we approach the airport, Hamza offered his final point about Yasir Qadhi and his followers. The sheikh insisted, "Really to be consistent with their teaching, they should leave; they shouldn't even be living here. You know, and I believe that. They need to go."[55]

Thrumming beneath the surface of this conversation (a conversation, by the by, between two white American men about the relative Americanness of a non-white American man – Qadhi is a natural-born US citizen) are a set of shared assumptions about good and bad Muslims, about what it means to be "particularly American," about what is foreign and what is "indigenous." The narrative Yusuf is spinning puts his approach to Islam and Zaytuna College at the heart of an adaptive process of Islam becoming rooted culturally, socially, politically, and pedagogically in America. In that familiar narrative, Qadhi, AlMaghrib, and Salafism represent something retrograde, maladaptive, alien. AlMaghrib might have instrumentally adopted some models of American education, but to Yusuf and Korb, Qadhi and his fellows are still purveyors of "culturally predatory Islamist ideologies from abroad."[56] They might be "in America," but there are severe doubts about whether they can ever be American Muslims.

Are Yusuf and Korb correct? Are the AlMaghrib teachers cultur- ally predatory wolves in American shaykhs' clothing? Can the Salafi discourse ever be truly acclimated to American culture? For all the democratic and egalitarian energy that surrounds the Salafi approach to scripture, are Salafis in actuality ideological foes to the American mainstream? It is to these questions we will turn with the next chapter.

5 How "American" Can Salafism Be?

In September 2011 – ten years after the 9/11 attacks – an American Salafi preacher living in Yemen was killed by a United States Predator drone strike ordered by President Barack Obama. His name was Anwar al-Awlaki, and, according to the Obama administration, he needed to be assassinated by drone because he was the Al Qaeda "network's leading English-language propagandist," who had also started operationally training and supporting suicide bombers.[1] Though he was a natural-born American citizen who was never charged with any terror-related crime, the government claimed he was an enemy soldier in the War on Terror who needed to be "removed from the battlefield."[2]

Just over a year later – on the eve of the 2012 American presidential election – Waleed Basyouni, another American Salafi preacher, a Houston imam and vice president of AlMaghrib Institute, in a low-tech, self-filmed video posted on YouTube and spread on Facebook, offered an endorsement of President Obama for reelection. Within the American Salafi-adjacent community and within the global Salafi discourse, Anwar's killing and Waleed's thirteen-minute video occasioned ripples of controversy and debates about Salafi theo-politics, about democracy and the elasticity of Salafism, and about what it means to be an American Muslim . . .

SALAFI *AND* AMERICAN?

Every chapter in this book holds Evangelical and Salafi thinkers and communities and tendencies side by side, but this chapter's comparison will be more implicit. No one seriously questions whether Evangelicalism is thoroughly ingrained in America. Some ideological opponents of Evangelicals might lament the presence of such a strong

Evangelical movement in America; they might say that Evangelical proselytizing or political maneuverings do not live up to the high ideals of American pluralism; but the *Americanness* of Evangelicalism is never in question. As we have seen, the same is not true of Salafism. The concern was raised in the last chapter's conversation between Hamza Yusuf and Scott Korb, and it is replicated in so much of the Security Studies literature on Salafism: Can Salafism ever *really* be at home in America? Is it fundamentally so antithetical to American values (the secular rule of law, democracy, pluralism, unity, etc.) that there will always be animus between Salafi Americans and their non-Salafi neighbors? Will Salafis always remain "in America" but never be "American"?

I am leery about even framing the question this way. I can already feel the eyes of my fellow humanities and religious studies scholars roll back in their collective skull. Of course, there is no objective, stable definition or set of criteria that makes something or someone qualitatively American. Whatever noble and distinctive "American values" we might name, they are often repeatedly historically problematized, at best, and callously violated by multitudes of real Americans, at worst. "America" is an idea and an identity that is itself discursive and contested. Moreover, religion is always embedded in culture. There is no Islam, no Salafism – indeed, no Evangelicalism – that exists *out there*, separate from culture or detachable from embodied communities in space and time. I will stipulate all of that.

But there are many voices, including voices of American Muslims like Hamza Yusuf, who express skepticism and trepidation about the incorporation of Salafism into the fabric of the American religious tapestry. When I tell Muslim acquaintances or audiences that I study Salafism, there is often a tensing up, a taken-abackness as they quickly intervene to remind me that Salafis are not in the mainstream – they are outsiders from the company of "good Muslims." So thorough has been this repudiation, as we have seen, that many Salafis (by most definitions) do not call themselves Salafis in America, they cast about for more respectable titles, less tarnished brands.

An ever-growing body of academic literature, think-tank reports, and media discourse on Salafism in "the West" (mostly focused on Europe with a few glancing references to American Salafism) raise questions again and again about whether "Western values" are compatible with Salafism, whether Salafis can integrate into democratic, non-Muslim majority political orders, and whether nonviolent Salafism is merely a breeding ground for violent extremism. For example, in a hearing in the Canadian Senate in 2015, two non-Salafi imams testified as to the origins of radicalism and terrorism among Muslims and laid the blame squarely on "a bunch of Wahhabis and Salafis who have nothing to do with Islam at all." The imams even invoke AlMaghrib Institute as an organization that is tacitly recruiting for ISIS and other terrorist causes.[3] Likewise, following the attacks in Paris in November 2015 for which ISIS claimed responsibility, French Prime Minister Manuel Valls told the National Assembly, "We have an enemy, and we have to identify it as such, it's radical Islam and one of its elements, Salafism."[4]

Jacob Olidort, a US security and foreign policy analyst who wrote his PhD dissertation on Albani, has argued that the notional distinction between so-called quietist Salafis and aggressive jihadist Salafis is really just that: notional.

> "Quietists," activists, jihadists, and other Salafis are all composed of the same theological DNA. They base themselves on texts and concepts developed over centuries by communities of established Muslim scholars. Indeed, this is a crucial component of the Salafi claim to authenticity. It is therefore not a big conceptual leap to go from quietism to jihadism.[5]

Implied is the possibility that congenial and culturally adept Muslims like Yasir Qadhi or the other AlMaghrib shaykhs merely need to have some invisible, internal switch flipped to become terrorists or terrorist sympathizers.

This academic and media conversation about Salafism and "the West" is pregnant with an inferred connection: Some Salafis are jihadists, some Salafis are terrorists, some Salafis have declared America and the West to be ideologically opposite and anathema to Islam and Salafism, so how could other Salafis honestly integrate into Western societies and accommodate Western identities? Indeed, in the backwash after 9/11 (the waters in which all of these analyses swim), jihadi Salafism has set the baseline of nearly all American and European epistemic judgments of Salafism. And lurking in the shadows of every one of these arguments in America in the past decade and a half is one man: Anwar al-Awlaki, that American imam turned Al Qaeda super-recruiter. This chapter has three parts: First, I will give a brief overview of contemporary Salafi theo-politics writ large and the outsize role America has played in global Salafi political theology; second, I will explore the looming case of Anwar al-Awlaki and his journey to join Al Qaeda; and, third, I will put forward Waleed Basyouni, the imam who endorsed Obama in 2012, as a means of envisaging a different possibility of intermingling Americanness and Salafism.

SALAFI THEO-POLITICS AND AMERICA

Much ink has been spilled since 9/11 examining global intra-Salafi political debates.[6] The most popular and widely cited – including by Jacob Olidort above – schema for organizing this discussion comes from Quintan Wiktorowicz who has suggested a tripartite taxonomy of the Salafi approaches to politics: "the purists, the politicos, and the jihadis."[7] In Wiktorowicz's analysis, *purist Salafis (aka quietists)*, who probably make up a majority of Salafis worldwide, conscientiously avoid contemporary political entanglements in favor of purging Islam of all the *bid'a* (innovation) and theological distortions that have crept in over the centuries. Despite their many theological and jurisprudential disagreements, he would include followers of Albani as well as conventional Wahhabis in this ostensibly apolitical coalition. Purists sit on the political sidelines; they typically avoid advocating for democracy or more participatory political orders, seeing them in and of themselves as Western, non-Islamic innovations.

Politico Salafis (a.k.a., activists) on the other hand, share some ideological turf with Muslims who are broadly labeled "Islamists," in that they believe that Islam (or, in this case, Salafism) contains immediate implications for how society should be organized and governed. The politicos are deeply frustrated by the corruption they see in governments in the Muslim world and by places in the world where Muslims seem to be mercilessly persecuted. So they are politically activated, calling for reforming society, sometimes democratically, sometimes from the top down, around Islamic principles and the Shari'a.

Jihadi Salafis (a.k.a., jihadists), in Wiktorowicz's arrangement, go a big step further than the politicos, determining that the corruption of faux Muslim rulers and the oppression of some Muslims warrant active warfare. They are willing to declare degenerate Muslim rulers "unbelievers" (*kafir*, pl. *kuffar*). With revolutionary language and recourse to violence, they aim to tear down all rotten and oppressive regimes.

Wiktorowicz's categories could be further complicated in several ways. For instance, many Salafis do not fit neatly into any of these buckets, and while overtly eschewing political participation, the purists often do tread into the realm of politicking and partisanship. But as a straightforward heuristic, Wiktorowicz offers a useful outline.[8] What is missed or elided when categories like Wiktorowicz's are taken as simply describing natural internal divisions within global Salafism is the historically contingent factors that have led to these divergences in the late twentieth century. To put a finer point on it, as I will explore in this chapter: The policies and actions of the *United States* since the 1980s have distinctly contributed to these internal fractures within Salafism.

But before we examine America's role in facilitating intra-Salafi discord, we need to have clarity on the term "jihad." The religion of

Islam, attached as it is to the historical life of the Prophet Muhammad and his community, emerged in a context of warfare, battles, religious persecution, and tribal conquest. Hence, the Qur'an and the Hadith both have extensive passages about "struggling or striving" (the root word of jihad) for the sake of Islam, whether it be the inner struggle to keep faith or outright defensive or offensive warfare, its just prosecution, or regulations for when and how and why it can be conducted.[9] As Salafis preeminently value and treasure these texts, conversations about jihad permeate Salafi discourse. To be abundantly clear: *This does not mean all or most Salafis are ready to take up arms to join some global jihad.* Many Muslims (Salafi or otherwise) who "preach about jihad" might be preaching against it or adjudicating abstractly over whether some contemporary circumstance could merit an armed struggle.

Like most Americans, most Salafis believe that some wars – some jihads – are just and merited and others are not.[10] Pre-9/11 (or, as we shall see, prior to 1996), this jihad discourse, when it ventured toward actual people taking up actual weapons, was not typically about America at all: It was about whether Salafis had a responsibility to come to the defense of their fellow Muslims in places like Afghanistan, Bosnia, Palestine, Chechnya, and Kashmir, places where Muslims were understood to be persecuted or where their territory had been invaded. The events of 9/11 cast everything before it in a different light, making any American Muslim who used the word seem like they were a part of a fifth column, plotting the destruction of America, instead of a Muslim talking about one of the many jurisprudential questions on which the Islamic tradition contains dense reflections and ideas.

Take the case of Afghanistan in the 1980s. When the Soviet Union made a heavy-handed land grab into Afghanistan, sending troops to occupy the majority Muslim population, this was seen not only by the international community but by the global Muslim community as an incursion against the Afghans' rights. In the guerrilla war of resistance that followed, tens of thousands of Muslims (Salafi and other) traveled to Afghanistan to join the jihad to push the atheistic invaders out. The asymmetrical warfare pursued by these *"Mujahideen"* (literally, "jihadists") was an effort famously backed by the CIA, financed with American dollars. From the late–Cold War, American intelligence perspective, they were drawing the Soviets into an expensive and unwinnable war – the Soviets' Vietnam. The Mujahideen not only recruited fighters from Muslim majority countries; they also openly came to American mosques to enlist American Muslims in the jihad in defense of the Afghans.[11] It is an irony explored in other places that a little more than a decade before 9/11, the "US government sponsored the largest and most successful jihad in modern history," a jihad that was the birthplace of an organization called Al Qaeda.[12] My point here is not so much to level a far-ranging critique of US foreign policy as to observe that the thing we call jihadi Salafism today was, during my own childhood, cultivated and gestated and valorized with American dollars and armed to the teeth with American weapons.

Turning to Wiktorowicz's "politicos:" Sometimes journalists write about Saudi Arabia as though it has no contentious politics, as though it was simply a static, theocratic monarchy. Yet through the 1970s and 1980s, in a departure from traditional Wahhabi quietism and avoidance of politics, a group of reformist, Muslim Brotherhood-influenced Salafi shaykhs in Saudi Arabia named the *Sahwa* ("Awakening") movement began calling and pressing for political reform to the Saudi autocratic, monarchical system. This movement was mostly contained and managed as a minority opinion within the broader swath of Wahhabi hegemony, but then, in the summer of 1990, Saddam Hussein's Iraq invaded its neighbor to the south, Kuwait. Soon after consolidating power in Kuwait, Hussein began making threatening overtures toward the neighboring Saudis, and Saudi King Fahd invited his ally, the United States, to send troops into Saudi Arabia to defend the border, thus inaugurating the Persian Gulf War. For the Sahwis (as the *Sahwa* shaykhs are sometimes called) this was highly objectionable: The Saud royal family's legitimacy was built upon its claim be the "Custodian of the Two Holy Mosques" in Mecca and Medina, the geographical and spiritual heart of Islam, and here they were asking for help from a – by the Sahwis' understanding, Christian – superior military power and inviting infidel (i.e., non-Muslim) soldiers to occupy the Land of the Two Holy Places.

The Sahwis' calls for reform that had been simmering for years boiled over into outright protests against the American troops. They organized a (rather polite and deferential, but pointed by Saudi standards) letter-writing campaign, gathering numerous scandalized Salafi shaykhs as signatories, to, in effect, violate the old Saudi-Wahhabi bargain: Religious leaders were openly criticizing the House of Saud. The Sahwis hoped to reform Saudi Arabia into a more participatory, representative "'conservative Islamic democracy' that would not speak its name."[13]

Naturally, this did not sit well with the Saudi royals or the Wahhabi establishment, and they started marshaling their own allies and Sahwi-critics. The royal family especially empowered a group of Salafi shaykhs centered around a disciple of Albani and an Islamic University of Medina professor named Rabi' al-Madkhali. As I noted in Chapter 3, al-Madkhali and his followers were famous for "vehemently opposing the Sahwa and demonstrating intense loyalty to the Saudi royal family."[14] For about three years, long after the conclusion of American operations in the Gulf War, the Sahwis and Madkhalis (politicos and purists) traded barbed treatises and lectures alternating condemnations and vindications of the royals' collaboration with America, until the royal family eventually banned the leading Sahwi shaykhs from speaking in public. When the Sahwis persisted, the Saudi powers that be had them fired from their university teaching jobs and, when still they didn't cease protesting, threw them in prison.[15]

All of this intra-Saudi controversy might seem, from American shores, like an abstruse theo-political debate taking place in a distant allied Muslim nation, but the "Sahwa insurrection" (as the Saudi government decided to call it) had two significant long-term impacts on America. First, the American troop presence was also deeply aggravating to a prosperous Saudi construction magnate, a Sahwi sympathizer, who had recently returned as a folk hero from the Afghanistan jihad, namely, Osama bin Laden. Bin Laden was fairly aimless after the Afghan victory, and he came to see the presence of US troops in Saudi Arabia as his new jihadi cause. He agitated and reconstituted his Al Qaeda network until, stripped of his Saudi citizenship and living under the protection of the then recently formed Taliban in Afghanistan, he would publish declarations proclaiming his agreement with the imprisoned Sahwi shaykhs and pronouncing the Saudi royal family illegitimate. In 1996, he went further, issuing a "Declaration of Jihad against the Americans Occupying the Land of the Two Holiest Sites," where he invokes the reformist complaints of the imprisoned Sahwis and cites the precedent of Ibn Taymiyya to acclaim the conflict, including against the Americans, a righteous jihad.[16] Though there had certainly been terrorist strikes against the USA before, this was the first serious, modern Salafi call for outright jihad against America and was the spark that grew into an inferno with 9/11 and the War on Terror.

To understand the second impact of the Sahwis' attempted reformation, we must return to the American domestic sphere. We have already seen that there was a burgeoning Salafi community in America pre-9/11. One might be inclined to assume that the thundering of Al Qaeda on the global horizon in the late 1990s would have had a significant impact on the *American* Salafi community, but that, again, would be a very post-9/11 assumption, reading magnitude backward on people who had no sense of the impending cataclysm. As far as I can tell, the vast majority of the pre-9/11 Salafi community thought very little about Al Qaeda, saw virtually no continuity between the international jihadi movement and their own.[17] Instead, the second significant impact of the Gulf War crisis of Saudi authority within America was driven not by Sahwis or Al Qaeda but by the personality of Rabi' al-Madkhali.

The pre-9/11 American Salafi community was largely centered around two communal hubs, "the Mecca and Medina" of American

Salafism.[18] The first was in Northern Virginia and the Washington DC suburbs and was predominantly made up of various immigrant groups (Arab, Somali, Afghan, South Asian, etc.) clustered around the Saudi government-funded Institute of Islamic and Arabic Sciences in America (IIASA), a satellite campus for the Saudi universities, as well as a variety of mosques, the largest being Dar al-Hijrah Islamic Center in Virginia.[19] The other hub was a mainly African American community in East Orange, New Jersey concentrated around the flourishing Islamic Center of America mosque. The East Orange community had satellite communities and mosques in Newark, NJ and Germantown, PA, as well as a few smaller sites.[20] While African American converts made up the majority of the Salafi community as a whole, by most accounts, in the early 1990s, there was good interchange among these communities, with African American, White, and Latino Salafis attending mosques and conferences along with the immigrant Muslim communities – especially those organized by the Qur'an and Sunnah Society (QSS) and the Islamic Assembly of North America (IANA). These energetic Salafi groups were beginning to be recognized within the larger Muslim community in the USA and encompassed smaller Salafi communities in most major US cities. Members and teachers would travel among communities to offer lectures or attend events and conferences. The American Salafis were early internet aficionados, creating websites, message boards, and audio-file upload sites to link together the geographically dispersed communities.[21]

A handful of Americans had taken advantage of the Saudi scholarships to study at the Saudi universities in the 1980s, but this ramped up significantly in the 1990s with dozens more undergoing training to become shaykhs and Salafi missionaries. Pre-9/11 American Salafis, in general, put Saudi and Arab culture on a pedestal. In their geographically remote Salafi quest to find *authentic* Islam, the lifestyle, dress, and details of Arab life – as funneled through the American shaykhs' experiences studying in Saudi Arabia – were interpreted as being real Islam. Thus many Salafi communities in America (and, indeed, many

Salafis globally today) were notably distinguishable by their attire: Not only were women traditionally covered with a head scarf (*hijab*) or full head covering (*niqab*) – a practice common in many Muslim cultures – but Salafi men were famous for wearing a thobe, a long flowing garment paired with trousers that stopped above the ankle, because this was traditional practice in Saudi Arabia and was thought to be how the Prophet himself dressed in the seventh century. The men also tended to grow out their beards longer, in conformity with Saudi/Salafi fashion.[22]

The timing of the 1990s surge in Americans studying at the Saudi universities happened to coincide with the internal Saudi fights between Sahwis and Madkhalis, and the elevation of Rabi' al-Madkhali at the Islamic University of Medina meant that most of these new students would study under the hard-line and Saudi-government-defending allies of al-Madkhali. Most of these Madkhali acolytes were African American because most of the earliest Americans to study in Saudi Arabia in the late 1980s and early 1990s were African American.[23]

As the Madkhali-trained and mostly Madkhali-aligned shaykhs began making their way back to America in the mid-1990s from their Saudi sojourns, they rhetorically and polemically amplified the Saudi-authenticity preoccupation among American Salafis while importing al-Madkhali's politics. As Umar Lee narrates:

> The zealots were also prone to banging brothers over the head on
> their position on the Saudi King. It was not good enough to
> recognize that Saudi Arabia printed copies of the Qur'ans and gave
> money to spread the dawah [Salafi message]. One – in these people's
> minds – must be loyal to and praise the Saudi rulers. You couldn't
> even remain silent on the issue.[24]

The Madkhali shaykhs' politics were fixated on Saudi Arabia, and they cared little for domestic American affairs. According to Rabi' al-Madkhali, democratic pluralism is "one of the deadly diseases that is imposed on [Muslims] to realise the West's interests, because the

West wants us to become divided."[25] Hence, the Madkhali shaykhs enjoined Salafis not to vote or involve themselves in American democracy because that wasn't the "real Salafi" way.

The arrival and ratcheting up of these Madkhali politics and polemics fractured the nascent American Salafi community in the late 1990s. Madkhali shaykhs claimed they were aligned with the "legitimate" Saudi scholars and gave voice to "true" Salafism. They demanded that "real" Salafis always identify themselves as Salafis (something about which there was little consensus at the time) and conform with their austere Madkhali interpretation. QSS, which had always had more of an African American/New Jersey affiliation, followed the Madkhali line, while IANA, which had more of an immigrant Salafi and Northern Virginia connection, was eventually denounced by the Madkhalis for not fitting their understanding of Salafism.[26] The Madkhali camp began creating lists of "deviant" Muslims and shaykhs, including others who had studied in Saudi institutions but who did not toe the Madkhali line, in what one participant in the movement has called an "Inquisition-like witch hunt that demanded groupthink."[27] As is not unusual in schismatic movements, some Madkhalis would later denounce even QSS for being insufficiently loyal to Madkhali principles.

This internal redefinition of the term "Salafi" in America in the late 1990s to mean, more or less, factional and Madkhali, is yet another factor in other American Muslims abandoning the Salafi label after 9/11. As I observed in Chapter 2, scripturalists can be very flexible with names and handles, so long as they retain their sense of scriptural devotion. The old-guard Madkhali communities, which are still mostly African American and rooted historically in New Jersey and Pennsylvania, kept the title of Salafi, while others, including the IANA crowd would, over time, jettison the Salafi title (though not the theology or their Saudi training) and consolidate after 9/11 around the fledgling AlMaghrib Institute.[28]

To summarize: Threaded through these intra-Salafi debates and dynamics are American policies, American assertions on the global stage, American alliances, and American Salafis themselves living in the slipstream created by Saudi and American policies. When we query "How American can Salafism be?" it is easy to treat those two specimens "America" and "Salafism" as clear-cut, dissociated subjects we are straining to conceptually fit together. In truth, the story of global Salafism – its internecine spats, its varied outlooks, its theo-political divergences – is stamped with America, intersecting again and again with American policies and identities. Now let us consider two actual American Salafi characters (Anwar al-Awlaki and Waleed Basyouni) to see how these intersections play out concretely.

ANWAR

Born to Yemeni parents in Las Cruces, New Mexico in 1971 while his father, a Fulbright scholar, was pursuing graduate studies in the USA, Anwar al-Awlaki grew up between the Middle East and America. Though he was a natural-born US citizen, his family went back to Yemen (the poorest Arab country and one of the poorest countries in the world) when Anwar was seven, so he spent most of his early life there, coming back to the USA for college. Like so many young people in the Muslim world in the 1980s, as a teenager in Yemen Anwar spent his time memorizing the Qur'an and was surrounded by stories lionizing the Mujahideen, the Muslim fighters from all over the world who were flocking to the jihad in Afghanistan.

Anwar's father, Nasser al-Awlaki, a very successful academic technocrat who served as Yemen's minister of agriculture and as chancellor of two universities, wanted to set his son on a similar path to his own. Anwar attended Colorado State University, where the lanky and paradoxically soft spoken but charismatic young man was elected the president of the Muslim Student Association. While still a college student in 1993, in the aftermath of the Mujahideen victory over the Soviets, he took a vacation trip to the fabled Afghanistan, bringing back an Afghan cap which he wore around campus with pride.[29] He graduated in 1994 with a degree in civil engineering. It was the only higher-learning degree he would ever finish.

Also while he was a student in Colorado, Anwar discovered a preternatural talent: He was a homiletical prodigy. He tried preaching a few Fridays at the small local mosque, and he was a rousing success. He had no formal training, but, having memorized the Qur'an, his fluency in English and Arabic meant he could switch back and forth between sacred text and practical lessons with ease. With his commonsense style, Anwar was American enough to connect with the interests of American audiences and Yemeni enough to feel authentically Arab.[30] Like Albani, the silver-tongued al-Awlaki was a Salafi autodidact. He voraciously read early Islamic history, studied the Hadith, and immersed himself as an amateur student of knowledge. Albani's Hadith expertise gained him entry into the abstract, bookish world of scholars; Anwar's learning brought him into the *minbar* (the pulpit in the mosque) to preach.

For the remainder of his twenties, Anwar's life would be pulled in three different directions: toward the educational pursuits his father wanted, toward his own virtuoso preaching talent, and toward his secret predilections. From Colorado, he moved to San Diego to begin a Master's in Educational Leadership at San Diego State University (never completed) and to serve as assistant imam at a San Diego mosque. His non-Muslim neighbors there remembered him as a devoted father of his young children, a passionate deep-sea fisher, and a friendly soul.[31]

The entrepreneurial imam discovered a way to monetize his eloquent homiletics: American and British Muslims loved his preaching, his calm, sincere, understated delivery, his capacity to link the situations of Muslims in the West with the era of the Salaf. Where Anwar excelled was as a storyteller, bringing the narratives of the life of the Prophet – the biography literature that is adjacent to the Hadith but less technically complicated – to life.[32] As one of Anwar's legion of American fans puts it, "Triple A [Anwar al-Awlaki] was able to bring the *ahadith* [hadiths] that were relevant to contemporary issues ... it would turn a light bulb on, and we would be like, 'I get why that's relevant now.' He was able to make that relatable."[33]

The content of his sermons was often critical of American foreign policy, advocating for embattled Muslims abroad, but it was also "very pro-American in some ways ... [praising] American exceptionalism and religious freedom."[34] He began selling cassette tapes and CDs of his prolific sermons – a fifty-three-CD box set on the life of Muhammad, a twenty-one-CD box set on the Lives of the Prophets, a twenty-two-CD box set on the Hereafter, etc. Before the Internet digitized Salafi learning, Anwar al-Awlaki was one of the foremost preachers filling the meritocratic niche of Anglophone Muslim scriptural exhortation.

Anwar also had a hidden life. Despite his preaching about the beauty and holiness of marriage and against the sin of fornication (pretty standard fare in conservative Muslim circles in America), twice in San Diego he was arrested by the police for soliciting prostitutes. He was fined and given probation. It was kept on the hush-hush.

In January 2001, twenty-nine-year-old Anwar took one of the most prestigious roles in the American Salafi community as the imam of Dar al-Hijrah, the crown-jewel mosque of the Northern Virginia Salafi hub. He entered into a ready-made network of mosques, Salafi charities and institutions, and eager believers. For most of 2001, to appease his father, he also took courses toward a doctoral degree in Human Resource Development at The George Washington University (never completed). At GWU, as the exciting new imam in the DC region, he was also invited to be the Muslim campus chaplain. Anwar arrived in DC the same month that George W. Bush was sworn in as president. "He told his father that he supported Bush in the 2000 election and hoped his new job might get him an invitation to the White House."[35]

There is a certain fun-house-mirror quality to many of the sources that exist today about Anwar's pre- and immediately post-9/11 activities (news articles, Security Studies reports, the 9/11 Commission Report, declassified FBI memos) as they spend an inordinate amount of time hashing over whether he was a jihad sympathizer or not *prior* to 9/11.[36] Two of the 9/11 hijackers visited

Anwar's mosque in San Diego and seemed to view him as a spiritual leader. One of those San Diego attendees and a third 9/11 hijacker also came to prayers at Dar al-Hijrah in 2001. No conclusive legal or testimonial evidence has ever been uncovered that Anwar knew anything about the 9/11 attacks before they occurred nor that he encouraged anyone to take up arms against the USA before 9/11. Indeed, all the evidence points to him being horrified after the attacks, speaking vociferously against the attackers and against Al Qaeda in public and in private. What many of these sources miss is just how small-town and inward-looking and fractured by the Madkhali provocations the Salafi community in America was in 2001. Moreover, it would be unsurprising that a Saudi or Yemeni Muslim of Salafi persuasion, as the 9/11 hijackers in question were, would visit the mosque of the local hotshot Salafi imam, the Yemeni kid preacher who's making it big.

When the FBI discovered that the hijackers had attended Anwar's mosque, agents showed up a few days after the attacks to interrogate him. They asked him whether he had ever preached about jihad, he said he had no comment on that question.[37] Of course, like most Salafi preachers, his sermons had touched on jihad, weighing the situations in Palestine, Kashmir, Bosnia, Chechnya, etc. Even at that transitional moment, Anwar seemed to recognize the shifting implication, the harsh recasting of Salafi discourse and norms that was underway.

For Anwar, 9/11 was a juncture of a different sort. As a high-profile, well-spoken imam in the DC area, after the attacks his opinion was sought out by government and media sources, and he repeatedly condemned the attacks. Along with Hamza Yusuf, he became, for a time, a go-to "moderate" Muslim leader who could unflappably explain Islam to a suddenly menacingly curious American public. The New York Times attested to him being "a new generation of Muslim leader capable of merging East and West."[38] He was even invited in early 2002 to speak at a luncheon at the Pentagon on "Islam and Middle Eastern Politics and Culture."

After 9/11, because of the fact that some of the hijackers attended Anwar's mosque and admired him, the FBI began surveilling him and following him everywhere, monitoring his cell phone, all unbeknownst to Anwar. After several months of 24-hour surveillance, "there was absolutely no indication that he was tied to al-Qaida or to terrorism or militancy."[39] But they did discover that Anwar was clandestinely soliciting different prostitutes in Washington, DC every week or so.

All of this came to an impasse in March 2002. Anwar was quickly becoming a Muslim celebrity, quoted in the *New York Times* and the *Washington Post*, being interviewed on Public Broadcasting Service (PBS). He was expressing hope in his sermons: "We came here to build, not to destroy ... We are the bridge between America and one billion Muslims worldwide."[40] Then the FBI conducted aggressive raids on a dozen Salafi institutions, charities, and the households of their leaders in Northern Virginia, including some of the Dar al-Hijrah congregants.[41] Like most of the American Salafi community, Anwar was furious about the post-9/11 crackdown on the American Muslim community, seeing it as an unnecessary backlash against many sympathetic American Salafis and other Muslims. His sermons, which had already had a sharp edge, became more strident. In one of his most angry Virginia sermons in March 2002, he recriminated,

> So this is not now a war on terrorism. We need to all be clear about this. This is a war against Muslims. It is a war against Muslims and Islam. Not only is this happening worldwide but it is happening right here, in America, that is claiming to be fighting this war for the sake of freedom, while it is infringing on the freedom of its own citizens, just because they are Muslims ...

> Maybe the next day the Congress will pass a bill that Islam is illegal in America. Don't think that this is a strange thing to happen; anything is probable in the world of today, because there are no rights unless there's a struggle for those rights, and the history of

America in that sense is very clear. African Americans in this
country had to go through a struggle; their rights were not handed
to them ... that's how slavery ended, and the struggle has to
continue.[42]

Even in his disillusionment, Anwar was still speaking the idealistic
American vernacular of moral political reform. The "jihad" (struggle)
in view was a parallel to the Civil Rights Movement, for Muslims to
claim their constitutional rights.[43]

A few days after that sermon, Anwar learned from the manager
of one of the escort services he had used that the FBI was following
him and that they knew all about his sex life and secret habits.
Despite his evident attachment to his life in Northern Virginia, he
was terrified of being exposed (and of being prosecuted).[44] So he left
America for Britain to go on a months-long preaching tour, capitaliz-
ing on his by then international CD-preacher fame.

In the UK, the progression of his alienation from America and
from the West continued apace with the ongoing War on Terrorism in
Afghanistan and – beginning March 2003 – Iraq. In one mosque in
London in 2003, he professed,

> Never, ever trust the kuffar [unbelievers, i.e., non-Muslims]. Do not
> trust them. Now you might argue and say "but my neighbor is such a
> nice person, my classmates are very nice, my coworkers, they're just
> fabulous people, they're so decent and honest ..." You know, these
> nice neighbors, wonderful coworkers and friends, all that it needed
> was for [Serbian President] Milošević to tell them the Muslims are
> evil people, all that was needed, and they pounced on the Muslims
> like wild beasts. This is in twentieth-century Europe.[45]

We can see, after 9/11 and his personal crisis, Anwar's theo-politics
shifting, becoming more desperate and more black and white. He
began preaching more about jihad, ruminating on what was legitimate
and what wasn't. Despite his ever-increasing fame for his preaching
and his CD sales, without the salary from Dar al-Hijrah, Anwar

couldn't make ends meet financially, and the FBI had dirt on him, making the USA fundamentally unsafe. So he and his family moved back with his parents in Yemen.[46]

He was arrested for ambiguous reasons by the Yemeni authorities in 2006.[47] During his imprisonment, he was interrogated by the FBI about his links to the 9/11 attackers, yet they never pursued a prosecution. Scott Shane, the *New York Times* reporter following Anwar's case, had officials from the Bush administration tell him that "the Yemenis asked them, 'This is an American citizen. We've got this American citizen. What do you want us to do with him?' And basically the Americans said, 'You know what? We wouldn't be *unhappy* if you kept him locked up.'" The FBI encouraged the Yemenis to hold Anwar for eighteen months without charges.[48]

To all appearances, it was there in the Yemeni prison that Anwar's views on jihad against America and the West solidified. He was held in solitary confinement almost the entire time, and he spent his lonely days immersing himself in reading Charles Dickens novels and in the Qur'an and the writings of Ibn Taymiyya and the Muslim Brotherhood revolutionary Sayyid Qutb on jihad.[49] After he was released in 2007, he launched a blog, and started recording sermons from Yemen outright endorsing Al Qaeda and encouraging European and American Muslims to take up arms against their countrymen and countrywomen. He even linked up with Al Qaeda in the Arabian Peninsula to launch *Inspire* magazine, an English-language publication aimed at recruiting Anglophone Muslims to the Al Qaeda cause.

Anwar's sermonizing reached a fever pitch in 2010 with his "A Call to Jihad," aimed squarely at his fellow American Muslims:

> To the Muslims in America I have this to say: How can your conscience allow you to live in peaceful co-existence with the nation that is responsible for the tyranny and crimes committed against your own brothers and sisters? How can you have your loyalty to a government that is leading the war against Islam and Muslims? ...

Muslims of the West, take heed and learn from the lessons of history: There are ominous clouds gathering in your horizon. Yesterday, America was a land of slavery, segregation, lynching, and [the] Ku Klux Klan, and tomorrow it will be a land of religious discrimination and concentration camps ... the war between Muslims and the West is escalating.[50]

In September 2011, at the age of forty, Anwar was hiding out in the backcountry of Yemen, posting clips of his sermons online along with pictures of himself ostentatiously posing with weapons, when US intelligence services discovered his whereabouts. President Obama had signed off on a kill order for him, and the drone strike killed him and several other militants. "[I]t was the first deliberate killing of a US citizen by its own government on presidential orders and without criminal charges or trial since the Civil War."[51] Two weeks later, Anwar's sixteen-year-old son, Abdulrahman, who had run away from the family home in search of his father, was also killed in a US airstrike.[52] Like Anwar, he was a US citizen, born while the family was in Colorado. In January 2017, days after Donald Trump took office, he ordered commandos to perform a dawn attack on an apparent Al Qaeda camp in Yemen to continue "our fight against the evil of radical Islamic terrorism." Thirty people, including ten women and children, were killed in the gun battle that ensued. Among the dead was Anwar's eight-year-old daughter, Nawar.[53]

Despite his wariness about Anwar's career path, his father, Nasser, has become something of an apologist for his son, denying before his death any connection to Al Qaeda:

My son is an engineer and an educationist. He studied in the best universities in the United States. But he is also a good Muslim. He published many books about Islam to teach young Muslims in English. His books are sold everywhere. Five million preaching tapes of Anwar Awlaqi have been sold in the west.[54]

Nasser has given statements to the press after each of the killings – his son, his grandson, his granddaughter – pleading with (and trying to legally force) the US authorities to cease remotely executing members of his family.[55]

Anwar's death and his family's tragedy have been cast as martyrdoms in Al Qaeda propaganda, and his success as a recruiter to jihad has only increased posthumously. Anwar's sermon recordings (including his early ones that were first on CD) have all been uploaded to Internet sites and YouTube. They continue to circulate and circulate and circulate, even though they are all now banned content on YouTube. And the sermons that are most shared, most mulled over, most discussed, are the ones after he left America, when he endorsed jihad. Some of his recordings were unofficially sold at AlMaghrib events even after the organization banned them in 2009.[56]

In terror attack after terror attack, foiled terrorist plot after foiled terrorist plot, in America and Britain, authorities find some connection, some inspiration tied to Anwar al-Awlaki: Umar Farouk Abdalmutallab, the so-called Christmas Day "Underwear Bomber" (who was also an AlMaghrib student) in 2009 traveled to Yemen to learn from Anwar and had been a fan of his preaching for years before that; one of the Tsarnaev brothers, who perpetrated the 2013 Boston Marathon bombings, said it was Anwar who persuaded him through his lectures of the need for violence; before Omar Mateen's 2016 attack on the Pulse nightclub in Orlando killing forty-nine people, he told a neighbor that he had been watching lots of videos of Anwar's sermons and found them "very powerful."[57] I could go on. In 2013, when ISIS launched its jihadi campaign to reestablish a caliphate, it also sought to co-opt the long-dead Anwar from Al Qaeda, reediting videos of him to make him appear to support their cause.[58]

I have spent years studying Salafism and intensively observing the American Salafi discourse, reading and listening to American Salafis who (though they might dissociate themselves from him now) found Anwar's worldview and presentation so compelling before and long after 9/11. I have listened to some of his sermons – his soft intonation, his measured phrasing, his connecting the dots among the darkest chapters of American history. Even as a non-Muslim, I can feel the poignant tug of his preaching, his obvious talent.

Many analyses of Anwar try to determine where he broke away from America, when he ceased being American, but I'm not sure such is possible. To me, Anwar's story – US-born immigrant kid who finds his voice in a free-wheeling religious atmosphere but gets into trouble and is done in by his own peccadillos and by the sweep of history – is irrepressibly American. To be sure, Anwar broke bad, and his undeniable talents have caused immense pain and many deaths, but I don't think he rejected America before he felt that America rejected him. For many Americans, Anwar's victims, the innocents killed by terrorist attacks in the West, are far easier to call to mind than the innumerable innocents who died in Afghanistan and Iraq and Yemen, collateral victims of our War on Terror.

I want to be clear on this point: *Anwar does not exemplify Salafism in America.* The dozens of people who have followed him down the byway of violent jihad are demographic outliers, fringy ideologues. But Anwar does represent something about America. I understand the temptation, especially for American Muslims, to overtly cabin off Anwar, to make him a persona non grata, a traitor, a fundamentalist, a non-American. But for me, Anwar holds up a mirror to post-9/11 American identity, our collective, thorny entanglement with Islam, our hard-stomping policies that have lamentably left many Muslims in the West and elsewhere longing for justice. Put simply, the lesson I draw from Anwar's dreadful example is that "How American can Salafism be?" is tied up with "How does America treat Salafis and Muslims *in America* and abroad?" Now let us turn from Anwar to a very different countenance of Salafism in America.

WALEED

Waleed Basyouni might well be the most pivotal Salafi in America, but no one talks about him. Outside of the Salafi-adjacent Muslim community, he's virtually unknown. Yasir Qadhi gets all the attention because he's punchy and eloquent and he speaks with a precision and staccato that means you have to listen. Yasir gets the long-form *New York Times Magazine* treatments, and he shows up in book after book on American Islam in the past ten years (including, I guess, this one). Yasir is a brand, a charismatic star preacher. Waleed, meanwhile, is not so snappy or such a media lightning rod. He's not as suave or hip as Saad Tasleem. He speaks more slowly, with a slight accent due to his growing up overseas and coming to the USA as an adult immigrant, though his slightly tentative English pace slips fluidly into his faster, native Arabic. While he's keenly aware of all the connotations attached to the term, he doesn't shy away from calling himself a Salafi. He's a shaykh's shaykh, garnering deep respect from his fellow AlMaghrib instructors, where they call him their "senior scholar" even though, as far as I can tell, he is not much older than his colleagues.[59] He has flown under the radar of so much of the extant analysis of Salafis in America. But I cannot think of another American Muslim who is more of an inverse from Anwar al-Awlaki than Waleed.

Like Anwar's youth spent in Yemen, Waleed grew up on the Arabian Peninsula, in neighboring Saudi Arabia. Like Anwar, in young adulthood Waleed developed a fascination with Salafism as a form of religion that was empowering and ideologically grounding. Like Anwar, Waleed was in high school during the jihad in Afghanistan, and he saw friends go to fight against the villainous Soviets. But that is about where the similarities dry up.

Even in their physical presence and evident personality, the two men are opposites: Anwar was sober and slender, forging his autodidact authority out of his smooth-spoken gravity. Waleed is prone to joke and tell personal anecdotes, to carry this deep learning lightly. He's a heavyset man with a ready smile.

Unlike Anwar, who continued to esteem the legendary Mujahideen from a distance, even traveling as a college tourist to celebrate their victory, Waleed's college experience was marred by a dark episode. One of his friends had departed from Saudi Arabia to

Afghanistan to fight, and when he returned during Waleed's freshman year at Imam Muhammad Ibn Saud Islamic University in Riyadh, the two got into an argument. The friend was more angry, more ideological, more combustible than Waleed remembered him, calling anyone around him who did not conform to his radical views a *kafir* (unbeliever), including his fellow Muslims. And one day, as they argued, the friend mirthlessly threatened to kill the teenage Waleed. This left a lasting impression, and, so, in the pre-9/11 era, when many of his fellow Salafis were debating about the wars in Bosnia, in Chechnya, in Palestine, and in Kashmir, as they wrangled theoretically over whether it was jurisprudentially merited to declare a new righteous war, Waleed saw things differently: "These jihadi ideologies – I'm very aware of them, and I see the evil of it."[60] As a Salafi student of knowledge, he spoke out against the rampant warfare language around him: "That's why I believe I'm not popular in many circles, because I used to talk about it very early when people don't want to talk about it."[61]

After finishing his undergraduate degree, Waleed went on to do what Anwar never did: complete a master's degree. His was in Islamic Theology, World Religions and Modern Religious Sects from the same university in Riyadh. Then Waleed did something unusual for people from his world – he emigrated to America. You see, the Saudi-Wahhabi educational project was to bring Muslims from all over the world, educate (some would say "indoctrinate") them, and send them back as missionaries to their home countries to disseminate the Saudi vision of Sunni Islam. But the Saudi-born-and-raised Waleed was attracted to America and especially to the vision of religious freedom and the separation of religion and state that America aspires to. So while many of his fellow Salafi shaykhs, perhaps begrudgingly, returned to their American homeland from the rhapsodized Saudi culture, Waleed's vision of America from the start was more sanguine and pluralistic:

> My understanding from day one, from 1997 when I came to the US until today: America is a state for everybody. That's one thing that

> I knew about America before I came to America. So I see America as a Christian state, as a Jewish state, as a Muslim state, as a Buddhist state, as an atheist state ... it is important for the state to be the place where we all feel belonging ... That's what makes America great, in my opinion. That's what makes America special.[62]

This might seem like an obvious point, capitalized upon by America's spiritual entrepreneurs for centuries: embracing religious disestablishment as a religious opportunity. But the story of Waleed's success in America is a story of subtle shifts in thought, stretching Salafism's flexible joints to adapt to new circumstances.

When Waleed arrived in the USA in 1997, he entered an American Salafi movement in the midst of an identity crisis. The fights and denunciations caused by the Madkhali shaykhs were in full effect. Coming from Saudi Arabia, Waleed was deeply aware of the Madkhali-Sahwi conflict, but he was also critical of both sides and had sparred with both in his time there – finding the Sahwis too eager to make hay out of opposing the American troop presence and the Madkhalis too obstreperous and parochial.[63] More importantly, while he continued to respect his teachers, Waleed was not overly infatuated with Saudi culture, having spent his entire early life there before deliberately leaving for America. Waleed took on the role of pushing the envelope of the Madkhali crowd and really challenging all of the Saudi-fixated tendencies of the American Salafi community.

Trading on his own Saudi credentials, he would receive invitations from Madkhali-aligned mosques or conferences, and intentionally wear a suit and tie instead of a thobe, just to provoke a reaction and have a conversation about what sort of Islamic fashion is appropriate for America. He recounts to me an encounter he had when he was invited to a mosque in Germantown, PA full of the "hardcore Madkhali-type of Salafi people:"

> They heard that this guy had come to America from Saudi Arabia, and he'd studied under Bin Baz and all these other big names they'd been hearing about ...

So, I came wearing pants and a shirt and jacket. Purposely,
I did that.

[chuckling] Oh my God! I still remember how they looked me up
and down and thought, "Where is this guy coming from? This guy
can't be Salafi!"

And when they heard the way I talked, it was everything, all the
buzzwords they are familiar with, all of the codes that I used, all the
references I used – it just goes check, check, check, check. The only
thing was how I'd dressed.

And then I told them, "Hey, Ibn Taymiyya – *rahimahullah* ["God
have mercy on him"] – said, 'If you live in the country which is non-
Muslim, you should not wear the Muslims' clothes. You should wear
the clothes that commonly exist in that society, because you don't
want to look odd, you know? You should be part of the society.'"

Oh my God, it was like … a big deal.[64]

Waleed's comfort and confidence within the Salafi discourse, his
Saudi credentials, his knowledge of the communal shibboleths, left
him in a position to poke and prod at the American Salafis' preoccu-
pations. From his perspective, the Madkhalis and many other pre-9/11
Salafis were wrongheadedly aiming to create a Saudi counterculture
within America, but his vision was for Salafis to become integrated
into American culture. Throughout our interviews, he keeps coming
back to that disarmingly simple phrase: "You should see yourself as
part of your society."[65] In my interviews with him, Waleed delights in
regaling me with these stories about the quibbles he received and the
confrontations he humorously blunted.

He tells me about a time after that when he was invited to
attend a meeting of the Madkhali-aligned Qur'an and Sunnah
Society in 1998 (the same conference that I noted in Chapter 1 where
Abu Muslimah had lectured a few years earlier), when Waleed initiated a controversy around voting. Democracy is a complicated

question for Salafis globally, and many of the respected Saudi shaykhs, particularly Rabi' al-Madkhali, have taken strong positions discouraging Muslim minorities from participating in secular elections. Waleed saw another opportunity:

> I heard this notion that we don't participate in democratic society, "Democracy is not Islam," blah blah blah. I said, "Obviously democracy is not Islam, but it is not *against* Islam. It's called democracy. It's a system."

> So a kind of clash happened between me and [the QSS] when I gave a *fatwa* [at their conference] on the importance of participating in elections and voting. And this was a shock for them, because they don't believe in being a part of the political system. They always believe that politics is dirty, corrupt, illegitimate; we should avoid it ... And I said, *"That's not the Salafi position."*

> Basically they kind of boycott[ed] me after that. Which is interesting because, the basic meaning for me of Salafism is pluralism. It's not a monolithic opinion.[66]

This final point is an important one. Many Salafis will straightforwardly assert that the model of the Salaf is singular and orderly. But Waleed (and other reformist Salafis) will point to disagreements and ideological battles among the Righteous Ancestors to illustrate how diversity of opinion has always been part of Islam, even at the cherished beginnings.

Waleed's amusement in his conflictual anecdotes is palpable. He could effortlessly quote the same scriptures, the same respected scholars (his own teachers or Ibn Taymiyya) as the Madkhalis were quoting and turn the tables on them. If Anwar found his pre-9/11 voice in America through preaching, Waleed found his as an instigator and a mind-opener – helping some American Salafis see how big and broad Salafism could be.

In fact, over the course of my conversations with Waleed, I've become convinced that part of what motivated his immigration to

America was a desire to expand the imagination of what Salafism might become. By his lights, loosened from the trappings of Saudi culture, Salafism could grow into a movement of open inquiry and reform in Islam:

> I always believed that the closest two groups to each other ever are the liberals and the Salafis. And I do believe that any Salafi who leaves Salafism, he ended up liberal, a progressive liberal person. Because it's the same mindset. It's the same idea.

> Salafism means you adopt an idea, not a person. So I'm not sold to any individual. It's not like, for example, the traditional Hanafi, Shafi'i, Maliki [madhhabs in] which is like you sell your brain to someone else. You have to basically follow one opinion and that's it. That's not Salafism . . .

> [Salafism] is very democratic because Salafism is also a very programmatic approach. You have to weight between advantage and disadvantage. And that's what democracy is.[67]

Waleed applied for and became a US citizen in 2001, just months before 9/11. Even though his parents had grown up in an autocratic Egypt and never voted, and Waleed himself had never had an opportunity to vote in his life in Saudi Arabia: "When I came to America, I just put my knowledge to action . . . I don't think I've ever missed an election day in my life."[68]

In his mellow, jocular, seasoned way, Waleed has sown the seeds of his vision of a capacious Salafism into the soil of the beleaguered American Salafi community for more than two decades. If Anwar's story post-9/11 was one of disintegration and slow-burn alienation from America, Waleed's post-9/11 trajectory was of ever-greater integration and inculturation. Like Anwar moving to take the imam job at Dar al-Hijrah, in 1999 Waleed moved his family to Houston, accepting the invitation to be the imam at the Taleem ul-Islam mosque. But, unlike the heavy-hitter image of Dar al-Hijrah, Taleem ul-Islam was not a Salafi hub or indeed a prominent community of any sort. Founded just a few years earlier in 1996, the small mosque community was then meeting in a strip mall across from NASA's massive Johnson Space Center. The mosque, which was eventually renamed the Clear Lake Islamic Center, has grown and matured along with Waleed in its "revivalist orthodox style" of Islam – one of the better paraphrases of "Salafi" I've found.[69] And it has been a space where he can slowly work out the implications of his broad-minded vision of American Salafism.

As Waleed has broken another Salafi norm and begun forging interfaith friendships and partnerships in Houston, the Clear Lake Islamic Center community has gone along with him, establishing interfaith collaborations with other Houston congregations. His set of friendships with local pastors (some of them Bible-belt Evangelicals) and rabbis is, as he puts it, "one of the best things to happen to me in America."[70] He tells me about going back to Saudi Arabia to see his teachers and friends there and hearing some of the antisemitic and anti-Israel sentiments that are latent in much of the Muslim Middle East: "I'm like, 'What do you guys talk about? The best people who help us in America are the Jews. You are out of your mind. Like my best allies and friends are Jews. My neighbors.'"[71] To be sure, Waleed is not belittling his old cohort – but his experience in America has given him relational knowledge that they lack. He's happy to share.

From his base at the Clear Lake mosque, Waleed's adroit but quiet influence kept expanding. In 2000, he helped found and serve as director of the Texas Dawah Convention, an older-sibling institution to AlMaghrib Institute: Drawing on many of the same shaykhs and ustadhs/ustadhas as the AlMaghrib ranks, TDC is similarly nondenominational in its demeanor. It also has a more devotion-bolstering, mega-conference ethos compared to AlMaghrib's educational-seminar emphasis. The annual convention draws upward of 3,000 Muslims from all over the country to Houston in December. There are bazaars, matrimonial programs (think: low-key, Islamically appropriate singles mingling), scavenger hunts, child-care programs for families, and, of course, inspirational keynote lectures by shaykhs and scholars disseminating scriptural knowledge and practical wisdom from the Qur'an and Hadith.

As it was for Anwar, 9/11 was a hinge event for Waleed. While Anwar experienced firsthand the early law-enforcement backlash against American Muslims and then fled the country, Waleed takes the long view: "9/11 forced the Muslim community to open up." He had already been outspoken against jihad from his experience in college, but,

> I became louder after 9/11. I became more [vocal] ... I saw, after 9/11, the reactions of our government [and how] it really opened the door for a lot of these jihadi groups to have a case and have a cause and start recruiting. And the message of Anwar al-Awlaki was a really popular message, getting popular, he speaks the language ... Violent extremism is an ideology. Ideologies and ideas must be countered by [other] ideologies.[72]

Anwar was ominously pursued (and, arguably, abused) by the off-kilter FBI, but Waleed began *voluntarily* working with the FBI to resist the influence of Anwar and other jihadi preachers. As he puts it, "I believe I'm part of society. I do believe that these law-enforcement agencies are not my enemies. I believe law enforcement [is] there to serve us."[73] For this, he has garnered dismay from different corners of the Muslim community – from jihadi sympathizers who have labeled Waleed as having a "House Negro mentality" (one of their favorite phrases taken from the rhetoric of Malcolm X) and have accused him of profiting off his collaboration with the FBI.[74] But Waleed's approach is also criticized by many progressive and activist Muslims, who are vigilant in protesting against law enforcement's past and present suspicion of the Muslim community and see what he is doing as "normalising the systemic discrimination we are forced to endure."[75]

Waleed's collaborative orientation does not mean that he is uncritical of American law enforcement:

> I don't want an FBI agent, I don't want the government of America to teach people what Islam is ... When I see some law enforcement

saying, "If you see a guy growing a beard or a sister wearing hijab or covered completely or wearing niqab, it means she's extremist ..." I said, "I reject that." Or, "Somebody became so religious, that means he's going to end up extremist ..." I reject that. This is nonsense.[76]

Waleed not only occasionally works with the FBI to speak to Muslim audiences about extremism, he also offers trainings for FBI and other local and federal agents to better understand the nuances and shadings within American Islam.[77] Over two decades now, Waleed has helped defuse some of the animosity and miscues between American law enforcement and Muslims that contributed so centrally to Anwar's dissolution.

In 2006, Waleed officially became one of the AlMaghrib shaykhs, joining the ranks of their popular instructors. But he quickly proved his wisdom and unique indispensability to the organization, and just two years later in 2008, Muhammad Alshareef, the entrepreneurial founder of AlMaghrib, announced he was putting "Shaykh Waleed in charge," while Alshareef pursued other projects, including developing a new Islamic life-coaching organization, DiscoverU.[78] Now as director of the institute (Waleed is careful not to elevate himself too high and refers to the other shaykhs as his "colleagues"), he is perched at the apex of American Salafism – or nondenominational post-Salafism, might be more apt – with a guiding hand in two of the most sizable, popular Salafi-adjacent educational institutions in the country.[79] He also sits on the influential Fatwa Committee of the Salafi-aligned Assembly of Muslim Jurists of America, a council of respected jurisprudential scholars who field questions through their website and hotline and offer Shariʿa-informed opinions to help American Muslims think through new circumstances and questions.

Which brings us back to that video of Waleed endorsing Barack Obama in 2012. At the time, much of the American Muslim community was angry with Obama over the extrajudicial killing of Anwar and his son, not to mention the hundreds of other American drone strikes that were killing uncounted numbers of Muslims in Pakistan and Afghanistan and Yemen. Waleed's logic in the video is domestic, pragmatic, and communal. He argues that he is not endorsing Obama's full platform of policies, but,

> I deeply believe that this is a very important election for us as Americans and for us as American Muslims as well ... We, as a Muslim community, we can make a difference this coming Tuesday ... Because it's about us as a community. It's about protecting our community's rights and to recognize the Muslim community as an element of this society ...

> This is our country. We live in it. We pay taxes. We share the future of it, and it's the place of generations to come for our community *insha' Allah t'ālā* [if God wills it, exalted is He]. We live in this country with everyone else. We share the same future.[80]

Having traced Waleed's journey, I read his Obama endorsement video as the culmination of his American acclimatization of Salafism: a sober, commonsensical plea with his fellow Salafi-leaning Muslims to weather the present storm, to lash themselves to the mast of American society for "generations to come." Waleed takes the long view.

When I ask him about how he determined to back Obama, he grounds his answer in American Muslim realities:

> A lot of social issues I don't agree with him on ... [But] working as an imam, we touch everybody's life. And so much of what defined [Obama's policies] at that time was healthcare, and I see a lot of my community would benefit from Obamacare, and his policy on immigration I believe is very good.

He's also critical of political purists and Muslims who make the perfect the enemy of the good, inveighing, "I do believe deeply that there is no 100 percent good [in politics], you know, that's an idea of Paradise, not this life."[81]

This short YouTube video sent small but serious shockwaves through the Salafi community both in America and abroad with a variety of reactions on social media and responses in online forums. Most people who follow Salafi theo-politics realized that Waleed was putting himself out on a limb: It is one thing for a Salafi shaykh to endorse *some* voting in particular circumstances to bring about a *more Islamic* societal order (something that is a topic of debate among the Saudi Salafi scholars); it is another thing entirely for a shaykh to publicly endorse a non-Muslim candidate who is, in the view of Anwar and many other politico and jihadi Muslims, waging war on fellow Muslims. Some liberal non-Salafi American Muslim leaders expressed joyful surprise that Waleed was being so forward looking – for a Salafi. But some of Waleed's colleagues at AlMaghrib stopped short of full-throatedly backing his new approach. Yasir Qadhi posted a link to the video on his public Facebook page (with its 900,000 followers) with the tepid comment:

> As for me, I'm in Tennessee, and it[']s a red state, so I don't feel the need to vote as it's already going to Romney. (And yes, personally I do feel that I don't want to endorse someone who is sending hundreds of thousands of drones overseas and killing thousands of people – but Sh. Waleed makes some good points as well).[82]

Harsh critiques of Waleed piled up both in America and elsewhere. Moosaa Richardson, a Madkhali-aligned imam in Pittsburgh, served up an especially blistering condemnation of Waleed over this video:

> These people are evil – AlMaghrib Institute instructors and those similar to them – they are evil. They pinch you off from the scholars. You are in the West with physical distance between you and the [Saudi] scholars ... the true scholars of Islam. This man, Waleed Basyouni, you'll hear him encouraging people to vote for this person and that person ... That is not our system, Waleed al-Basyouni [sic]! That is the system of America! That is the system of democracy, which is *kufr* [unbelief], outside of Islam![83]

Underlying Richardson's exasperation is a formal authority distinction that many Saudis and Madkhalis make: From the perspective of the Saudi establishment, the American graduates of the Salafi universities are generally preachers and missionaries (du'āt), not scholars ('ulama'). While the AlMaghrib instructors might hold the title of "shaykh" among their American students, Richardson is, in true Madkhali fashion, pointing back to the Saudi turf as the land of the *real* scholars of Islam.[84] Waleed – who is an edge case here because he grew up in Saudi Arabia and did not attend IUM, and who like Qadhi picked up an American PhD in Islamic Studies along the way – sees himself as a scholar, someone qualified to offer counsel to his fellow American Muslims that might depart from the Saudi consensus.[85]

The YouTube and social media rants like Richardson's and other Madkhali criticisms are easy for Waleed to brush (or laugh) off, but that is not the limit of the vitriol he has received. A few years after his Obama endorsement, ISIS, that same nascent jihadi state that was seeking to claim Anwar's posthumous legacy, put out a death threat against Waleed for his work with the FBI and for a specific *fatwa* he offered invalidating Muslims' traveling to Syria to join their jihad. In their English-language publication, *Dabiq*, the ISIS leaders expressly named Waleed and several other American Muslim leaders and called for jihadis to "kill ... [these] apostates, including the imams of kufr [unbelief], to make an example of them, as all of them are valid – rather obligatory – targets according to Sharī'ah."[86] So long as ISIS remained a going concern, Waleed had to get extra security for himself, his family, and his mosque, in fear that someone in Houston might take their instructions to heart.

For all the complaints people have about Salafis not being "American" enough, Waleed flashes like a warning hazard light against such blithe assertions. If we're in the business of gauging Americanness and if I'm being candid, Waleed's creative, high-reaching, courageous Americanness puts my prize-from-the-cereal-box, to-the-manner-born Americanness to shame. It is difficult for me to put into respectable academic-speak how much I like Waleed, how something about his vision of American Salafism speaks to something deep in my American Protestant soul. I know I'm breaking the fourth wall of scholarly objectivity pretty blatantly now, so let me go a little further: The thought has crossed my mind that, if I were Muslim, I would give serious consideration to moving to Houston to be a part of his mosque community. I was not expecting that when I began studying American Salafism.

CONCLUSION

Returning to Wiktorowicz's categories, it is apparent that, after 9/11, Anwar ended up in the jihadi camp. It wasn't that he had some switch randomly flipped, nor was he "self-radicalized," as the parlance has it. He didn't, as far as I can discern from a review of the documentary evidence of his life, have some smoldering teleology of terrorism. His violent radicalization occurred at the hands of a high-strung American security state and from the personal demons and contradictions he was carrying around – favorite son of Yemen (one of the world's most troubled and impoverished countries) *and* citizen of America (global hegemon); puritanical preacher *and* customer of sex workers; jihadi hero-worshipper *and* idealistic American.

Anwar's story isn't exactly unique to him: Other American Muslims and American Salafis, wrenched by their own contradictions and loyalties, have followed him down the dark road to treacherous jihad. They loom large for their fearsomeness in the popular American imagination. They are infamous but far from representative, not at all a good basis for forming a judgment of American Salafism on the whole. I'm confident each of their life stories contain subtleties and incongruities like Anwar's. If the American Muslim community comprises several million people, and Salafi and Salafi-adjacent communities in America contain, conservatively, hundreds of thousands, the handful of operative, anti-American jihadi Salafis are a rounding error, the margin of the margin. Waleed stands on the other side of that calculus. Through Texas Dawah Convention, AlMaghrib, his online *fatwas*, his Muslim-focused media appearances, his FBI-collaboration campaigns, his YouTube videos, Waleed has reached tens of thousands of Salafi-sympathetic American Muslims, taught them to stretch and find the play in the joints of their religion in America.

When I speak at churches about Islam, people often question me about the "moderate Muslim leaders" (a term, incidentally, the media once tried to apply to Anwar): "When will they speak up about all this jihad stuff?" That unending Western quest to find the ideal, mushy, unobtrusive Muslim. "Moderate," in this context, is a word that assumes a threshold Islamophobia – no one asks me if I'm a "moderate Christian." I will say this: In the panoply of prominent Salafi and post-Salafi shaykhs and thought leaders in America, Waleed is about as respected as they come.

Of course, as we began this chapter observing, there is no essential, objective "Americanness." Indeed, in people like Anwar and Waleed the discourse of Americanness and the discourse of Salafism intersect and blend in complicated ways. Even in his most "jihadi" mode, Anwar is still articulating his *cri de cœur* in the language of American protest and with appeals to American history. And, by any plausible provisional rendition of "Americanness" (at least any one that is not premised on some chauvinistic Christian nationalism), Waleed's style of religion is thoroughly American.

So, how do we categorize Waleed according to Wiktorowicz's esteemed groupings? He is certainly not a jihadi – to the degree that the jihadis have put out death orders on him. Neither is he a "purist" or "quietist" Salafi, splitting his religion from his politics or kowtowing to the distant House of Saud. As we were wrapping up one of our conversations, Waleed said to me, off the cuff: "Salafis don't, in general, have a good PR machine. The only country that really adopted Salafism was Saudi Arabia, and Saudi Arabia has a *very poor* PR machine. It is propaganda. It just has its own problems. That's why it is a failure."[87] No, he's not a quietist or backdoor Saudi apologist.

Which leaves us with the politicos, the Sahwis, the revivalist, political reform-minded Salafis, whose apparent ambition is an

Islamically normative (probably illiberal) conservative democracy in Muslim majority countries – a tolerably egalitarian, thoroughly religious state. Waleed does indeed have some Sahwi friends from his time in Saudi Arabia, and if we had to put him in a bucket, he might end up a "politico," inasmuch as he fits the basic definition of a politically engaged Salafi. However, he somewhat dismissively, tells me, "Those people [the Sahwis], they pick and choose from the scholars ... They are very political, more than religious."[88] Waleed sees himself as a scholar, a public intellectual in global Salafism.

I believe that Waleed embodies, and who knows how widespread or successful it will be, something that doesn't fit cleanly into Wiktorowicz's categories, something that is not described in any of the extant literature on Salafi theo-politics: an indigenization of Salafism to an environment of pluralistic, liberal democracy. Waleed is moving the Overton Window of Salafi theology of culture, extending the range of what is in-bounds.

Slowly, methodically, institutionally, collegially, Waleed has pulled American Salafism (especially, AlMaghrib-style post-Salafism) in his direction. And, I think, he's setting his targets even higher – on the global Salafi discourse itself. He says,

> There is a problem I see, with anyone who belongs to the Salafi background or ideology: The moment they begin progressing and learning – like myself, I developed myself a lot and all these changes happened to me, and I matured in many areas – the problem is, when those people become like this ... they don't try to identify themselves as part of this ideology anymore. Good example: Yasir Qadhi. He's completely denounced Salafism, blah blah blah. And I said, "Yasir, you're nothing but that. Your whole entire, growing up ..."

> I told him, "Yasir, if me and you just denounce and start attacking Salafism, we're never going to fix it. And it's never going to go away." That's one of the things that I think is important. I don't tell people that I'm Salafi, but also I don't mind embracing it, and

I believe in the principle of Salafism as a principle. And I'm willing to explain what that means. Because I do believe that Salafism is just a pure version of Islam.[89]

"It's never going to go away" – so much hangs on the antecedent of that pronoun. If I'm interpreting him correctly, "it" is the state of purported enmity between Salafism and the West. "It" is the world where jihadism has epistemically defined Salafism. Waleed, of all people, knows the dark edges of Salafism, the dangerous alleyways that the Osama bin Ladens and Anwar al-Awlakis of the world have taken it down, but he's determined to stay in the discourse, to widen its orbit, to actually win Salafi hearts and minds, to show how different Salafism can be.

6   Empowered by Common Sense

Ify Okoye is a gay, Nigerian American, feminist, hijabi, (post-)Salafi, Muslim woman, and she carries the interlacing of those identities with an admirable equanimity. In late August 2001, Ify – it's pronounced "Eefee" – had just finished high school and was taking a year off before college. She'd moved from where she'd grown up in upstate New York to Northern Virginia. Then, less than two weeks later, the 9/11 attacks occurred. She recalls picking up her neighbor's kids from school because the neighbor worked at the Pentagon and couldn't get home in the chaos after the attack. There she was sitting with the neighbor's kids, watching the incessant TV coverage, seeing the Twin Towers, a familiar site as a native New Yorker, aflame and collapsing; she says, "To see them on fire was stunning."[1]

Ify had grown up in a nondenominational Christian church in New York, which she'd abandoned in high school, but 9/11 sparked an interest, a longing within her to find meaning and purpose in her life. Like so many religiously unmoored-but-seeking American young adults, on September 12, 2001, Ify began reading up on the world religions, including Islam, and within a couple of months she'd decided to convert.[2] As she explains it, "the essentials of Islam accorded with my *fitra* (nature)."[3] This concept, *fitra*, is an important one in Islamic theology: Unlike most strands of Western Christianity where human beings are born into a state of original sin and separation from God, Islamic theology emphasizes how human beings are naturally born in a state of submission (*islam*) with an instinctual connection to God (*fitra*) and only later do they fall away from that through external influences or poor choices. *Fitra* can also have connotations of an intuitive moral sensibility, a congenital rationality that, if followed, will lead one back to God. This is why many people who adopt Islam in adulthood, people like Ify, call themselves "reverts" rather than converts – they are reverting back to their original religious state.

At any rate, in the spring of 2002, the same time that Anwar al-Awlaki was seeing his American dreams imploding at Dar al-Hijrah in Northern Virginia, the same time that Muhammad Alshareef was founding AlMaghrib Institute in nearby suburban Maryland, Ify began exploring different mosques in the greater Washington DC region. All of the mosques seemed nice, with friendly people, but Ify found herself most at home with the Salafi folks. Salafism seemed, to her revert's eyes, the most authentic and accessible – albeit rigorous and intellectually exacting – style of Islam. If there was some irony that, on 9/11, a group of Salafi Muslims attacked her country and her home state of New York, and then she converted and adopted Salafi Islam, it is an irony that was swaddled in the profundity of the experience of connection, learning, and meaning she found.

The mosques were fine and all, but where Ify found her truest sense of belonging and purpose was with AlMaghrib. She began taking courses when it was just a fledgling organization under Alshareef's leadership still housed at the Salafi-aligned Dar-us-Salaam mosque in College Park.[4] She loved the courses; the rigor of the learning; the confident and congenial shaykhs; the scriptural knowledge she gained through each lecture and seminar; the way her faith was bolstered with each weekend devoted to learning. As AlMaghrib's orbit grew, Ify would even travel to other parts of the country to take courses. She became an ameerah (the female leader paired up with a male leader) of the Maryland qabeela (tribe/chapter) of AlMaghrib.

Like many other gifted and opinionated young communicators in the first decade of the new millennium, Ify began blogging, at first under the pseudonym "Muslim Apple" and then, as she grew more confident in her own voice, under her own name.[5] Her blog, running from 2006 to 2017, in many ways reads as an insider account of the evolutions and metamorphoses that American Salafism and post-Salafism have undergone that I've explored in the last few chapters. Particularly from

2006 to 2010, Ify's blog reveals an ardent and sponge-like student of knowledge, transcribing inspiring quotes from AlMaghrib shaykhs, posting favorite Hadith passages, highlighting local mosque or AlMaghrib educational opportunities. She was even invited to become a regular contributor to *Muslim Matters*, an online magazine co-founded by Yasir Qadhi in 2007 that serves as a hub of socially conservative and the "not-salafi but salafi" Islamic discourse in America.[6]

Her 2006 blog post protesting Anwar al-Awlaki's "secret detention" in Yemen captured the consensus among Salafi Americans at the time. It garnered dozens of comments that were markedly supportive of Anwar and outraged at the US government's treatment of the then-still-beloved imam.[7] Many of the commenters speak glowingly of the influence that Anwar's preaching had exerted on the their faith lives. Yet, a few years later, as Anwar's rhetoric became more hard-bitten, as he openly endorsed jihad against America, Ify dramatically about-faced in her evaluation of the erstwhile imam:

> I know some Muslims, particularly those that are fans of the old Anwar al-Awlaki that we used to know when he lived in this area will not want to say anything, thinking they are doing good by abstaining from saying anything but I believe those sort of attitudes are harmful. When people make foolish and/or dangerous statements, one should not just sit back quietly and twiddle one's thumbs. This is how nonsense goes unchecked in many of our communities. If you have a mind, don't be afraid to use it, if you have critical thinking capabilities, utilize them, and don't be like sheep docilely being led to the slaughter.[8]

I would note here that beneath the surface of this bracing commentary is, again, a sense of *fiṭra* and innate rationality. In his transformation into an out-and-out jihadi preacher, Anwar's words had become "foolish," "nonsense," an affront to "critical thinking." "If you have a mind, don't be afraid to use it," Ify exhorts.

Throughout this time, Ify would have proudly called herself a Salafi, and her attraction to other women was not something that she spoke of openly or blogged about. Then internal dissonance began to ripple under the surface for her, breaking into the open in 2010. It's unclear which domino fell first. One transformational event was at IlmSummit, an intensive conference organized by AlMaghrib, led by Yasir Qadhi and Waleed Basyouni. It was a sort of AlMaghrib boot camp for the most promising students from all over North America. At IlmSummit, the shaykhs sought, as much as possible for a condensed time, to recreate the experience of studying with *their* shaykhs at the Saudi universities.[9] The students of knowledge stayed at a hotel in Houston, and had "access to our teachers virtually 24/7 ... it wasn't uncommon to find two or more instructors out at 2 or 3 a.m. in the morning, answering questions, sharing knowledge, and benefiting the students."[10] At IlmSummit, Yasir Qadhi offered a session for advanced students of knowledge amusingly entitled "Sects in the City: Heresiology," where he let his hair down a little to reveal some of his own process, emerging from his PhD program at Yale, of historicizing Salafism as a modern movement and not the sole, unbroken, authentic path back to the Prophet.

For Ify, who had spent her whole Muslim life engrossed in the Salafi discourse, this was a revelatory – and, perhaps, liberatory – experience, and it was after this that, like Shaykh Yasir, she stopped calling herself Salafi. As I tried to elucidate in Chapter 2, this did not mean that she stopped *thinking* or *practicing* like a Salafi. I ask her about her present feelings about Salafism, and she muses,

> When I drive to upstate New York, when I drive past some places like Binghamton, it feels like home. I don't live there – haven't lived there in 17 or 18 years – but it still feels like home, because it's where I grew up. And I feel the same thing about Salafism; I grew up there ...
>
> I'm [still] very grounded in the theology of Salafism ... in that understanding and in that practice of Islam. It's the Islam I grew up in and feels very [much] like home. I'd say that [it's still present] in my outward practice: my praying, my fasting, my clothing choices.[11]

I break into my interview with Ify here, and we go back and forth for a while as I talk about my own inescapable Evangelical upbringing, pondering correspondences. She's a kindred spirit. As I've argued in earlier chapters, we never fully leave behind the places we come from, the formative experiences that shape our habits of mind.

Around that same 2010 timeframe, Ify's feminist streak – which had been quietly, internally churning for a few years as she observed how Muslim women were treated as second-class citizens in many US mosques – broke out into the open. Generally, in mixed gender settings Muslim women pray behind the men in mosques, often with a barrier of separation between them. This is typically justified as preserving modesty and allowing men and women to pray in an undistracted manner. But, as Ify and some of her female friends observed, the actual practice in many mosques in America was to have women pray in a separate room, sometimes a poorly furnished basement. Ify took to calling these "separate and unequal, if not downright shoddy and dangerous accommodations for sisters," the "penalty box."[12] This blog post, which was also published on *Muslim Matters*, triggered some heated exchanges in the comments section, with many women (and some men) affirming Ify's points and many men (and some women) pushing back and accusing Ify of advancing an anti-male, feminist agenda. In response to a user named Abd-Allah, who pressed for Ify to "quote what an **actual scholar** has to say on this issue" so as "to find out what is the correct Islamic view about this," she offered a sharp rejoinder:

> I don't need a fatwa to tell me that it is not only possible but Islamically acceptable to treat women better and afford them better accommodation. These things are common sense. In Islam, we respect the people of knowledge [i.e., scholars and shaykhs] and defer to them to guide us and our actions as they are the inheritors of the prophets, yet Allah has also given us laypeople an intellect with the capacity for critical thinking.[13]

Ify's discursus here pointedly illustrates the interchange between students of knowledge ("laypeople") and scholars ("people of knowledge") that I sketched in Chapter 4, though this instance has a definite gender overlay. Implied in Abd-Allah's challenge is that Ify, as a woman, cannot be or become an "actual scholar" or categorically infer "the correct Islamic view" and so must perpetually buoy her arguments by appeals to the shaykhs and teachers. Having spent years studying under Yasir Qadhi, Waleed Basyouni, and the other AlMaghrib shaykhs, Ify *does* often cite the shaykhs (or scripture directly) in defense of her positions, but she also regularly grounds her arguments in a more elemental, intuitive knowledge: common sense.

Throughout 2010 and 2011, Ify and a few of her friends began staging "Pray-in" protests at several DC-area mosques (including Dar al-Hijrah and Dar-us-Salaam), where they would intentionally and provocatively line up behind the men, with no intervening barrier, in the main prayer room. In one case, a verbal confrontation between the praying men and Ify and her fellow protesters grew so heated that the police were eventually called. Ify and her comrades argued that there were no barriers separating men from women – much less consigning women to a different room entirely – in the time of the Prophet, hence the Sunna (the precedent of the Prophet and the Salaf) was on their side against these "cultural practices" which have made their way into Islam.[14] These protests set off spirited debates in the Muslim community, leading Ify to take to her blog to defend her position, which is worth quoting at length:

> There's a problem with the way Islam is taught in orthodox
> conservative circles in the East and West. While laudably trying to
> inculcate a respect for the textual sources of Quran and hadith and
> what are seen as the more authentic or authoritative
> interpretations, there also tends to be an enormous emphasis placed
> on rote memorization and repetition of other people's actual
> ingenuity and critical thinking ...

The struggle of Islam in the western countries in the 21st century will be to imbue Muslims in these lands with an authentic and uniquely western vision of Islam. It must be organic – rising from these lands and not cheap copy-pastes or immigrant culture-based Islam ...

The religion is easy, we all have to find our baseline and above that there is so much fluidity and expansiveness built into the shariah because it's a divine message made for all people at all times. There are matters that [are] well-known and even if you never encountered a scholar in your life, you would still be able to discern through the use of your God-given critical thinking capacity ... These things are well-known, it's part of the pure and natural *fitra* (human nature).[15]

Note, again, how Ify's egalitarian and American vision of Islamic faith and practice (the Shari'a) is undergirded by a powerful deployment of commonsense rationality and *fitra*. Though Ify was, in this phase of her life, moving away from calling herself a Salafi, her anti-clericalism, her derision of rote learning and blind following, her impulse toward fresh evaluation of scriptural sources, her appeal to the practice of the Prophet's community, and her sense of lay empowerment are all deeply Salafi. Nonetheless, as controversy piled up around the "Pray-in" protests, *Muslim Matters* disinvited Ify from her role as a regular contributor.

Where Ify really upset the Muslim apple cart was when she came out of the closet in 2012. But we'll get to that in the next chapter. Before we go there, I want to pause in this chapter to consider the *style and idiom* of Ify's theologizing and interpretation. At every stage of her religious evolution, her realizations and choices – from conversion to feminist protesting to, as we shall see, her coming out – have been guided and articulated with powerful invocations of intuitive reasoning. Her rational nature (*fitra*) draws her to Islam; she rejects Anwar's jihadism not merely as dangerous but as foolish and nonsensical; her opposition to the mosques' "penalty-box" practices is shaped by "common sense," whether she has a fatwa to back her up or not; her feminism is bolstered by her "God-given critical thinking capacity." Common sense is, for Ify, not merely an intuitive practicality but rather a profoundly empowering guiding light steering her religious sensibility.

In fact, this style of reasoning and confident interpretive assertion we hear throughout Ify's journey, is by no means peculiar to her. American Salafi (and post-Salafi) discourse, as the keen reader will have noticed over the past few chapters, is permeated with a rhetoric of common sense – appealing to the *obviousness* of certain understandings, to the *self-evidence* of scriptural texts, against the *nonsense* of wrong-headed ideas, to the *straightforward* interpretation of any fair-minded, rational person. What is striking is how much this parallels the rhetorical stylings of American Evangelicals, who for nearly 300 years have linked together powerful notions of common sense and direct scriptural encounter. This is, I now recognize retrospectively, what first drew me to resonate with the American Salafi idiom; it chimed in my Evangelical-attuned mind, producing the déjà vu feelings that occasioned this book.

So the question for this chapter is: Whence comes this resonance? To phrase it starkly: *Why do post-Salafis in America, like Ify, sound so much like American Evangelicals in their interrelating of common sense and scripture?* Do my Evangelical déjà vu sensations from listening to American Salafis have any grounding in history and shared experience? Or, to depersonalize it a little, has America and proximity to American Evangelicalism left a stylistic mark on otherwise distinct Salafi expressions?

The answer I want to offer for these questions, after long reflection, is not a simple one, but rather it braids together three different overlapping theories of convergence among which, illustratively, Ify sits at the center. Returning to the evolutionary metaphor I introduced earlier, I see three potential explanations for how American Salafis arrived at this idiomatic resemblance: First, Evangelicals have no monopoly on commonsense-style rhetoric.

Commonsense appeals could simply be innate to Salafi discourse in general, responsive to Salafism's distinct origins and twentieth-century emergence, regardless of the language, so that, as Salafi conversations are translated into or conducted in English, such phrasings occur naturally. This might be called the *coincidence theory* of Salafi-Evangelical convergence: It is possible that Salafis and Evangelicals independently and in parallel developed these similar styles.

Second, the similar Salafi and Evangelical idioms might both be shaped by a shared American culture and milieu. As I will explore below, America's distinct vernacular of common sense was forged by the particular Enlightenment philosophies and ideas that got baked into the nation's identity in the colonial and antebellum periods. This might be termed the *osmosis theory* of Salafi-Evangelical rhetorical correlation, with both movements absorbing their commonsense parlances from a pervading American dialect.

Third, American Salafis like Ify might have learned and borrowed the commonsense style from Evangelicals. Given Evangelicals' very public and boisterous mode of proclaiming their truth (and uplifting the Bible) in the American public square, flooding the country's religious airwaves with Evangelical discourse, it would be unsurprising to find Salafis imitating a demonstrably successful American scripturalist mode. We can call this the *mimesis theory* of Evangelical-Salafi concurrence.

As I believe the case of Ify handily exhibits, these three possibilities might all be mutually operating and reinforcing. She is plausibly translating genuine Salafi and Islamic ideas (*fiṭra*, humanity's rational nature) into an English commonsense phrasing, while also participating in America's characteristic wisdom-of-the-common-man dialect, while *also* drawing on her own nondenominational Evangelical upbringing to verbalize her egalitarian, Salafi/post-Salafi way of being Muslim. On the level of theory, in order to analyze and interpret a case of convergent evolution, as we observe in the Evangelical-Salafi case, we need not isolate a single mechanism or mutation but instead we can attend to all the operative genetic and environmental forces at play. If there is a commonsense affinity between Evangelicals and Salafis in America, the goal here is to hypothesize three connected whys and hows of that affinity.

COINCIDENCE: SALAFISM'S CONGENITAL COMMONSENSE INSTINCTS

In a marvelous essay examining the occurrence of commonsense-style reasoning across human cultures, the anthropologist Clifford Geertz calls common sense "one of the oldest suburbs of human culture," a pedestrian mode of anti-elite appeal to the savvy of the everywoman and everyman that is "an everywhere-found cultural form."[16] In Geertz's analysis, the *content* of common sense varies widely by province and locality, inescapably shaped by cultural atmospherics, but there are certain tropes – he names "'naturalness,' 'practicalness,' 'thinness,' 'immethodicalness,' and 'accessibleness'" – that can be identified across these different contexts.[17] Belief in common sense is, it seems, a human phenomenon: earthy conventional wisdom, the lucid thinking of the rank and file.

Hence, the observation that Salafis and Evangelicals both evince a commonsensical style of rhetoric applied to scripture is not necessarily extraordinary. Indeed, the fact that, at a macro scale, Evangelicalism and Salafism share similar goals – spreading theological originalism through the empowerment and enlistment of everyday Christians and Muslims in the study of scripture – it is unsurprising that, despite their very different geographical, cultural, and historical evolutions, both movements would land upon regular appeals to common sense as a way of popularizing scripture study. What is interesting about this, though, is that there is no single word or phrase in Arabic, Salafism's mother tongue and lingua franca, that uniformly translates as "common sense."[18] Instead what we find in Anglophone Salafi discourse is shaykhs and laypeople like Ify taking a constellation of phrases and ideas from Arabic and rendering them "common sense." And if you cock your head and stare closely at that constellation, you can see the face of that medieval Salafi forefather: Ibn Taymiyya.

When I pointed out to Yasir Qadhi how frequently he importunes "common sense" (or its synonyms) and links it to the Qur'an and the Hadith in his lecturing and teaching, he responded, "I actually read that in Ibn Taymiyya, and I've adopted it from him."[19] Yet when I tried to pin him down on the exact phrase or concept from Ibn Taymiyya he was translating, he was noncommittal, signaling that it came from several different words and concepts in Ibn Taymiyya's thought. I received similar responses from other Salafi shaykhs who would readily acknowledge the commonsensical element in their Salafi hermeneutics, and would likewise point to Ibn Taymiyya for its genesis, but then direct me toward a cluster of ideas in the medieval shaykh's thought. Yasir indicated that the Taymiyyan phrase ṣarīḥ al-ʿaql (roughly, "clear or unequivocal mindedness") was probably the closest to "common sense."[20] Hatem al-Haj, a respected Salafi shaykh who serves on the Fatwa Committee of the Assembly of Muslim Jurists of America with Waleed, when I asked him about the roots of a commonsense approach to scripture in Salafism, primarily highlighted the importance of balancing reason (ʿaql) and revelation (naql) in Ibn Taymiyya's writings.[21] To the same question, Waleed called my attention to Ibn Taymiyya's paramount commitment to stick to the plain sense (ẓāhir – often translated as "literal") of the Qur'anic or Hadith texts.[22]

So too, many Salafis like Ify will translate fiṭra as simply "common sense," which is actually putting a tellingly Taymiyyan spin on that facet of Islamic theology. You see, the concept of fiṭra is somewhat open to interpretation because it occurs only once in the Qur'an (Q 30:30). It is, by most Muslim interpretations, a pristine, natural state of innocence and submission to God. As the Prophet says in a key hadith, "Every newborn is born in his true nature (fiṭra). Then his parents make him a Jew, Christian, or Zoroastrian. This is like the way animals produce their young with their limbs perfect. Do you see anything deficient in them?"[23] In non-Salafi Islam, fiṭra is a theological precept about human nature's alignment with Islam, but it does not necessarily carry a connotation of rationality or intelligence. *Fiṭra* for most Muslims does not have a noetic or intellectual function. It is more primal and instinctual than that.[24]

Yet, as with so many parts of the Sunni tradition, Ibn Taymiyya had his own take on *fiṭra*, and he amplified the concept to make it more of an innate moral sense. His reinterpretation of *fiṭra* opens a host of new possibilities in understanding human nature and our capacity to know and recognize truth. Consider how he explains the above hadith:

> The *fiṭrah* is to the truth as the light of the eye is to the sun. *Everyone who has eyes* can see the sun if there are no veils over them. The erroneous beliefs of Judaism, Christianity and Zoroastrianism act like veils, preventing people from seeing the truth. It is *common experience* that people whose *natural sense* of taste is not spoiled love sweets; they never dislike them unless something spoils the sense of taste ... This *power to know and to act* which develops into Islam when there is nothing to obstruct it or affect its working is the *fiṭrah* on which God has created man.[25]

The analogies employed are far-reaching. *Fiṭra* functions, in Ibn Taymiyya's formulation, like one of the five senses if unimpeded by outside forces. It is a sort of spiritual and moral sixth sense: the "power to know and to act." It is less that humans have built-in knowledge content, and more that we are intrinsically sensible, innately drawn to truth and rightness.[26] As one contemporary Ibn Taymiyya scholar puts it, the shaykh "expands [the scope of *fiṭra*] to include the moral sphere and regards it as a fully reliable guide to truth ... The role of prophets is not to introduce anything fundamentally new to *fiṭra* but to clarify, strengthen, and perfect it."[27] Our internal rational sense, if undeterred, will relay accurate data to us, and this moral sense will be drawn to the good. In truth, for Salafis, fashioned as they are in the mold of Ibn Taymiyya, "common sense" is actually a pretty good English translation of *fiṭra*.

All of this points to an important – though difficult to answer – question: If "common sense" is just the best way in English to capture this constellation of Taymiyyan ideas, wouldn't it stand to reason that all Anglophone Salafis would correspondingly use this phrasing? Put another way, is there any sort of distinctly *American* common sense accent to Salafism that sets the American Salafi scripturalist discourse apart from that in the UK, Australia, etc.? If Geertz is correct that commonsense reasoning is "an everywhere-found cultural form," is there anything peculiarly American about Ify's and other American Salafis' commonsense idiom? As we look toward our next theory of rhetorical convergence (that Salafis and Evangelicals in America are both absorbing commonsense stylings by osmosis from American culture) it is worth asking: Are there vernacular markers America has left on Salafis in the last thirty-odd years?

The challenge in answering this question is that there are no clear national boundaries in cyberspace between English-speaking Salafis in, say, Canada, the UK, Australia, and the USA. Salafi shaykhs, like the AlMaghrib instructors, are now international scripturalist celebrities, lecturing and teaching courses all over the Anglophone world. Plus, most of the Internet-quickened, Anglophone Salafi discourse (from message boards to YouTube videos) overlaps those different geographies, and a hundred others where Salafis might speak English as a second or third language. If you want to find the American Salafi dialect, how do you separate out what is American signal in all that noise?

I think about the case of Tarek Mehanna. Mehanna was a twenty-nine-year-old American pharmacist and former AlMaghrib student convicted in Pittsburgh in 2011 of "providing material support" for al-Qaeda and conspiring to kill US soldiers in Iraq.[28] The case was much-discussed in the media at the time, because Mehanna did not have any direct connection to al-Qaeda, and the lion's share of the evidence marshaled against him was online speech he had made on message boards, websites, and private chats. In those postings, in addition to hostility against America and American foreign policy, he argued vehemently for the right of Muslims in Afghanistan and Iraq to wage defensive jihad against the invading American troops. By his own account, he had never supported al-Qaeda, but he *had* translated popular classical jihad treatises from Arabic into English, which Mehanna's lawyers (and many legal scholars) argued was protected under the First Amendment, but which federal prosecutors convinced the jury had benefited al-Qaeda in its recruitment efforts.[29] The case was even appealed to the US Supreme Court, which declined to hear it.

Without adjudicating the justness of Mehanna's conviction, my interest lies in a speech Mehanna gave before the judge at his sentencing hearing. The entire speech was posted and reposted in Salafi message boards and social media, and it is a master stroke of American rhetoric, tying together Paul Revere, Tom Paine, Harriet Tubman, John Brown, Rosa Parks, and Malcolm X all in defense of people's duty to resist oppression. Mehanna, speaking directly to the judge, compares the Minutemen of the American Revolution to the mujahideen in Afghanistan, and, he passionately intones:

> I was born and raised right here in America and this is something which angers many people: How is it that I can be an American and believe the things I believe, take the positions I take? Everything a man is exposed to in his environment becomes an ingredient that shapes his outlook, and I'm no different. So, in more ways than one, it's because of America that I am who I am ...

> [Muslims defending their countries] is not terrorism, and it's not extremism. It's the simple logic of self-defense. It's what the arrows on that seal above your head represent: defense of the homeland. So, I disagree with my lawyers when they say that you don't have to agree with my beliefs – no! Anyone with common sense and humanity has no choice but to agree with me. If someone breaks into your home to rob you and harm your family, logic dictates that you do whatever it takes to expel that invader from your home. But when that home is a Muslim land, and that invader is the US

military, for some reason the standards suddenly change. Common sense is renamed "terrorism" and the people defending themselves against those who came to kill them from across the ocean become "the terrorists" who are "killing Americans."[30]

Mehanna's speech was utterly unpersuasive to the judge, who sentenced him to seventeen years in prison, but it is pretty clear why the speech was so attractive to Salafis in America and abroad: Mehanna was eloquently reversing the polarity of the War on Terror. In his telling, the American soldiers, who have gone abroad to be "greeted as liberators" (in Dick Cheney's infamous phrase), are the terrorists and colonizers, while the Muslims who are fighting against those soldiers are defenders of the homeland, the bearers of common sense, à la the American Revolution. Mehanna is both de-centering America as righteous homeland and re-appropriating the commonsense American example of revolutionary freedom.

What is telling in Mehanna's speech is the sort of common sense he is calling forth. His immediate audience is not his fellow Salafis; it is an American judge, and at a slight remove, an American public whose fabled history he is obliquely re-narrating. He foregrounds the Americanness of his ideas and his values, even as he expresses befuddlement that his fellow Americans do not see his logic. He even looks forward in the speech to the day when he will be vindicated in the eyes of the American people, when common sense will be restored: "... history repeats itself. One day, America will change and people will recognize this day for what it is."[31] While Mehanna is fluent in Arabic and skilled in translation between Arabic and English, if notions of *fiṭra* or consonant Taymiyyan conceptions of innate rationality are present in his rhetoric, they have taken a back seat to a fine-tuned American accent and idiom. Mehanna is, to recover a phrase that is often used to denigrate or castigate immigrants or ethnic minorities in America, *speaking American*. He is using the emblems and jargon of America to deftly redefine American common sense. This and myriad other instances of

American Salafi invocations of common sense, from Ify Okoye to Yasir Qadhi, have convinced me that Ibn Taymiyya's foundational understandings of human rationality and *fiṭra*, which are ubiquitous for contemporary Salafis, are a necessary but not a sufficient explanation for the Salafi commonsensical parlance in America. No, to fully understand the influence *American* discourse has had on American Salafism, we have to go back, like Mehanna, through the long stretch of American history.

OSMOSIS: THE FOUNDATIONS OF AMERICA'S COMMONSENSE ECOLOGY

A pivotal moment in the intellectual founding of the United States occurred in a small village outside of Aberdeen, Scotland when a Protestant pastor read a new book. Thomas Reid was a parish minister in the Church of Scotland in the 1740s when he first encountered his fellow Scotsman David Hume's *A Treatise of Human Nature*; it left Reid badly shaken. Hume, a philosophical prodigy who was one year younger than Reid, had started the earth-shaking *Treatise* at the age of twenty-three, and published it six years later in 1740. Reading Hume's *Treatise* would set Reid on a path that would lead him to become a celebrated philosophy professor and spend the rest of his life refuting Hume.

What was so distressing for Reid about the *Treatise* was not just Hume's evident atheism. He could not easily see any way around Hume's logic. In the *Treatise*, and in his later works, Hume poked holes in the confident empiricism of his own time which assumed the data coming from the five human senses to be the veritable building blocks of all knowledge. Hume took the scientific method with its empirical mode that was all the rage since Francis Bacon and Isaac Newton's pioneering work in the previous century, and he turned the method inward. He asserted that if all of the then-fledgling scientific and academic fields are to be conducted by human minds, then "the science of man [i.e., study of human nature and the inner workings of the human mind] is the only solid foundation for the other sciences."[32] Such an inquiry, like any scientific pursuit, must rely not on theoretical speculations or a priori assumptions but on "experience and observation," here of the mind itself.[33]

What Hume found, as he pursued this line of questioning is that the human mind is not merely a well-oiled machine for processing reality. No, the data that enter a person's mind through the five senses are shaped, sorted, and shaded by the mind itself. This skeptic's insight into how the mind's workings are full of "manifest paradoxes and contradictions" represented "a turning point in the history of modern epistemology."[34] Our imaginings, sentiments, and passions affect our knowing and our experience of the world, and our filtering beliefs may or may not be true, but they are not necessarily empirically arrived at or founded on objective reason. Hume's skepticism drove the sharp end of the wedge between simple cause and effect, between sensory perception and reality, between certitude and probability.[35] With his circumspect logic, Hume "quietly cut away all ontological certainties."[36]

Several trajectories of Hume's skepticism are momentous: Immanuel Kant would notably write at the end of his life that "the remembrance of *David Hume* was the very thing that many years ago first interrupted my dogmatic slumber and gave a completely different direction to my researches in the field of speculative philosophy." [37] The awakened Kant would inaugurate a new stage in Western epistemology as, in his *Critique of Pure Reason* (1781), he distinguished between the essence of things (the *noumena*), which remains beyond human apprehension, and the experienced reality (the *phenomena*). Kant titled his approach "transcendental idealism" and he self-graded it as "a complete solution to the Humean problem."[38] In the next generation, Jeremy Bentham would read Hume's *Treatise*, especially its treatment of virtue, and he "felt as if scales had fallen from my eyes."[39] He would go on to found the philosophical current of Utilitarianism.

Kant and Bentham (and numerous other philosophers after them) found ways to incorporate or allow the sting of Hume's epistemic skepticism to push them onto new paths, but Thomas Reid opted for outright rebuttal. By Reid's estimation, if you granted the premise of "[t]he ingenious author of that treatise" that there is a disjunction between the objective world and the subjective human mind, then you thereby enter into "a system of scepticism which leaves no ground to believe any one thing rather than its contrary."[40] Reid left his ministerial position in 1752 to become a professor at King's College, Aberdeen, and he began writing his refutation of Hume's *Treatise*. More than a decade later, as Reid was in the process of moving to the University of Glasgow to take over the respected Professorship in Moral Philosophy from Adam Smith (yes, *that* Adam Smith), he published his *An Inquiry into the Human Mind on the Principles of Common Sense*.

Compared to Hume's dense *Treatise*, Reid's *Inquiry* is a relatively easy read, and his argument is not difficult to follow. For Reid, human experience is not merely grounded in the individual mind processing objective reality through its own ideas and passions and sentiments. Instead, ideas and logic and language are all communal, arising out of the shared experience and communication of humankind:

> If there are certain principles, as I think there are, which the constitution of our nature leads us to believe, and which we are under a necessity to take for granted in the common concerns of life, without being able to give a reason for them; these are what we call the principles of common sense; and what is manifestly contrary to them, is what we call absurd.[41]

In other words, everyone knows and everyone lives on the basis of: Up is up, down is down, water when frozen becomes ice. Ideas are not merely locked away in solitary human minds and prey to the individual's idiosyncratic passions and whims; basic ideas are public and communal, grounded in the shared reality and shared wisdom of all humanity. In substance, Reid argued that "the mind is structured in such a way that it is impossible not to act and think as if our perceptions revealed the real world to us."[42] Philosophy, for Reid, is built upon this foundation of common sense, on the "common apprehensions of mankind," not on abstract cogitations or the skeptical hole-poking emitting from Hume's idiosyncratic intellect.[43]

In the long term, Hume's "system of scepticism" has proven far more impactful on the field of philosophy, and that's why today his writings are standard fare on Introduction to Philosophy syllabi, whereas Reid is often treated by sophisticated philosophers as more of an Enlightenment curiosity. But in eighteenth-century Scotland, Reid was more highly regarded, and a whole school of philosophy formed around him, with other philosophers expounding on the power of common sense and piling on with critiques of Hume. This school has gone by various labels: Scottish Realism, Scottish Common Sense, or, in an obvious discourtesy to Hume, the Scottish Philosophy.

What made Scottish Realism so popular was not only that it was accessible and empowering to the everywoman and everyman, but it was also uniquely suited to the mid-to-late-eighteenth-century zeitgeist: "at once amenable to science, Christian beliefs, the rise of the modern public sphere, and democratic politics."[44] And these Scottish debates and concepts, along with all the other European Enlightenment currents, quickly made their way across the Atlantic to the American colonies, where they mingled with the experimental, revolutionary, and republican sentiments coming out of the First Great Awakening.[45]

It has been well-established by intellectual historians that Scottish Common Sense shaped the intellect of the American colonies and the young nation.[46] It is no coincidence that Thomas Paine's best-selling, eve-of-the-Revolution pamphlet (which Mehanna implicitly invoked in his sentencing speech) was titled "Common Sense," as he tied together the virtues of democracy with this "mundane, invisible, but increasingly valuable standard of truth" in his time.[47] Nor is it an accident that a favorite phrase of the Scottish Realists, "self-evident," is attached to the acclaimed truths – life, liberty, and the pursuit of happiness – in the first line of the

Declaration of Independence. "It was the Scottish Enlightenment, not the French, that the Americans found most congenial to their democratic institutions."[48]

After the American Revolution, Reid and the other Scottish Realists became, if anything, even more influential, as American colleges, universities, and seminaries promoted the Scottish Enlightenment, somewhat ignoring the other important philosophical developments emanating from Europe. The post-Revolution curricula of the College of Philadelphia (today's University of Pennsylvania), Yale College, Harvard College, and the College of New Jersey (today's Princeton University) were all built around the Scottish Realist philosophers, so that generation after generation of intellectual leaders in the young republic were inculcated with Reid's Common Sense.[49] Indeed, the philosophical flourishing and debates of Europe's other Enlightenments, the posterity of Kant and others provoked by Humean skepticism, did not full-fledgedly cross the Atlantic and enter the American academy until after the Civil War. Instead, for the first four score and seven years of the American republic, American intellectual life was incubated rhetorically, politically, philosophically, and democratically in the intuitive knowledge of the common man and common woman. The soil of Antebellum America was implanted not with the deep-rooted skepticism of David Hume or the high-branching idealism of Immanuel Kant but with the rhizomatic, egalitarian, scientific-but-not-too-technical, self-evident logic of Thomas Reid.

This prolonged American heyday of Scottish Common Sense came to an end after the Civil War. Darwin's theory of evolution, increased scholarly cross-pollination with Europe, and the restructuring of university curricula all led to a wider variety of philosophies being taught in higher education settings. As one of the founders of the field of American Studies, Perry Miller, crisply observes,

> It is a curious fact that one of the most radical revolutions in the history of the American mind took place in the two or three

decades after the Civil War without exciting appreciable comment: The philosophy and philosophers of Scottish Realism vanished from the American colleges, leaving not even a rack behind, and were swiftly replaced by expounders of some form of Idealism.[50]

Over the ensuing century and a half, America's ambit of philosophical inquiry has diversified and pluralized.

Still, Scottish Realism left its indelible mark on America: From Tom Paine to Donald Trump, from the Abolitionists campaigning against slavery to the Suffragettes campaigning for women's enfranchisement to the pro-life activists pleading with women outside abortion clinics, American politics and persuasion is stamped with the idiom of common sense. Sophia Rosenfeld trenchantly notes how the rhetoric of common sense functions in American life as both a "banal and often elite, political weapon," but also as a form of empowerment for the demeaned and depreciated: "Our faith in common sense ... offers a space from which ordinary people and nonexperts, whether women, members of marginalized groups, or simply people of humble origins, can dare to speak to and for their fellow citizens' public concerns."[51]

Which brings us back to Ify Okoye and Tarek Mehanna and the other American Salafis. I'm fairly certain the vast, vast majority of them have never read Thomas Reid, but their appeals to their own straightforward powers of intuitive reason are, like so much of American discourse, idiomatically downstream from the Scottish Realists. The empowerment Ify feels to vocalize a form of post-Salafi Islamic feminism participates in a long tradition of a distinctly American dialect that has its headwaters in eighteenth-century Scotland. Mehanna's skipping-stone, tour de force of historic American champions of justice against oppressors – from Tom Paine to Malcolm X – culminates in himself; his common sense participates in the long tradition of American jeremiad and man-on-the-street reasoning.

Put simply, Salafis' appropriation of the American common-sense slang for conducting intra-Salafi discussions and for their presentation of themselves to outsiders serves as further evidence of what I argued in the last chapter about the flexibility and indigenization of the Salafi discourse as it has entered the American environment. Over the course of the four decades since Salafism came to American shores, Salafis and Salafi-adjacent communities have grown ever more fluent in the American vernacular. The thematic connection between Thomas Reid and Ify Okoye and Tarek Mehanna may be as unexceptional as the fact that Ify and Mehanna are *Americans*, breathing in an American intellectual biosphere oxygenated by Scottish Common Sense. I would even contend, based on the divergent examples of Waleed Basyouni in the last chapter and Tarek Mehanna here, that 9/11 acted as an accelerant of this idiomatic appropriation – the intimidating government scrutiny, the need to transmute Salafi discourse into less expatriate language, and the responsive establishment of post-Salafi institutions like AlMaghrib have given these communities a crash course in *speaking American*.

MIMESIS: THE AMERICAN EVANGELICAL PRECEDENT

All of this leads us to our third theory. We can see that Salafism has been bequeathed a reachably rational theological temperament from Ibn Taymiyya, which has become accelerated and transliterated as "common sense" within America's abiding Scottish Realist climate. What about the possibility of Salafis seeing and imitating the blending of American common sense and scripture from Evangelicals?

If the rhetorical markers of Scottish Realism are still vaguely detectable in American culture in general, American Evangelicalism has kept the Scottish Realist flame alive with a particular passion. The advent of Scottish Common Sense as the *"lingua franca* of American intellectual life until after the Civil War"* meant that the style and reasoning of the Scottish Philosophy was adopted across the board by American Protestants, evangelical and traditional alike.[52] A major part of Reid and his cohort's motive for gainsaying and undercutting Hume was theological: They feared that Hume's skepticism would enfeeble all confident belief and epistemically hollow out

Christian faith. If Hume's "science of man" and other forms of Enlightenment rationalism contributed to the growth of atheism and deism, Scottish Common Sense provided "precisely the kind of apologetic philosophy that Christians in the Age of Reason needed."[53] The anti-scholastic, anti-clerical, anti-hierarchical dispositions of the Protestant Reformations, amplified by the individualized spirituality and direct-to-the-Bible ethos of the Great Awakening, made a diverse Protestant colonial public magnetized to a respectable way to participate in the Enlightenment fervor without abandoning their basic theological premises.

Antebellum American Christians of all stripes embraced this rhetoric of common sense as a way of holding together faith, republicanism, and intellectual respectability. It is worth remembering that the eminent, historic American universities of today were, in the early nineteenth century, principally still operating as denominational seminaries: Yale for Congregationalists, Harvard for Unitarians, Brown for Baptists, Princeton for Presbyterians. As the "Scottish Philosophy" took pride of place in all of these foundational theological institutions of America, Scottish-style Common Sense "defined mental habits for Protestants North and South, for dignified urban ministers and enterprising preachers on the frontier, for sober doctrinal conservatives and populist democratic polemicists."[54]

Indeed, the preaching of the Second Great Awakening, the revivalist engineering of Charles G. Finney, the surge in American biblicism that were the historical antecedents of Evangelicalism were all expedited in the provincial dialect of common sense. [55] As I laid out in Chapter 3, Finney's down-home rhetoric and plain-sense biblical acclamations, his mastery of the *"language of common life,"* were the basis for his popularity and success, and all of these could truly flourish as they did particularly in a culture steeped in Scottish Realism.

After the Civil War, as American intellectual life opened up, as the Scottish Philosophy fell out of vogue, modernizing Protestants (who would eventually title themselves "Mainline") followed the culture and explored greener idealist philosophical pastures, but one tribe of Americans remained true believers in Reidian Common Sense: Fundamentalists and Evangelicals. The Scottish Realists continued to be read and studied in Fundamentalist and Evangelical seminaries and colleges well into the mid-twentieth century, decades after they had disappeared from non-evangelical academies.[56] "Thus the Common Sense philosophy, with its confidence in the rational judgments of ordinary people, became fused with the American evangelical heritage."[57] Generation after generation of lay Evangelicals have been empowered by common sense to pick up their Bibles and start studying and interpreting, giving evangelical culture and oration in the twentieth and twenty-first centuries an aura of "timewarp – a subculture holding to principles of thought that the larger culture had dismissed."[58] In Mark Noll's analysis, "the Common Sense tradition has not so much provided American evangelicals with theological principles as it has given distinctive shape to the style, the apologetics, and the biblical shape of an already existing faith."[59] To paraphrase that in the language of this book: Common sense is less the superstructure of Evangelical theology than the idiom of Evangelical discourse.

I cannot resist observing a historical correlate: The intuitively rational, but soundly religious feminism of Ify Okoye is by no means unprecedented. In accord with Rosenfeld's observation above about common sense accrediting marginal voices, countless American Evangelical women have used culturally resonant appeals to commonsense knowledge and to the plain meaning of the Bible to challenge the patriarchal customs of America (and American Evangelical Christianity) and argue for their rights and equality. One who especially comes to mind vis-à-vis Ify is Hannah Whitall Smith, whose 1875 devotional book *The Christian's Secret of a Happy Life* has been cherished by generations of Evangelicals. Smith, whose later works include *Everyday Religion, or the Common-Sense Teaching of the Bible*, never mentions Reid or the other Scottish Realists, so far as I can tell, but, like Finney, her power to persuade hinges on an intellectual culture shaped by the Scottish Philosophy.[60] Though Smith had no formal religious training to speak of, she masterfully used her down-to-earth, practical-wisdom-from-the-Bible stylings to carve out a respected religious authority and a reading audience in postbellum America. Feeling ensnared in an unhappy marriage, she became one of the principal American women leaders in "temperance, women's suffrage, and improving the plight of all women, near and far."[61] Toward the end of her life, Smith wrote a theological autobiography titled *The Unselfishness of God*, where she, quite at odds with most turn-of-the-century evangelical theology, maternalizes God, drawing on her own experience as a mother to intuitively discern "the mother-heart of God" that embraces all of humanity.[62] Like her earlier works, Smith's feminist manifesto is littered with references to the Bible and, in one of Smith's favorite phrases, "plain common-sense."[63] Smith died in 1911, a lifetime before Ify would be born, but they are both instances in a long succession of American women empowered from the margins by commonsense scripturalism.

So ... are American Salafis just mimicking the discourse of Evangelicals? While I would hesitate to put it that baldly, such a possibility cannot be dismissed out of hand, as American culture is replete with Evangelical biblical reasoning. Anyone who has ever driven through rural America scanning for a stable radio station – or clicked through local television channels just about anywhere in America – knows the experience of encountering an Evangelical preacher mid-sermon. Moreover, methodological borrowing, especially in an entrepreneurial religious field, is a regular occurrence.[64] A number of recent analyses of Salafis (and other religious media figures) in the Arab world have noted the rise of a form of what Yasir Qadhi himself has called "Islamic televangelism" that patently models itself on televised religious preaching pioneered by Western Evangelicals.[65] Anecdotally, Umar Lee confidently told me (his sourcing itself appeared secondhand) about Muhammad Alshareef, the founder of AlMaghrib, studying Prosperity Gospel, Evangelical-lite preachers like Joel Osteen and Benny Hinn, not just for their preaching style but to imitate their business models with his own enterprises.[66] These ambitious, public-facing, proselytizing scripturalist discourses are not hermetically sealed but are intensely public, and the Salafis I've met are highly aware of Evangelicals and their influence in America. How could they not be?

On a more human and lived-identity level, many American converts to Islam, like Ify and Umar Lee, grew up in Christian and Evangelical families and churches. Lee, who was raised in a Southern Baptist church, laughingly opines to me that the best American Muslim preachers are the converts/reverts who grew up in church:

> You know the African Americans, like a Shadeed Muhammad [an imam in Philadelphia and Islamic University of Medina graduate], I mean, he grew up in church, so there's a certain knowledge of delivery and stuff ... I grew up with fire-and-brimstone Baptists. Those were good preachers ... And that's why a Siraj Wahhaj [an imam in Brooklyn who studied at another Saudi university] gets so popular – he can preach. He grew up in the Baptist church. Suhaib [Webb, a former AlMaghrib instructor, whose grandfather was an Evangelical preacher] can preach – grew up in the church.[67]

No one epitomizes this Evangelical-Salafi transference so well as Yusha (Joshua) Evans. He was raised Evangelical; participated in Young Life, an Evangelical parachurch ministry for high school students; and was planning on attending Bob Jones University, the prototypical conservative Evangelical-Fundamentalist Bible college. Yet, after discovering many inconsistencies while repetitively reading the Bible, he found himself disillusioned with his Christian faith. He eventually discovered the Qur'an, converted pre-9/11, and is now a Salafi preacher who travels around the USA narrating his testimony to Muslim groups with a lecture titled "How the Bible Led Me to Islam: The Story of a Former Christian Youth Minister."[68] Evans is my age, and we grew up in the same 1990s subculture of conservative Evangelicalism. I attended some Young Life meetings in high school. I share some of his disgruntlement with the conception of the Bible

I was taught as a child. I can picture myself on a path like his, making a lateral move like his. I would say that Yusha Evans changed religion and swapped scriptures, but he traded scripturalism for scripturalism, commonsense discourse for commonsense discourse.

In truth, the ubiquity of Evangelical biblicism and commonsensical appeals in America means that our last two theories – of *osmosis* (soaking up the lingering droplets of Scottish Realism in American culture in general) and *mimesis* (consciously or subconsciously imitating efficacious Evangelical entreaties to workaday wisdom and scripture) – can bleed and blend together. In fact, surveys consistently find that approximately 17 percent of American Muslims will also mark that they are "'born again' or evangelical" in addition to being Muslim![69] Who knows how many of these "evangelical Muslims" are reverts or are Salafi or Salafi-adjacent? I offer it merely as a sign of how religious language and identities are fluid and fill the shape of the cultural and phraseological setting into which they are poured. Recasting an image from Michael Muhammad Knight that I quoted in Chapter 2 about the blurred borders between Salafism and other strands of American Islam: "Ideas and practices can dig tunnels under the borders, and not every [Salafi] who expresses a[n] [Evangelical]-influenced thought would necessarily identify that thought as '[Evangelical].'"[70]

CONCLUSION

This chapter has been a wild ride, bounding from Ibn Taymiyya to Tarek Mehanna to Yusha Evans, from Thomas Reid to Hannah Whitall Smith to Ify Okoye. Idiom is an ephemeral and elusive quarry to track. Let me see if I can tie it all together here. The echoes I heard when I first encountered American Salafis centered on a stylistic convergence, a commonsense American dialect that links notions of innate rationality to scriptural interpretation, first engendered among Evangelicals and now, somehow, replicated among Salafis. My aim in the foregoing analysis is to interrogate that "somehow" – how is it that we find Salafis in America picking up, playing with, retooling, and deploying idioms of commonsense scripturalism that have a 250-plus year history of association with American Evangelicalism? I will close with three points.

First, drawing together this chapter's analysis with Chapter 2, when we think about Evangelicalism and Salafism as discourses rather than as neatly bounded theologies or movements of explicit belonging, we can begin to take note of the amorphous mutations and hybrids that form at their boundaries. Just as Evangelicalism merges and mingles with other permutations of Christianity, just as Salafism merges and mingles with other permutations of Islam, so too, Evangelicalism and Salafism can merge and mingle with each other in a mutual cultural and dialectical environment. Evangelicals in America have welded together common sense and scriptural interpretation for centuries. Salafism's rational theological anthropology, courtesy of Ibn Taymiyya, primed the pump for Salafis in America to appropriate the American dialect of common sense that emerged from Scottish Realism. The mimetic influence of American Evangelicalism on Salafism is probably the most speculative of the three theories outlined here, but, especially when the phenomena of conversion with figures like Ify Okoye, Umar Lee, and Yusha Evans comes into view, we can see specific paths that the idiom may have trod. They are embodied figures of colloquial transmutation.

Second, we saw in Chapter 4 that Evangelicalism and Salafism can have quite sophisticated scholarly expressions, in which scripturalist intellectuals may retain their originalist assumptions and literalist hermeneutics, but they can hold their own in any Christian or Muslim religious-academic environment. Yet the pedagogical ambitions of Salafism and Evangelicalism, particularly in an egalitarian and literate cultural space like America, stretch them to build vast educational networks of amateur scripture handlers. This chapter substantiates that, in America, the rhetoric and theologization of common sense has been a major means of articulating, facilitating, and justifying this dispersal of knowledge and interpretation. Common sense bridges the trained world of scholars, shaykhs, and pastors with the dabbling or asymptotically learning world of the students of knowledge. To borrow a phrase from Ify, common sense serves as the "baseline ... be[ing] able to discern through the use of your God-given critical thinking capacity." For the American Scripture People (of both varieties), what separates the religious elites from the multitude is knowledge, not capacity; it's training, not intelligence. Common sense is the lay-person-empowering, scripture-is-accessible, grassroots-activating hook and loop of the scripturalist discourses.

Third, I would be remiss not to remark here, after long observation, that there is a latent problem with all of this talk of common sense, and it is signposted in the conflicts Ify has encountered: *There is no such thing as common sense.* Or, to nuance it a bit, common sense is local and communal. As the Jesuit philosopher and theologian Bernard Lonergan has remarked, "there are very many brands of common sense. Common sense is common, not to all men [and women] of all places and times, but to the members of a community successfully in communication with each other."[71] In other words, common sense is objectively not a universal, ahistorical human sensibility that unfailingly guides all people to the same conclusions. Common sense is discursive and colloquial. Common sense is consensus.

Ify's common sense leads her and her friends to protest the injustice of the "penalty box," where many other American Muslim men *and women* see nothing objectionable there. Tarek Mehanna's common sense impels him to advocate defensive jihad by Muslims in Iraq and Afghanistan, and he is exasperated that his fellow Americans (much less his fellow American Muslims) can't all see his irrefutable logic. On some level, common sense is a fine thing to assert in practical arguments over everyday concerns, but it is a pretty thin epistemic basis for a philosophical, theological, or moral system.

There's an aphorism that I've heard all my life and that Yasir Qadhi recited to me in one of our interviews: Common sense isn't so common.[72] It's an attempt to explain the gap between the theory of common sense and the fact of perpetual, thoroughgoing disagreement among otherwise "sensible" people. But it's worse than that. On this point, at least, David Hume was correct: Human beings may have some base ability to instinctually reason, but everything, *everything*, that enters our minds is affected by the idiosyncrasies of our being, our passions, desires, upbringing, habits of mind, communities of belonging, theological presuppositions, and quirks. We can sort ourselves into communities where there is so much inferential overlap that it feels like common sense – I grew up in a community like that. The assumptions, the particular biblical interpretations, the understandings of sexuality, the image of America as a Christian nation – all of this felt self-evident to me, until I stepped out of that small corner of Southern California Evangelicalism.

By enlisting and staking so much of their interpretive assuredness on notions and rhetoric of common sense, the Scripture People *do* empower and invigorate the masses, but they also sacrifice communal coherence. Ironically, the very universal that Salafis and Evangelicals beseech – innate human rationality – fractures and fragments the movements. When tradition is pushed aside in favor of the direct sacred text, when both sides in an interpretive debate agree on the import and plainness of that text, and when both sides are invoking common sense, there is no way of adjudicating disagreements. There is no higher court of appeal.

Who speaks for Evangelicalism? What structures Salafi thought? Ify learned from Salafism to trust her rational *fiṭra*, but what happens when her innate rationality and her most fundamental sense of herself as a gay woman puts her at odds with almost everyone else in the AlMaghrib community? That is the topic of our final chapter.

7 Can We Call Salafism (or Evangelicalism) a Movement?

Things were simpler when the Skrift town charter was written. The residents were enthusiastic about the experiment in direct democracy upon which they were embarking. The town would have no mayor or judge or formal hierarchy, but instead a civic council of rotating elected citizens would adjudicate all disputes and guide the community through consensus and persuasion. Any major decision could come before the whole township in a referendum. Since the detailed town charter had been passed unanimously by all citizens, there was trust that, in perpetuity, any disagreement among the Skrift folk would be resolved straightforwardly through reference to the charter. Sentiments abounded that the plain meaning of the charter, which, after all, had been written by and for the people, combined with the steady, collective wisdom of the community, would keep everything on the right track.

Things began to spiral within a few years. There was an ambiguity in one clause of the charter where the absence of a comma led to two conflictual readings on the question of expanding Skrift's borders. The majority of the council determined that such a change would require the whole town's vote, but one council member, an entrepreneurial businesswoman who had already purchased land and begun building a shopping center traversing the town border, read the charter as inscribing her business in all the rights and privileges of the town. She was not alone – a number of her fellow citizens and employees saw it as clearly *right there* in the charter that the adjoining property be included. After months of disputes, and when she could see no way past her fellow council members' "ridiculous" reading of the charter, unable to individually convene a general vote, she determined to take her group of supporters and secede. Their new adjacent town would preserve the same charter – after all, it *was* unanimous and clear – as they built a new democratically governed village abutting Skrift.

This process repeated itself: Everyone loved the perspicuous charter, but, as disagreements arose, as interpretive tempers flared, as interests diverged, as the personalities of council members and prominent citizens came to the fore, divergent understandings of the Skrift charter proliferated. Time and again groups broke off – splinter towns splintered again, new neighborhoods formed their own municipalities, and each and every one would readopt the same charter, but their own parochial, "obvious" reading of that shared text would govern their tiny democracy.

It didn't happen fast, but over several generations, the birds-eye view of the Skrift landscape showed something quite striking; what had once been a coherent town with a central square where all could gather was now an archipelago of small, decentralized villages. Over time, the core principles of consensus and charter originalism had fractured and gerrymandered the community, so that each autonomous village was populated by those who abided within that village's agreed-upon reading of the charter. They were all governed by that same initial text but by wildly different understandings of it. The citizens of the villages would generally socialize with one another, and business and interchange continued among them. There was still a vaguely identifiable Skriftian character to the region, but inter-village debates about the charter always surfaced intramural quarrels and subterranean fault lines. The core similarity that connected and affiliated all the Skrift folk was simultaneously the very thing that left them internally frayed and discordant.

I use this parable to depict a conundrum I've been puzzling over since I first stepped out of Evangelicalism. I've been mulling over it even more intensely since I started studying and conversing with America's Salafis. To read much of the extant media coverage and a good deal of the academic analysis of Evangelicals and Salafis is to be left with two contradictory impressions. On the one hand, many in-anutshell analyses assert, Evangelicals are unified by shared experiences (i.e., being born again), shared theological claims, shared purposes, shared politics, and, most of all, a shared, vaguely literalist approach to the Bible. This is borne out by the socio-graphic evidence with 22 percent of Americans (a number that is arrestingly close to where most demographers would peg Evangelical adherence) agreeing with the statement: "The Bible is the actual word of God and is to be taken literally, word for word."[1] Likewise, news and scholarly articles that touch on Salafism teem with descriptions about what conjoins Salafis: esteem for the thought of Ibn Taymiyya; anti-Sufi attitudes; valuing the model of the Salaf over intermediating traditions and *madhhabs*; and, most concretely, a direct and literal approach to interpreting the Hadith and the Qur'an. Reading these descriptions, you are left with the firm impression that to use the terms Salafism and Evangelicalism is to speak about coherent theological and behavioral communities of religious believers marching, more or less, in lock step in accordance with their interpretation of their sacred texts.

On the other hand, just to dip your toes into the discussions among Salafis and among Evangelicals, even in a fairly delimited cultural space like America, is to discover a raging ferment of dispute and disagreement and manifest heterogeneity. Salafis who are ostensibly reading and citing *the same* texts and professedly using *the same* methods and interpretive assumptions reach radically different conclusions. As different as Waleed cooperating with the FBI and Anwar declaring jihad on America, as different as Ify and her friends protesting for women's Sunna-equality in the mosque and many other female mosque attendees disparaging them for being troublemakers. As Yasir Qadhi, wearing his academic hat, puts it, "What you find, actually, is very, very diverse, contradictory, and competing claims of truth within the movement, to the extent that, at times, what separates these strands within Salafism is more significant than what unites them."[2] The same, or at least a consonant, phenomenon is evident among Evangelicals, where we can see what Christian Smith has termed "pervasive interpretive pluralism": "[t]he undeniable fact of entrenched, ubiquitous disagreements among biblicists about what scripture teaches on most issues, large and small."[3] American Evangelicals may agree that the Bible is a clear document and a reliable guide for life, but the movement is internally fractured, roiled by debates about the different "literal" meanings individuals and communities find in the Bible.

Attempts to comprehensively taxonomize all of the different sub-groupings of Salafis and Evangelicals result in a sort of reductio ad absurdum: How do you enumerate the clusters of grass in a verdant field? One effort to categorize the different strands of Evangelicalism in the 1970s came up with fourteen "subcultural evangelical groups," and even there the author admits that his project is by no means exhaustive, with countless further subdivisions possible.[4] Think of all of the different flavors of Salafism we have seen in the preceding chapters: the paramosque devotional education of AlMaghrib; the African American Salafism that can have a polemical Madkhali mood or not; the entrepreneurialism of Muhammad Alshareef that is reproducing Prosperity Gospel preaching and life-coaching salesmanship; the disillusioned and eloquent jihadism of Anwar al-Awlaki; the incorporationist Americanism of Waleed Basyouni; the academically respectable post-Salafism of Yasir Qadhi; the Ex-vangelical certitude of Yusha Evans; the enterprising hipsterism of Saad Tasleem; the outraged global citizenry of Tarek Mehanna; and, of course, the *fiṭra* feminism of Ify Okoye. All of these people are ostensibly in the Salafi discourse, interpreting and applying the Qur'an and Hadith and living within the bounds of American culture, but their inhabitations and interpretations of Salafism vary staggeringly.

This decentralized, rhizomatic, discursive temperament means that Salafism and Evangelicalism do not move like movements – coordinated and unified – but rather they operate more like a flock of birds, splitting and merging, moving somehow in every direction at once. To steal a splendidly onomatopoetic word from ornithology: Salafism and Evangelicalism are less movements and more

ILLUSTRATION 7.1 A flock of starlings (murmuration)

murmurations, the cacophonous and chaotically beautiful dancing flight of a flock of starlings (see Illustration 7.1).

This also means, as we have seen in the many case studies of the preceding chapters, that these movements are also highly susceptible and adaptable to their environments. Without an arboreal trunk or deep root structure, the grass grows in any salutary direction. Without a set flight plan or single leader, the flock murmurates and gyrates and whirls to and fro around the sky.

In this final chapter, I want to audit this process of scriptural-interpretive topsy-turviness by following a debate that has fragmented both communities of American Scripture People in the 2010s: gay inclusion and gay marriage. To the arms-length observer, gay rights and gay inclusion would seem to be the rare issue on which all Salafis and all Evangelicals are unanimous in opposition. Though neither Salafism nor Evangelicalism is premised on the authority of tradition (see Chapter 3), Evangelicals and Salafis can both draw upon (until recently) almost universal customs of scriptural interpretation in their respective Western Christian and Sunni traditions that reject homosexual behavior. There is very, very little in the Qur'an or Hadith or the Christian Bible that has historically been construed as being accepting of homosexuality. Moreover, the idiomatic consolidation of American Evangelicals and Salafis around appeals to common sense should presumably serve as a bulwark against incorporating any new understandings of gender and sexuality. As Clifford Geertz notes in his sharp essay on common sense that I highlighted in the previous chapter, conventions around sexuality and gender are among the most common of commonsensical postulations: "the network of practical and moral conceptions woven about those supposedly most rooted of root realities: maleness and femaleness."[5]

Nonetheless, the porousness, the malleability of these scripturalist discourses means that, as the American public's views on gay rights and gay marriage have dramatically flipped over the past few decades, there have been correspondent shifts inside Salafi and Evangelical communities. We can see LGBTQ individuals coming out of the closet within communities of Evangelicals and Salafis, upholding their queer identities with commonsense and scriptural arguments, and finding allies there. And we see countervailing forces pushing back. What I aim to offer here is not some grand thesis about the inevitable future of LGBTQ inclusion and affirmation by mainstream Salafis and Evangelicals – that is far from certain. Instead, I want to use these debates to anatomize two cases of evolution and adaptation: How is it that a new local consensus, a mutation in the body scripturalist, a new outlying village still holding to the scriptural charter, forms?

THE TURNING TIDE OF AMERICAN COMMON SENSE ABOUT HOMOSEXUALITY

It is difficult to overstate how fast the shift in American public opinion on gay rights and gay marriage has been in the early twenty-first century. In 1988, the biennial General Social Survey speculatively asked about approval of gay marriage, finding that a mere 11 percent of all Americans agreed that "homosexuals should have

[the] right to marry." Yet as the USA entered a new millennium and the topic of gay rights came more and more to the fore, we see an accelerating trend line every time the question was asked: 35 percent approve in 2006, 48 percent in 2012, 68 percent in 2018. The data also show an extraordinary shift in how young people (age 18–34) view the issue, so that, by 2018, 79 percent supported gay marriage and only 13 percent opposed it.[6] Coupled with this (or, perhaps, *driven by* this) climactic change in American attitudes was the landmark Supreme Court *Obergefell* v. *Hodges* decision in 2015 that ruled that it was a constitutional right for same-sex couples to marry.

Now imagine the experience of that rapidly changing reality *from within culturally conservative religious communities.* In my childhood in the 1980s, a small fraction of Americans supported gay marriage and gay rights. Gay marriage especially was seen as a fringe political cause, a talking point used by Religious Right mobilizers to stoke Evangelical and Fundamentalist fears, but a nonetheless very remote possibility. By my thirties in the 2010s, a solid and ever-growing majority had reoriented in favor of it. Hidden in these numbers are tens of millions of changed minds, legions of transformed perspectives (including my own) in apprehending the dignity of – and supporting full equality for – gay people.

Following on the last chapter's attention to the historical role of common sense in American discourse, it is perhaps unsurprising that these tidal shifts around Americans' understandings of gay dignity and gay marriage were also verbalized in the idiom of common sense. In the Pew Research Center's massive Religious Landscape survey, conducted in 2007 and again in 2014, the demographers actually included a question about where Americans look for guidance on right and wrong, with four options: religion, philosophy/reason, common sense, or science. The lingering effects of Scottish Realism on America are still evident here with a majority (52 percent) of respondents in 2007 and a plurality (45 percent) in 2014 saying that they look primarily to common sense to guide their morality.[7]

What is fascinating – given the point that I was arguing at the end of the previous chapter that common sense is actually just malleable, provincial consensus – is that when you correlate the answers of those Americans who prioritize common sense in determining morality from 2007 to 2014, you can see, in plain numbers, American common sense around homosexuality shifting and re-sorting in a relatively short period of time. What we find is that in 2007, among those Americans who said that common sense was their primary guide on moral questions, 59 percent thought that homosexuality "should be accepted." By 2014, that number had jumped to 72 percent of commonsense Americans supporting gay inclusion and dignity. Though Pew's researchers did not ask about gay marriage in 2007, they did ask about it in 2014 and found that 63 percent of Americans who prioritize commonsense morality also support same-sex marriage. Even more telling: Across the board among all the different forms of moral guidance – religion, philosophy/reason, common sense, or science – the majority (53 percent) of the people who said they favor gay marriage were those in the common sense camp.

What the professional watchers of public opinion were observing throughout the first two decades of the twenty-first century was a sea change in American views on social acceptance of gay people and societal acceptance of gay marriage. In what might be one of the fastest moral thought revolutions in American history, what would have seemed commonsensical and upstandingly moral to a middle-of-the-road American born in the 1970s about the unacceptability and need for exclusion of gay people from the institution of marriage, was, for the average child born in the first decade of the twenty-first century, the exact opposite – that the full inclusion, equal rights, and human dignity of gay people was obvious, uncontroversial, and anything less would be immoral.

Public opinion, common sense, and the Supreme Court were all trending in the same direction, instantiating a new consensus in American culture at large. But what about the common sense morality that obtained among the scripturalists? How did Evangelicals and

Salafis – who, to reiterate, had no precedent for a major reversal in their conventional thinking about human sexuality in either theology or epistemology – respond to this turning tide of broader American opinion?

MATTHEW VINES' "CREDIBLE" CASE

In March 2012, twenty-one-year-old Matthew Vines delivered a lecture at a church in his hometown of Wichita, Kansas titled "The Gay Debate: The Bible and Homosexuality," which he then posted as a video on YouTube.[8] In the sixty-seven-minute video, Vines is visibly nervous, but also steadfast, offering an emotional and biblical argument that makes a positive case for Bible-believing Christians to affirm monogamous gay marriage. Vines, who had a conservative Evangelical background and had been an undergraduate at Harvard University, dropped out of college for a year prior to the lecture in order to grapple with his internal awareness of being gay and to reconcile that awareness with his Evangelical faith and understanding of the Bible. Six months after the lecture, when the *New York Times* published a profile of Vines in its Fashion section, the video had accumulated more than 350,000 views, occasioned almost 7,000 YouTube comments, and been translated into six different languages.[9] Vines' video, and his follow-up book *God and the Gay Christian: The Biblical Case in Support of Same-Sex Relationships*, which was published two years later, crashed like a powerful wave against the sea wall of biblical common sense in American Evangelical culture.

What made Vines' approach to understanding gayness vis-à-vis the Bible compelling to so many people was its straight-over-home-plate, Evangelical pitch. He weaves together personal testimony and Bible talk. Walking the viewer through each biblical passage that has been used to condemn gay people, he delves into the Greek and Hebrew and original context to find new ways of reading the verses that defang them of their anti-gay bite. At no point in the lecture (and only sparingly in the book) does he cite elite theologians or appeal to any authority or interpreter outside of the Bible itself. To be sure, the vast majority of Vines' arguments are not original; after all, the lecture and book are the work of an adept undergraduate. Instead, he draws heavily on interpretations and exegesis prefigured by a number of gay-affirming theologians from progressive and liberal Protestant traditions.[10] Vines' ingenuity lies in how he translates these ideas and interpretations into the Evangelical idiom, invoking Evangelical shibboleths about the Bible. As he writes,

> many Christians now support same-sex relationships. But those who do tend to see Scripture as a helpful but dated guidebook, not as the final authority on questions of morality and doctrine.
>
> That is not my view of Scripture.
>
> Like most theologically conservative Christians, I hold what is often called a "high view" of the Bible. That means I believe all of Scripture is inspired by God and authoritative for my life.[11]

Vines is locking in his Evangelical bona fides. He invokes his "high view" of the Bible over and against other less biblically loyal, pro-gay interpreters. He labels himself "theologically conservative," knowing that the immediate charge that could be used by some to discard his argument is that he is simply a theological liberal pretending to care about the authority of the Bible. He knows that his interpretation of the Bible is running against the consensus of the vast majority of the Evangelical community, and he is seeking a fair hearing. Indeed, he summarizes his project thus:

> My goal has not been to break new ground, but to bring credible, often-overlooked insights to light, and to synthesize those insights in clear and accessible ways for a broad audience ... *Christians who affirm the full authority of Scripture can also affirm committed, monogamous same-sex relationships.*[12]

There is another, subtler message here: The implication of these passages and, indeed, of Vines' lecture and book overall, is that there is some sub-sect of Evangelicals who *want* to be able to read the Bible in a gay-affirming way. His search for a "credible" argument implies that there is a credulous and willing audience. In Vines' own lifetime, the American cultural consensus has congealed around favoring gay rights, and Vines is offering Evangelicals a plausible – *"can also affirm"* – path to their participation in that broader cultural communal sensibility.

His argument targets the heart of the Evangelical discourse – not the scholars but the educated and scripturally literate lay person. In his action steps at the end of the book for gay-affirming Christians who hope to influence their churches toward their own views, he counsels, "I encourage you to lead a careful study of Scripture before asking people to change their position ... Invite church members to participate in a Bible study to explore the issue."[13] Could there be anything more Evangelical? Vines sends people, lay people, invested students of knowledge, back to the Bible to discuss it again.

Indeed, Vines' intuition that there is a willing audience for such biblical, inclusive, pro-gay messages among Evangelicals is corroborated in the Religious Landscape surveys: In 2014, Pew found that 28 percent of Evangelicals were supportive of legalizing gay marriage and 36 percent of Evangelicals thought homosexuality "should be accepted by society." Tellingly, those Evangelicals who look first to common sense for their guidance on moral questions were more likely to support gay rights and inclusion: 43 percent supported legalizing gay marriage and a majority (53 percent) thought homosexuality should be accepted.[14] American Evangelical common sense, because it is *American*, is permeable to the broader cultural consensus.

To be sure, there is a difference between accepting homosexuality or gay marriage at a societal or civic level and theologically embracing gay people (e.g., allowing gay marriage ceremonies or openly gay leaders in one's church), a distinction that is not captured in many surveys' phrasings. But Vines' search for a "credible"/"can also affirm" biblical argument in favor of gay marriage and inclusion in Evangelical churches certainly found a receptive audience in many corners of American Evangelicalism, and he became one of the fore-most voices in the Evangelical discourse championing the cause.

Given what we've already seen of scripturalist pedagogical cul-ture, Vines represents a predictable mutation – a studious and articu-late lay person interpreting the Bible persuasively against the consensus of Evangelical scholars but in line with rapidly shifting, widespread American common sense – and the Evangelical shaykh class (if I may be so bold) reacted swiftly. As Vines' video gained popularity and reach, Evangelical pastors and Bible scholars took to their sermons, blogs, podcasts, and airwaves to refute Vines' argu-ments and interpretations. In their torrent of denunciations, many of his critics ambled again over the familiar ground of the same Bible passages, quibbling with his hermeneutics, his use of Greek and Hebrew, his contextualizations, his lack of formal credentials. But Vines' basic Evangelical premises – that this debate hinged on the Bible and easily accessible rationality alone – went unquestioned.[15]

For instance, one of Vines' more prominent early critics was James R. White, an Evangelical apologist and garrulous online debater. Within weeks of Vines' video emerging on YouTube, White took to his radio show and podcast to spend five hours refuting Vines' lecture. He plays Vines' YouTube recording in full, pausing after every few sentences to add his own gloss of interpretation and rebuttal. White – who had a decade earlier written a book attacking gay-affirming theology via the "clear teaching of the Bible" – backhandedly compli-ments the much younger man for having given an "erudite speech," and then proceeds to, somewhat mockingly, take Vines' thesis apart piece by piece.[16] White rehashes the same passages as Vines, asserting his own conventional reading, while rejecting Vines' interpretations as an "excellent example of the kind of handling of the scripture that is absolutely necessary for those who would turn the moral system of the scripture on its head, and that's exactly what someone who would call themselves a 'gay Christian' [is] doing."[17]

A more substantial and scholastic response to Vines' book came in the form of an e-book, written collectively by a group of professors from the Southern Baptist Theological Seminary, titled *God and the Gay Christian? A Response to Matthew Vines*. The book is edited and introduced by Albert Mohler, president of SBTS, and a theologian whom *Time* magazine once (questionably) called the "reigning intellectual of the evangelical movement in the US."[18] The arguments put forward in the e-book are, like White's, unsurprising: that the plain sense of the Bible and the history of Christian interpretation denounce homosexuality. What is noteworthy about the book is not its innovative arguments, but its ambient, apprehensive awareness of the shifting sands of Evangelical consensus on this matter. As Mohler warns,

> There are a great host of people, considered to be within the larger evangelical movement, who are desperately seeking a way to make peace with the moral revolution and endorse the acceptance of openly gay individuals and couples within the life of the church. Given the excruciating pressures now exerted on evangelical Christianity, many people – including some high-profile leaders – are desperately seeking an argument they can claim as both persuasive and biblical. The seams of the evangelical fabric are beginning to break, and Vines now comes along with a book that he claims will make the argument so many are seeking.[19]

This characterization of the grounds of the debate illumines the potency of Vines' plea: An articulate case for a biblical, gay-affirming theology, offered in an Evangelical idiom, could split the movement. Mohler is cagey on whether those fence-sitters who are craving a message like Vines' are really Evangelicals or merely "considered to be within the larger evangelical movement," but the book is written to win over that wavering crowd. Without resorting to White's polemical tone, Mohler can declare that Vines' "argument, however, is neither true nor faithful to Scripture."[20] Common sense and cultural consensus outside the Evangelical movement have already shifted on the issue of gay marriage, and Mohler makes shoring up the provincial consensus of the Evangelical community an utmost priority.

What fascinates me about this and several further exchanges between Vines and White and between Vines and the SBTS professors is that they are all conducted within the scripturalist horizons, with both sides acclaiming the Bible's full authority, debating about the same passages, and arguing that each has the correct, moral reading of the text. Both readings are lucid and rational and plausible, and neither is presented in bad faith. Yet the debate cannot be resolved, and the two sides speak past one another, because, despite their shared theological and hermeneutical commitments, what is common sense to Vines and what is common sense to White and the SBTS scholars cannot be reconciled.

When I left Evangelical ministry in 2010 to pursue a PhD studying Islam, I was already seeing a growing retrenchment among Evangelical communities and institutions against this rising tide of gay-affirming common sense. Some Evangelical churches and para-church institutions softened their stance on gay inclusion, a few even embraced gay marriage, but many Evangelical institutions circled the wagons. My own *alma mater*, Fuller Theological Seminary, long considered one of the more forward-leaning, ecumenical Evangelical schools in the country, after the *Obergefell* decision in 2015, began expelling any students it discovered were legally same-sex married.[21] Matthew Vines, for his part, has founded his own parachurch organization, The Reformation Project, whose vision is "a global church that honors Scripture and fully affirms LGBTQ people."[22] And so, a new, gay-affirming encampment in the landscape of American Evangelicalism is established, demanding enfranchisement, hailing the clarity of the original charter.

AN AMERICAN RIP VAN WINKLE IN MEDINA

Saajid Lipham's story recapitulates many tropes of the American Salafi experience we've seen over the last few chapters but with a twist. He grew up in Fort Meade, Maryland, a standard-issue, white, nominally Christian, military-family kid in the Baltimore-DC corridor. He was in high school on 9/11, and the attacks and the inconveniently increased security he saw all around him at Fort Meade left him with a low-grade negativity toward Islam: "To me it was just common sense that Islam was this religion of terrorist lunatics."[23]

When he went to a nearby public university, like many undergraduates, he began asking big philosophical questions and searching for meaning. He read various books, took college classes on religion and sought answers anywhere he could find. Then: "One night it just hit me – I just remembered my *fitra*. I remembered when I was young how natural and how sure I was that God existed. I remembered that feeling I had ... that innate understanding that there is a Creator, there is one God."[24] He started intently exploring Christianity and Judaism without finding any deeper insight there.

At some point he had the thought that he had never read the Qur'an, so he googled it, and started reading an English translation online. "As soon as I started reading this book, I knew that this was from the Creator ... I got chills. I knew as clear as day, as clear as the sun is bright, I knew ... this was what I had been looking for all these years ... It was reaffirming my *fitra*."[25] He converted in 2008, fell in with the American Salafis, and started doing *da'wa* – calling all his friends and family to Islam. By 2010, the same time that Ify's feminist activism in DC-area mosques was beginning to make waves, Lipham was leaving the USA to study at the Islamic University of Medina.

From 2010 to 2018, he was in Saudi Arabia, learning Arabic, getting a bachelor's in Salafi *da'wa* and theology, and then like dozens of American IUM *du'āt* (missionaries) before him, it was time to come back to America to spread the scriptural knowledge and faith, the love of the Qur'an, that had come to define his life. Like any entrepreneurial young *ustadh* looking to gain a following back in the States, while he was still in Medina, Lipham created a website, but he also made sure to create a YouTube channel to broadcast his scriptural and other insights. Online media had progressed since Ify's blogging days. Lipham's YouTube persona is casual and candid. With his long Salafi beard, most videos have him speaking straight to camera, often wearing a baseball cap, sometimes recording quick reflections from his car. But what strikes me most about Lipham's videos after his long sojourn in the heart of the global Salafi discourse is his tone: The best word I can find for it is *flabbergasted*.

Lipham has returned to an American post-Salafi scene that is unrecognizable compared to what he was learning in Medina. His fellow IUM alumni, many of whom graduated fifteen or twenty years earlier, are now running life-coaching organizations! Some of them are openly offering opinions and fatwas that make no reference to (and appear to contradict) the teachings of the Saudi shaykhs and scholars! Some of them, like Yasir Qadhi, have not only stopped calling themselves Salafis, but they've started working hand in hand with Sufis and with Traditional Muslims like the professors at Zaytuna College! AlMaghrib shaykhs are not only endorsing American presidential candidates – one of them is even speaking at Bernie Sanders rallies and leading prayers in the US House of Representatives! AlMaghrib shaykhs are forming local interfaith coalitions with rabbis and pastors and bringing their mosques into ongoing congregation-to-congregation interfaith partnerships! And most scandalous, in Lipham's view, many of his fellow IUM alums, the supposed leaders of Salafism in America, have softened their stances and rhetoric on LGBTQ issues! Lipham's mood vacillates through his frequent YouTube videos from bemused to outraged, as he tries to reconcile his own hot-off-the-press Saudi Salafi training with the reality on the ground in Salafi-adjacent America.

What happened in the eight years between when Saajid Lipman left for IUM and when he returned to America? Some of this story we know already: Yasir Qadhi's charismatic popularity has continued to grow as his Salafism metamorphoses into an ecumenical, nondenominational, conservative American Islam. Waleed Basyouni's open-hearted, culture-friendly leadership at AlMaghrib and Texas Dawah Convention has pulled some segments of American Salafi theo-politics further and further from the aggrieved exhortations of Anwar al-Awlaki or the Islamic State and more and more toward pluralist, democratic participation. But what about Lipham's foremost complaint: How did the American Salafi discourse lighten up about LGBTQ issues? For that part of the story, we need to return to Ify Okoye.

IFY'S STORY, CONTINUED

Ify was actually one of the hundreds of thousands of people who watched Matthew Vines' "The Bible and Homosexuality" lecture on YouTube. In 2012, she was grappling with her own decision of whether and when to come out of the closet. Her outright feminist activism and advocacy for women's equality in mosque prayers had already gotten her disinvited as a contributor to *Muslim Matters*, but she was also on track to finish her course of studies at AlMaghrib in the fall of 2012. There was no one in the AlMaghrib circle who was openly gay-affirming, especially not among the shaykhs. Ify was, by this point, inching toward publicly revealing her sexual orientation. In early 2012, she contributed a personal account of a romance she'd had with another Salafi woman to a volume titled *Love, InshAllah: The Secret Love Lives of American Muslim Women*. She published her story under a pseudonym, not quite ready to have her own gay identity see the light of day.[26]

Ify tells me, "I have always been gay. I tried very hard not to be, I tried to get married to some men, and I was like, 'OK, I'm just going to suppress this thing forever.'" At some point, as she recounts in the pseudonymous story, she decided that she was going to romantically pursue other women, even if she wasn't out of the closet. Looking back on it now, she registers a comic irony:

> One of the interesting things about conservative Muslim communities – and I think this is [true of] conservative communities, religious communities across the board, and it's maybe just the reality of the world: It was an incredible dating pool! Dar-us-Salaam, Dar al-Hijrah – there are so many gay women there in these really conservative communities, negotiating these same

things, trying to negotiate their faith and their identity. I think people never appreciate when I say that. Because they're like, "Yes, gender segregation" [intoning ominously], and I'm like, "Yes! Gender segregation is great for dating!" You know, generally, I'm very for equality and lack of segregation, but . . .[27]

Then, one Friday at prayers, the imam was exhorting the community to sign a petition for a statewide referendum banning gay marriage. This was certainly not the first anti-gay message Ify had heard in a Friday *khutba* (sermon), but it struck a chord in her that day. The imam recited a common wisecrack against gay marriage: "We all know that God made Adam and Eve, not Adam and Steve." (Even this little quip is evidence of idiomatic borrowing from Evangelicals among conservative American Muslims. It's a joke that only makes sense in English; moreover, while the figure of Eve is mentioned in the Qur'an's creation account, she is not named. In the Hadith, she is called Hawwā.[28]) Somehow, the confluence of this imam's joke, an exhortation about the importance of coming out of the closet from the lesbian newscaster Rachel Maddow, and her own pseudonymous story being published impelled Ify to bring her sexual identity out into the open.

She came out officially, naturally, on her blog. Her post is emphatic: After quoting Maddow and explaining her reasoning in coming out, her frustration with the homophobia she's seen in American Muslim spaces, and how she provisionally understands sexuality in relation to faith, Ify offers her own comeback to the imam's Adam and Eve joke: "God not only made Adam and Eve but he also made Steve and me." In other words, if you accept the idea that some people are born gay, then the joke doesn't make sense, because, by theistic definition, if something exists the creator must have created it. Ify resolutely ends the post: "I am not giving up my faith."[29] With such an overtly religious affirmation of her gayness by an AlMaghrib insider and influential blogger, Ify kindled a very public conversation in Salafi and post-Salafi communities in America about

LGBTQ inclusion, about the possibility of being unqualifiedly gay and Muslim, and about what is tolerable in theological and jurisprudential debate. She knew that on this front, even more than with her feminist provocations, she was way outside of the consensus of the community.

While some of Ify's friends and blog followers jumped into the comment thread on her post to affirm her choice to come out, she got a great deal of pushback from other commenters, from some *Muslim Matters* writers, and from friends who couldn't assimilate this newly revealed dimension of her. Even Ify's (male) ex-fiancé chimed into the comments to cite the Qur'an and some hadiths to prove that homosexuality is incompatible with Islam. I find it impressive how, in the comment section of her blog and in subsequent posts about her gay identity, Ify doesn't disengage. She patiently, levelheadedly, and personally deliberates with her critics, using scripture, theology, all of her AlMaghrib training, and her own irrefutable experience to explain how her queerness assimilates into the whole picture of her life.

Unlike Matthew Vines, Ify was already pretty well-versed in Islamic and Salafi theology and jurisprudence having spent the better part of a decade in AlMaghrib seminars, so she appeared comfortable theologically coming out without a verse-by-verse exegesis. She instead embraces her gayness paradoxically. For example, one commenter on her blog responded to Ify's original coming-out post with a quintessential scripturalist line of attack: "Why would there be verses in the Quran and hadiths that are apparently against homosexuality if people are born with a homosexual orientation? How do you personally deal with these verses and hadiths?" Ify responds,

> As a Muslim, I believe God has the most exalted and sublime attributes, among these include mercy, love, justice, and wisdom. Therefore, in my opinion, asking why God has chosen to do something is a bit beside the point. Once we accept these attributes, we accept that God as the Creator has created everything for a purpose, even if we don't fully understand it.[30]

This is actually a quite sophisticated interpolation that draws upon that defining Salafi debate from early Islam. This debate, going back to Ibn Taymiyya and Ibn Hanbal (see Chapter 1), surrounds how to interpret God's attributes and the Qur'an's apparently corporeal language – God sitting on a throne, God having a hand, etc. – without slipping into idolatry by casting God in humanity's image. The Salafi scripturalist theological reasoning goes that humans cannot logically resolve that tension, but instead should say, "We affirm the truth – the ẓāhir, the literal or plain meaning – of scripture's language about God and God's attributes, corporeal as it may appear, bilā kayfa [without asking how]." Human apprehension, Salafi theology reasons, is not the measure of God. In summary, Ify is arguing that God is God, God created her thus, and she accepts her gayness bilā kayfa – without asking how.

In the lead-up to her post and afterward as she debated with her online critics, Ify also found herself doing a good deal of reading in Christian and Jewish gay-affirming theology, which is where she encountered Matthew Vines' lecture. She found a lot of inspiration in the work of Orthodox rabbi Steven Greenberg, who had kicked up great controversy in his own community by coming out in 1999 and with his 2004 book Wrestling with God and Men: Homosexuality in the Jewish Tradition.[31] Many gay people who have come of age in conservative communities, when they come out, decide to seek out greener pastures and more liberal, gay-affirming communities, but what links Ify and Vines and Greenberg is that they did not. They chose to not leave their respective, culturally conservative religious communities, but instead to pull the discourses toward themselves – to publicly merge their scriptural-vernacular, community-of-belonging, and sexual identities. She tells me a story about a time, after she came out, that she was invited to offer the khutba (the sermon or exhortation) during Friday prayers at a progressive, LGBTQ-affirming mosque in Toronto. After the khutba, a woman came up to her and said, "Your khutba was very Salafi ... like the style." Ify says, "Because that's the style I know."[32]

After Ify came out of the closet, Yasir Qadhi reached out to her multiple times, trying to get her to retract or at least clarify her blog post. In her recounting,

> He tried to call me and tell me, "Ify, you have a standing here in the community. You're well known. You represent AlMaghrib. You represent *Muslim Matters*. People know you. I don't think this is a good idea ... I think you should write another post with all of these qualifications to say, even though you are attracted to women, you believe in the Qur'an and Sunna, and you believe [homosexuality] is a sin and a test and a trial ..." Just a whole bunch of nonsense, and I was like, "No thank you."[33]

As we talk, I do ask Ify about her view nowadays of the AlMaghrib shaykhs, the leaders she once esteemed so highly and followed around the country, and her response is respectful and cool at the same time:

> Being gay is part of who I am, and my faith is also part of who I am. I don't negotiate them anymore. I think that was really a challenge, to come to a place where I could say, "You know what? I hear Yasir and Waleed and Muhammad Alshareef and all these people in my ear, and they can't be my teachers *here*. They're not my teachers, because they have no experience with what I'm talking about." And they will always say, that you have to follow authority – "You've got to follow authority, you can't follow your desires ..."
>
> I don't accept that because of common sense; my *fiṭra* is telling me that that's not right. Like the way women are treated in mosques: not right. So I felt very comfortable just stepping out on my own, and actually it was very liberating psychologically to do so.[34]

Even this choice, to tune out the opinions of her teachers, can be understood as an extension of a principle that Yasir himself has emphatically articulated for preferring the opinions of local Western scholars who inhabit one's own context and experience over those who live overseas in far different cultural contexts. He advises:

> Who do we turn to for spiritual and moral guidance in times of
> crisis ... for these modern issues we're facing as a community? ...
> We need to start giving preference to our local people of knowledge,
> those who reside here and understand our situation ... There is
> "book knowledge," knowledge that has been discussed and
> codified ... but there is another type of knowledge, and that is the
> knowledge of the reality of the situation, and that knowledge
> cannot be studied in a book, it can only be experienced. Only those
> who are living in a land can understand the real pros and cons.[35]

He goes on (predictably) to invoke a precedent from the life of Ibn
Taymiyya as an example. Ify has evidently come to a similar conclusion as Yasir, except where he applies the principle of seeking out
scholars with experiential knowledge to geography and culture, she
extends the same principle to sexuality.

At the end of the day, the scriptural knowledge and the invocations of commonsense rationality that appealed to and empowered Ify
to become a consummate student of knowledge, an AlMaghrib
protégé, also empowered her to come out of the closet and forge a
Salafi-ish gay-affirming theology. Like Vines, she is in uncharted
waters, but Ify didn't start a new paramosque organization to advance
the cause. She's more content to stay out of the limelight.

She rarely attends mosque prayers anymore, in part because she
doesn't want to be "pushed into the women's space" and, in part,
because she knows she'll stand out. "I'm just going to show up in
jeans and a shirt, which is already putting you out there in these
conservative communities." When I ask her how she'd describe the
form of Islam she's practicing today, she fires back quickly, "DIY
[Do-it-yourself]."[36]

GAY RIGHTS, ALMAGHRIB, AND ALMAGHRIB 2.O

It is difficult to know the full impact of Ify's public coming out. From
the comments on her gay-positive blog posts, it's clear that they were
read by hundreds and probably thousands of Salafi-adjacent Muslims.

She's also obviously not the only gay American Muslim arguing for their own dignity and Islamic integrity, though she's the only one I've found doing so in such a clear Salafi accent. As I have previously observed, the relative smallness of the American Muslim population (roughly 1 percent of all Americans) combined with the limited set of questions that demographers tend to be interested in asking Muslims leave us without much fine-grained numerical insight into American post-Salafi and Salafi-adjacent communities. We do have *some* data about American Muslims in general though: Pew's Religious Landscape in 2014 found 42 percent of American Muslims supporting gay marriage (52 percent opposed), and a Public Religion Research Institute survey in 2018 found 51 percent supporting (34 percent opposed).[37] Similarly, the Institute for Social Policy and Understanding found in 2020 that 39 percent of American Muslims (as compared with 16 percent of white Evangelicals) support working in coalition with LGBTQ groups on shared political goals.[38] It is safe to say that the socially conservative Salafi-adjacent communities would fall on the less gay-friendly part of this spectrum, but these surveys do not usually distinguish among different types of Muslims and their samples of Muslims are often small enough that it's difficult to know how much to read into these numbers regarding American Salafism. No, to understand how post-Salafi communities in America have reacted to the gay inclusion and gay marriage debates, as with so much in this book, the best route at our disposal is to look at what was so troubling to Saajid Lipham, that Medinan Rip Van Winkle returning to his American homeland: We must look at the American post-Salafi institutions and thought leaders.

An indicative case for what Lipham is reacting against came up in one of my interviews with Waleed. I was observing to him how much homosexuality and debates about gay inclusion had become a live issue in the conservative American Muslim world in the late 2010s, and Waleed agreeingly volunteered a recent anonymous example: A graduate student at AlMaghrib was nearing completion of her degree, but she was also "an open, practicing lesbian." One of the program administrators approached Waleed, as director of the

Institute, to just hintingly double check that this was really going forward. Waleed relates their conversation:

> He said, "She's going to be graduating … She's going to have an Islamic studies degree from AlMaghrib Institute, and she's openly gay?"
>
> I said, "Did she finish all of her course materials?"
>
> And he said, "Yes."
>
> So I said, "I will sign her certificate. As simple as that."
>
> I think that's society, and that's the nuance. That's not my business what kind of sexual orientation she has, I'm not a judge over her.[39]

Waleed presents this story to me as a perfectly judicious, accommodating, commonsensical outcome, but, in truth, it represents a huge shift in approach from where AlMaghrib began. I doubt Saajid Lipham has heard this story, but I do not doubt that he would be scandalized by it.

For certain, Waleed's "none of my business" response is still quite a distance from a theological affirmation of gay identity of the sort Ify is advancing. Though when I relay Waleed's anecdote to her, she reflects:

> I think in the early 2000s if you had asked that question, they would have been like, "No, you're not getting the certificate." But the country changes. The Islam that was taught in pre-9/11 or just post-9/11 won't work with the community today … Waleed's even like, "Vote for Hillary" in 2016! The community changes as the culture changes … It's interesting to see.[40]

I will just observe in passing that Waleed's simple decision to let "an open, practicing lesbian" student complete her course of studies is a bridge that my own ostensibly forward-looking Evangelical *alma mater*, Fuller Seminary, has refused to cross.

Here on the cusp of concluding this book, I need to introduce two more characters to our cast of Salafi thought leaders in America, because I believe they encapsulate the branching futures of post-Salafi Islam. The first is one of the rising star AlMaghrib shaykhs named Omar Suleiman. Suleiman is the whole package: He has Saad Tasleem's youthful charisma and good looks, Muhammad Alshareef's entrepreneurial spirit, and Waleed Basyouni's genial, irenic, and acculturating instincts. He preaches with a warm smile. Suleiman did not study at the Islamic University of Medina or any other Saudi university, instead cobbling together his education through a variety of institutions in the United Arab Emirates, Malaysia, and the United States. While many of his mentors and friends are Salafis, I cannot find any instances of Suleiman directly using that term to describe himself – he seems content to exist in the vaguely Hanbali, "orthodox Islam" polysemy that Yasir Qadhi and the other AlMaghrib shaykhs have ushered in.

Though he remains a respected next-generation AlMaghrib shaykh, in 2016, Suleiman created a new paramosque platform for the transferal of scriptural knowledge by founding Yaqeen Institute for Islamic Research, based in Dallas. Yaqeen is less a competitor for AlMaghrib's sprawling educational empire and more what I would call "AlMaghrib 2.0." Where AlMaghrib disseminates scriptural knowledge by drawing tens of thousands of students to in-person intensive seminars, Yaqeen vaporizes that same knowledge to make it even more communicable: creating online curricula, comprehensible and brief articles, slickly edited videos, and digestible bites of Qur'an and Hadith insights. If AlMaghrib has a Salafi-leaning-but-nondenominational cast to its shaykhs, Yaqeen is as big-tent, conservative Islam as you can find: Zaytuna College professors, self-identified Salafi scholars, prominent Islamic Studies academics, AlMaghrib shaykhs, and conventional Sunnis populate the sizable team of advisers, researchers, fellows, and staff who contribute to Yaqeen's expansive online content. Where AlMaghrib trades on the charismatic, preacher-teacher devotional exhortation of its shaykhs, Yaqeen has more of an academic-lite ethos – a theological think tank where Muslim apologetics accompany studious-but-accessible position papers and videos. It is ecumenical, mainstream American post-Salafism made manifest.

In an ill-fated personnel decision, Suleiman, as he was gathering the team that would staff Yaqeen in 2016, decided to hire a prolific but polemical American Muslim blogger named Daniel Haqiqatjou (pronounced "ha-kee-kat-joo"). Haqiqatjou is a Houston native who grew up at Waleed's Clear Lake Islamic Center. He did his undergraduate degree at Harvard (major in physics, minor in philosophy), and then obtained a Master's in Philosophy from Tufts University. I belabor his educational background because of what it's lacking: any sort of conventional Islamic training. In 2007, Haqiqatjou had been invited, like Ify, to be a regular columnist at *Muslim Matters*, carving out a niche for himself writing about philosophy of science from a layman's Muslim scripturalist perspective. Suleiman hired him as the Director of Religion and Scientism (i.e., the ideologization of science), with his first Yaqeen articles attacking the legitimacy of the theory of evolution.[41] With the unparalleled confidence of someone possessing a Master's in Philosophy, Haqiqatjou casts himself as both a student of knowledge and an expert in the Islamic critique of Western science and Western philosophy. In less than a year, Haqiqatjou and Yaqeen had parted ways, his departure shrouded in HR mystery, but leaving a simmering resentment between Haqiqatjou and Suleiman. These might seem like esoteric staffing decisions at a fledgling start-up, but it presages one of the great online antagonisms of American Islam in the late 2010s.

Omar Suleiman's star has continued to rise. With dual platforms from AlMaghrib and Yaqeen, he has become the most celebrated of the celebrity shaykhs. In fact, Suleiman has even broken out of the insider "shaykh" orbit to become a straight up Islamic celebrity, adopting the more easily digestible title "imam" to make sense to non-Muslims. As the commencement of the Trump Era coincided with the founding of Yaqeen, he has even styled himself as a civil rights leader, making common cause throughout the Trump presidency with other activists. He was arrested at the US Capitol protesting against Trumpian abuses of immigrants in 2018.[42]

Where Waleed could unsolicitedly endorse Barack Obama with a YouTube video from the margins, Democratic politicians now seek out Suleiman's favor. Beto O'Rourke, in his unsuccessful bid for a Texas Senate seat in 2018, made sure to be seen dining and consulting with Suleiman and earned his endorsement.[43] When Beto ran for president in 2019, Suleiman helped introduce him at a major campaign rally, all while quoting Martin Luther King, Jr. and Malcolm X and denouncing Trump's "manufactured fears against Muslims."[44]

In a moment that reverberated across Muslim American social media, during Ramadan in 2019, Suleiman was invited to offer the invocation prayer in the US House of Representatives – "Let us not be overcome by the darkness of evil nor the slumber of indifference that turns human beings into hashtags and neighbors into enemies …"[45] And, yes, it was Suleiman who I mentioned earlier speaking at a Bernie Sanders rally in 2020, linking together the plight of Muslim refugees denied entrance by Trump's Muslim Ban, African American victims of police shootings, innocent Afghans killed in American drone strikes, and Latin American immigrants blocked at the US border. "We intend to fulfill that promise of America – of unity, equitability, prosperity, magnanimity – of love."[46] Some right-wing Islamophobes, who fastidiously track and systematically misconstrue every development at AlMaghrib, have taken to derisively calling Suleiman the prototype of a new "'woke,' modernist Salafism."[47]

All of this, the political exposure, the media attention, the adulation of American Muslims across the theological and political spectrum, the alliances with Democratic activists, has put Omar Suleiman in an awkward position vis-à-vis gay rights. What is consensus and common sense about homosexuality in his socially conservative, post-Salafi community flies in the face of the new American common sense about LGBTQ inclusion, dignity, and rights equality, much less the prevailingly progressive views among Suleiman's fellow Democratic and social justice activists. From the beginning of Yaqeen, he has tried different ways of untying this Gordian knot, hitherto, I would argue, unsuccessfully.

For example, in 2017 Yaqeen published an article by Jonathan Brown (Director of Research at Yaqeen) and a rejoinder from Shadee Elmasry (a popular Traditional Islam shaykh in the mold of Hamza Yusuf) titled, "LGBTQ and Islam Revisited: The Days of the Donald." There Brown makes the case that while Islamic jurisprudence has always forbidden homosexual acts, Orthodox American Muslims can support LGBTQ rights and gay civil – i.e., not Islamically sanctioned – marriage, because LGBTQ individuals are fellow citizens and fellow minorities in a shared lifeboat threatened by Trumpism and the "White (Protestant) Christian" majority in America. In essence, Brown argues, Muslims can maintain their theological and jurisprudential scruples against homosexuality, while finding common cause and not "laps[ing] into thinking that supporting someone's rights is an all-or-nothing relationship."[48] Elmasry dutifully argues the traditional counter position. Yaqeen Institute published this experimental debate, evidently hoping to instigate a broader reconsideration and push the envelope of acceptable positions regarding LGBTQ alliances.

Similarly, Suleiman has written several pieces in mainstream media (in addition to his regular Yaqeen and *Muslim Matters* fare) offering a rationale for socially conservative Muslims to be included within an otherwise progressive political coalition without being asked to "abandon mainstream Islamic beliefs." He cites as a model the Black church which "still maintains socially conservative positions while remaining at the forefront for social justice work."[49] In an interview explaining his approach, he casts his views on homosexuality as more personal and private: "If a person has conservative views that they uphold within their own family life, so long as that does not lead to denying, belittling, or dehumanizing someone else, then I don't think that's particularly problematic."[50]

In his Yaqeen publications directed toward culturally conservative Muslim audiences, he has articulated a jurisprudence of social justice activism that makes space for what he calls "conditional allyship," arguing from Hadith accounts that the Prophet Muhammad participated in a pact in Mecca to

> stand with the oppressed regardless of what tribe they were from … The [non-Muslim Meccans] at this time maintained all sorts of idolatry, lewdness, and oppressive practices, but that didn't stop the Prophet from joining them in achieving this specific good. He wasn't normalizing their practices, he was addressing the specific harm of one of those practices that had tainted them collectively.[51]

This offers, in Suleiman's analysis, a Sunna precedent for alliances in specific human- and Muslim-rights causes with communities (i.e., LGBTQ advocates and progressive politicians) with whom the conservative Muslims have major disagreements: "Isolation is a losing strategy for Orthodox Muslims."[52] He has said he is hoping to write a book on this subject.[53]

Suleiman's social justice activism is both a furtherance and a refinement of the logic that Waleed put forward in his endorsement of Obama – finding space in American pluralism and liberal politics for Muslim scripturalist voices. To repeat, Waleed Basyouni and Omar Suleiman are still quite distant from the position proposed by Ify Okoye, theologically vindicating her gayness, but their positions regarding LGBTQ rights and alliances are *also* a far cry from the views that I can find in Salafi discourse anywhere outside of America. Hence Saajid Lipham's flabbergastedness.

What Omar Suleiman seems to have not anticipated in his activist-ally evolution was how much it left his right flank exposed, and here is where Daniel Haqiqatjou reenters the narrative. Since his short-lived tenure at Yaqeen, he had returned to blogging, posting on YouTube and social media, and, of course, setting up an alternate scriptural-educational paramosque institute named Alasna Institute. Expanding beyond his previous science-and-philosophy focus, Haqiqatjou has staked out hard-line positions on women and hijabs, homosexuality, secularism and liberalism, feminism, homeschooling, the #MeToo movement, abortion, political correctness, and just about any other Muslim and American culture war issue you can imagine. He was bitterly critical of trends he saw among celebrity shaykhs who "are habitually saying things that are religiously incorrect, misleading, subversive, even noxious but you remain within the bounds of political correctness ... You can accrue tons of praise, headline all the Muslim conferences, raise large sums of money for your causes, and everyone wants to 'march' with you."[54] The targets of his ire are fairly obvious, but he held back from naming names. Then in 2019 the simmering feud boiled over.

What exactly triggered the ruckus is unclear, but Haqiqatjou took to social media, to his blog, and to every podcast that would have him on to denounce Omar Suleiman, Yaqeen Institute, and any of the other "compassionate imams" (this was not a compliment) who had, in his view, compromised on LGBTQ rights. Citing the rapid change of consensus in American culture – like the SBTS professors refuting Matthew Vines – he sounded the alarm that the otherwise "commonsensical" views of orthodox Muslims are vulnerable to persuasion by these compromising shaykhs to enter this landslide of pro-LGBTQ public opinion.[55] Haqiqatjou accused Suleiman of supporting same-sex marriage; posted pictures of him on stage with liberal politicians and LGBTQ activists, insinuating that he must agree with their views; and took a scorched-earth approach to taking down his former employer. What has ensued is a battle royal in the landscape of American Muslim social media.

The AlMaghrib shaykhs leaped to support their colleague Omar Suleiman, and Suleiman himself took to *Muslim Matters* and social media to defend his own position, complicated and subtle as it may be. Emblematic of these defenses was a Facebook post by Yasir Qadhi, who at one point had mentored Haqiqatjou and co-written articles with him on *Muslim Matters*. He doesn't name Haqiqatjou. Given the atmospherics, he doesn't have to:

It's sad to see the toxic neo-Madhkhalism that is rearing its ugly head online for the last few years. Those of us who have lived through the original (and I most definitely did, in the 90s in Madinah) see ALL of its signs in this new vulture-culture.

Neophytes, who lack proper Islamic training and experience, read in the worst into others who have more knowledge, age and experience than them ... by taking righteous Muslims as the real enemies, they ignore the far bigger problems that the Ummah [community] is facing, and the actual people who wish to oppose Allah and His Messenger and harm the believers ...

Just FYI, this status wasn't really about my critics – they don't bother me. But I would like to give a shout out to my dear friend Sh. Omar Suleiman, someone whom I thank Allah for blessing all of us with. He's a great asset to our national community. And yes, for the record, I do sometimes disagree with his opinions and positions, and when I do, I advise him directly.[56]

While this is not my dogfight, I would respectfully opine here that I actually think Yasir's Madkhali analogy, while interesting, is not the best one available. Not only has Haqiqatjou denied any connection to or inspiration from Rabi' al-Madkhali, he shows no signs of the avowed Saudi theo-politics that are definitional for Madkhalism.[57] I think there's a better comparative metaphor to be had: Daniel Haqiqatjou might be the first Muslim that I actually feel comfortable calling a Fundamentalist, not in the threadbare, colloquial sense of lurid and foreign "Islamic fundamentalism," but in the anchored, historical American Protestant sense. Haqiqatjou's barrages against liberalism, modernism, secularism, evolution, the sexual revolution, cultural decay; his nuanceless but singularly confident proclamation of the plain truths of Islamic scripture and tradition; his leveraging of technological platforms to tempestuously denounce his co-religionists, even if they agree with him on 95 percent of issues; his simultaneous reliance upon and rejection of the intellectual architecture of Western philosophy – all of these signal his embeddedness in broader American debates about religion, science, and society whose table was set by Fundamentalism in the early twentieth century. I think Yasir Qadhi's instinct to connect the origins of Haqiqatjou's antipathy back to Old World Salafi debates is misbegotten.[58] To me, Haqiqatjou represents a full-fledged *American* reactionary Salafism, a mutation of Salafi discourse that is hard to conceive of outside of a twenty-first-century American ecosystem.

The debate that had begun about LGBTQ rights and Omar Suleiman spiraled out, as Haqiqatjou took to lambasting the other AlMaghrib shaykhs and Yaqeen scholars who were defending his former boss. Suddenly everything was fair game: the shaykhs' politics; their empowerment of female leaders and ustadhas; their departure from earlier Saudi-influenced views; their celebrity statuses; how they made their money. As with all things Salafi, the subtext was always "What is the authentic Islam?" In one interview, challenged with Yasir's "neo-phyte" accusation, Haqiqatjou pulls a classic scripturalist student-to-scholar retort, "I don't have the *ijaza*, the formal degree or certificate, I haven't graduated from an *'alim* [Islamic scholar] program, but that doesn't mean that I am not learned or I haven't studied ... That is, I feel, a big distraction from the issue to bring up someone's credentials."[59] Once again, the very scriptural-interpretive meritocratic values that legitimize the autodidactic Albanis of the world, also can uphold your Matthew Vineses, your Ify Okoyes, and, yes, your Daniel Haqiqatjous.

Saajid Lipham, who does have some claim to IUM credentials, jumped into the fray, using his YouTube channel to interview and argue on the side of Daniel Haqiqatjou, against his fellow Islamic University of Medina alumni, all the while expressing a continuous befuddlement at how these strange ideas and values had entered the Salafi discourse. As of my writing this, the social media back-and-forth continues unabated with no clear end in sight.

CONCLUSION

If this chapter contributes nothing else, I hope that it cements in the readers' minds how claims or accusations of "literalism" are, empirically, a red herring. All of the skirmishing personalities of this chapter – indeed, the whole cast of scripturalist characters of this book – would likely sign on to some avouchment of the literal truth of scripture. "Literalism" sets the boundaries of the battlefield; the authority and clarity of scripture are table stakes in their disputes; the plain truth of the Bible or the Qur'an/Hadith is the premise that makes the rest of the argument consequential. In other words, attestations of literalism may be among the least interesting aspects of scripturalist communities, because they tell you almost nothing about what actual scripturalists believe or how they operate in the world.

While they could plausibly all be labeled American Salafis, to say that Omar Suleiman, Ify Okoye, and Daniel Haqiqatjou are all part of the same *movement* is to enter into Saajid Lipham's existential discombobulation. Instead, if we try to attain a birds-eye view of American post-Salafism, we see a cluster of quarrelsome, centerless villages, networked by a provincial patois of scriptural citation, ostensibly governed by the same original Qur'an-and-Hadith charter, but whose parochial interpretations of that charter depart so radically as to be irreconcilable. New eddies of common sense spin off; new boroughs form.

Surveying the fracas between Daniel Haqiqatjou and Omar Suleiman, I can begin to imagine a day when an American Salafi or "revivalist Orthodox" shaykh or imam will adopt an Ify Okoye-like affirmation of gay identity and maybe even gay marriage. It might not be Waleed Basyouni or even Omar Suleiman, but, if and when it does happen, his – let's be realistic, if it's a shaykh, it'll probably be a *he* – his reinterpretation will be presented as a straightforward apprehension from scripture. Like Matthew Vines, he will declare at the outset his unmitigated loyalty to the sacred texts, then offer a hermeneutic that bridges to the broader American cultural common sense about gay equality. Perhaps he'll use Ify's "without asking how" (*bilā kayfa*) argument, or not. Inevitably, there will be a real brawl on social media, as the different townships reposition themselves, shore up their consensuses. Daniel Haqiqatjou will go ballistic. Newly minted IUM graduates will balk. The flock of students of knowledge will murmurate as they do. Some of them will join the new settlement. Recriminations will be traded. And the discourse will move on.

Conclusion

America is a strange place to do religion. It was ever so. From the multifarious mix of dissenting and establishment Protestants – the flotsam and jetsam of the warring Reformations – who came to settle European colonies on the stolen lands of native peoples to the multitudes of Central and Eastern European Jews and Irish-Italian-Polish Catholics who came yearning to breathe free, escaping famine and persecution from the Old World; from the Black churches that managed to forge, out of the slavers' religion, a tradition of empowerment, hope, and liberation, to the various Black Muslims who have reconstituted and reinhabited pre-slavery Islamic identities; from the legions of immigrant communities who have brought and adapted their religions on American shores to the countless spiritual innovators who have alloyed and invented new American styles of religious belonging: Mormons, Christian Scientists, Jehovah's Witnesses, Scientologists, Seventh-day Adventists, New Agers, Nation of Islam adherents, Theosophists, and Pentecostals – if you can say nothing else about American religion, it's energetic, entrepreneurial, and eclectic.

When you stack the United States up against its fellow developed-world, wealthy, industrialized nations, its strangeness becomes even more apparent. Americans, on average, identify as more religious, pray more, believe in God more, attend more religious services, and say that religion is more important to their lives than survey respondents in any peer country.[1] And threaded through all of this American religious fervor is the galvanizing force of Protestant revivalism and biblicism that we today call Evangelicalism, which encompasses, give or take, a quarter of the American population, and which has exerted its influence on American politics, American rhetoric, American pop culture, and American media for centuries. To offer a slightly provocative analogy: America is the Saudi Arabia of Evangelicalism – the intellectual and discursive nerve center for a global scripturalist movement, whose seminaries attract international students from all over the globe, whose universities churn out Evangelical scholars and pastors, whose well-funded Evangelical missionaries have encircled the globe with influence and pedagogy.

And America's pattern of religious strangeness extends to Salafism too. When I read the academic literature about Salafis in Canada, Europe, Australia, etc., I'm perpetually struck by how eccentric the movement is that I've spent these years observing in America. Salafism in Europe and other Western countries is commonly characterized as antagonistic toward secular authorities, chauvinistically competing with other Islamic strands and communities, alienated from local politics and government, riven by Madkhali shaykhs' stringency, fixated on Saudi debates and Saudi theo-politics, and piously isolationist.[2] Having never directly studied these distinct Salafi contexts, I will refrain from commenting beyond noting that this is also something the American Salafis I've interviewed sometimes remark upon, especially in connection with British Salafism, where linguistic barriers are low, where interchange among traveling shaykhs is frequent, and where they see a very different mood of English-speaking Salafism in practice. For instance, Waleed recounted to me several anecdotes about his experiences setting up the AlMaghrib branch in the UK – how marginalized Salafis feel in British culture, how much pushback he got over AlMaghrib's practice of having men and women learn together and over their policy of having a male *and female* leader for each qabeela – "They expect us to just be a Salafi group coming to do a class," he grouses.[3]

What explains this apparent divergence between other "Western" experiences of Salafism and the AlMaghrib-style American post-Salafi integration? I can envision a bouquet of theories:

- the relative economic stability and comfortability of America, in general, and of the American Muslim community, in particular, facilitating incorporation;

- *or* America's geographical isolation from other Salafi communities leading to experimentation;
- *or* the distinct US immigration system and comparatively well-integrated Muslim community fostering American Salafism's more cosmopolitan character;
- *or* America's constitutionally protected religious freedom allowing Salafis the breathing room to reformulate their identities;
- *or* the existence of an older and more deeply rooted African American Muslim (and Salafi) population making American acclimatization easier.

All of these are plausible, and, I believe, worthy of further exploration and theorization.

In this book, I have chosen to home in on and theorize two of these uniquely American factors that have contributed to American Salafism's evidently distinct qualities – one obvious and the other counterintuitive. The obvious element that sets the American Salafi experience apart from other Western Salafi experiences is *9/11 and its aftermath.* The counterintuitive factor that I have tried to excavate interreligiously through my own background and moments of recognition is *the presence of American Evangelicalism.*

SHARED ECOLOGIES

As I have argued throughout this book, Salafism and Evangelicalism are phenotypically somewhat similar in their scripturalist-revivalist habits, but evolutionarily quite different. Salafism emerged out of the turbulent, authenticity-seeking, post-colonial world of the Middle East and South Asia, drawing on a deeply rooted countertradition of Hanbali-Taymiyyan-Wahhabi scripture-based reform and reinterpretation in Sunni Islam. Through Saudi funding and institution building, the global Salafi intellectual current has come to flow most prominently through the Arabian peninsula, though it has many other native locales. Evangelicalism, on the other hand, grew up with the American nation, bundling together the revivalist instincts and love for the Bible from various Protestant sects and denominations to form a competitive, coalitional, traditionless, perpetually renewing form of modern Christian identity. From America, Evangelical missionaries and parachurch ministries have spread Evangelical born-again messages and biblicism internationally, but American culture and religion remain marked by Evangelicalism's rambunctious original emergence.

Salafism came to American shores in the 1980s and 1990s without non-Muslims like myself taking much notice. Just as the nascent movement was beginning to get off the ground – building Qur'an and Hadith educational networks among African Americans and immigrant Muslims, umbilically tied through sojourner shaykhs to Saudi paradigms and debates – 9/11 intervened.

In the immediate aftermath of the attacks, Salafism and Evangelicalism appeared to be on a glide path to global religious war, with George W. Bush, America's most Evangelical of presidents, declaring that "this crusade, this War on Terrorism is going to take a while," because "we're facing a new kind of enemy … We haven't seen this kind of barbarism in a long period of time. No one could have conceivably imagined suicide bombers, burrowing into our society and then emerging all on the same day … This is a new kind of evil."[4] As American forces moved into Afghanistan to root out the Al Qaeda mujahideen that the American government had, less than two decades earlier, funded against the Soviets, Osama Bin Laden, in a statement delivered in November 2001, eagerly picked up on Bush's imagery, keen to reciprocate the bellicose rhetoric:

> … This war is fundamentally religious in nature. The Muslims of the East have responded to and sympathized with other Muslims against the Crusader people of the West … they are resisting the strongest, fiercest, most dangerous and violent Crusader campaign against Islam since Muhammad was sent … Bush left no room for the doubts or media opinion. He stated clearly that this is a Crusader war.[5]

Watching this escalation of bombast and budding apocalyptic confrontation take shape in the fall of 2001, it is understandable that many right-leaning observers feared Huntington's predicted "Clash of Civilizations" while left-leaning watchers fretted over a burgeoning, religiously inflected "Clash of Fundamentalisms."[6] Security Studies scholars and experts jumped into the fray to offer their threat analysis, in the process boiling Salafism down to a question of security threat or not.

As the FBI dismantled American Salafi institutions and strong-armed vulnerable Muslims into cooperation, Anwar al-Awlaki and a handful of other American Salafis bought into this narrative, eventually enlisting in what they took to be the Muslim side of the war that Bush had declared. Similarly, many Evangelicals and other Americans, including Muslims, enlisted in the US Armed Forces, Homeland Security, and intelligence services to fight terrorism and, on some level, Islamic fundamentalism or Radical Islam.[7] Afghanistan, Iraq, the Islamic State of Iraq and Syria, drone strikes, Yemen, terrorist attacks in the USA and Europe – history is littered with the consequences of those narratives. And so much of the extant Western literature on Salafism implicitly and explicitly participates in and perpetuates these narratives: Salafism is something threatening, rigid, foreign, evil, barbaric, antipathetic to Western norms and values.

And yet, when we look at what has happened among the vast majority of American Salafis, a different narrative materializes. The US government's crackdown on domestic Salafi institutions and communities upended the incipient movement and forced some American Salafis to reinvent themselves. The tragedy of 9/11 cast a pall over the "Salafi" identity in America, including within the Muslim community, but this freed Salafi-trained shaykhs and leaders to seek other monikers and build nondenominational institutions like AlMaghrib, Texas Dawah Convention, and Yaqeen Institute. The American government's (over)reaction to 9/11 did lead, I have argued, to Anwar al-Awlaki's fragmentation but also contributed to Muhammad Alshareef, Waleed Basyouni, Yasir Qadhi, Omar Suleiman, and Ify Okoye plotting a course toward an integrated American post-

Salafism of the future. All of this – the divergent American Salafi responses to 9/11 and the government's crackdown, the influence of these educational institutions for disseminating a hitherto unseen form of popularized, nondenominational post-Salafism – is, I think, pretty transparent from the evidence presented in the foregoing chapters.

The more eccentric connection I have theorized is the thematic and stylistic convergence between this post-Salafism and Evangelicalism in America. My starting point is the déjà vu-inducing echoes I continually hear in the American Salafi idiom, and I have set in parallel in these pages the very Protestant inheritance that Salafis themselves analogize to in describing their own intuitions of familiarity. If I was working from the comparative fundamentalism frameworks of old, I might have asserted some essential similarity (say, "literalism" or "discomfort with modernity" or just "being fundamentalists") that categorically explains these similarities. But instead, I have looked to the shared ecology of America, to the very particularities and strangeness of the American religious landscape, to discover why Evangelicals and Salafis sound so much alike here.

I contend that it is less that Salafis have consciously observed, analyzed, and mimicked Evangelical styles of American religion (though that is, as we have seen, at least a piece of the puzzle), and more that Evangelicalism set the model and defined the evolutionary niche of how a thriving, egalitarian, revivalist, un-traditional, scripture-based religious movement can inhabit America's distinctively pluralistic, entrepreneurial, and competitive ecosystem. Over the past forty years, Salafism has entered into an American religious environment ready-made to elicit Salafis' built-in interpretive flexibility, technological adaptiveness, and scriptural-popularizing instincts, because Evangelicals have been drinking at those watering holes for many decades. Evangelicals have evolved parachurch institutions and commonsense rhetorical stylings that negotiate the space between exclusivist theological confidence and American religious pluralism (and between elite scholars and the aspiringly knowledgeable masses), and Salafis have built analogous paramosque institutions and adapted similar idioms to fit their own needs.

This is not to imply that Salafis and Evangelicals experience anywhere near equal cultural power in America today. Evangelicals may express perceptions of embattledness, of the abating influence of the Bible in American society, but they are, by no means, a disempowered or marginal religious community in present-day America. Evangelical voters hold sway over one of the two American political parties, and by sheer demographic heft, political alliance, and institutional power, Evangelical voices feature prominently, albeit often stridently, in American public life. Salafis and Salafi-adjacent communities and leaders are, by contrast, a minority within a minority of American Muslims. Evangelicals *feel* embattled; Salafis and post-Salafi communities *are* embattled. Muslims in America experience real Islamophobia and xenophobia, and the rhetoric of the War on Terrorism mingled with the Security Studies dominance in the Western academic analysis of Salafism have served to internally *other* American Salafis. They exist and operate in an America that is still largely white, still largely Christian, and still largely hostile to Islam.

A DIFFERENT INTERRELIGIOUS FUTURE

Let me end with a somewhat hopeful vignette: Do you remember James R. White, the Evangelical apologist? I spent a paragraph in Chapter 7 profiling his rapid-response, less-than-generous podcast reaction to Matthew Vines' "The Bible and Homosexuality" lecture. Well, James R. White has a surprising friendship with, of all people, Yasir Qadhi.

It started because White was doing research for a series of public apologetic debates he was having with Muslim clerics and he was writing a book on the Qur'an for Christians, but he didn't understand Islamic theology. So someone connected him to Qadhi, then still a PhD student at Yale and a recent addition to AlMaghrib. Qadhi, not quite sure what to make of a Christian apologist seeking knowledge of Islamic theology, sent White a series of CDs from his recorded lectures in an AlMaghrib course. White was so eager for more that he petitioned Qadhi to share his lectures on the Hadith, which Qadhi was pleased to do. They struck up a regular correspondence about Islamic scripture and its interpretation.

In 2013, when an Islamophobic website spliced together clips of several of Qadhi's lectures to make it sound like he was endorsing violent jihad against Jews and Christians, White, unprompted, came to his defense, recording his own YouTube video vindicating the shaykh.[8] They continued corresponding.

Both men were disturbed by Donald Trump's election in 2016 and what it augured for the future of America. So, in January 2017, a few days after Trump's inauguration, White and Qadhi met in person for the first time. White came to the shaykh's hometown in Memphis, and he invited Yasir to do a dialogue event at a local Bible church, to have him explain his view of Islam to an Evangelical audience. The next night, Qadhi invited White to do a similar event at his mosque across town, to allow him to explain Evangelical theology to conservative Muslims.

In both events – which, of course, are posted on YouTube – White and Qadhi go back and forth about the namby-pamby sentiments that suffuse most interfaith dialogue spaces. They commiserate on how liberal Christians and liberal Muslims want to avoid their real differences in belief and practice and consume some thin gruel of interreligious sameness. They make it clear to their church and mosque audiences that while they aren't there to debate or argue, neither are they there to minimize the deep disagreements between "mainstream" Christians and "mainstream" Muslims. Each of them admit at different points that he would like to see the other converted to his own religion, but, for now, they're content to have a good-humored and respectful friendship.

White introduces the first evening's discussion and Qadhi, thus:

> The reason I specifically sought him out, is that I sense such a
> kindred spirit on the other side of the chasm that divides us with

regards to our theology and our beliefs. He is a consistent Muslim; he believes what he says. He wants to seek for consistency amongst his people and his own practice. And so, you have two believing people – one Christian, one Muslim – come together and say, "We need to discuss not only what divides us, but also, where do we have similarities? How can we live in the same community?"[9]

Before the Evangelical church audience, White uses his own cultural power to uplift and substantiate Qadhi's positive portrayal of Islam. He takes pains to vouch for Yasir, to highlight the shaykh's strong opposition to ISIS and terrorism, and to push back on the Islamophobic stereotypers who have tried to delegitimize Qadhi online. He urges the Bible church attendees toward empathy with the plight of Muslims in America, inviting Qadhi to candidly comment on, "What's it like to be Muslim in America post-9/11?"

Qadhi, in introducing White at his mosque, likewise searches for a way of expressing his deep respect and affection for the man without compromising in any way what he himself believes:

> A lot of times the people that we [Muslims] meet with [in interfaith spaces] are following understandings of Christianity that we don't really sympathize with. It's rare to meet an expert and an erudite, learned scholar who is faithful to the tradition and is willing to share with us his interpretation and his understanding of Christianity . . .
>
> It was so impressive and refreshing really to meet somebody who was taking the time to research what we actually believe from the sources. And then he began asking me questions about Hadith, so I sent him my online series of Hadith lectures I gave about the sciences of Hadith. So he's studying *muṣṭalaḥ al-ḥadīth*, the terminology of Hadith, you know, *ṣaḥīḥ* and *ḥasan* and *ḍaʿīf* and whatnot. I mean it's very impressive to meet somebody who's going to be so dedicated to actually learn the sources . . .
>
> I find a kindred spirit in James, here, and I literally consider him a brother in a *faithfulness* that is similar to mine – *it's not the same*

faith, but I do not question his integrity, and I do not doubt his commitment, and I do not doubt his sincerity.[10]

The words "Evangelical" and "Salafi" never come up in the two events, but those identities linger in the background the whole time.[11]

Through their three and a half hours on stage together, both White and Qadhi cast about for a word to describe their commonality, what exactly it is that is *kindred* about their spirits: "Conservative," "faithful," "consistent," and "mainstream" are all thrown out as potential congruities. As someone who has spent some time on this language question, I would hazard to point out that there are plenty of *conservative* Christians and Muslims who would not see eye to eye with White or Qadhi respectively. White is, like me, an alumnus of Fuller Theological Seminary, an arguably mainstream *Evangelical* school, but he also adheres to a distinctive Calvinistic Baptist corner of Evangelical theology and is hardly what most Mainline Protestants or Catholics would call a *mainstream Christian*; and many American Muslims, Hamza Yusuf chief among them, would take exception with applying that word to Qadhi's Islam.

What Qadhi expressly admires about White is his willingness to go directly to the sources of Islamic law and theology. He marvels at one point that White has read through the entire voluminous Hadith collections of al-Bukhari and Muslim, while the vast majority of Muslims at his mosque haven't even done the same. When White goes to explain the Christian doctrine of the Trinity to the Muslim audience, he makes clear that he is not relying on hidebound tradition or creeds, but instead he is a "biblical Trinitarian." Similarly, what White admires in Qadhi is not merely his mastery of the Islamic tradition, but his facility with Islamic scripture. He is awed by Qadhi's memorization of the Qur'an and quick ability to directly access the Hadith in defense of his views. In all humility, I would suggest that their kindredness is not that they are "consistent," or "faithful," or "conservative," or "mainstream." I believe the word they are looking for is *scripturalist*.

After the two dialogue events, it was White's turn in the hot seat, as a number of his fellow Evangelicals dredged up every negative clip or Islamophobic article they could find about Qadhi to portray White as a "useful idiot for Islamism." As one aggressive critic summarized:

> Qadhi is a Salafist, an ultraconservative sect of Islam associated with, but predating[,] Saudi Wahhabism. Osama bin Laden was a Salafist ...
>
> Qadhi is both Dean of Academic Affairs and [an] instructor at the Al Maghrib [sic] Institute, which has produced numerous jihadis.[12]

Qadhi, for his part, leaped on his Facebook page to defend his engagement with White and to defend White himself, writing,

> ... apparently, these Far Right individuals truly believe that Muslims are so dangerous, so evil, so deadly, that the mere fact that Mr. White can sit with us, and essentially humanize us as people who believe in our faith, entails that Mr. White is in fact helping and abetting the Muslim Brotherhood, Salafis, Al-Qaeda and other groups ...
>
> For the record, I did not personally receive any negative comments from any Muslim for inviting Mr. White into our masjid (although I'm sure some Muslims online and in other parts of the world might object) ...
>
> James, if you're reading this, know that I strongly disagree with your views on Islam ... [but] I will defend you against your fellow Christians as they smear your name and accuse you of all types of falsehoods.[13]

Their friendship continues.

Undeniably, there are aspects of the dialogue between Qadhi and White that raise my liberal hackles. The common ground they describe is not merely in their approach to scripture. They also together lament the normalization of homosexuality and the decline of respect for the normative dimension of God's law in American culture. I think both men find it easier to empathize across the Muslim-Christian divide than across the gay-straight divide with their co-religionists.

But there are spaces where the boundaries between these hulking, unwieldy entities that we call the "world religions" become thin, when déjà vu and echoes of familiarity can play across the gaps and produce moments of mutual recognition and respect. Someone sees something familiar that resonates deeply and piques curiosity and, maybe, friendship. I think the kindred spirit and dialogue between White and Qadhi (not to mention the interfaith friendships and alliances that Waleed Basyouni and Omar Suleiman are forging or the mutuality that emerges for Ify Okoye with gay, religiously conservative Christians and Jews) betokens a different possible inter-religious future in America, one where dialogue and mutual affection can occur even among communities that exhibit stark, exclusivist disagreements. It is pluralism with room for sharp elbows. Such a future is, to be sure, not a conventional interfaith huddle of agreement, deference, and polite platitudes, but it is a far cry from a Clash of Civilizations or, for that matter, a Clash of Fundamentalisms.

Afterword

I submitted the original manuscript of this book with all the above chapters to the publisher for review on the morning of January 6, 2021. A few hours later, I was experiencing a different sort of déjà vu, transfixed by the TV screen just as I had been twenty years earlier. This time I watched as American Evangelicalism experienced its own 9/11-type mortification. Watching hordes of rioters, many carrying "Jesus 2020" flags and Bibles and crosses, singing Evangelical-style worship songs, storming the seat of the US government, I think I felt just an inkling of what American Salafis might have felt that September morning, seeing their religion weaponized, their familiar symbols and words become totems of hate. Of course, given the immensity of Evangelical cultural power, I didn't have to worry that the entirety of the American security state would come crashing down on my Evangelical family and friends in the aftermath.

Some of the insurrectionists even wore shirts and carried flags emblazoned with crusader crosses, silently invoking the same inheritance of low-grade Christian bellicosity toward Muslims that had tumbled out of George W. Bush's mouth two decades before. Unlike the 9/11 attackers, the insurrectionists of 1/6 were not very well organized nor focused, probably accounting for the blessedly low but still tragic death count. But like the 9/11 attackers, many of them were overtly motivated by their religion – as well as by their politics and individual psychologies. Like the 9/11 attackers, the motley crew of Evangelical and Pentecostal and Charismatic and Catholic and QAnon Christians who stormed the Capitol thought they were on the side of justice and righteousness.

Never one to miss an opportunity to affirm his full-toned, progressive Americanness, while the insurrection was still unfolding,

Omar Suleiman tweeted an image of the rioters inside the Capitol, with the caption:

> These are your terrorists. Don't you dare compare them to anyone else. They are the culmination of the white supremacy that has nourished this nation since it's [sic] inception.
>
> If this was a BLM [Black Lives Matter] protest, this would've been... [a] massacre.
>
> Outrageous.[1]

Captured in that tweet is not only an irony but an axial shift. Recall that Suleiman himself was arrested less than three years earlier at the Capitol building protesting the anti-immigrant policies of Trump and other Republicans. Many right-wing Islamophobic websites have repetitively delighted in pointing out how the immensely popular Imam Suleiman shares some Salafi theological DNA and maybe intellectual genealogy with the 9/11 hijackers, but 1/6 revealed a jarring truth to anyone inclined to participate in that blame-the-Salafis game: the threat to American stability and rule of law turned out to not be Salafi-adjacent Muslims or creeping Shari'a. It was, instead, something truly homegrown.

What has become apparent in the aftermath of 1/6 and the near miss of Trumpian American autocracy is that the massive security apparatus of the United States had, in the twenty years since 9/11, lost sight of a festering menace of white supremacy, right-wing extremism, and Christian radicalization at home. The microscope focus on Salafism and Islamism and chasing down and deradicalizing putative "Radical Islam" left American law enforcement and counterterrorism agencies woefully incognizant of a different sort of extremism, one that is deeply tied to American history and the legacy of white and Christian supremacy in the nation's past.

Watching many of my friends and former colleagues ease away from calling themselves Evangelicals in the Trump and post-Trump era leads me to wonder whether "Evangelical" is rapidly becoming the new "fundamentalist," a moniker that is not fit for polite society as more and more political connotations accrue. Perhaps. But forswearing the "Evangelical" name would be just another in a long line of scripturalist evolutions, molting one skin, one title for another with their approach to (and claiming of) the Bible intact.

The Capitol Riot is a scarring reminder that no religious tradition is immune to violent ideologization, just as no democracy is so well-established as to foreclose the threats of insurrection and authoritarian takeovers. If human beings are to persist in the building of religiously and racially plural democracies – and I sincerely hope that we will, for the alternatives are grim in a globalized world – we must cultivate dialogue, fellow-feeling, friendships amid disagreements, interreligious explorations, and spaces where Muslims and Christians (two-thirds of the globe's population) in particular can find amiable, if not theological, mutuality.

Notes

INTRODUCTION

1 Pew Research Center, "The Future of World Religions: Population Growth Projections, 2010–2050," April 2, 2015, www.pewforum.org/2015/04/02/religious-projections-2010-2050/.

2 Nicholas Vinocur, "Manuel Valls Takes on Islam," *Politico Europe*, August 1, 2016, www.politico.eu/article/manuel-valls-takes-on-islam-france-islam-extremist-terrorism/, and The New Arab Staff, "French Elections: Far-right Presidential Candidate Marine Le Pen Backs Down on Hijab Ban," *The New Arab*, April 17, 2022, https://english.alaraby.co.uk/news/french-elections-le-pen-backs-down-hijab-ban-proposal.

3 Jonathan Z. Smith, "In Comparison a Magic Dwells," in *Imagining Religion: From Babylon to Jonestown* (Chicago: University of Chicago Press, 1982), 22.

4 Freiberger calls this a "scholar-centered" framework for interreligious comparison, that foregrounds the identity and interests of *me*, the comparativist. Oliver Freiberger, *Considering Comparison: A Method for Religious Studies* (Oxford: Oxford University Press, 2019), 103.

5 Maureen Fiedler, "Salafi Muslims: Following the Ancestors of Islam," *Interfaith Voices*, interview with Yasir Qadhi, February 21, 2013, http://interfaithradio.org/StoryAudio/Salafi_Muslims__Following_the_Ancestors_of_Islam.

6 Joshua Dubbler, "Salafi Muslims," in the *Encyclopedia of Muslim-American History*, ed. Edward E. Curtis (New York: Facts on File, 2010), 500. The quote actually continues "Salafi Muslims reject such categorizations," though I have not found this to be the case. Several of my Salafi interviewees with whom I discussed this comparison expressed interest and even agreement with the comparison.

7 This line from the US Marines Hymn was written in reference to the ensuing Barbary Wars in the early 1800s. See Glenn Tucker, *Dawn of Thunder: The Barbary Wars and the Birth of the US Navy* ([no place]: Bowsprit Books, 2018), 274.

8 Joel Barlow (trans.), "Treaty of Peace and Friendship, Signed at Tripoli, November 4, 1796," Yale Law School: The Avalon Project, https://avalon .law.yale.edu/18th_century/bar1796t.asp.

9 James McHenry, "From James McHenry," in *Memoirs of the Administrations of Washington and John Adams: Edited from the Papers of Oliver Wolcott, Secretary of the Treasury*, Vol.2, ed. George Gibbs (New York: William Van Norden, 1846), 36. Emphasis original. Fort McHenry is the famous site of the battle during the War of 1812 that led to the penning of the American national anthem, originally a poem titled "Defence of Fort M'Henry."

10 John Fea, *Was America Founded as a Christian Nation? A Historical Introduction* (Louisville: Westminster John Knox, 2011), 4. On the ongoing impact of the Barbary piracy incidents and the Barbary Wars on American literature and Americans' views of Islam, see David D. Grafton, *An American Biblical Orientalism: The Construction of Jews, Christians, and Muslims in Nineteenth-Century American Evangelical Piety* (Lanham, MD: Lexington Books, 2019), 32 ff.

11 Baylor Religion Survey, Wave 5 (2017), www.thearda.com/Archive/Files/ Analysis/BRSW5ED/BRSW5ED_Var71_1.asp, and Baylor Religion Survey, Wave 6 (May 2021), www.baylor.edu/baylorreligionsurvey/doc.php/ 376255.pdf, 57.

12 PRRI Staff, "Competing Visions of America: An Evolving Identity or a Culture Under Attack? Findings from the 2021 American Values Survey," Public Religion Research Institute, November 2021, www.prri.org/ research/competing-visions-of-america-an-evolving-identity-or-a-culture-under-attack/.

13 On the origins and mutations of this concept, see Mark Silk, "Notes on the Judeo-Christian Tradition in America," *American Quarterly* 36, no. 1 (Spring 1984), and K. Healan Gaston, *Imagining Judeo-Christian America: Religion, Secularism, and the Redefinition of Democracy* (Chicago: University of Chicago Press, 2019).

14 This tri-faith approach to defining American religion is most famously formulated in Will Herberg's *Protestant-Catholic-Jew: An Essay in American Religious Sociology* (Chicago: University of Chicago Press, 1955). On the broader historical context of this idea, see Kevin M. Schultz, *Tri-faith America: How Catholics and Jews Held Postwar America to Its Protestant Promise* (New York: Oxford University Press, 2011).

15 For instance, contrast Stephen Prothero's exposition of the Judeo-Christian concept in *American Jesus: How the Son of God Became a National Icon* (New York: Farrar, Straus, and Giroux, 2003), 259ff, with Anya Topolski, "The Dangerous Discourse of the 'Judaeo-Christian' Myth: Masking the Race-Religion Constellation in Europe," *Patterns of Prejudice* 54, no. 1–2 (2020).

16 Besheer Mohamed, "New Estimates Show US Muslim Population Continues to Grow," Pew Research Center, January 3, 2018, www .pewresearch.org/fact-tank/2018/01/03/new-estimates-show-u-s-muslim-population-continues-to-grow/.

17 On attempts to update and expand the Judeo-Christian framework to include Muslims after 9/11, see Gaston, *Imagining Judeo-Christian America*, 251–255.

18 Bernard Lewis, "The Roots of Muslim Rage," *The Atlantic* (Sept 1990), www.theatlantic.com/magazine/archive/1990/09/the-roots-of-muslim-rage/304643/.

19 Samuel P. Huntington, "The Clash of Civilizations?," *Foreign Affairs* (Summer 1993): 22–49.

20 Samuel P. Huntington, *The Clash of Civilizations and the Remaking of the World Order* (New York: Simon & Schuster, 1996). To be fair to Huntington, while Lewis centrally invokes the term "Judeo-Christian," Huntington uses it much more cautiously, and only when quoting others, such as Lewis. Huntington is much more comfortable with phrases like "Western Christian," Western Christianity," and "Western civilization."

21 Huntington, *The Clash of Civilizations*, 258 and 210.

22 For a good reception history of Huntington's thesis, see, Jeffrey Haynes, "From Huntington to Trump: Twenty-Five Years of the 'Clash of Civilizations,'" *The Review of Faith & International Affairs* 17:1 (Feb 2019).

23 For instance, see David Holloway, *9/11 and the War on Terror* (Edinburgh: University of Edinburgh Press, 2008), 7–11.

24 Peter Steinfels, "Ideas and Trends; There's Nothing Monolithic about Evangelical Politics," *New York Times*, March 13, 1988.

25 For one tone-setting instance, see Martin E. Marty, "Fundamentalism Reborn: Faith and Fanaticism," *Saturday Review*, May 1980.

26 BL 238 is by no means the only repository for books about religious fundamentalism, with many books on "Islamic fundamentalism" also falling in the BP 60 subject heading.

27 On the expansion and eventual implosion of the comparative fundamentalism academic endeavor, see Matthew D. Taylor, "A Cautionary Tale for Interreligious Studies from Comparative Fundamentalism: Who is at the Table?," *The Journal of Interreligious Studies* 21 (October 2017), https://irstudies.org/index.php/jirs/article/view/279/259.

28 The exemplar of this literature (both in the sense of its most advanced and highbrow form and yet filled throughout with this tone of categorical antipathy) is the five-volume Fundamentalism Project, edited by Martin Marty and R. Scott Appleby, beginning with *Fundamentalisms Observed* (Chicago: University of Chicago Press, 1991).

29 Google Books NGram Viewer, 2020.

30 For a prime example of how loose (and liberal-Protestant-based) definitions of Islamic fundamentalism are, see Ruud Koopmans, "Fundamentalism and Out-group Hostility," *WZB Mitteilungen*, December 2013, www.wzb.eu/system/files/docs/sv/iuk/koopmans_englisch_ed.pdf.

31 For instance, Vinay Lal, "Postscript 9-11, or the Terrorism That Has No Name," in *Empire of Knowledge: Culture and Plurality in the Global Economy* (London/Sterling, VA: Pluto Press, 2002), 183–201; and Joseph B. Tamney, "American Views of Islam, Post 9/11," *Islamic Studies* 43, no. 4 (2004): 599–630.

32 National Commission on Terrorist Attacks Upon the United States, "The 9/11 Commission Report," July 22, 2004, www.9-11commission.gov/report/911Report.pdf, 50. The Commission was citing Marty and Appleby's aforementioned *Fundamentalism Observed*.

33 This phrase seems to have occurred to multiple people, including several before 9/11. Most prominently, it was the title of Tariq Ali's book responding to 9/11 and the ensuing War in Afghanistan, *The Clash of Fundamentalisms: Crusades, Jihads, and Modernity* (London: Verso, 2002).

34 Nicholas Kristof, "Jesus and Jihad," *New York Times*, July 17, 2004, www.nytimes.com/2004/07/17/opinion/jesus-and-jihad.html.

35 US House Permanent Select Committee on Intelligence and US Senate Select Committee on Intelligence, "Report of the Joint Inquiry into the Terrorist Attacks of September 11, 2001," December 2002, www.intelligence.senate.gov/sites/default/files/documents/CRPT-107srpt351-5.pdf, 4–5.

36 See Barry Buzan and Lene Hansen, *The Evolution of International Security Studies* (Cambridge, UK: Cambridge University Press, 2009), 226–255.

37 I would point here especially to the foundational work of Quintan Wiktorowicz, to which I return in Chapter 5, who was one of the first American analysts to accurately and insightfully explore the concept of Salafism, especially his widely cited, "A Genealogy of Radical Islam," *Studies in Conflict & Terrorism* 28 (2005): 75–97, and "Anatomy of the Salafi Movement," *Studies in Conflict & Terrorism* 29 (2006): 207–239.

38 What I am broadly calling the Security Studies genre of studies of American Salafism actually ranges from careful think-tank style reports like Alexander Meleagrou-Hitchens' *Salafism in America: History, Evolution, Radicalization*, The George Washington University Program on Extremism, October 2018, https://extremism.gwu.edu/sites/g/files/zaxdzs2191/f/ Salafism%20in%20America.pdf, to more alarmist texts such as Chris Heffelfinger, *Radical Islam in America: Salafism's Journey from Arabia to the West* (Dulles: Potomac Books, 2011), to comprehensive battle plans including Michael W. S. Ryan, *Decoding Al-Qaeda's Strategy: The Deep Battle Against America* (New York: Columbia University Press, 2013), to autobiographical accounts like Daveed Gartenstein-Ross, *My Year Inside Radical Islam: A Memoir* (New York: Jeremy P. Tarcher/Penguin, 2007).

39 I am thinking here particularly of Anabel Inge's *The Making of a Salafi Muslim Woman: Paths to Conversion* (New York: Oxford University Press, 2017), which draws on ethnographic research among Salafi women's groups in the UK, and Susanne Olsson's *Contemporary Puritan Salafism: A Swedish Case Study* (Bristol, CT: Equinox Publishing, 2019).

40 For instance, Graeme Wood, "What ISIS Really Wants," *The Atlantic*, March 2015, www.theatlantic.com/magazine/archive/2015/03/what-isis-really-wants/384980/, and Andrea Elliott, "Why Yasir Qadhi Wants to Talk about Jihad," *The New York Times Magazine*, March 17, 2011, www .nytimes.com/2011/03/20/magazine/mag-20Salafis-t.html.

41 Brian Naylor, "Radical Islam or Radical Islamism? It Depends Whom You Ask," NPR News, June 14, 2016, www.npr.org/2016/06/14/482011041/ radical-islam-or-radical-islamism-it-depends-who-you-ask. On the contested history between the concepts "fundamentalism" and "Islamism" in studies of Islam, see Martin Kramer, "Coming to Terms: Fundamentalists or Islamists," *Middle East Quarterly* (Spring 2003): 65–77.

42 While many scholars' work has informed my chosen approach, I have taken special inspiration from Tanya Luhrmann's ethnographic method in *When God Talks Back: Understanding the American Evangelical*

Relationship with God (New York: Vintage Books, 2012), and Saba Mahmood's piercingly personal self-extension to understand Salafi-adjacent Islamists in Egypt in her *Politics of Piety: The Islamist Revival and the Feminist Subject* (Princeton: Princeton University Press, 2005). On comparative theology, see Francis X. Clooney, *Comparative Theology: Deep Learning Across Religious Borders* (Oxford: Wiley-Blackwell, 2010).

43 This concept "scripturalist/-ism" in English was seemingly coined to characterize and criticize certain types of radical Protestants in the eighteenth century – *Oxford English Dictionary*, Online ed., s.v. "scripturalism" (Oxford: Oxford University Press, 2014) – but it has never gained wide usage or taken on the polemical edges of "fundamentalism." Clifford Geertz used the term scripturalist to describe the nascent purist Salafi movements he saw coalescing in diverse majority-Muslim contexts in the middle of the twentieth century: "the turn toward the Koran, the Hadith, and the Sharia, together with various standard commentaries upon them, as the only acceptable bases of religious authority." *Islam Observed: Religious Developments in Morocco and Indonesia* (Chicago: University of Chicago Press, 1968), 65. A number of analysts of Islam have employed it since then.

44 George R. McGhee Jr., *Convergent Evolution: Limited Forms Most Beautiful* (Cambridge, MA: MIT Press, 2011), 7.

45 An alert reader of Smith's generative "In Comparison a Magic Dwells" essay, will note that I am concocting an admixture of what he terms the "ethnographic" method of interreligious comparison with the – in his evaluation, largely unexplored – "evolutionary" method.

46 "The aim of such a comparison [of two religious phenomena] is the redescription of the exempla (each in light of the other) and a rectification of the academic categories in relation to which they have been imagined." Jonathan Z. Smith, "Epilogue: The 'End' of Comparison: Redescription and Rectification," in *A Magic Still Dwells: Comparative Religion in the Postmodern Age*, Kimberly C. Patton and Benjamin C. Ray, eds. (Berkeley: University of California Press, 2000), 239.

CHAPTER I

1 Smith, "In Comparison a Magic Dwells," 35.

2 G. R. Evans, *The Roots of the Reformation: Tradition, Emergence, and Rupture* (Downers Grove: InterVarsity Press Academic, 2012), 187.

3 On other continuities between the early Protestants and their predecessors, see also Heiko Oberman, *Forerunners of the Reformation: The Shape of Late Medieval Thought*, trans. Paul L. Nyhus (Cambridge, UK: James Clarke & Co, 2002).

4 *Oxford English Dictionary*, Online ed., s.v. "evangelical" (Oxford: Oxford University Press, 2014). B. A. Gerrish, *The Old Protestantism and the New: Essays on the Reformation Heritage* (Chicago: University of Chicago Press, 1982), 29ff. I am choosing to use the non-capitalized form "evangelical" to denote use of the less particular adjective until the mid-twentieth century when the identity "Evangelical" or "Evangelicalism" congealed into a self-affirming nounal form. I use a similar capitalization scheme with salafi vs. Salafi/Salafism.

5 On how "evangelical" took on the meaning "anti-Catholic" in the Reformation and afterward, see Lindon D. Fisher, "Evangelicals and Unevangelicals: The Contested History of a Word, 1500–1950," *Religion and American Culture* 26, no. 2 (Summer 2016), 188–192.

6 Contrary to popular usage, *sola Scriptura* did not mean the Reformers entirely discarded all previous Christian teachings or traditions for the pure, unmediated text. Richard Bauckham, "Tradition in Relation to Scripture and Reason," in *Scripture, Tradition, and Reason: A Study in the Criteria of Christian Doctrine*, Richard Bauckham and Benjamin Drewery, eds. (Edinburgh: T&T Clark, 1988), 123.

7 See Peter H. Wilson, "The Causes of the Thirty Years War 1618–1648," *The English Historical Review* 123, no. 502 (June 2008): 554–586, and Daniel Philpott, "The Religious Roots of Modern International Relations," *World Politics* 52, no. 2 (Jan, 2000): 206–245.

8 Thomas S. Kidd, *The Great Awakening: The Roots of Evangelical Christianity in Colonial America* (New Haven: Yale University Press, 2007), 50. On the American origins of the concept of Protestant denominations, see Sidney E. Mead, *The Lively Experiment: The Shaping of Christianity in America* (New York: Harper & Row, 1963), 103ff.

9 Jonathan Edwards, "Importance and Advantage of a Thorough Knowledge of Divine Truth," in *The Works of Jonathan Edwards, A.M., with an Essay on His Genius and Writings*, ed. Edward Hickman (London: John Childs and Son, 1839), Vol. 2, 161.

10 Mark A. Noll, *America's God: From Jonathan Edwards to Abraham Lincoln* (New York: Oxford University Press, 2002), 44.

11 See Mark A. Noll, *In the Beginning Was the Word: The Bible in American Public Life, 1492–1783* (New York: Oxford University Press, 2016), 271ff. Following Noll (pp. 11–13), I am using the term biblicist to describe an appeal to the authority of "the Bible alone." Though sometimes more rhetorical than real, this is a stronger claim than the original Protestants' *sola Scriptura* slogan, which was more akin to "the Bible supreme among all authorities."

12 Randall Balmer, *The Making of Evangelicalism: From Revivalism to Politics and Beyond* (Waco: Baylor University Press, 2010), 17.

13 Richard T. Hughes and C. Leonard Allen, in *Illusions of Innocence: Protestant Primitivism in America, 1630–1875* (Chicago: University of Chicago Press, 1988), observe how the desire to recover "original" Christianity linked together the otherwise disparate Mormons, Landmark Baptists, Shakers, Disciples of Christ, and the "Christian" movement of the early nineteenth century.

14 Jill Lepore, *These Truths: A History of the United States* (New York: W. W. Norton & Company, 2018), 190.

15 Roger Finke and Rodney Stark, *The Church of America, 1776–2005: Winners and Losers in Our Religious Economy* (New Brunswick: Rutgers University Press, 2005), 55.

16 See Nathan O. Hatch, *The Democratization of American Christianity* (New Haven: Yale University Press, 1989).

17 Finke and Stark, *The Church of America*, 57.

18 George Marsden, *The Evangelical Mind and the New School Presbyterian Experience: A Case Study of Thought and Theology in Nineteenth-Century America* (Eugene: Wipf & Stock, 1970), 14–16.

19 Robert Baird, *Religion in America; or, an Account of the Origen, Progress, Relation to the State, and Present Condition of the Evangelical Churches in the United States with Notices of the Unevangelical Denominations* (New York: Harper & Brothers, 1844), 270.

20 Mark Noll, *The Civil War as a Theological Crisis* (Chapel Hill: University of North Carolina Press, 2006).

21 For discussion of this shift from evangelical "postmillennialism" to "premillennialism," see George M. Marsden, *Fundamentalism and American Culture*, 2nd ed. (New York: Oxford University Press, 2006), 49–51.

22 See Marsden, *Fundamentalism and American Culture*, 11–31.

23 Harry Emerson Fosdick, "Shall the Fundamentalists Win?," Sermon at First Presbyterian Church, New York, NY, May 21, 1922, http://historymatters.gmu.edu/d/5070/.

24 On the development of "Fundamentalist" as epithet, see Susan Harding, "Representing Fundamentalism: The Problem of the Repugnant Cultural Other," *Social Research* 58, no. 2 (Summer 1991): 373–393.

25 See Joel A. Carpenter, *Revive Us Again: The Reawakening of American Fundamentalism* (New York: Oxford University Press, 1997), 63.

26 With the language of "disruption," I am consciously referencing here, the evolutionary principle of "disruptive selection," where a species (i.e., nineteenth-century evangelical Christians) has variable traits that environmental factors push toward extreme phenotypical expressions as opposed to more intermediate balanced ones. See David Pfennig and Karin Pfennig, *Evolution's Wedge: Competition and the Origins of Diversity* (Berkeley and Los Angeles: University of California Press, 2012), 112ff.

27 On the origins and ideological counter-positioning of Mainline Protestantism and Fundamentalism/Evangelicalism, see Elesha Coffman, *The Christian Century and the Rise of Mainline Protestantism* (New York: Oxford University Press, 2013), esp. 213ff.

28 On the shifting connotations and grammatical forms of "evangelical," see Thomas S. Kidd, *Who is an Evangelical? The History of a Movement in Crisis* (New Haven: Yale University Press, 2019), 9ff.

29 George Marsden, *Reforming Fundamentalism: Fuller Seminary and the New Evangelicalism* (Grand Rapids: Eerdmans, 1987).

30 On the Evangelical quest for intellectual respectability, see Molly Worthen, *Apostles of Reason: The Crisis of Authority in American Evangelicalism* (New York: Oxford University Press, 2014).

31 In this concise summary of Evangelicalism, I do not have time nor space to introduce what is arguably the third and even more complicated subspecies of American Evangelicalism, namely, Pentecostalism.

32 See Randall Balmer, *Bad Faith: Race and the Rise of the Religious Right* (Grand Rapids: Eerdmans, 2021).

33 George Marsden, *Fundamentalism and American Culture*, 231–257.

34 Stanley Grenz, "Nurturing the Soul, Informing the Mind: The Genesis of the Evangelical Scriptural Principle," in *Evangelicals & Scripture: Tradition, Authority and Hermeneutics*, edited by Vincent Bacote, Laura

C. Miguélez, and Dennis Okholm (Downers Grove: InterVarsity Press, 2004), 21.

35 For one such paradigmatic encounter, see Kimlyn J. Bender, *Confessing Christ for Church and World: Studies in Modern Theology* (Downers Grove: InterVarsity Press, 2014), 66.

36 Daniel A. Madigan, "People of the Word: Reading John with a Muslim," *Review & Expositor* 104, no. 1 (2007): 81–95.

37 Sahih al-Bukhari, Vol. 4, Book 54, Hadith 535, https://sunnah.com/ bukhari/59/124. The symbol after the word "Prophet" is Arabic script invoking "Peace be upon him."

38 Sahih al-Bukhari, Vol. 2, Book 23, Hadith 398, https://sunnah.com/ bukhari/23/70.

39 Jonathan Brown, *Misquoting Muhammad: The Challenge and Choices of Interpreting the Prophet's Legacy* (London: Oneworld, 2014), 37.

40 This parallel is also suggested by Wilfred Cantwell Smith, *What is Scripture? A Comparative Approach* (Minneapolis: Fortress Press, 2005), 46.

41 Someone might intelligently assert that the entire Islamic tradition, built as it is around the Qur'an as the locus of divine communication, is a *scripturalist* tradition. But, if the word scripturalism is to be meaningful in describing an ideological orientation (i.e., an -ism), it must mean something relative to other things: Who are the people who are exceptional in the Islamic community through history in advancing direct appeal to the Qur'an *and Hadith* as the definitive mainstay for all Islamic knowledge and practice?

42 Put differently, Christian debates generally center on God's nature where Islamic debates mostly focus on God's will. Mark L. Movsesian, "*Fiqh* and Canons: Reflections on Islamic and Christian Jurisprudence," *Seton Hall Law Review* 40 (2010): 862–863.

43 On a technical level, Shari'a refers to the Divine Law – God's will from all eternity – whereas *fiqh* – Islamic jurisprudence – is the flawed and constrained human effort to attain some understanding of the Shari'a. See Wael Hallaq, *Sharī'a: Theory, Practice, Transformations* (Cambridge, UK: Cambridge University Press, 2009) and Jonathan Brown's more approachable *Misquoting Muhammad*.

44 Daniel Brown, *Rethinking Tradition in Modern Islamic Thought* (Cambridge, UK: Cambridge University Press, 1996), 12ff. See also Yasir Qadhi, "Salafī-Asha'rī Polemics of the 3rd & 4th Islamic Centuries," *The Muslim World* 106 (July 2016): 433–447.

45 Hodgson charmingly terms this group the "Ḥadīth folk" and socio-politically situates their "textualist tendencies" and "traits of populism" in the late ninth and early tenth centuries. Marshall G. S. Hodgson, *The Venture of Islam: Conscience and History in a World* Civilization, Vol. 1 (Chicago: University of Chicago Press, 1974), 386–392.

46 Ibn al-Jawzī, *Virtues of the Imām Aḥmad ibn Ḥanbal*, Vol. 1, trans. Michael Cooperson (New York: New York University Press, 2013), 93.

47 Ibn al-Jawzī, *Virtues of the Imām*, 359.

48 For overviews of this process, see John Burton, *Introduction to the Hadith* (Edinburgh: Edinburgh University Press, 1994) and Jonathan Brown, *Hadith: Muhammad's Legacy in the Medieval and Modern World*, 2nd ed. (Oxford: Oneworld, 2018).

49 In technical terms, this is the classical distinction between *ijtihad* (the independent effort of the scholar to develop an original response to a question from the Hadith and Qur'an rather than relying on juristic precedent) and *taqlid* (defaulting to the precedents of previous generations of scholars). As Marshall Hodgson piercingly observes, "Ḥanbalism had never really been primarily a school of fiqh [jurisprudence] at all. It remained a comprehensive and essentially radical movement ... Ijtihād inquiry remained alive among the Ḥanbalīs; each major teacher felt free to start afresh, according to the needs of his own time for reform in a puritan direction." *The Venture of Islam: The Gunpowder Empires and Modern Times*, Vol. 3 (Chicago: The University of Chicago Press, 1974), 160.

50 "Written sources make it clear that medieval scholars used the notion of *madhhab al-salaf* primarily in theological contexts, where it served as an authoritative and prestigious synonym for the – Hanbali creed (*aqīda*)." Henri Lauzière, "The Construction of Salafiyya: Reconsidering Salafism from the Perspective of Conceptual History," *International Journal of Middle East Studies* 42 (2010): 372.

51 Henri Lauzière makes the compelling case that this adjective *"salafī"* (or the more common early phrasing *"madhhab al-salaf "*) was not a noun or formal identity, but rather one among several means that people who were Hanbali in their creedal theology (*aqīda*) used to signal their primal connection to the earliest Muslim theological community. *The Making of Salafism: Islamic Reform in the Twentieth Century* (New York: Columbia University Press, 2016), 28.

52 Ovamir Anjum, *Politics, Law, and Community in Islamic Thought: The Taymiyyan Moment* (New York: Cambridge University Press, 2012), 188.

53 Paul Heck, *Skepticism in Classical Islam: Moments of Confusion* (New York: Routledge, 2014), 152–189.

54 See Elliott Bazzano, "Ibn Taymiyya, Radical Polymath, Part 1: Scholarly Perceptions," *Religion Compass* 9/4 (2015): 105.

55 Sherman Jackson, "Ibn Taymiyyah on Trial in Damascus," *Journal of Semitic Studies* 39, no. 1 (Spring 1994): 64.

56 Jon Hoover, "Ibn Taymiyya between Moderation and Radicalism," in *Reclaiming Islamic Tradition: Modern Interpretations of the Classical Heritage*, eds. Elisabeth Kendall and Ahmad Khan (Edinburgh: Edinburgh University Press, 2016), 178–180.

57 Guido Steinberg, "Muhammad ibn ʿAbd al-Wahhab (1703–1792)" in *Global Salafism: Islam's New Religious Movement* (New York: Columbia University Press, 2009), 430–431. On Ibn ʿAbd Al-Wahhab's broader milieu, see Ahmad S. Dallal, *Islam without Europe: Traditions of Reform in Eighteenth-Century Islamic Thought* (Chapel Hill: University of North Carolina Press, 2018).

58 Ahmad S. Dallal, "The Origins and Objectives of Islamic Revivalist Thought, 1750–1850," *Journal of the American Oriental Society* 113, no. 3 (July–Sept, 1993), 350.

59 "Ibn ʿAbd al-Wahhāb produced no unprecedented opinions, and Saudi authorities regard him not as a mujtahid [practitioner of *ijtihad* – the independent reasoning of a scholar/jurist] in fiqh [jurisprudence], but rather in *daʿwa* or religious awakening." Frank Vogel, *Islamic Law and Legal System: Studies of Saudi Arabia* (Leiden/Boston: Brill, 2000), 75–76. See also Natana DeLong-Bas, *Wahhabi Islam: From Revival and Reform to Global Jihad* (New York: Oxford University Press, 2004), 110–111.

60 For instance, Eamon Murphy, *The Making of Terrorism in Pakistan: Historical and Social Roots of Extremism* (London/ New York: Routledge, 2013), 96.

61 For a more sympathetic reading of Ibn ʿAbd al-Wahhab's conception of jihad, see DeLong-Bas, *Wahhabi Islam*, 34–35.

62 "Wahhabi" is seen as an insulting name by many of the followers of Ibn ʾAbd al-Wahhab, but Wahhabi is the name that has stuck to the movement. For those seeking a more neutral term, the "Najdi movement" or "Najdi daʿwa" is a preferred descriptor.

63 Reinhard Schulze, *A Modern History of the Islamic World* (New York: New York University Press, 2002), 69–72.

64 See Roel Meijer, "Introduction," in *Global Salafism: Islam's New Religious Movement*, ed. Roel Meijer (New York: Columbia University Press, 2009), 9–13.

65 This phrasing comes from Ovamir Anjum, "Salafis and Democracy: Doctrine and Context," *The Muslim World* 106 (July 2016): 473.

66 Abu Muslimah, "Distinguishing the Truth," Lecture at Qur'an and Sunnah Society of North America, 8th Annual Conference, 1994, https://archive.org/details/AbuMuslimah/AM+-+Distinguishing+the+Truth+(8th +QSS+-+1994).mp3. The hadith he cites (a Salafi favorite) is widely attested, for instance Sahih al-Bukhari, Vol. 8, Book 76, Hadith 437, https://sunnah.com/bukhari/81/18.

67 These estimated numbers come from Jeff Diamant, "Engagement and Resistance: African Americans, Saudi Arabia, and Islamic Transnationalisms, 1975 to 2000" (PhD diss., City University of New York, 2016), 25. When the original Nation of Islam disintegrated in the mid-1970s following the death of Elijah Muhammad, his son, Warith Deen Mohammed, took over leadership and sought to bring the movement into alignment with conventional Sunni Islam. Louis Farrakhan endeavored to reconstitute the organization under the original name and his leadership. But, as Diamant observes, a number of post-NOI African American Muslims like Abu Muslimah looked to Salafism and the Saudi educational system as a source of authentic Islam.

68 See especially, Umar Lee, *The Rise and Fall of the Salafi Dawah in North America* (St. Louis: Self-published, 2014); and Dawud Adib, "History of the Salafi Da'wah in America Pt 1," YouTube.com, June 18, 2011, https://youtu.be/tixXMlFkgms.

69 This textualist/Hanbali school of theology also sometimes goes by the name *Athari* [from *athar*, commonly translated as "tradition," a synonym for "hadith"], see Qadhi, "Salafī-Ashʿarī Polemics," 434, n. 2.

70 John Voll, *Islam: Continuity and Change in the Modern World* (Syracuse: Syracuse University Press, 1994), 161–190. These various reform movements included the nineteenth-century proto-Salafi, Ahl-i-Hadith movement in South Asia, which shared a lot of intellectual lineage and beliefs with the eventual more Saudi-aligned Salafis. See Daniel Brown, *Rethinking Tradition*, 32–36.

71 See Brown, *Hadith: Muhammad's Legacy*, 251–256. The "Modernist Salafis" were the Salafis that attracted the attention of American and European scholars, and, reading Western academic literature about Islam in the twentieth century, one could be forgiven for thinking that Salafism was a synonym of progressive, modern reformism.

72 David Commins, *The Wahhabi Mission and Saudi Arabia* (New York: I. B. Tauris & Co, 2006), 152–153.

73 On contextual adaptations from IUM alumni in Nigeria, see Alexander Thurston, *Salafism in Nigeria: Islam, Preaching, and Politics* (Cambridge/New York: Cambridge University Press, 2016).

74 See Stéphane Lacroix's *Awakening Islam: The Politics of Religious Dissent in Contemporary Saudi Arabia*, trans. George Holoch (Cambridge, MA: Harvard University Press, 2011).

75 On the Islamic University of Medina as a hub of this pluralization, see Michael Farquhar, *Circuits of Faith: Migration, Education, and the Wahhabi Mission* (Stanford: Stanford University Press, 2017).

76 Frank Vogel, "Saudi Arabia: Public, Civil, and Individual Shariʿa," in *Shariʿa Politics: Islamic Law and Society in the Modern World*, ed. Robert W. Hefner (Bloomington: Indiana University Press, 2011), 55–93.

77 Edward E. Curtis IV, *Muslims in America: A Short History* (New York: Oxford University Press, 2009), 73.

78 58 percent are immigrants and 18 percent the children of immigrants. Pew Research Center, "US Muslims Concerned about Their Place in Society, but Continue to Believe in the American Dream," July 16, 2017, www.pewresearch.org/religion/wp-content/uploads/sites/7/2017/07/U.S.-MUSLIMS-FULL-REPORT-with-population-update-v2.pdf. Estimates on the size of the American Muslim community also come from Besheer Mohamed, "Muslims Are a Growing Presence in US, But Still Face Negative Views from the Public," Pew Research Center, September 1, 2021, www.pewresearch.org/fact-tank/2021/09/01/muslims-are-a-growing-presence-in-u-s-but-still-face-negative-views-from-the-public/.

79 Jeff Diamant, "Engagement and Resistance." See also, Shadee Elmasry, "The Salafis in America: The Rise, Decline and Prospects for a Sunni Muslim Movement among African-Americans," *Journal of Muslim Minority Affairs* 30, no. 2 (June 2010): 217–236.

80 National Commission on Terrorist Attacks, "The 9/11 Commission Report," 362.

CHAPTER 2

1 Pew Research Center, "The Diminishing Divide … American Churches, American Politics," June 25, 1996, www.pewresearch.org/wp-content/uploads/sites/4/legacy-pdf/126.pdf; and Christian Smith, *American Evangelicalism: Embattled and Thriving* (Chicago: University of Chicago Press, 1998), 236. Smith's 1996 survey allowed Protestants to initially select multiple identities and then choose a primary identity among them, thereby disaggregating within the Fundamentalist–Evangelical spectrum who leaned toward which of those two factions.

2 Pew Research Center, "Faith-Based Funding Backed, But Church–State Doubts Abound," April 10, 2001, www.pewresearch.org/wp-content/uploads/sites/4/legacy-pdf/15.pdf.

3 Anna Greenberg and Jennifer Berktold, "Evangelicals in America," *Religion and Ethics Newsweekly*, April 5, 2004, wwwtc.pbs.org/wnet/religionandethics/files/2008/10/results.pdf.

4 Pew Research Center, "US Religious Landscape Survey," June 1, 2008, www.pewresearch.org/wp-content/uploads/sites/7/2008/06/report2-religious-landscape-study-full.pdf. The methodology of the Religious Landscape survey focuses on denominational identity, so it sorts people identifying as Fundamentalist into two different sub-Evangelical categories: "Nondenominational Fundamentalist" (0.3 percent of all Americans) and "Other Evangelical/Fundamentalist" (also 0.3 percent of the population). Because this latter category includes several other identity configurations (including "Bible-believers" and "Charismatic"), the two percentages combined would be less than 0.5 percent self-affirming Fundamentalists.

5 Pew Research Center, "America's Changing Religious Landscape," May 12, 2015, www.pewforum.org/wp-content/uploads/sites/7/2015/05/RLS-08-26-full-report.pdf.

6 This was not an immediate shift, as we can see even the most stalwart of Fundamentalist institutions – Bob Jones University – casting about a few months after 9/11 for a new title "because of the media's penchant for lumping Christian Fundamentalists in the same heap as Islamic Fundamentalists." Ted Olsen, "The End of Christian Fundamentalism?," *Christianity Today*, March 1, 2002, www.christianitytoday.com/ct/2002/marchweb-only/3-11-53.0.html.

7 For example, a 2004 Pew Research study found a strong contingent of what they called "Traditionalist Evangelicals" (12.6 percent of all Americans),

which held down the right wing of Evangelicalism, but included a lot of Evangelicals from non-Fundamentalist backgrounds. John C. Green, "Religion and the 2004 Election: A Pre-election Analysis," Pew Research Center, September 2004, www.pewresearch.org/wp-content/uploads/sites/7/2004/09/green-full.pdf.

8 For instance, Robert Parham, "911 Ends Christian Fundamentalism, Clouds Future Christian Leadership," *Good Faith Media*, January 31, 2002, https://goodfaithmedia.org/911-ends-christian-fundamentalism-clouds-future-christian-leadership-cms-282.

9 Rosemary R. Corbett, "Islamic 'Fundamentalism': The Mission Creep of an American Religious Metaphor," *Journal of the American Academy of Religion* 83, no. 4 (December 2015): 977–1004.

10 E.g., Mark Lilla, "Extremism's Theological Roots," *New York Times*, October 7, 2001, www.nytimes.com/2001/10/07/opinion/extremisms-theological-roots.html; and Andrew Sullivan, "This Is a Religious War," *New York Times Magazine*, October 7, 2001, www.nytimes.com/2001/10/07/magazine/this-is-a-religious-war.html.

11 I am grateful to George Marsden for sharing his intuition about this post-9/11 dimension in the decline of the positive Protestant "Fundamentalist" identity.

12 Caryle Murphy, "For Conservative Muslims, Goal of Isolation a Challenge," *Washington Post*, September 5, 2006, www.washingtonpost.com/wp-dyn/content/article/2006/09/04/AR2006090401107_pf.html.

13 Muslim Link Staff, "Responses to Washington Post Piece on Dar-us-Salaam Vary," *The Muslim Link*, September 17, 2006, www.muslimlinkpaper.com/community-news/community-news/590-Responses to Washington Post Piece on Dar-us-Salaam Vary.html.

14 Lee, *The Rise and Fall of the Salafi Dawah*, part 9.

15 See commentary from Irtiza Hasan on Imran Muneer, Mahin Islam, Murtadha Siddiqui, and Amir Saeed, "EP 027: The AlMaghrib Origin Story with Irtiza Hasan," *The Mad Mamluks*, September 11, 2016, https://themadmamluks.com/the-almaghrib-origin-story-irtiza-hasan. *The Mad Mamluks* is a podcast hosted by four, now-middle-aged AlMaghrib alumni who often reflect back on their educational experiences there, offering a helpful lens into the identities and dynamics around the institute's evolution from the student level.

16 Zareena Grewal, *Islam Is a Foreign Country: American Muslims and the Global Crisis of Authority* (New York: New York University Press, 2014), 330.

17 On *The Mad Mamluks* podcast, the hosts categorize AlMaghrib as a "much more mild version of Salafi Islam." Muneer et al., "The AlMaghrib Origin Story."

18 Pew Research Center, "America's Changing Religious Landscape."

19 Different demographers count these groups differently, especially by introducing more racial categories to separate out "white Evangelicals," and come up with different statistics. See Daniel Cox and Robert P. Jones, "America's Changing Religious Identity," *PRRI*, September 6, 2017, www .prri.org/research/american-religious-landscape-christian-religiously-unaffiliated.

20 Frank Newport and Joseph Carroll, "Another Way to Look at Evangelicals in America Today," *Gallup*, December 2, 2005, www.gallup.com/poll/20242/another-look-evangelicals-america-today.aspx. For a more recent update to these surprisingly stable "Evangelical Catholic" numbers, see Ryan P. Burge, "The Curious Case of Born-Again Catholics," *Religion in Public*, July 18, 2019, https://religioninpublic.blog/2019/07/18/the-curious-case-of-born-again-catholics.

21 Pew Research Center, "US Muslims Concerned about Their Place in Society."

22 Ibid.

23 Ihsan Bagby, "The American Mosque 2011: Basic Characteristics of the American Mosque Attitudes of Mosque Leaders," *CAIR*, January 2012, pp. 18–20, www.cair.com/images/pdf/The-American-Mosque-2011-part-1 .pdf.

24 Umar Lee, interview, March 2, 2017. A more wild-eyed estimate from an anti-Salafi, Sufi shaykh – Hisham Kabbani – who spoke at the US State Department in 1999 and asserted that 80 percent of US mosques are influenced by or vulnerable to "extremist ideologies," especially "the Wahhabi cult originating in Arabia ... who prefer to use the more respectable name Salafi." Islamic Supreme Council of America, "Revealing the Roots of Militant Extremism," February 1999, https://wpisca.wpengine .com/?p=152. These comments were denounced as inaccurate and inflammatory by nearly every major American Muslim organization. Laurie Goodstein, "A Nation Challenged: The Cleric; Muslim Leader Who Was Once Labeled an Alarmist Is Suddenly a Sage," *New York Times*, October 28, 2001, www.nytimes.com/2001/10/28/us/nation-challenged-cleric-muslim-leader-who-was-once-labeled-alarmist-suddenly.html.

25 Michael Muhammad Knight, *Why I Am a Salafi* (Berkeley, CA: Soft Skull Press, 2015), 17. A more paranoid and Islamophobic analysis of this same phenomenon can be found in Freedom House, "Saudi Publications on Hate Ideology Fill American Mosques," *Center for Religious Freedom*, 2005, http://derafsh-kaviyani.com/english/saudipub .pdf.

26 Bebbington, *Evangelicalism in Modern Britain: A History from the 1730s to the 1980s* (Grand Rapids, MI: Baker, 1989), 2–3.

27 Bob Smietana, "Many Who Call Themselves Evangelical Don't Actually Hold Evangelical Beliefs," *LifeWay Research*, December 6, 2017, https:// lifewayresearch.com/2017/12/06/many-evangelicals-dont-hold-evangelical-beliefs.

28 See also Mark Noll, "Defining Evangelicalism," in *Global Evangelicalism: Theology, History, and Culture in Regional Perspective*, ed. Donald M. Lewis and Richard V. Pierard (Downers Grove, IL: InterVarsity Press, 2014), 25.

29 Bernard Haykel, "On the Nature of Salafi Thought and Action," in *Global Salafism: Islam's New Religious Movement*, ed. Roel Meijer (New York: Columbia University Press, 2009), 35.

30 Haykel, "On the Nature of Salafi Thought and Action," 38–39.

31 Aaron Rock-Singer, *In the Shade of the Sunna: Salafi Piety in the Twentieth-Century Middle East* (Oakland: University of California Press, 2022), 9. Singer's book highlights a number of these distinctive Salafi practices in operation in Egypt, and, while he does not specifically draw out the Salafi mode of scriptural engagement as one of these, the very title of his book signals the centrality of the Hadith (the Sunna) for buttressing Salafi piety and identity.

32 Haykel, "On the Nature of Salafi Thought and Action," 39n15.

33 Emad Hamdeh, "Shaykh Google as Ḥāfiẓ al-ʿAṣr: The Internet, Traditional ʿUlamāʾ, and Self Learning," *American Journal of Islam and Society* 37, nos. 1–2 (2020): 67–102.

34 Interview, February, 18, 2017.

35 On Salafi's low-to-the-ground scriptural theologizing, see Yasir Qadhi, "Salafī-Ashʿarī Polemics," 439.

36 Ockenga, "The Unvoiced Multitudes,' in *A New Evangelical Coalition: Early Documents of the National Association of Evangelicals*, ed. Joel A. Carpenter (New York: Garland, 1988), 33.

37 Robert Wuthnow, *Communities of Discourse: Ideology and Social Structure in the Reformation, the Enlightenment, and European Socialism* (Cambridge, MA: Harvard University Press, 1989), 16. On defining discourse, see also Jan Renkema, *Introduction to Discourse Studies* (Amsterdam: John Benjamins Publishing, 2004), 48.

38 Fisher makes a similar point, describing Evangelicalism as "a Protestant-inflected way of being in the world … a flexible and dynamic idiom, intended to communicate a relative biblical authenticity by those who wielded it." "Evangelical and Unevangelical," 186.

39 The use of the term "discourse" in contemporary scholarship often invokes the historiographical analysis of Michel Foucault. While Foucault is valuable and useful in his own right, I am not intentionally referencing or aligning my analysis with the entirety of his correlation of power and knowledge. Likewise, I am cognizant of Talal Asad's insightful definition of Islam itself as "a discursive tradition." Talal Asad, "The Idea of an Anthropology of Islam," Center for Contemporary Arab Studies, Georgetown University, Occasional Paper Series, March 1986, p. 14. In Chapter 3, I take up the question of whether Salafism (and, for that matter, Evangelicalism) can reasonably be considered a "tradition."

40 On the boundaries of discourse, see Sara Mills, *Discourse* (London: Routledge, 1997), 62.

41 Frank Newport, "Who Are the Evangelicals? Estimates Vary Widely," *Gallup*, June 24, 2005, https://news.gallup.com/poll/17041/who-evangelicals.aspx. On non-Protestants and even non-Christians identifying as Evangelical, see also Ryan P. Burge, "Do You Have to Be Protestant to Be Born Again?," *Religion in Public*, May 7, 2018, https://religioninpublic.blog/2018/05/07/do-you-have-to-protestant-to-be-born-again.

42 See Meleagrou-Hitchens, *Salafism in America*, 45, 64, 90.

43 Yasir Qadhi (writing as Yasir Kazi), "Reconciling Reason and Revelation in the Writings of Ibn Taymiyya (d. 728/1328): An Analytical Study of Ibn Taymiyya's *Darʾ al-taʿāruḍ*" (PhD diss., Yale University, 2013).

44 Andrea Elliott, "Why Yasir Qadhi Wants to Talk about Jihad," and Yasir Qadhi, "GPU'08 with Yasir Qadhi: When Islamophobia Meets Perceived Anti-Semitism," *Muslim Matters*, November 10, 2008, https://muslimmatters.org/2008/11/10/gpu-08-with-yasir-qadhi-when-islamophobia-meets-perceived-anti-semitism/. See also Grewal, *Islam Is a Foreign Country*, 332.

45 Qadhi, interview, February 18, 2017.

46 For instance, Joe Kaufman, "Muslim Who 'Apologized' for Cursing Jews Featured at Terror-Linked Banquet," *FrontPage Magazine*, February 5, 2016, https://archives.frontpagemag.com/fpm/muslim-who-apologized-cursing-jews-featured-terror-joe-kaufman.

47 Yasir Qadhi, "On Salafi Islam," *Muslim Matters*, April 22, 2014, http://muslimmatters.org/2014/04/22/on-salafi-islam-dr-yasir-qadhi. While Qadhi has been circumspect about avoiding precise labels for his post-Salafi identity, he has been very explicit in his denunciation of his early career defense of Ibn ʿAbd al-Wahhab, arguing that the "fanaticism" of the eighteenth-century reformer was a theological precursor for ISIS. Imran Muneer, Mahin Islam, Murtadha Siddiqui, and Amir Saeed, "EP 166: Salafis and Ibn Abd Al-Wahhab, Science and Miracles, Yajuj and Majuj," *The Mad Mamluks*, interview with Yasir Qadhi, October 4, 2019, https://themadmamluks.com/dryasirqadhi.

48 Yasir Qadhi, "Have You Left the Way of the Salaf?," April 9, 2015, www.youtube.com/watch?v=8GYkedPkxlI. Qadhi posted this video on his own YouTube channel.

49 Yasir Qadhi, email correspondence, ISLAMAAR group, July 18, 2019.

50 I am not the first to suggest this "post-Salafism" category, and Qadhi himself has recently commented that "there's an element of truth to that" label. Qadhi on Muneer et al., "EP 166: Salafis and Ibn Abd Al-Wahhab." On a different but pertinent use of the term "post-Salafi" with regard to the shifting political and religion-and-state architecture of Saudi Arabia since the elevation of crown prince Muhammad Bin Salman, see Besnik Sinani, "Post-Salafism: Religious Revisionism in Contemporary Saudi Arabia," *Religions* 13 (2022): 340–356.

CHAPTER 3

1 Saad Tasleem, "My Story! Path to Knowledge, Intentions, Sincerity, Motivations," YouTube.com, May 9, 2020, https://youtu.be/mXcUGVlDG0U.

2 Brett McCracken, *Hipster Christianity: When Church and Cool Collide* (Grand Rapids: Baker, 2010).

3 Saad Tasleem, "My iPath," YouTube: AlMaghrib Institute, September 22, 2013, https://youtu.be/EFXX7-DeF4M.

4 Tasleem, "My iPath."

5 Tasleem, "My iPath."

6 A translation slippage can be important for understanding how the term "traditional" gets (mis)applied to Salafis: The word *Hadith* can sometimes be translated as "the traditions of the Prophet." Hence, Hadith specialists can sometimes be described as having "traditional" training or even be rendered awkwardly in English as "traditionists." Paradoxically, some of the so-called Traditional Salafis are among the most untraditional Muslims you can find. See Hodgson, *The Venture of Islam*, Vol. 1, 390 n. 11.

7 Olivier Roy, *Globalised Islam: The Search for the New Ummah* (London: Hurst and Company, 2004), 1, and "The Varieties of American Evangelicalism," USC Center for Religion and Civic Culture, November 1, 2018, https://crcc.usc.edu/report/the-varieties-of-american-evangelicalism.

8 Quoted in Gamaliel Bradford, *D. L. Moody: A Worker in Souls* (Garden City, NY: Doubleday, Doran & Co., 1927), 36.

9 Alister E. McGrath, "Faith and Tradition," in *The Oxford Handbook of Evangelical Theology*, ed. Gerald R. McDermott (New York: Oxford University Press, 2010), 91.

10 In fact, Finney might be credited as the one who originated the term "Burned Over District," see Charles G. Finney, *Charles G. Finney: An Autobiography* (Westwood, NJ: Fleming H. Revell, 1876), 78.

11 Finney, *An Autobiography*, 4.

12 Finney, *An Autobiography*, 7.

13 Finney, *An Autobiography*, 45.

14 See Alice Felt Tyler, *Freedom's Ferment: Phases of American Social History to 1860* (Minneapolis: University of Minnesota Press, 1944), 29. Finney slightly misquotes Dow's verse in *Lectures on Revival of Religion* (New York: Leavitt, Lord, & Co., 1835), 190.

15 Finney, *An Autobiography*, 42.

16 Finney, *An Autobiography*, 54. For locating Finney's idiosyncratic theology on the classic Calvinist-Arminian continuum of Protestant theology, see George Redfield's preface to Charles G. Finney, *Lectures on Systematic Theology*, ed. J. H. Fairchild (New York: George H. Doran Company, 1878), vii.

17 Balmer, *The Making of Evangelicalism*, 19–25.

18 Finney, *Lectures on Revival of Religion*, 192.

19 Finney, *An Autobiography*, 89.

20 New York Historical Society Museum and Library, "Guide to the Broadway Tabernacle Church and Society Papers 1835–1980," October 19, 2011, http://dlib.nyu.edu/findingaids/html/nyhs/broadwaytabernacle/bioghist.html.

21 Hatch, *Democratization*, 197.

22 Finney, *Lectures on Revival*, 255.

23 Balmer, *Making of Evangelicalism*, 22.

24 Charles G. Finney, *Reflections on Revival*, compiled by Donald Dayton (Minneapolis: Bethany House, 1979), 113–114.

25 Charles E. Hambrick-Stowe, *Charles G. Finney and the Spirit of American Evangelicalism* (Grand Rapids: William B. Eerdmans, 1996), 200–201.

26 See Finney, *An Autobiography*, 347ff, 393, 451.

27 Finney, *An Autobiography*, 84. See also Hatch, *Democratization*, 199.

28 Hofstadter, *Anti-intellectualism in American Life* (New York: Vintage Books, 1962), 91–92.

29 Emad Hamdeh, "Qurʾān and Sunna or the *Madhhab*s?: A Salafi Polemic against Islamic Legal Tradition," *Islamic Law and Society* 24 (2017): 6.

30 Stéphane Lacroix, "Al-Albani's Revolutionary Approach to Hadith," *Institute for the Study of Islam in the Modern World* 21 (Spring 2008): 7. On tendencies toward hierarchical authority within the purportedly egalitarian and meritocratic Salafi-Wahhabi movement, see Roel Meijer, "Politicising *al-Jarḥ wa-l-Taʿdīl*: Rabīʿ b. Hādī al-Madkhalī and the Transnational Battle for Religious Authority," in *The Transmission and Dynamics of the Textual Sources of Islam: Essays in Honour of Harald Motzki*, eds. Nicolet Boekhoff-van der Voort, Kees Versteegh, and Joas Wagemakers (Leiden: Brill, 2011), 378–379.

31 This debate circles around the thorny methodological question of *ijtihad* (independent effort to sift the sources in Qurʾan and Hadith to answer a practical question) versus *taqlid* (relying on precedents from previous scholars). *Ijtihad*, or claims to practice it, carries an air of radical reform and perpetual rethinking. On Wahhabis' use (or lack) of *ijtihad*, see Vogel, *Islamic Law and Legal System*, 76.

32 Daniel Brown, *Rethinking Tradition*, 40–41 and 115. See also Jonathan Brown, *Hadith*, 251–256.

33 Emad Hamdeh, "The Formative Years of an Iconoclastic Salafi Scholar," *The Muslim World* 106 (July 2016): 419.

34 Hamdeh, "Formative Years," 420–425.

35 Jacob Olidort, "In Defense of Tradition: Muḥammad Nāṣir al-Dīn al-Albānī and the Salafi Method" (PhD diss., Princeton University, 2015), 83. See also Emad Hamdeh, *Salafism and Traditionalism: Scholarly Authority in Modern Islam* (Cambridge/New York: Cambridge University Press, 2021), 59–74.

36 On the influence of modernist Salafis on al-Albani's "purist" Salafism, see Joas Wagemakers, "Salafism's Historical Continuity: The Reception of 'Modernist' Salafīs by 'Purist' Salafīs in Jordan," *Journal of Islamic Studies* 30, no. 2 (2019): 214–216.

37 Lacroix, *Awakening Islam*, 83.

38 Since the time of Ibn Hanbal, a basic rule was that evaluators should focus on the chain of oral transmission (*isnād*) and not on the content of the individual hadith (the *matn*). See Burton, *Introduction to the Ḥadīth*, 110–116. Part of what was controversial about Rida and other modernists' suggestions about a wholesale reevaluation of the Hadith was that they implicitly and explicitly argued that new, modern categories (empirical sciences or modern reason) be retroactively applied to the content – *matn* – of ancient hadiths to produce some new means of evaluation. Albani chose instead to regenerate the more mainstream work of *isnad* criticism, though he prioritized the morality of the transmitters over other qualities (memory, correspondence with other accounts, etc.). Lacroix, *Awakening Islam*, 83. On whether *matn* criticism had subtly occurred prior to modernity, see Jonathan Brown, "How We Know Early Ḥadīth Critics Did *Matn* Criticism and Why It's So Hard to Find," *Islamic Law and Society* 15 (2008): 143–184.

39 On other scholars rejecting the authority of the *madhhab*s, see Qadhi, "On Salafi Islam."

40 I am here paraphrasing his argument defending Salafism as quoted in Hamdeh, "Qur'ān and Sunna or the *Madhhab*s?", 13–14.

41 Jonathan Brown, *Hadith*, 297.

42 Lacroix, "Al-Albani's Revolutionary Approach." On other scholars who were forerunners to the eventual Salafi position and were willing to call the classical Hadith collections into question, see Jonathan Brown, *The Canonization of al-Bukhārī and Muslim: The Formation and Function of the Sunnī Ḥadīth Canon* (Leiden/Boston: Brill, 2007), 316.

43 On Albani's "quietist" political vision and hope for a pure Islamic government, see Lauzière, *The Making of Salafism*, 226.

44 While Albani's ideas were controversial, important groundwork had been laid for his views in Saudi Arabia, including with Bin Baz himself, by the influence of the Indian Ahl-i-Hadith movement and its previous cross-pollination with Wahhabism. See Stéphane Lacroix, "Between Revolution and Apoliticism: Nasir al-Din al-Albani and His Impact on the Shaping of Contemporary Salafism," in Global Salafism, 61–62.

45 Qadhi, "On Salafi Islam." On the interface between Rashid Rida and Saudi Salafism, see Lauzière, The Making of Salafism, 60ff.

46 The city of Medina was called Yathrib in the early seventh century until Muhammad and his community migrated there (the Hijra), after which it was renamed "Madīnat an-Nabī" – City of the Prophet.

47 Hamdeh, "Formative Years," 429.

48 Hamdeh, "Qurʾān and Sunna or the Madhhabs?", 2 n. 3.

49 Lacroix, Awakening Islam, 84.

50 Lacroix, "Between Revolution and Apoliticism," 66.

51 Interview with a former follower of Albani in Lacroix, "Between Revolution and Apoliticism," 67.

52 Lacroix, Awakening Islam, 72.

53 Analysts also sometimes call the school of al-Albani "scientific Salafism" (al-Salafiya al-ʿIlmiya) because of the way the Albanian shaykh reinvigorated focus on the science of Hadith. See Robert G. Rabil, Salafism in Lebanon: From Apoliticism to Transnational Jihadism (Washington, DC: Georgetown University Press, 2014), 34–35.

54 Richard Gauvain, Salafi Ritual Purity: In the Presence of God (London: Routledge, 2012), 102.

55 Mohammad Abu Rumman and Hassan Abu Hanieh, "Jordanian Salafism: A Strategy for the 'Islamization of Society' and an Ambiguous Relationship with the State," (Amman: Friedrich-Ebert-Stiftung, 2010), 43, http://library.fes.de/pdf-files/bueros/amman/07758-book2.pdf. Humorously, given the core argument of this chapter, this report alternates between calling al-Albani's strand of Salafism either "conservative" or "traditional."

56 Quintan Wiktorowicz, The Management of Islamic Activism: Salafis, the Muslim Brotherhood, and State Power in Jordan (Albany: State University of New York Press, 2001), 133ff.

57 Lacroix, "Between Revolution and Apoliticism," 58.

58 See, for instance, https://sunnah.com/.

59 Richard Gauvain, "Salafism in Modern Egypt: Panacea or Pest?" *Political Theology* 11, no. 6 (2010), 809. Lacroix is more restrained, but still acknowledges the atmospheric change made by Albani: "al-Albani's ideas would rapidly become a means for Salafi religious entrepreneurs from outside the Wahhabi aristocracy to challenge the existing hierarchy." "Al-Albani's Revolutionary Approach," 7.

60 I cannot find anywhere that Tasleem even explicitly identifies himself as a Salafi. He does mention Albani in the materials for one of his AlMaghrib courses, where he calls him "one of the *Dhahiri* [Ẓāhirī – literalist] scholars from Syria" and characterizes the Albanian's fatwa on beard length as "slightly strange." Saad Tasleem, "Trends: Professional Notes," (Chicago: Qabeelat Wasat/AlMaghrib Institute, November 2017), www.qwasat.org/wp-content/uploads/2017/11/Qabeelat-Wasat-Trends-Updated.pdf.

61 Jonathan Brown clarifies that while Albani "telescoped the normative dimension of time in Islamic religious history," he was not "rejecting the work of classical Muslim scholars; indeed al-Albānī relied entirely on earlier criticisms of ḥadīths and their transmitters in his reevaluation of the contents of famous works." *Canonization*, 323–324.

62 For a profound example of such, see James K. Wellman Jr., Katie E. Corcoran, and Kate J. Stockly, *High on God: How Megachurches Won the Heart of America* (New York: Oxford University Press, 2020), xii.

63 On the deep roots of Evangelical easy-access "Biblicism," see Marsden, *Fundamentalism and American Culture*, 224.

64 Jacob Olidort, "The Politics of 'Quietist' Salafism," The Brookings Project on US Relations with the Islamic World, Analysis Paper no. 18 (February 2015).

65 This group also goes by the title "Jamis" after Shaykh Muhammad Aman al-Jami, another Albani disciple and professor at the Islamic University of Medina. See Lacroix, *Awakening Islam*, 211ff and Farquhar, *Circuits of Faith*, 106–107.

66 Sunan Abu Dawud, 38, 4278, http://sunnah.com/abudawud/39/1.

67 Sunan Abu Dawud, 37, 4273, http://sunnah.com/abudawud/38/8. See Lacroix, *Awakening Islam*, 99.

68 Robin Wright, *Sacred Rage: The Wrath of Militant Islam* (New York: Simon and Schuster, 2001), 148.

69 Thomas Hegghammer and Stéphane Lacroix, "Rejectionist Islamism in Saudi Arabia: The Story of Juhayman Al-'Utaybi Revisited," *International Journal of Middle East Studies* 39, no. 1 (Feb 2007), 106–109.

70 Rabil, *Salafism in Lebanon*, 38–39.

CHAPTER 4

1 See Randall Balmer, "Awana Clubs International," in *Encyclopedia of Evangelicalism* (Louisville: Westminster John Knox Press, 2002), 39.

2 Ummie's Kiddie Kottage, Advertisement in *al-Minhaj Magazine* 1, no. 3 (July 2016): 57.

3 Hamza Yusuf, "Hadith Collections Written for Scholars Not Common People," YouTube, August 9, 2018, https://youtu.be/Wlhevh6bujc.

4 See Brown, *Hadith: Muhammad's Legacy*, 32–35.

5 Emad Hamdeh, *Salafism and Traditionalism*, 67. On gradations within the *ijaza* system, see Brown, *Hadith*, 45–46.

6 Grewal, *Islam Is a Foreign County*, 164. Grewal does excellent work contextualizing and analyzing Yusuf's many incarnations and his appeal to diverse Muslim audiences, see especially, 159–171 and 305–313.

7 For a pointed instance of Yusuf brandishing his *ijaza* to contrast himself with Salafis, see Graeme Wood, *The Way of the Strangers: Encounters with the Islamic State* (New York: Random House, 2017), 232–233. On Yusuf's place in a global constellation of "contemporary Sufis who are also political reformers and cultural critics who speak out against Wahhabism, Salafism, and Islamic fundamentalism," see Scott Kugle, *Rebel between Spirit and Law: Ahmad Zarruq, Sainthood, and Authority in Islam* (Bloomington and Indianapolis: Indiana University Press, 2006), 16.

8 Kasper Mathiesen, "Anglo-American 'Traditional Islam' and Its Discourse of Orthodoxy," *Journal of Arabic and Islamic Studies* 13 (2013): 191–219; and Ron Geaves, "Learning the Lessons from the Neo-revivalist and Wahhabi Movements: The Counterattack of the New Sufi Movements in the UK," in *Sufism in the West*, Jamal Malik and John Hinnells, eds. (New York: Routledge, 2006), 142–159.

9 See Sadek Hamid, *Sufis, Salafis, and Islamists: The Contested Ground of British Islamic Activism* (London/New York: I. B. Tauris, 2016), 81.

10 Grewal, *Islam Is a Foreign Country*, 308.

11 Jonathan Kaufman, "'Rock Star' of New Muslim Generation Also Happens to Be White Suburbanite," *Wall Street Journal*, February 15, 2002, www .wsj.com/articles/SB1013726525977751060. Timur R. Yuskaev uses Yusuf as a case study of the evolution of a Muslim American public intellectual in "Muslim Public Intellectuals and Global Muslim Thought," in *The Cambridge Companion to American Islam*, edited by Juliane Hammer and Omid Safi (New York: Cambridge University Press, 2013), 266–278.

12 Scott Korb, *Light without Fire: The Making of America's First Muslim College* (Boston: Beacon Press, 2012), 88.

13 Zareena A. Grewal and R. David Coolidge, "Islamic Education in the United States: Debates, Practices, and Institutions," in *The Cambridge Companion to American Islam*, Juliane Hammer and Omid Safi, eds. (New York: Cambridge University Press, 2013), 259. For a more detailed intellectual biography of Yusuf and Shakir and analysis of the neo-traditional Islamic underpinnings of Zaytuna, see Nathan Spannaus and Christopher Pooya Razavian, "Zaytuna College and Construction of an American Muslim Identity," in *Modern Islamic Authority and Social Change*, Vol. 2, Masooda Bano, ed. (Edinburgh: Edinburgh University Press, 2018), 39–71.

14 Seyyed Hossein Nasr, whose work has been a touchstone of the Traditional Islam movement, also employs the tree metaphor for the Islamic tradition: "Tradition, therefore, is like a tree, the roots of which are sunk through revelation in the Divine Nature and from which the trunk and branches have grown over the ages." *Traditional Islam in the Modern World* (London/New York: Kegan Paul International, 1987), 13.

15 Korb, *Light without Fire*, 187.

16 Aja Frost, "Zaytuna Becomes First Accredited Muslim College in the US," *USA Today*, March 18, 2015, www.usatoday.com/story/college/2015/03/18/ zaytuna-becomes-first-accredited-muslim-college-in-the-us/37401387/.

17 Zaytuna brochure, quoted in Grewal, *Islam Is a Foreign Country*, 313.

18 Muneer et al., "The AlMaghrib Origin Story." This comment was made by Mahin Islam.

19 Waleed Basyouni, who is the director of AlMaghrib and is based in Houston, clarified for me in an interview that the international headquarters of the Institute is in Toronto, where the Houston headquarters is basically their accounting office and US headquarters. Though even there, the mailing address provided in Toronto leads to a

mailbox service in a pharmacy. There is no physical center of AlMaghrib: The administrative workers and shaykhs and chapters are distributed in a very Internet-age manner. Interview, July 23, 2020.

20 An online message board commentator offers this word-on-the-street summary: "Al-Maghrib is probably the biggest and largest salafi organization in North America. There is no doubt that all the AlMaghrib scholars are salafi, whether or not they follow a madhab [sic] in fiqh, they still are. There is nothing wrong in that, but for them to 'run' away from the salafi label is like hiding from what they are really. I like to say that Al-Maghrib are the moderate and cool salafis." Mujahideen Ryder in *Islamic Awakening* Forum, January 31, 2007, AZSecure-data.org version, https://dibbs.ai.arizona.edu/dibbs/azsecure-forums-darkweb/IslamicAwakening.zip.

21 Grewal, *Islam Is a Foreign Country*, 336.

22 In Anglophone Salafi and other Muslim usage, "shaykh" usually connotes someone who has training in one or more of the classical Islamic sciences – *fiqh* (jurisprudence), *aqida* (theology), Hadith, etc. – whereas *ustadh* carries more of a sense of "instructor" or "master," someone still in the process of acquiring knowledge. While there have certainly been women who have earned the honorific *shaykha* in Islamic history, I have never found Salafis or post-Salafis using the feminine form. The two current female AlMaghrib instructors are listed as *ustadha*s.

23 AlMaghrib claims on its website that its classes "[cater] to more than 120,000 unique students." It is unclear how many of those are American versus participants abroad. AlMaghrib Institute, "About Us," www.almaghrib.org/about.

24 Grewal and Coolidge, "Islamic Education in the United States," 262.

25 Zaytuna College, "College Catalog: Academic Year 2021–2022," https://zaytuna.edu/assets/pdf/Zaytuna-College-Catalog-2021-22-Oct-27-compressed.pdf.

26 Riffing on the trope of non-Muslims calling for a "Protestant Reformation" in Islam and on the frequent comparison of Salafis to the Protestant Reformers, Yusuf has retorted, "These people that say Islam needs a Reformation have never read Christian history. This *is* the Reformation! What we need is a Council of Trent. We need a Counter Reformation." Mehdi Hasan interview with Hamza Yusuf, "Why Do People Join ISIL?" *AlJazeera English*, November 21, 2015, https://youtu.be/nzccNMui3cg.

27 AlMaghrib Institute, "Seminar Catalogue," www.almaghrib.org/seminars.

28 Yasmin Mogahed, "Transformed – Not Losing on Life," AlMaghrib Institute Channel, YouTube.com, May 11, 2016, https://youtu.be/mCn4uNErd5o.

29 Muneer et al., "The AlMaghrib Origin Story." This comment was made by Amir Saeed.

30 For an overview of these often localized tensions, see Lloyd Ridgeon, ed., *Sufis and Salafis in the Contemporary Age* (New York: Bloomsbury Academic, 2015).

31 Yasir Qadhi, "Update! Pledge of Mutual Respect and Cooperation," *Muslim Matters*, September 25, 2007, https://muslimmatters.org/2007/09/22/pledge-of-mutual-respect-and-cooperation/.

32 Anonymous, "Al-Maghrib Institute 'Watch,'" Wordpress, https://sunni1.wordpress.com/al-maghrib-institute-exposed/.

33 AlMaghrib Institute, "About," https://web.archive.org/web/20181205065556/www.almaghrib.org/about.

34 Korb, *Light without Fire*, 49, 51.

35 See Grewal, *Islam Is a Foreign Country*, 164.

36 Qadhi, "Update! Pledge of Mutual Respect." On how Qadhi was challenged to square this statement with his own previous views and the consensus among Saudi Salafis who saw this as an ideological betrayal, see Farquhar, *Circuits of Faith*, 179–180.

37 Interview, January 16, 2016.

38 Quoted in Grewal, *Islam Is a Foreign Country*, 313.

39 Zaytuna College, "Master of Arts Program," https://zaytuna.edu/academics/masters-degree.

40 Society for Biblical Literature website, www.sbl-site.org/default.aspx. See Mark A. Noll, *Between Faith and Criticism: Evangelicals, Scholarship, and the Bible in America*, 2nd ed. (Vancouver: Regent College Publishing, 2004), 122ff.

41 Not only was the IUM not structured around the conveyance of individualized *ijaza*s from scholars, its leaders expressly built their curriculum around this missionary formation goal. Farquhar, *Circuits of Faith*, 109–114, 160.

42 On this disjunction between Salafi democratizing rhetoric and reality, see Jonathan Brown, "Is Islam Easy to Understand or Not?: Salafis, The Democratization of Interpretation and the Need for the Ulema," *Journal of Islamic Studies* 26, no. 2 (2015): 117–144.

43 California Lutheran University, "The Lutheran Education Experience," www.callutheran.edu/about/lutheran-experience.html.

44 California Lutheran University, "2019–2020 Undergraduate Catalog," https://catalog.callutheran.edu/undergraduate/coursesofinstruction/religion/#courseinventory.

45 Biola University, "First-time College Admission Process," www.biola.edu/admissions/undergrad/first-time.

46 Biola University, "Academic Catalog | 2020–21," http://catalog.biola.edu/.

47 Larry Poston coined the term "paramosque" in his *Islamic Daʿwah in the West: Muslim Missionary Activity and the Dynamics of Conversion to Islam* (New York/Oxford: Oxford University Press, 1992), 93ff. Though with Poston's use of this term (non-mosque organizations that facilitate Muslim activities and communities), his emphasis is much more on *daʿwah* (calling/invitation) as an outward facing orientation in activism and proselytism. I am suggesting here a wider range of what "paramosque" activities might entail, including a strong intra-Muslim educational dimension.

48 Korb, *Light without Fire*, 26.

49 He discloses in the introduction to the book, "My own background and religious training was in Christian theology, which over the years I'd paired with a fair sampling of Judaism … With the present book … I set out to write something I didn't know." *Light Without Fire*, xxii.

50 Korb, *Light without Fire*, 189.

51 Yahya Birt, "Blowing in the Wind: Trumpism and Traditional Islam in America," *Medium.com*, February 14, 2017, https://yahyabirt.medium.com/https-medium-com-yahyabirt-blowin-in-the-wind-trumpism-and-traditional-islam-in-america-40ba056486d8. See also, Jayson Casper, "Muslims Join Evangelical Theology Conference," *Christianity Today*, November 20, 2020, www.christianitytoday.com/news/2020/november/islam-christianity-evangelical-theology-society-ets.html.

52 The Center for Justice and Accountability, "United States: Human rights coalition rejects report issued by State Department's Commission on Unalienable Rights," July 19, 2020, https://cja.org/united-states-human-rights-coalition-rejects-report-issued-by-state-departments-commission-on-unalienable-rights/. See also, Ali Rogin, "Members of New Pompeo Task Force Have Previously Praised Human Rights Abusers," *PBS NewsHour*, July 10, 2019, www.pbs.org/newshour/world/members-of-new-pompeo-task-force-have-previously-praised-human-rights-abusers.

53 Quoted in Walaa Quisay and Thomas Parker, "On the Theology of Obedience: An Analysis of Shaykh Bin Bayyah and Shaykh Hamza Yusuf's Political Thought," *Maydan: Islamic Thought*, January 8, 2019, https://themaydan.com/2019/01/theology-obedience-analysis-shaykh-bin-bayyah-shaykh-hamza-yusufs-political-thought/. See Hamza Yusuf, "When Evil Fails and Goodness Prevails: Regarding the Recent Coup Attempt in Turkey," Sandala.org, July 31, 2016, https://sandala.org/when-evil-fails/, and "Hamza Yusuf Hurtful Comments on Syrians," YouTube.com, September 11, 2019, https://youtu.be/1xDF2yW7cQg.

54 The heading for this debate among Salafis comes from the Arabic phrase *al-walā' wa-l-barā'* which can be translated as "loyalty [*walā'*] (to God, Islam, and the Muslim community) and disavowal [*barā'*] (of all others)." Qadhi spoke extensively about this question at the AlMaghrib seminar I attended with him, and he has written about it as well: "Divided Loyalties or Imagined Conflicts? Muslims in America," MuslimMatters.org, January 15, 2010, https://muslimmatters.org/2010/01/15/divided-loyalties-or-imagined-conflicts/. See also, Yasir Qadhi, "Yasir Qadhi: A Proud, Patriotic, Shariah Practicing American," MuslimMatters.org, March 11, 2011, https://muslimmatters.org/2011/03/11/yasir-qadhi-a-proud-patriotic-shariah-practicing-american/.

55 Korb, *Light without Fire*, 144–145. The "balance our loyalties" quote comes from Yasir Qadhi, "The Lure of Radicalism and Extremism Amongst Muslim Youth," MuslimMatters.org, October 18, 2010, https://muslimmatters.org/2010/10/18/yasir-qadhi-the-lure-of-radicalism-amongst-muslim-youth/.

56 Korb, *Light without Fire*, 26. This quote is actually taken by Korb from an essay by another white American revert to Islam, Umar Faruq Abd-Allah, "Islam and the Cultural Imperative," The Oasis Initiative, 2004, www.theoasisinitiative.org/islam-the-cultural-imperative. Abd-Allah does not mention Salafism or Wahhabism in the essay; it is Korb who makes that connection.

CHAPTER 5

1 Scott Shane and Benjamin Weiser, "Court Papers Reveal Qaeda Operative's Work as Trainer and Bomb Expert," *New York Times*, May 10, 2016, www.nytimes.com/2016/05/11/world/middleeast/anwar-al-awlaki-qaeda.html.

2 Scott Shane, "The Lessons of Anwar al-Awlaki," *New York Times Magazine*, August 30, 2015, www.nytimes.com/2015/08/30/magazine/the-lessons-of-anwar-al-awlaki.html.

3 Senate of Canada, "The Standing Committee on National Security and Defence," 41st Parliament, 2nd Session, February 2, 2015, https://sencanada.ca/en/Content/Sen/committee/412/secd/51874-e.

4 Quoted in Rik Coolsaet, "'All Radicalisation is Local': The Genesis and Drawback of an Elusive Concept," Egmont Royal Institute for International Relations, June 2016, 30, www.egmontinstitute.be/content/uploads/2016/05/ep84.pdf?type=pdf.

5 William McCants and Jacob Olidort, "Is Quietist Salafism the Antidote to ISIS?," Brookings Markaz, March 13, 2015, www.brookings.edu/blog/markaz/2015/03/13/is-quietist-salafism-the-antidote-to-isis/.

6 To name just a few exemplars of this genre: Joas Wagemakers, *Salafism in Jordan: Political Islam in a Quietist Community* (New York: Cambridge University Press, 2016); Gilles Kepel, *Jihad: On the Trail of Political Islam*, trans. Anthony F. Roberts (Cambridge, MA: Belknap Press, 2000); Daniel Lav, *Radical Islam and the Revival of Medieval Theology* (New York: Cambridge University Press, 2012); and Francesco Cavatorta, ed., *Salafism After the Arab Awakening: Contending with People's Power* (New York: Oxford University Press, 2017).

7 Wiktorowicz, "Anatomy of the Salafi Movement," 208. Though he doesn't cite Wiktorowicz for his own schema Peter Mandaville similarly trilaterally divides Salafis up into "Salafi quietists," "Salafi Islamists," and "Salafi jihadis." *Global Political Islam* (London/New York: Routledge, 2007), 248–249.

8 See Joas Wagemakers, "Revisiting Wiktorowicz: Categorising and Defining the Branches of Salafism," in *Salafism After the Arab Awakening*, 8. Alternative political taxonomies include ones developed by Yasir Qadhi himself in "On Salafi Islam," and Noah Salomon, "The Salafi Critique of Islamism: Doctrine, Difference and the Problem of Islamic Political Action in Contemporary Sudan" in *Global Salafism: Islam's New Religious Movement*, ed. Roel Meijer (New York: Columbia University Press, 2009), 147.

9 See Asma Afsaruddin, *Striving in the Path of God: Jihad and Martyrdom in Islamic Thought* (New York: Oxford University Press, 2013), and Michael Bonner, *Jihad in Islamic History: Doctrines and Practices* (Princeton: Princeton University Press, 2006).

10 Dominic Tierney recalls that close to 80 percent of Americans supported the 2001 invasion of Afghanistan and around 70 percent supported the war in Iraq two years later. "Do Americans Love War?" *The Atlantic*, January 24, 2011, www.theatlantic.com/national/archive/2011/01/do-americans-love-war/70068/.

11 See Christian Parenti, "America's Jihad: A History of Origins," *Social Justice* 28, no . 3 (85) (Fall 2001): 31–38. The hosts of The Mad Mamluks podcast recount memories of such Mujahideen recruiting efforts in America during their youth on Imran Muneer, Mahin Islam, Murtadha Siddiqui, and Amir Saeed, "EP 195: The Failure of Establishing the Caliphate with Mazin Abdul Adhim," *The Mad Mamluks* podcast, August 2, 2020, https://themadmamluks.libsyn.com/ep-195-the-failure-of-establishing-the-caliphate-mazin-abdul-adhim.

12 George Criles, *Charlie Wilson's War: The Extraordinary Story of the Largest Covert Operation in History* (New York: Atlantic Monthly Press, 2003), 165. On the effects of the Afghan jihad on intra-Salafi discourse, see Quintan Wiktorowicz, "The Salafi Movement: Violence and the Fragmentation of Community," in *Muslim Networks from Hajj to Hip Hop*, eds. Miriam Cooke and Bruce B. Lawrence (Chapel Hill: University of North Carolina Press, 2005), 216ff.

13 Lacroix, *Awakening Islam*, 173. Lacroix's whole book is an excellent exploration of the impetus behind, the dynamics within, and the reactions to the Sahwa movement.

14 Lacroix, *Awakening Islam*, 215. On the subtleties of Madkhali politics in non-Saudi contexts, see Zoltan Pall, *Salafism in Lebanon: Local and Transnational Movements* (Cambridge, UK: Cambridge University Press, 2018), 20ff.

15 These punishments were most conspicuously meted out on the two leading Sahwis, Salman al-Ouda and Safar al-Hawali. See Mamoun Fandy, "Safar al-Hawali: Saudi Islamist or Saudi nationalist?," *Islam and Christian–Muslim Relations* 9, no. 1 (1998): 5–21.

16 Though he was not a trained jurist, Bin Laden presented this document in the form of a fatwa. Osama bin Laden, "Declaration of Jihad against the Americans Occupying the Land of the Two Holiest Sites," Combating Terrorism Center at West Point, August 1996, https://ctc.usma.edu/harmony-program/declaration-of-jihad-against-the-americans-occupying-the-land-of-the-two-holiest-sites-original-language-2/. For some reason

the English translation on this page renders Ibn Taymiyya as "Ibn Tamimah."

17 Umar Lee paints a picture of the insular nature of the pre-9/11 American Salafi community, "While we were living in our bubble, all that mattered was trying to 'go study,' 'spread the dawah [message],' and/or 'establish classes' ... During the good times, Salafis were blissfully unaware of the latest American (or world) economic or social trends ... Many of the things that mattered to salafis, mattered little to the rest of the world." *Rise and Fall of the Salafi Dawah*, Part 8.

18 The "Mecca and Medina" image comes from Elmasry, "The Salafis in America," 225. Elmasry's article is one of the best extant academic resources charting the dissolution of the pre-9/11 Salafi community.

19 IIASA was colloquially known as "the *ma'had*" (institute), and was utilized as a primary education resource by many American Salafis. Elmasry, "The Salafis in America," 222–224. See also, Caryle Murphy and Susan Schmidt, "US Revokes Visas of 16 at Islamic Institute," *Washington Post*, January 29, 2004, www.washingtonpost.com/archive/politics/2004/01/29/us-revokes-visas-of-16-at-islamic-institute/56b9b643-3046-4dce-9408-67242b0fc7e3/.

20 Diamant's dissertation ("Engagement and Resistance") is rooted in close historical and ethnographic study of this New Jersey African American Salafi community.

21 Lee, *Rise and Fall of the Salafi Dawah*, Parts 4 & 5.

22 Lee, *Rise and Fall of the Salafi Dawah*, Part 6. On the historical development of these distinctive Salafi sartorial practices, see Rock-Singer, *In the Shade of the Sunna*, 170–227.

23 Yasir Qadhi has commented that a dozen or more Americans had gone to study at IUM in the 1990s before he arrived there in 1996, and all of those who preceded him were African American. Yasir Qadhi, Comments during "Salafism, a Growing Islamic Movement" panel, American Academy of Religion, San Antonio, TX, November 2016. On al-Madkhali's influence in African American Salafi communities, see Diamant, "Engagement and Resistance," 230–235.

24 Lee, *Rise and Fall of the Salafi Dawah*, Part 6. While Lee never uses the term Madkhali or Jami to label this group, the specific content of their political theology is a dead giveaway.

25 Quoted in Meijer, "Politicising *al-Jarḥ wa-l-Ta'dīl*," 385.

26 Elmasry, "The Salafis in America," 230. Lee, *Rise and Fall of the Salafi Dawah*, Parts 6 & 7.

27 Tariq Nelson, interview with Andrea Useem, "Surviving Salafism: An American Muslim Recovers from Extremism and Makes a Difference," December 12, 2007, https://web.archive.org/web/20080828070734/www .religionwriter.com/islam-in-america/surviving-salafism-an-american- muslim-recovers-from-radicalism-and-makes-a-difference/.

28 Iman Dawood observes a similar phenomenon at work in the UK, where Madkhali adherents have come to monopolize the Salafi identity, causing others who previously identified as Salafis to seek other labels. Iman Dawood, "Who is a 'Salafi'? Salafism and the Politics of Labelling in the UK," *Journal of Muslims in Europe* 9 (2020): 240–261.

29 Scott Shane and Souad Mekhennet, "Imam's Path from Condemning Terror to Preaching Jihad," *New York Times*, May 8, 2010, www.nytimes .com/2010/05/09/world/09awlaki.html.

30 An American Muslim who knew him describes "the common sense that Awlaki brought to religious texts" in Scott Shane's *Objective Troy: A Terrorist, A President, and the Rise of the Drone* (New York: Crown Publishing Group, 2015), 99. On Awlaki's bi-cultural charisma, see Angela Gendron, "The Call to Jihad: Charismatic Preachers and the Internet," *Studies in Conflict and Terrorism* 40, no. 1 (2017): 44–61.

31 Shane and Mekhennet, "Imam's Path from Condemning Terror."

32 See Alexander Meleagrou-Hitchens, *Incitement: Anwar al-Awlaki's Western Jihad* (Cambridge, MA: Harvard University Press, 2020), 85–90.

33 This quote came from Murtadha Siddiqui, one of the cohosts of the Mad Mamluks podcast in the midst of a nostalgic conversation about al-Awlaki where all four cohosts reminisced about the role his preaching played in their pre-9/11 development. In Siddiqui's evaluation, al-Awlaki was and is peerless among English-language Islamic preachers: "Yasir Qadhi doesn't even come close." Imran Muneer, Mahin Islam, Murtadha Siddiqui, and Amir Saeed, "EP 198: Ali Timimi Freed, Peace with Israel, David Wood Eats Quran, Bilal Abdul Kareem Arrested!" *The Mad Mamluks* podcast, August 19, 2020, www.youtube.com/watch?v=dkdKTM3ffrc.

34 Scott Shane, "Anwar al-Awlaki, Yemen, and American Counterterrorism Policy," Brookings Institution, Washington, D.C., September 17, 2015, 3, www.brookings.edu/wp-content/uploads/2015/08/20150917_awlaki_ yemen_transcript.pdf.

35 Shane, "The Lessons of Anwar al-Awlaki."

36 Shane's *Objective Troy*, 109ff, has a good rundown of the legal, circumstantial, and anecdotal evidence for and against al-Awlaki's radicalization prior to 9/11. He concludes: "When all the evidence is considered, the notion of Awlaki having a well-hidden secret life in Al Qaeda is unpersuasive" (115).

37 Shane, *Objective Troy*, 83.

38 Laurie Goodstein, "A Nation Challenged: The American Muslims; Influential American Muslims Temper Their Tone," *New York Times*, October 19, 2001, www.nytimes.com/2001/10/19/us/nation-challenged-american-muslims-influential-american-muslims-temper-their.html.

39 Shane, "Anwar al-Awlaki, Yemen, and American Counterterrorism Policy," 6.

40 Shane, "The Lessons of Anwar al-Awlaki."

41 See Shane, *Objective Troy*, 103ff.

42 Quoted in Alexander Meleagrou-Hitchens, "As American As Apple Pie: How Anwar al-Awlaki Became the Face of Western Jihad," International Centre for the Study of Radicalisation and Political Violence (2011), 41, https://icsr.info/wp-content/uploads/2011/09/ICSR-Report-As-American-As-Apple-Pie-How-Anwar-al-Awlaki-Became-the-Face-of-Western-Jihad .pdf.

43 Meleagrou-Hitchens reads this and other sermons as evidence that al-Awlaki was firmly in Wiktorowicz's activist/politico Salafi strand. See *Incitement*, 65ff.

44 It is unclear what al-Awlaki knew about his legal situation, but Scott Shane has uncovered FBI files showing that they intended to leverage charging al-Awlaki with crossing state lines (from Virginia to DC) to solicit prostitutes in hopes of making him an informant or discrediting him as a preacher with his fellow Muslims. See Shane, *Operation Troy*, 108–109, 117, 119.

45 Quoted in Meleagrou-Hitchens, "As American as Apple Pie," 49. Slobodan Milošević was the leader of the Serbian (Orthodox Christian) faction in the Bosnian War that proceeded from the breakup of Yugoslavia. He oversaw the ethnic cleansing of Bosnian Muslims. Incidentally, the Bosnian War (1992–1995) was another conflict that some Muslim clerics declared was a legitimate jihad, and many Muslims from around the globe traveled to Bosnia to defend their coreligionists, covertly supported by American

intelligence services. See Richard J. Aldrich, "America Used Islamists to Arm the Bosnian Muslims," *The Guardian*, April 21, 2002, www .theguardian.com/world/2002/apr/22/warcrimes.comment.

46 Once al-Awlaki moved to Yemen in 2003 or 2004, there is evidence that he went to neighboring Saudi Arabia to study (or, at least, converse) with Salman al-Ouda, one of the Sahwi leaders, though al-Ouda had declared the war against the Americans in Iraq to not be a legitimate jihad. Shane, *Objective Troy*, 157–158.

47 Al-Awlaki claimed he had intervened in a kidnapping, a tribal dispute, and was arrested on that pretext. The US authorities claimed he was "imprisoned … on charges of kidnapping for ransom and being involved in an al-Qa'ida plot to kidnap a US official." US Department of the Treasury, " Treasury Designates Anwar Al-Aulaqi, Key Leader of Al-Qa'ida in the Arabian Peninsula," press release, July 16, 2010, https://home.treasury .gov/news/press-releases/tg779. No paperwork formally describing or substantiating those charges has ever surfaced. See Shane, *Operation Troy*, 165 and Meleagrou-Hitchens, *Incitement*, 36–37.

48 Shane, "Anwar al-Awlaki, Yemen, and American Counterterrorism Policy," 9. See also Meleagrou-Hitchens, "As American as Apple Pie," 30.

49 Shane and Mekhennet, "Imam's Path from Condemning Terror to Preaching Jihad."

50 Quoted in Melagrou-Hitchens, "As American as Apple Pie," 75–76.

51 Scott Shane, "The Enduring Influence of Anwar al-Awlaki in the Age of the Islamic State," *Combating Terrorism Center Sentinel* 9, no. 7 (July 2016), https://ctc.usma.edu/the-enduring-influence-of-anwar-al-awlaki-in-the-age-of-the-islamic-state/.

52 Abdulrahman's cousin (Anwar's nephew) was also killed in the attack. This second attack was evidently focused on another medium-value target from Al Qaeda in the Arabian Peninsula (AQAP) who was not even present. Seven people in total died, and President Obama told a close aide that the whole thing was a "fuck up." Shane, *Objective Troy*, 296.

53 Mohammed Ghobari and Phil Stewart, "Commando Dies in US Raid in Yemen, First Military Op OK'd by Trump," *Reuters*, January 29, 2017, https://uk.reuters.com/article/uk-usa-yemen-qaeda-idUKKBN15D094.

54 Hakim Almasmari, "Interview: Dr. Nasser Awlaqi Father of Sheikh Anwar Awlaqi," *YemenPost*, April 10, 2010, www.yemenpost.net/ Detail123456789.aspx?ID=100&SubID=1781&MainCat=4.

55 See Tom Finn and Noah Browning, "An American Teenager in Yemen: Paying for the Sins of His Father?," *Time*, October 27, 2011, http://content .time.com/time/world/article/0,8599,2097899,00.html. On Nasser al-Awlaki's effort to prevent his son's execution, see Al-Aulaqi v. Obama, 727 F.Supp.2d 1 (2010).

56 See Grewal, *Islam is a Foreign Country*, 331.

57 Mohammed A. Malik, "I Reported Omar Mateen to the FBI. Trump Is Wrong That Muslims Don't Do Our Part," *The Washington Post*, June 20, 2016, www.washingtonpost.com/posteverything/wp/2016/06/20/i-reported-omar-mateen-to-the-fbi-trump-is-wrong-that-muslims-dont-do-our-part/. On Abdalmutallab and AlMaghrib, see Paul Cruickshank and David Mattingly, "Terror Suspect Attended 2008 'Knowledge Fest' in Houston," *CNN*, December 30, 2009, www.cnn.com/2009/US/12/30/terror.suspect .seminar/index.html. The Counter Extremism Project has a database of American and European Muslim extremists who have some connection to or draw inspiration from al-Awlaki: www.counterextremism.com/anwar-al-awlaki. See also Donald Holbrook, "The Spread of Its Message: Studying the Prominence of al-Qaida Materials in UK Terrorism Investigations," *Perspectives on Terrorism* 11, no. 6 (December 2017): 89–100.

58 Scott Shane, "The Enduring Influence of Anwar al-Awlaki."

59 AlMaghrib Institute, "Waleed Basyouni," Instructor Profiles, www .almaghrib.org/instructors/waleed-basyouni.

60 Interview, July 23, 2020. For Basyouni's more general reflections on seeing dozens of people he knew come back changed from the jihad in Afghanistan, see Waleed Basyouni, "Violence in the Name of God," 2008, https://youtu.be/DN7KRgvS9Cw.

61 Interview, July 23, 2020.

62 Interview, July 23, 2020.

63 Basyouni was mentored by, among others, the man who originally invited Albani to Saudi Arabia, Shaykh Abd al-Aziz Bin Baz. For Basyouni's reflections on his mentorship by Bin Baz, see Waleed Basyouni, "Chai Chat with Shaykh Waleed Basyouni," YouTube: Green Lake Masjid Channel, August 30, 2019, www.youtube.com/watch?v=GR3fZ49w_gM. Basyouni also described to me in an interview a "very smart" back and forth he had with Salman al-Ouda, one of the principal Sahwis, about the American troops during the Persian Gulf crisis, when Basyouni was an undergraduate and al-Ouda was a master's student in Riyadh. Interview, December 5, 2018.

64 Interview, July 23, 2020.

65 Interview, July 23, 2020.

66 Interviews, February 28, 2017 and December 5, 2018.

67 Interview, December 5, 2018. To be fair to the Muslims who devotedly follow a *madhhab*, Basyouni is being polemical here – there is real flexibility and a range of opinion on many questions within each of these *madhhab*s.

68 Interview, December 5, 2018.

69 Clear Lake Islamic Center, "Our History," https://web.archive.org/web/20160326182722/www.themasjid.org/our-history/.

70 Interview, July 23, 2020.

71 Interview, February 28, 2017. See Farquhar, *Circuits of Faith*, 133–134.

72 Interview, July 23, 2020.

73 Interview, July 23, 2020. Basyouni has also spoken more extensively on his views on cooperating with law enforcement in an interview: Chelby Daigle, "Waleed Basyouni on Extremism," *Muslim Link Canada*, March 31, 2015, https://muslimlink.ca/stories/waleed-basyouni-extremism.

74 This comment was posted in response to a video of Basyouni's "Violence in the Name of God" lecture, "That's American Islam for you. The old House Negro mentality." Daniel, "Waleed Basyouni Exposed," in *Islamic Awakening* Forum, August 23, 2008, AZSecure-data.org version, https://dibbs.ai.arizona.edu/dibbs/azsecure-forums-darkweb/IslamicAwakening.zip. Elsewhere, another commenter on one of Basyouni's lectures says, "He doesnt [sic] have to toe the line of Kuffar [unbelievers] unless he wants to be on their payroll." Naeem Muhammad Khan, comment on "Inside the Mind of a Muslim Terrorist," HalalTube.com, October 30, 2009, www.halaltube.com/inside-the-mind-of-a-muslim-terrorist. This same commenter negatively compares Basyouni with al-Awlaki whom he views as having integrity in this regard.

75 Asim Qureshi, "Open Letter to Muslim Activists and Organizations in the US on Engagement with the Structures of Policing," *Muslim Matters*, September 24, 2020, https://muslimmatters.org/2020/09/24/open-letter-to-muslim-activists-and-organisations-in-the-us-on-engagement-with-the-structures-of-policing/. Qureshi does not mention Basyouni or AlMaghrib by name, but they are clearly included in the trend he is taking issue with. A more sustained form of this argument is advanced in Arun Kundnani, *The Muslims Are Coming!: Islamophobia, Extremism, and the Domestic War on Terror* (London/New York: Verso, 2014).

76 Interview, July 23, 2020.

77 On the broader context of tension between the FBI and the American Muslim community, including misperceptions about Islam within the FBI, see Michael Barkun, "The FBI and American Muslims after September 11," in *The FBI and Religion: Faith and National Security Before and After 9/11*, edited by Sylvester A. Johnson and Steven Weitzman (Oakland: University of California Press, 2017), 244–255.

78 Muhammad Alshareef, "AlMaghrib's New VP: Shaykh Waleed Basyouni," AlMaghrib Blog, June 26, 2008, https://web.archive.org/web/ 20080812045529/www.almaghrib.org/blog/2008/06/almaghribs-new-vp- shaykh-waleed.html. Yasir Qadhi had been appointed Dean of Academic Affairs at AlMaghrib in March 2008.

79 While Alshareef was still listed as the President of AlMaghrib and Waleed as the "Vice President," after Waleed's incorporation into the administration, Alshareef settled abroad and focused on DiscoverU, https://discoveru .online/courses/. See Imran Muneer, Mahin Islam, Murtadha Siddiqui, and Amir Saeed, "EP 150: Supercharger Alma Mater with Muhammad AlShareef," *The Mad Mamluks* podcast, May 4, 2019, www.youtube.com/ watch?v=mMg_JCaEZpg. On AlMaghrib's tax filings since 2012, Basyouni is listed as "Director and Vice President," see AlMaghrib Institute, Inc., Form 990 (2012), https://projects.propublica.org/nonprofits/display_990/ 270091991/2013_12_EO/27–0091991_990_201212. He has more recently taken on more of a senior adviser role with Texas Dawah Convention, allowing others to run the day-to-day organization.

80 Waleed Basyouni, "Shaykh Waleed Basyouni's Endorsement for President," YouTube.com, November 5, 2012, https://youtu.be/30Y-lxDcwyg.

81 Interview, December 5, 2018.

82 Yasir Qadhi, Facebook post, November 5, 2012, https://facebook.com/ yasir.qadhi/posts/346149342147109.

83 Moosaa Richardson, "Voting, Democracy, the Ikhwani Manhaj and Waleed Basyouni," YouTube.com, September 22, 2013, www.youtube .com/watch?v=5kVabUqtzuM.

84 An important recent study on the dynamics around what counts as a scholar among American Madkhali Salafis is Emily Goshey, "No Scholars in the West: Salafi Networks of Knowledge from Saudi Arabia to Philadelphia," *American Journal of Islam and Society* 29, nos. 1–2 (2022): 41–71.

85 Basyouni earned his PhD from Graduate Theological Foundation in 2007. Like Qadhi's, his dissertation was on Ibn Taymiyya.

86 Islamic State in the Levant, "Kill the Imāms of Kufr in the West," *Dabiq* no. 14, April–May 2016, 16–17. Yasir Qadhi and Hamza Yusuf were also on this ISIS death list.

87 Interview, December 5, 2018.

88 Interview, December 5, 2018.

89 Interview, December 5, 2018.

CHAPTER 6

1 Ify Okoye, interview, August 26, 2020.

2 There is both anecdotal and quantitative evidence of a surge in converts to Islam in America after 9/11. See Jodi Wilgoren, "A Nation Challenged: American Muslims; Islam Attracts Converts by the Thousand, Drawn Before and After Attacks," *The New York Times*, October 22, 2001, www .nytimes.com/2001/10/22/us/nation-challenged-american-muslims-islam-attracts-converts-thousand-drawn-before.html, see also Amy Melissa Guimond, *Converting to Islam: Understanding the Experiences of White American Females* (New York: Palgrave Macmillan, 2017), 7.

3 Ify Okoye, "The Mormoms [sic] Helped Me Become Muslim," *IfyOkoye. com* (blog), June 6, 2009, https://ifyokoye.com/2009/06/06/mormons-witnesses-shahadah-twice-almaghrib/.

4 On the contested identification of Dar-us-Salaam with Salafism, see Chapter 2. Interestingly, Okoye herself participated in that controversy in 2006 about whether the *Washington Post* had accurately identified Dar-us-Salaam as Salafi. See Ify Okoye (posting as Muslim Apple), "Dar us Salaam Salafi? The Goal is Not Isolation," *IfyOkoye.com* (blog), September 8, 2006, https://ifyokoye.com/2006/09/08/dar-us-salaam-salafi-%E2%80% 93-the-goal-is-not-isolation/.

5 For a comparison of Okoye's blog with other feminist Muslim bloggers see, Krista Melanie Riley, "'You Don't Need a Fatwa': Muslim Feminist Blogging as Religious Interpretation," (PhD diss, Concordia University, 2016).

6 Amad Shaikh, Qadhi's co-founder at *Muslim Matters*, jokes that it emerged out of the American Muslim blogosphere that was trying to capture "the 'orthodox voice' or at the time [the] 'not-salafi but salafi

voice.'" Amad Shaikh (posting as Abu Reem), "How a Blog Was Born: MuslimMatters Origins," May 21, 2012, https://muslimmatters.org/2012/05/21/how-a-blog-was-born-muslimmatters-origins/. Alternatively, Umar Lee summarizes: "What Muslim Matters is trying to do is try to create a mainstream that is Salafi or that is conservative." Interview.

7 Ify Okoye, "Anwar al-Awlaki Jailed," *IfyOkoye.com* (blog), November 8, 2006, https://ifyokoye.com/2006/11/08/anwar-al-awlaki-jailed/.

8 Ify Okoye, "Update: What's Up with Anwar al-Awlaki?," *IfyOkoye.com* (blog), November 10, 2009, https://ifyokoye.com/2009/11/10/whats-up-with-anwar-al-awlaki/.

9 Yasir Qadhi, "The Vision of IlmSummit: Keynote Lecture at IlmSummit 2008," November 30, 2012, https://youtu.be/9UB4OF2F6pA.

10 Siraaj Muhammad, "Ilm Summit 2009: A Day in the Life," *Muslim Matters*, August 19, 2009, https://muslimmatters.org/2009/08/19/ilm-summit-2009-a-day-in-the-life/.

11 Okoye, interview.

12 Ify Okoye, "The Penalty Box: Muslim Women's Prayer Spaces," *Muslim Matters*, February 8, 2010, https://web.archive.org/web/20100212124810/https://muslimmatters.org/2010/02/08/the-penalty-box/.

13 Muslim Apple, February 9, 2010, comment on Ify Okoye, "The Penalty Box." The emphasis in Abd-Allah's comment is his own.

14 See Ify Okoye, "Pray in Accordance to the Sunnah: Muslim Women Protest Against Marginalization," *Muslim Matters*, June 7, 2010, https://muslimmatters.org/2010/06/07/pray-in-accordance-to-the-sunnah-muslim-women-protest-against-marginalization/. On local media coverage of the protests and their reception in the Muslim community, see William Wan and Michael Laris, "Mosque Pray-ins against Segregation of Sexes are Springing Up," *The Washington Post*, May 22, 2010, www.washingtonpost.com/wp-dyn/content/article/2010/05/21/AR2010052104253.html, and Muslim Link Staff, "Breaking the Ranks or Peaceful Protest?", June 3, 2010, Muslim Link, www.muslimlinkpaper.com/community-news/community-news/2193-breaking-the-ranks-or-peaceful-protest.html.

15 Ify Okoye, "Use Your Mind: You Don't Need a Fatwa for Everything," *IfyOkoye.com* (blog), January 19, 2011, https://ifyokoye.com/2011/01/19/use-your-mind-you-dont-need-a-fatwa-for-everything/.

16 Clifford Geertz, *Local Knowledge: Further Essays in Interpretive Anthropology* (New York: Basic Books, 1983), 77, 85. In his suburb

metaphor, Geertz is riffing on a passage from Wittgenstein comparing language (and, for Geertz, culture) to an old city with maze-like streets that only gradually becomes rationalized into more neatly ordered outlying suburbs.

17 Geertz, *Local Knowledge*, 85. He keeps these "somewhat unstated properties" in quotes to convey that, like notions of common sense themselves, these qualities participate in the assumption that common sense is real and meaningful.

18 This is not to say that the concept or idea of common sense is impossible to express in Arabic. Various phrases can approximate the idea of common sense, usually through some combination of four trilateral roots: *f-ṭ-r* (the same root as *fiṭra*, connoting nature, creation, innate dispositions), *n-ṭ-q* (connoting logic, speaking, articulation), and *f-k-r* (connoting thought, reflection, and holding something in one's mind), with the root *s-l-m* (the same root as Muslim and Islam, with a range of meaning from soundness and security to submission and consent). Thus any of the phrases *al-fuṭrat al-salīma*, *manṭiq salīm*, or *tafkīr salīm* can be used to convey the idea of common sense.

19 Qadhi, interview, January 16, 2016.

20 Yasir Qadhi, email correspondence, January 20, 2016. For a counter argument that "common sense" is an inadequate translation of *ṣarīḥ al-ʿaql*, see Anke von Kügelgen, "The Poison of Philosophy: Ibn Taymiyya's Struggle for and against Reason," in *Islamic Theology, Philosophy and Law*, Birgit Krawietz and Georges Tamer, eds. (Berlin/Boston: De Gruyter, 2013), 298.

21 Hatem al-Haj, interview, March 2, 2017. This correlation of *ʿaql* and *naql* in the thought of Ibn Taymiyya is also the topic of Yasir Qadhi's Yale PhD dissertation: Qadhi, "Reconciling Reason and Revelation."

22 Basyouni, interview, February 28, 2017. The *ẓāhir* of a scriptural passage is the unadorned meaning. See Ibn Taymiyya, *Ibn Taymiyyah Expounds on Islam: Selected Writings of Shaykh al-Islam Taqi ad-Din Ibn Taymiyyah on Islamic Faith, Life, and Society*, trans. and ed. Muhammad ʿAbdul-Haqq Ansari (n.p., n.d.), 154, https://archive.org/details/IbnTaymiyyahExpoundsOnIslam-Alhamdulillah-library.blogspot.in.pdf. *Fatāwā* 6:355–372.

23 Sahih Muslim Vol. 2, Book 23, Hadith 398, https://sunnah.com/muslim/46/34. This translation is taken from Ibn Taymiyya, *Ibn Taymiyyah*

Expounds on Islam, 3, so that the connection with the following analysis can be clear. This hadith itself appears to be aiming to interpret that lone use of the noun *fiṭra* in the Qur'an.

24 See Camilla Adang, "Islam as the Inborn Religion of Mankind: The Concept of *Fiṭra* in the Works of Ibn Ḥazm," *Al-Qantara* XXI (2000): 391–410. See also Yasien Mohamed, *Fitrah: The Islamic Concept of Human Nature* (London: Ta Ha Publishers, 1996).

25 Ibn Taymiyya, *Ibn Taymiyyah Expounds on Islam*, 3–4. *Fatāwā* 4:247. Emphasis added.

26 See Jon Hoover, *Ibn Taymiyya's Theodicy of Perpetual Optimism* (Leiden/Boston: Brill, 2007), 43–44.

27 Jon Hoover, *Encyclopaedia of Islam*, 3rd. ed., s.v. "Fiṭra." See also Frank Griffel, "Al-Ghazālī's Use of the 'Original Human Disposition" (*Fiṭra*) and Its Background in the Teachings of al-Fārābī and Avicenna," *The Muslim World* 102 (January 2012): 28.

28 See Marco Werman, "Tarek Mehanna Found Guilty," PRI's *The World*, December 20, 2011, www.pri.org/stories/2011-12-20/tarek-mehanna-found-guilty, and Tarek Mehanna v. United States, 35 F.3d 32 (Supreme Court 2013).

29 For more on Mehanna's trial and its implications for free-speech curtailment in America, see Andrew F. March, "A Dangerous Mind?", *The New York Times: Opinion*, April 21, 2012, www.nytimes.com/2012/04/22/opinion/sunday/a-dangerous-mind.html, and Ross Caputi, "Tarek Mehanna: Punished for Speaking Truth to Power," *The Guardian*, April 16, 2012, www.theguardian.com/commentisfree/cifamerica/2012/apr/16/tarek-mehanna-punished-speaking-truth.

30 Tarek Mehanna, "Tarek Mehanna's Sentencing Statement," *HistoryIsAWeapon.com*, April 12, 2012, www.historyisaweapon.com/defcon1/tarekmehannasentencingstatement.html.

31 Mehanna, "Sentencing Statement."

32 Hume, *A Treatise of Human Nature Being: A Critical Edition* (Oxford: Clarendon Press, 2007), 4.

33 Hume, *Treatise*, 4.

34 T. Heiner Klemme, "Skepticism and Common Sense," in *The Cambridge Companion to the Scottish Enlightenment*, ed. Alexander Broadie (New York: Cambridge University Press, 2003), 118.

35 There *were* limits to Hume's skepticism. He did, in later writings make space for "*excessive* skepticism" to be "corrected by common sense and

reflection." David Hume, *An Enquiry Concerning Human Understanding*, ed. Peter Millican (Oxford/New York: Oxford University Press, 2007), 161. On Hume's views on common sense, see Marion Ledwig, *Common Sense: Its History, Method, and Applicability* (New York: Peter Lang Publishing, 2007), 79ff.

36 D. H. Meyer, "The Uniqueness of the American Enlightenment," *American Quarterly* 28, no. 2 (Summer 1976): 169.

37 Immanuel Kant, *Prolegomena to Any Future Metaphysics with Selections from the Critique of Pure Reason*, ed. and trans. Gary Hatfield (Cambridge, UK: Cambridge University Press, 2004), 10. Emphasis his.

38 Kant, *Prolegomena*, 106.

39 Bentham, *A Comment on the Commentaries and a Fragment on Government*, J. H. Burns and H. L. A. Hart, eds. (Oxford: Clarendon Press, 1977), 440. On the interrelationship between Hume and Bentham's thought, see José L. Tasset, "Bentham on 'Hume's Virtues,'" in *Happiness and Utility: Essays Presented to Frederick Rosen*, eds. Georgios Varouxakis and Mark Philp (London: University College London Press, 2019), 81–97.

40 Thomas Reid, *An Inquiry into the Human Mind on the Principles of Common Sense* (Edinburgh: Anderson, MacDowall, and Robertson, 1818), vi–vii.

41 Reid, *Inquiry into the Human Mind*, 59.

42 Mark A. Noll, "Common Sense Traditions and American Evangelical Thought," *American Quarterly* 37, no. 2 (Summer 1985): 220.

43 Reid, *Inquiry into the Human Mind*, 59. E. Brooks Holifield concisely phrases this the "Scottish turn to the presuppositions implicit in experience." *Theology in America: Christian Thought from the Age of the Puritans to the Civil War* (New Haven: Yale University Press, 2003), 178.

44 Benjamin W. Redekop, "Reid's Influence in Britain, Germany, France and America," in *The Cambridge Companion to Thomas Reid*, eds. Terence Cuneo and René van Woudenberg (Cambridge, UK: Cambridge University Press, 2004), 313.

45 Noll points out that Reid himself was building on a foundation laid by another Scottish Enlightenment figure, Francis Hutcheson, who was a generation older than Hume and Reid, and who had argued that human beings are endowed with a universal, innate moral sense. Hutcheson, because of his age and stature, was far more impactful on American philosophy prior to the Revolution, whereas Reid's Common Sense had its

American flowering after the Revolution. See Noll, *America's God*, 107–109.

46 For a good overview, see Samuel Fleischacker, "The Impact on America: Scottish Philosophy and the American Founding," in *The Cambridge Companion to the Scottish Enlightenment*, 316–337. See also Daniel N. Robinson, "The Scottish Enlightenment and the American Founding," *The Monist* 90, no. 2 (April 2007): 170–181, and Henry F. May, *The Enlightenment in America* (Oxford: Oxford University Press, 1976).

47 Sophia Rosenfeld, *Common Sense: A Political History* (Cambridge, MA: Harvard University Press, 2011), 138.

48 Meyer, "Uniqueness of the American Enlightenment," 178.

49 See Fleischacker, "The Impact on America," 328–333, and Noll, *America's God*, 109 and 113.

50 Perry Miller, "Introduction," in *American Thought: Civil War to World War I* (New York: Holt, Rinehart and Winston, 1954), ix.

51 Sophia Rosenfeld, "Tom Paine's Common Sense and Ours," *The William and Mary Quarterly* 65, no. 4 (October 2008): 667.

52 Noll, "Common Sense Traditions," 219.

53 Sydney E. Ahlstrom, *A Religious History of the American People* (New Haven and London: Yale University Press, 1975), 356.

54 Noll, *America's God*, 103. E. Brooks Holifield in *The Gentlemen Theologians: American Theology in Southern Culture, 1795–1860* (Eugene, OR: Wipf and Stock, 1978, 110–126) spends a whole chapter divining the ways Scottish Realism became embedded in antebellum Southern theology across the Protestant denominations.

55 On the role of common sense and Evangelical scriptural populism in developing the American ethos of religious individualism, see Hatch, *Democratization of American Christianity*, 162–189.

56 See Noll, "Common Sense Traditions," 222. On contemporary Evangelical reappropriations of Reid, see Peter Byrne, "Reidianism in Contemporary English-Speaking Religious Epistemology," *European Journal for Philosophy of Religion* 3/2 (Autumn 2011): 267–284, and Nicholas Wolterstorff, *Thomas Reid and the Story of Epistemology* (New York: Cambridge University Press, 2001).

57 Marsden, *Fundamentalism and American Culture*, 251.

58 Noll, "Common Sense Traditions," 233.

59 Noll, "Common Sense Traditions,"226.

60 See Smith, *Every-Day Religion, or the Common-Sense Teaching of the Bible* (London and Edinburgh: Fleming H. Revell, 1893), vi.

61 Debra Campbell, "Hannah Whitall Smith (1832–1911): Theology of the Mother-Hearted God," *Signs* 15, no. 1 (Autumn 1989): 95. On Smith's complicated marriage, see M. J. D. Roberts, "Evangelicalism and Scandal in Victorian England: The Case of the Pearsall Smiths," *History* 95, no. 4 (October 2010): 437–457.

62 Hannah Whitall Smith, *The Unselfishness of God: A Spiritual Autobiography* (London and Edinburgh: Fleming H. Revell, 1903), 215.

63 Smith, *The Unselfishness of God*, 15, 82, 85, 150, 176, 197.

64 As Martin Riesebrodt has insightfully observed, "On the one hand, religions often become conscious of themselves by demarcating themselves from and arguing against other religions. On the other hand, interacting religions also borrow elements from one another and assimilate to one another ... Phases of demarcation and polemics, on the one hand, and phases of assimilation, unification, and identification, on the other, often flow seamlessly into one another and overlap." Martin Riesebrodt, *The Promise of Salvation: A Theory of Religion*, trans. Steven Rendell (Chicago: University of Chicago Press, 2010), 23.

65 Yasir Qadhi, "Rethinking Salafism: Shifting Trends and Changing Typologies Post Arab Spring," Prince Alwaleed bin Talal Center for Muslim-Christian Understanding, Georgetown University, April 17, 2019, https://youtu.be/hOTDNkHTEnU. See also Yasmin Moll, "Islamic Televangelism: Religion, Media, and Visuality in Contemporary Egypt," Arab Media and Society 10 (Spring 2010), www.arabmediasociety.com/islamic-televangelism-religion-media-and-visuality-in-contemporary-egypt/; Tuve Floden, "Televangelists, Media *Du ʿā*, and *ʿUlamā*: The Evolution of Religious Authority in Modern Islam" (PhD diss., Georgetown University, 2016); and Ibrahim Saleh, "Islamic Televangelism: The Salafi Window to Their Paradise," in *Global and Local Televangelism*, Pradip Ninan Thomas and Philip Lee, eds. (New York: Palgrave Macmillan, 2012), 64–83.

66 Lee, interview.

67 Lee, interview.

68 Yusha Evans, "How the Bible Led Me to Islam: The Story of a Former Christian Youth Minister," YouTube.com, September 9, 2009, https://youtu.be/IYMKQKSV0bY. Evans openly identifies with the Salafi *manhaj* (methodology) saying that "they are on the true path, the righteous

guidance" in a 2012 video. Yusha Evans, "Misconception about 'Salafi (Ahlul Hadees)' by Former Christian Youth Minister 'Yusha Evans'.flv," YouTube.com, April 23, 2012, https://youtu.be/r1ck3jHUKW0.

69 Ryan P. Burge, "What's Up with Born-Again Muslims? And What Does That Tell Us About American Religion?," *Religion in Public*, March 2, 2021, https://religioninpublic.blog/2021/03/02/whats-up-with-born-again-muslims-and-what-does-that-tells-us-about-american-religion/.

70 Knight, *Why I Am a Salafi*, 17.

71 Bernard Lonergan, *Method in Theology* (New York: Herder and Herder, 1972), 154.

72 Interview, February 18, 2017. Qadhi attributed this quote to one of his teachers.

CHAPTER 7

1 Lydia Saad, "Three in Four in US Still See the Bible as Word of God," Gallup Politics, June 4, 2014, www.gallup.com/poll/170834/three-four-bible-word-god.aspx.

2 He made this comment in reference to different Salafi approaches to politics around the world, but shortly prior to that, he acknowledges that similar diversity inhabits Salafi arguments about theology and law in general. Yasir Qadhi, "Rethinking Salafism: Shifting Trends and Changing Typologies Post Arab Spring."

3 Christian Smith, *The Bible Made Impossible: Why Biblicism Is Not a Truly Evangelical Reading of Scripture* (Grand Rapids: Brazos Press, 2011), 67.

4 Robert E. Webber, *Common Roots: The Original Call to an Ancient-Future Faith* (Grand Rapids: Zondervan, 1978), 56–57.

5 Geertz, *Local Knowledge*, 81.

6 General Social Survey, "Homosexuals Should Have Right to Marry (Agree/ Disagree)," GSS Data Explorer, https://gssdataexplorer.norc.org/trends/ Gender%20&%20Marriage?measure=marhomo.

7 Pew Research Center, "America's Changing Religious Landscape."

8 Matthew Vines, "The Gay Debate: The Bible and Homosexuality," YouTube.com, March 10, 2012, https://youtu.be/ezQjNJUSraY.

9 See Douglas Quenqua, "Turned Away, He Turned to the Bible," *New York Times*, September 16, 2012, http://query.nytimes.com/gst/fullpage.html? res=9C00E6DA1E31F935A2575AC0A9649D8B63&pagewanted=all.

10 Vines has cited as influential thinkers on his own approach the Finnish theologian and Hebrew Bible scholar Martti Nissinen – especially his *Homoeroticism in the Biblical World: A Historical Perspective*, trans. Kirsi Stjerna (Minneapolis: Fortress Press, 1998); the Episcopalian Yale New Testament scholar Dale Martin; and the Episcopalian Yale historian John Boswell. See Douglas Quenqua, "Turned Away." In his book, he relies heavily on the Reformed Church of America theologian James V. Brownson's *Bible, Gender, Sexuality: Reframing the Church's Debate on Same-Sex Relationships* (Grand Rapids: Wm. B. Eerdmans, 2013), which was published in the year between Vines' lecture and his own book. Brownson serves as a board member at the nonprofit, The Reformation Project, that Vines founded.

11 Matthew Vines, *God and the Gay Christian* (New York: Convergent Books, 2014), 1–2.

12 Vines, *God and the Gay Christian*, 3. Emphasis his.

13 Vines, *God and the Gay Christian*, 175.

14 Pew Forum, "America's Changing Religious Landscape."

15 For a telling traditional-Catholic exception that proves the rule, see Joshua Gonnerman, "Why Matthew Vines is Wrong about The Bible and Homosexuality," *First Things*, October 10, 2012, www.firstthings.com/web-exclusives/2012/10/why-matthew-vines-is-wrong-about-the-bible-and-homosexuality. Gonnerman, a Catholic PhD student, seems to misconstrue the entire intra-Evangelical culture and appeal of Vines' argument and chastises him for not looking to (Catholic) church tradition to guide his biblical interpretation.

16 See James R. White and Jeffrey D. Niell, *The Same Sex Controversy: Defending and Clarifying the Bible's Message about Homosexuality* (Minneapolis: Bethany House, 2002), 57, 97, 151, 166, 179.

17 James R. White, "'Gay Christianity' Refuted, Part 1," Alpha and Omega Ministries, May 23, 2012, www.aomin.org/aoblog/the-dividing-line/gay-christianity-refuted/.

18 Broward Liston, "Interview: Missionary Work in Iraq," *Time*, April 15, 2003, http://content.time.com/time/world/article/0,8599,443800,00.html.

19 R. Albert Mohler Jr., ed., *God and the Gay Christian? A Response to Matthew Vines*, Kindle edition (Louisville: SBTS Press, 2014), location 31–44.

20 Mohler, *God and the Gay Christian?*, location 57.

21 See Elizabeth Redden, "A Seminary, Same-Sex Marriage and Student Privacy," *Inside Higher Ed*, November 25, 2019, www.insidehighered.com/news/2019/11/25/former-student-sues-seminary-claiming-she-was-expelled-after-officials-obtained-tax. Fuller's relationship to LGBTQ inclusion is complicated: In 2013, it became the first Evangelical seminary to allow an official LGBT student club; see AP, "LGBT Group Finds Acceptance at Evangelical College," *USA Today*, July 13, 2013, www.usatoday.com/story/news/nation/2013/07/13/lgbt-group-finds-acceptance-at-evangelical-college/2514629/. Yet in 2015, Professor J.R. Daniel Kirk was denied tenure for taking a pro-gay marriage stance. J.R. Daniel Kirk, "Fuller and Me," *Storied Theology*, June 29, 2015, https://web.archive.org/web/20150917154307/www.jrdkirk.com/2015/06/29/fuller-and-me/.

22 The Reformation Project, "Mission," 2020, https://reformationproject.org/mission/.

23 Saajid Lipham, "My Journey to Islam," July 28, 2018, https://youtu.be/UdydAKi8NBw.

24 Lipham, "My Journey."

25 Lipham, "My Journey."

26 Ify Okoye (writing as Tolu Adiba), "A Prayer Answered," in *Love, InshAllah: The Secret Love Lives of American Muslim Women*, Ayesha Mattu and Nura Maznavi, eds. (Berkeley, CA: Soft Skull Press, 2012): 18–27. Once Ify came out later that year, the following imprints of the book included her true name without the pseudonym. While Ify doesn't explicitly say in the piece that her love interest, "Hafsa," is Salafi, there are several subtle contextual Salafi cues that strongly suggest such, including that Ify and "Hafsa's" first meeting involves an exchange of gift books by Ibn Qayyim al-Jawziyya, the most prominent disciple and inheritor of Ibn Taymiyya (pg. 21).

27 Interview.

28 See Q 2:35 and Q 7:19.

29 Ify Okoye, "Yes, I Am,"*IfyOkoye.com* (blog), August 21, 2012, https://ifyokoye.com/2012/08/21/yes-i-am/.

30 Ify Okoye, August 27, 2012, comment on Ify Okoye, "Yes I Am," August 21, 2012, https://ifyokoye.com/2012/08/21/yes-i-am/.

31 Steven Greenberg, *Wrestling with God and Men: Homosexuality in the Jewish Tradition* (Madison: University of Wisconsin Press, 2004).

32 Interview.

33 Interview.

34 Interview.

35 Yasir Qadhi, "Toward Establishing a Vision for the Muslims in the West," January 8, 2014, https://youtu.be/xXuJXcM9bIU.

36 Interview.

37 Pew Forum, "America's Changing Religious Landscape." Robert P. Jones et al., "Emerging Consensus on LGBT Issues."

38 ISPU, "American Muslim Poll 2020," April 22, 2020, www.ispu.org/wp-content/uploads/2020/09/Appendix-III.-Data-tables.pdf?x89973.

39 Interview, July 23, 2020.

40 Interview.

41 Haqiqatjou has claimed in several online posts that his title was "Director of Research" at Yaqeen, but I cannot find any concrete evidence of such a title or promotion in his short tenure there. See Muslim Skeptic Team, "Reviewing Yaqeen Institute: A Source of Certainty or Doubt?," *The Muslim Skeptic*, April 20, 2020, https://muslimskeptic.com/2020/04/20/yaqeen-institute-review/.

42 Sarah Sarder, "Dallas Muslim Leader Omar Suleiman Arrested during DACA Protest on Capitol Hill," *The Dallas Morning News*, March 6, 2018, www.dallasnews.com/news/immigration/2018/03/06/dallas-muslim-leader-omar-suleiman-arrested-during-daca-protest-on-capitol-hill/.

43 Omar Suleiman, Twitter Post, October 27, 2018, https://twitter.com/omarsuleiman504/status/1056192898881019904?lang=en.

44 Beto O'Rourke, "Rally Against Fear – Live from Dallas, TX," October 17, 2019, www.facebook.com/watch/live/?v=3066288886776131&ref=watch_permalink.

45 Yaqeen Institute, "Imam Omar Suleiman Delivers Opening Prayer in US House of Representatives," YouTube.com, www.youtube.com/watch?v=JiCAPZcjlWg.

46 Omar Suleiman, "Imam Omar Suleiman at Bernie Sanders Rally," Facebook Post, February 15, 2020 www.facebook.com/imamomarsuleiman/videos/605975899961879.

47 Sam Westrop, "Flexible Salafis: The Growing Political Power of 'Woke,' Modernist Islamism," *Middle East Forum*, May 9, 2020, www.meforum.org/60924/flexible-salafis.

48 Jonathan Brown and Shadee Elmasry, "LGBTQ and Islam Revisited: The Days of the Donald," Yaqeen Institute, December 14, 2017, https://

yaqeeninstitute.org/jonathan-brown/lgbtq-and-islam-revisited-the-days-of-the-donald. Qadhi has made a similar, though less openly pro-LGBTQ, argument separating civic and religious laws around gay marriage. Yasir Qadhi, "What Should Be the Muslim Response to Gay Marriage," AlMaghrib Institute: YouTube, July 23, 2015, www.youtube.com/watch?v=o0oxJ-wfJZo.

49 Omar Suleiman, "Muslims and the Left: Can Social Conservatives Work on Social Justice?," *HuffPost*, July 29, 2017, www.huffpost.com/entry/muslims-and-the-left-can-social-conservatives-work_b_597cdcc5e4b0c69ef70528a7. See also Omar Suleiman, "One Year After the Travel Ban, I Am Not Your American Muslim," *CNN.com*, January 24, 2018, www.cnn.com/2018/01/24/opinions/travel-ban-anniversary-suleiman-opinion/index.html.

50 Dom DiFurio, "Q&A: Islamic Scholar Omar Suleiman on the Quran and Homosexuality," *The Dallas Morning News*, June 16, 2016, www.dallasnews.com/opinion/commentary/2016/06/16/qa-islamic-scholar-omar-suleiman-on-the-quran-and-homosexuality/.

51 Omar Suleiman, "Faithful Activism: A Sunnah Framework," Yaqeen Institute, October 30, 2020, https://yaqeeninstitute.org/omar-suleiman/faithful-activism-a-sunnah-framework.

52 Suleiman, "Faithful Activism."

53 Omar Suleiman, "Questions about My Political Activism," *Muslim Matters*, October 17, 2019, https://muslimmatters.org/2019/10/17/questions-about-my-political-activism-imam-omar-suleiman/.

54 Daniel Haqiqatjou, Facebook Post, October 10, 2017, www.facebook.com/haqiqatjou/posts/2037745503110828.

55 Daniel Haqiqatjou, "Omar Suleiman, Which LGBT Rights Do You and Yaqeen Want Muslims to Support?," Facebook Post, October 17, 2019, www.facebook.com/watch/live/?v=444571316409191&ref=watch_permalink.

56 Yasir Qadhi, Facebook Post, October 17, 2019, www.facebook.com/yasir.qadhi/posts/its-sad-to-see-the-toxic-neo-madhkhalism-that-is-rearing-its-ugly-head-online-fo/10157196198383300/.

57 Dilly Hussain, "[BBUK] EP 39: The Beef with Yaqeen | Daniel Haqiqatjou," YouTube.com, June 29, 2020, www.youtube.com/watch?v=JD5mt90_tyY.

58 Qadhi has himself tacitly labeled Haqiqatjou an "uber-fundamentalist," though his definition – "the retreat of the intellectual cowards; they just

quickly jump to the tradition, in their mind, and then 'khalas' [Done! Finished!] all conversations end" – leads me to believe that he means it in the more generic sense rather than the American Protestant parallel I am drawing. Qadhi on Muneer et al., "EP 166: Salafis and Ibn Abd Al-Wahhab."

59 Hussain, "The Beef with Yaqeen."

CONCLUSION

1 For example, see Jonathan Evans, "US Adults Are More Religious Than Western Europeans," *Pew Research Center: Fact Tank*, September 5, 2018, www.pewresearch.org/fact-tank/2018/09/05/u-s-adults-are-more-religious-than-western-europeans/, and Dalia Fahmy, "Americans Are Far More Religious Than Adults in Other Wealthy Nations," *Pew Research Center: Fact Tank*, July 31, 2018, www.pewresearch.org/fact-tank/2018/07/31/americans-are-far-more-religious-than-adults-in-other-wealthy-nations/.

2 This literature includes: Mohamed-Ali Adraoui, *Salafism Goes Global: From the Gulf to the French Banlieues* (New York: Oxford University Press, 2020); Hamid, *Sufis, Salafis, and Islamists: The Contested Ground of British Activism*; Olsson, *Contemporary Puritan Salafism: A Swedish Case Study*; Roy, *Globalised Islam: The Search for a New Ummah*; Wood, *The Way of the Strangers*; and numerous think-tank reports, security studies documents, and media articles. On Madkhali influence in Europe, see Dawood, "Who is a 'Salafi'?" and Meijer, "Politicising *al-Jarḥ wa-l-Taʿdīl*," 381–382.

3 Interview, July 23, 2020.

4 George W. Bush, "Remarks on Arrival at the White House and an Exchange with Reporters," Government Publishing Office, September 16, 2001, www.govinfo.gov/content/pkg/WCPD-2001-09-24/html/WCPD-2001-09-24-Pg1322.htm. A White House spokesman later attempted to clarify that Bush meant the word crusade in "the traditional English sense of the word, a broad cause." See Peter Waldman and Hugh Pope, "'Crusade' Reference Reinforces Fears War on Terrorism Is against Muslims," *The Wall Street Journal*, September 21, 2001, www.wsj.com/articles/SB1001020294332922160.

5 Osama Bin Laden, *Messages to the World: The Statements of Osama Bin Laden*, ed. Bruce Lawrence, trans. James Howarth (New York: Verso, 2005), 134–135.

6 On the apocalyptic aspects of Bush's post-9/11 rhetoric, see Matthew Avery Sutton, *American Apocalypse: A History of Modern Evangelicalism* (Cambridge, MA: Harvard University Press, 2014), 370–371.

7 Pew found a slight, though not necessarily statistically significant, uptick of identification as born-again or Evangelical among US veterans who served after 9/11 (39 percent) as compared with those who served pre-9/11 (37 percent). Paul Taylor, "The Military-Civilian Gap: War and Sacrifice in the Post-9/11 Era," Pew Research Center, October 5, 2011, www .pewresearch.org/wp-content/uploads/sites/3/2011/10/veterans-report .pdf.

8 James R. White, "James White Slams Robert Spencer for Calling Dr. Qadhi a Hate Preacher," *The Dividing Line,* August 28, 2014, https://youtu.be/ voTRdlVW0I0.

9 James White and Yasir Qadhi, "Christian Muslim Dialogue, Pt. 1," Memphis Islamic Center, January 28, 2017, https://youtu.be/ L2NBcVAV038.

10 James White and Yasir Qadhi, "Christian Muslim Dialogue, Pt. 2,' Memphis Islamic Center, January 28, 2017, https://youtu.be/ r2tPHLOej1w.

11 White is well aware of Qadhi's association with Salafism, mentioning it in his Qur'an book, and calling Salafism "a very conservative Sunni branch ... [that] is at the heart of today's worldwide Muslim resurgence." James L. White, *What Every Christian Needs to Know about the Qur'an* (Bloomington, MI: Bethany House, 2013), 58.

12 James Simpson, "When Evangelicals Become Useful Idiots for Islamism," *American Thinker,* June 24, 2017, www.americanthinker.com/articles/ 2017/06/when_evangelicals_become_useful_idiots_for_islamism.html.

13 Yasir Qadhi, Facebook Post, June 30, 2017, www.facebook.com/yasir .qadhi/posts/many-of-you-are-aware-that-i-had-a-dialogue-with-james- white-a-reformed-baptist-/10155063223833300/.

AFTERWORD

1 Omar Suleiman, Twitter Post, January 6, 2021, https://twitter.com/ omarsuleiman504/status/1346921607638306816.

Bibliography

Abd-Allah, Umar Faruq. "Islam and the Cultural Imperative." *The Oasis Initiative* (2004). www.theoasisinitiative.org/islam-the-cultural-imperative.

Abu Rumman, Mohammad, and Hassan Abu Hanieh. "Jordanian Salafism: A Strategy for the 'Islamization of Society' and an Ambiguous Relationship with the State." Amman: Friedrich-Ebert-Stiftung (2010). http://library.fes.de/pdf-files/bueros/amman/07758-book2.pdf.

Adang, Camilla. "Islam as the Inborn Religion of Mankind: The Concept of Fiṭra in the Works of Ibn Ḥazm." *Al-Qantara* XXI (2000): 391–410.

Adraoui, Mohamed-Ali. *Salafism Goes Global: From the Gulf to the French Banlieues*. New York: Oxford University Press, 2020.

Afsaruddin, Asma. *Striving in the Path of God: Jihad and Martyrdom in Islamic Thought*. New York: Oxford University Press, 2013.

Ahlstrom, Sydney E. *A Religious History of the American People*. New Haven, CT: Yale University Press, 1975.

Ali, Tariq. *The Clash of Fundamentalisms: Crusades, Jihads, and Modernity*. London: Verso, 2002.

Anjum, Ovamir. *Politics, Law, and Community in Islamic Thought: The Taymiyyan Moment*. New York: Cambridge University Press, 2012.

Anjum, Ovamir. "Salafis and Democracy: Doctrine and Context." *The Muslim World* 106 (July 2016): 448–473.

Asad, Talal. "The Idea of an Anthropology of Islam." Center for Contemporary Arab Studies, Georgetown University. Occasional Paper Series (March 1986): 14.

Bacote, Vincent, Laura C. Miguélez, and Dennis Okholm *Evangelicals & Scripture: Tradition, Authority and Hermeneutics*. Downers Grove, IL: InterVarsity Press, 2004.

Bagby, Ihsan. "The American Mosque 2011: Basic Characteristics of the American Mosque Attitudes of Mosque Leaders." *Council on American Islamic Relations* (January 2012). www.cair.com/images/pdf/The-American-Mosque-2011-part-1.pdf.

Baird, Robert. *Religion in America; or, an Account of the Origen, Progress, Relation to the State, and Present Condition of the Evangelical Churches in the United States with Notices of the Unevangelical Denominations*. New York: Harper & Brothers, 1844.

Balmer, Randall. *Bad Faith: Race and the Rise of the Religious Right.* Grand Rapids, MI: Eerdmans, 2021.

Balmer, Randall. *Encyclopedia of Evangelicalism.* Louisville, KY: Westminster John Knox Press, 2002.

Balmer, Randall. *The Making of Evangelicalism: From Revivalism to Politics and Beyond.* Waco, TX: Baylor University Press, 2010.

Bano, Masooda, ed. *Modern Islamic Authority and Social Change*, vol. 2. Edinburgh: Edinburgh University Press, 2018.

Bauckham, Richard, and Benjamin Drewery, eds. *Scripture, Tradition, and Reason: A Study in the Criteria of Christian Doctrine.* Edinburgh: T&T Clark, 1988.

Baylor Religion Survey. Wave 5 (2017). www.thearda.com/Archive/Files/Analysis/ BRSW5ED/BRSW5ED_Var71_1.asp.

Baylor Religion Survey. Wave 6 (May 2021). www.baylor.edu/baylorreligionsurvey/ doc.php/376255.pdf.

Bazzano, Elliott. "Ibn Taymiyya, Radical Polymath, Part 1: Scholarly Perceptions," *Religion Compass* 9, no. 4 (2015): 100–116.

Bebbington, David. *Evangelicalism in Modern Britain: A History from the 1730s to the 1980s.* Grand Rapids, MI: Baker, 1989.

Bender, Kimlyn J. *Confessing Christ for Church and World: Studies in Modern Theology.* Downers Grove, IL: InterVarsity Press, 2014.

Bentham, Jeremy. *A Comment on the Commentaries and a Fragment on Government.* Edited by J. H Burns and H. L. A. Hart. Oxford: Clarendon Press, 1977.

Bin Laden, Osama. "Declaration of Jihad against the Americans Occupying the Land of the Two Holiest Sites." *Combating Terrorism Center at West Point* (August 1996). https://ctc.usma.edu/harmony-program/declaration-of-jihad-against-the-americans-occupying-the-land-of-the-two-holiest-sites-original-lan guage-2.

Bin Laden, Osama. *Messages to the World: The Statements of Osama Bin Laden.* Edited by Bruce Lawrence. Translated by James Howarth. New York: Verso, 2005.

Boekhoff-van der Voort, Nicolet, Kees Versteegh, and Joas Wagemakers. *The Transmission and Dynamics of the Textual Sources of Islam: Essays in Honour of Harald Motzki.* Leiden: Brill, 2011.

Bonner, Michael. *Jihad in Islamic History: Doctrines and Practices.* Princeton, NJ: Princeton University Press, 2006.

Bradford, Gamaliel. *D.L. Moody: A Worker in Souls.* Garden City, NY: Doubleday, Doran, 1927.

Broadie, Alexander, ed. *The Cambridge Companion to the Scottish Enlightenment.* New York: Cambridge University Press, 2003.

Brown, Daniel. *Rethinking Tradition in Modern Islamic Thought.* Cambridge: Cambridge University Press, 1996.

Brown, Jonathan. *The Canonization of al-Bukhārī and Muslim: The Formation and Function of the Sunnī Ḥadīth Canon.* Leiden: Brill, 2007.

Brown, Jonathan. *Hadith: Muhammad's Legacy in the Medieval and Modern World.* 2nd ed. Oxford: Oneworld, 2018.

Brown, Jonathan. "How We Know Early *Ḥadīth* Critics Did *Matn* Criticism and Why It's So Hard to Find." *Islamic Law and Society* 15 (2008): 143–184.

Brown, Jonathan. "Is Islam Easy to Understand or Not? Salafis, the Democratization of Interpretation and the Need for the Ulema." *Journal of Islamic Studies* 26, no. 2 (2015): 117–144.

Brown, Jonathan. *Misquoting Muhammad: The Challenge and Choices of Interpreting the Prophet's Legacy.* London: Oneworld, 2014.

Brown, Jonathan, and Shadee Elmasry. "LGBTQ and Islam Revisited: The Days of the Donald." *Yaqeen Institute* (December 14, 2017). https://yaqeeninstitute .org/jonathan-brown/lgbtq-and-islam-revisited-the-days-of-the-donald.

Brownson, James V. *Bible, Gender, Sexuality: Reframing the Church's Debate on Same-Sex Relationships.* Grand Rapids, MI: Eerdmans, 2013.

Burge, Ryan P. "The Curious Case of Born-Again Catholics." *Religion in Public* (July 18, 2019). https://religioninpublic.blog/2019/07/18/the-curious-case-of-born-again-catholics.

Burge, Ryan P. "Do You Have to Be Protestant to Be Born Again?" *Religion in Public.* (May 7, 2018). https://religioninpublic.blog/2018/05/07/do-you-have-to-protestant-to-be-born-again.

Burge, Ryan P. "What's Up with Born-Again Muslims? And What Does That Tell Us about American Religion?" *Religion in Public* (March 2, 2021). https:// religioninpublic.blog/2021/03/02/whats-up-with-born-again-muslims-and-what-does-that-tells-us-about-american-religion.

Burton, John. *Introduction to the Hadith.* Edinburgh: Edinburgh University Press, 1994.

Bush, George W. "Remarks on Arrival at the White House and an Exchange with Reporters." *Government Publishing Office* (September 16, 2001). www.govinfo .gov/content/pkg/WCPD-2001-09-24/html/WCPD-2001-09-24-Pg1322.htm.

Buzan, Barry, and Lene Hansen. *The Evolution of International Security Studies.* Cambridge: Cambridge University Press, 2009.

Byrne, Peter. "Reidianism in Contemporary English-Speaking Religious Epistemology." *European Journal for Philosophy of Religion* 3, no. 2 (Autumn 2011): 267–284.

Campbell, Debra. "Hannah Whitall Smith (1832–1911): Theology of the Mother-Hearted God." *Signs* 15, no. 1 (Autumn 1989): 79–101.

Carpenter, Joel A., ed. *A New Evangelical Coalition: Early Documents of the National Association of Evangelicals*. New York: Garland, 1988.

Carpenter, Joel A., *Revive Us Again: The Reawakening of American Fundamentalism*. New York: Oxford University Press, 1997.

Cavatorta, Francesco, ed. *Salafism after the Arab Awakening: Contending with People's Power*. New York: Oxford University Press, 2017.

Clooney, Francis X. *Comparative Theology: Deep Learning across Religious Borders*. Oxford: Wiley-Blackwell, 2010.

Coffman, Elesha. *The Christian Century and the Rise of Mainline Protestantism*. New York: Oxford University Press, 2013.

Commins, David. *The Wahhabi Mission and Saudi Arabia*. New York: I. B. Tauris & Co, 2006.

Cooke, Miriam and Bruce B. Lawrence, eds. *Muslim Networks from Hajj to Hip Hop*. Chapel Hill: University of North Carolina Press, 2005.

Coolsaet, Rik. "'All Radicalisation Is Local': The Genesis and Drawback of an Elusive Concept." Egmont Royal Institute for International Relations. June 2016. www.egmontinstitute.be/content/uploads/2016/05/ep84.pdf?type=pdf.

Corbett, Rosemary R. "Islamic 'Fundamentalism': The Mission Creep of an American Religious Metaphor." *Journal of the American Academy of Religion* 83, no. 4 (December 2015): 977–1004.

Cox, Daniel and Robert P. Jones. "America's Changing Religious Identity." Public Religion Research Institute. September 6, 2017. www.prri.org/research/american-religious-landscape-christian-religiously-unaffiliated/.

Criles, George. *Charlie Wilson's War: The Extraordinary Story of the Largest Covert Operation in History*. New York: Atlantic Monthly Press, 2003.

Cuneo, Terence and René van Woudenberg. *The Cambridge Companion to Thomas Reid*. Cambridge, UK: Cambridge University Press, 2004.

Curtis, Edward E. ed. *Encyclopedia of Muslim-American History*. New York: Facts on File, 2010.

Curtis, Edward E. *Muslims in America: A Short History*. New York: Oxford University Press, 2009.

Dallal, Ahmad S. *Islam without Europe: Traditions of Reform in Eighteenth-Century Islamic Thought*. Chapel Hill: University of North Carolina Press, 2018.

Dallal, Ahmad S. "The Origins and Objectives of Islamic Revivalist Thought, 1750–1850." *Journal of the American Oriental Society* 113, no. 3 (July–Sept, 1993): 341–359.

Dawood, Iman. "Who Is a 'Salafi'? Salafism and the Politics of Labelling in the UK." *Journal of Muslims in Europe* 9 (2020): 240–261.

DeLong-Bas, Natana. *Wahhabi Islam: From Revival and Reform to Global Jihad.* New York: Oxford University Press, 2004.

Diamant, Jeff. "Engagement and Resistance: African Americans, Saudi Arabia, and Islamic Transnationalisms, 1975 to 2000." PhD diss., City University of New York, 2016.

Elliott, Andrea. "Why Yasir Qadhi Wants to Talk about Jihad." *The New York Times Magazine*, March 17, 2011. www.nytimes.com/2011/03/20/magazine/mag-20Salafis-t.html.

Elmasry, Shadee. "The Salafis in America: The Rise, Decline and Prospects for a Sunni Muslim Movement among African-Americans." *Journal of Muslim Minority Affairs* 30, no. 2 (June 2010): 217–236.

Evans, G. R. *The Roots of the Reformation: Tradition, Emergence, and Rupture.* Downers Grove, IL: InterVarsity Press Academic, 2012.

Evans, Jonathan. "US Adults Are More Religious Than Western Europeans." *Pew Research Center: Fact Tank.* September 5, 2018. www.pewresearch.org/fact-tank/2018/09/05/u-s-adults-are-more-religious-than-western-europeans/.

Fahmy, Dalia. "Americans Are Far More Religious Than Adults in Other Wealthy Nations." *Pew Research Center: Fact Tank.* July 31, 2018. www.pewresearch.org/fact-tank/2018/07/31/americans-are-far-more-religious-than-adults-in-other-wealthy-nations/.

Fandy, Mamoun. "Safar al-Hawali: Saudi Islamist or Saudi nationalist?" *Islam and Christian-Muslim Relations* 9, no. 1 (1998): 5–21.

Farquhar, Michael. *Circuits of Faith: Migration, Education, and the Wahhabi Mission.* Stanford: Stanford University Press, 2017.

Fea, John. *Was America Founded as a Christian Nation? A Historical Introduction.* Louisville, KY: Westminster John Knox, 2011.

Fiedler, Maureen. "Salafi Muslims: Following the Ancestors of Islam." *Interfaith Voices.* Interview with Yasir Qadhi. February 21, 2013. http://interfaithradio.org/StoryAudio/Salafi_Muslims__Following_the_Ancestors_of_Islam.

Finke, Roger and Rodney Stark. *The Church of America, 1776–2005: Winners and Losers in Our Religious Economy.* New Brunswick, NJ: Rutgers University Press, 2005.

Finney, Charles G. *Charles G. Finney: An Autobiography.* Westwood, NJ: Fleming H. Revell, 1876.

Finney, Charles G. *Lectures on Revival of Religion.* New York: Leavitt, Lord, & Co., 1835.

Finney, Charles G. *Lectures on Systematic Theology.* Edited by J. H. Fairchild. New York: George H. Doran Company, 1878.

Finney, Charles G. *Reflections on Revival.* Compiled by Donald Dayton. Minneapolis, MN: Bethany House, 1979.

Fisher, Lindon D. "Evangelicals and Unevangelicals: The Contested History of a Word, 1500–1950." *Religion and American Culture* 26, no. 2 (Summer 2016): 184–226.

Floden, Tuve. "Televangelists, Media Duʻā, and ʻUlamāʼ: The Evolution of Religious Authority in Modern Islam." PhD diss., Georgetown University, 2016.

Fosdick, Harry Emerson. "Shall the Fundamentalists Win?" Sermon at First Presbyterian Church, New York, NY. May 21, 1922. http://historymatters .gmu.edu/d/5070/.

Freedom House. "Saudi Publications on Hate Ideology Fill American Mosques." Center for Religious Freedom. Washington, DC, 2005. http://derafsh-kaviyani .com/english/saudipub.pdf.

Freiberger, Oliver. *Considering Comparison: A Method for Religious Studies.* Oxford: Oxford University Press, 2019.

Gartenstein-Ross, Daveed. *My Year Inside Radical Islam: A Memoir.* New York: Jeremy P. Tarcher/Penguin, 2007.

Gaston, K. Healan. *Imagining Judeo-Christian America: Religion, Secularism, and the Redefinition of Democracy.* Chicago, IL: University of Chicago Press, 2019.

Gauvain, Richard. *Salafi Ritual Purity: In the Presence of God.* London: Routledge, 2012.

Gauvain, Richard. "Salafism in Modern Egypt: Panacea or Pest?" *Political Theology* 11, no. 6 (2010): 802–825.

Geertz, Clifford. *Islam Observed: Religious Developments in Morocco and Indonesia.* Chicago, IL: University of Chicago Press, 1968.

Geertz, Clifford. *Local Knowledge: Further Essays in Interpretive Anthropology.* New York: Basic Books, 1983.

Gendron, Angela. "The Call to Jihad: Charismatic Preachers and the Internet." *Studies in Conflict and Terrorism* 40, no. 1 (2017): 44–61.

General Social Survey. "Homosexuals Should Have Right to Marry (Agree/ Disagree)." GSS Data Explorer. https://gssdataexplorer.norc.org/trends/Gender %20&%20Marriage?measure=marhomo.

Gerrish, B. A. *The Old Protestantism and the New: Essays on the Reformation Heritage.* Chicago, IL: University of Chicago Press, 1982.

Goshey, Emily. "No Scholars in the West: Salafi Networks of Knowledge from Saudi Arabia to Philadelphia." *American Journal of Islam and Society* 29, nos. 1–2 (2022): 41–71.

Grafton, David D. *An American Biblical Orientalism: The Construction of Jews, Christians, and Muslims in Nineteenth-Century American Evangelical Piety.* Lanham, MD: Lexington Books, 2019.

Greenberg, Anna and Jennifer Berktold. "Evangelicals in America." *Religion and Ethics NewsWeekly.* April 5, 2004. wwwtc.pbs.org/wnet/religionandethics/files/2008/10/results.pdf.

Greenberg, Steven. *Wrestling with God and Men: Homosexuality in the Jewish Tradition.* Madison: University of Wisconsin Press, 2004.

Grewal, Zareena. *Islam Is a Foreign Country: American Muslims and the Global Crisis of Authority.* New York: New York University Press, 2014.

Griffel, Frank. "Al-Ghazālī's Use of the 'Original Human Disposition' (*Fiṭra*) and Its Background in the Teachings of al-Fārābī and Avicenna." *The Muslim World* 102 (January 2012): 1–32.

Guimond, Amy Melissa. *Converting to Islam: Understanding the Experiences of White American Females.* New York: Palgrave Macmillan, 2017.

Hallaq, Wael. *Sharīʿa: Theory, Practice, Transformations.* Cambridge, UK: Cambridge University Press, 2009.

Hambrick-Stowe, Charles E. *Charles G. Finney and the Spirit of American Evangelicalism.* Grand Rapids, MI: William B. Eerdmans, 1996.

Hamdeh, Emad. "Qurʾān and Sunna or the *Madhhabs*?: A Salafi Polemic against Islamic Legal Tradition." *Islamic Law and Society* 24 (2017): 6.

Hamdeh, Emad. *Salafism and Traditionalism: Scholarly Authority in Modern Islam.* New York: Cambridge University Press, 2021.

Hamdeh, Emad. "Shaykh Google as Ḥāfiẓ al-ʿAṣr: The Internet, Traditional ʿUlamāʾ, and Self Learning." *The American Journal of Islam and Society* 37, no. 1–2 (2020): 67–102.

Hamdeh, Emad. "The Formative Years of an Iconoclastic Salafi Scholar." *The Muslim World* 106 (July 2016): 149–176.

Hamid, Sadek. *Sufis, Salafis, and Islamists: The Contested Ground of British Islamic Activism.* New York: I. B. Tauris, 2016.

Hammer, Juliane and Omid Safi, eds. *The Cambridge Companion to American Islam.* New York: Cambridge University Press, 2013.

Harding, Susan. "Representing Fundamentalism: The Problem of the Repugnant Cultural Other." *Social Research* 58, no. 2 (Summer 1991): 373–393.

Hatch, Nathan O. *The Democratization of American Christianity.* New Haven, CT: Yale University Press, 1989.

Heck, Paul. *Skepticism in Classical Islam: Moments of Confusion.* New York: Routledge, 2014.

Heffelfinger, Chris. *Radical Islam in America: Salafism's Journey from Arabia to the West*. Dulles, VA: Potomac Books, 2011.

Hefner, Robert W. *Shari'a Politics: Islamic Law and Society in the Modern World*. Bloomington: Indiana University Press, 2011.

Hegghammer, Thomas and Stéphane Lacroix. "Rejectionist Islamism in Saudi Arabia: The Story of Juhayman Al-'Utaybi Revisited." *International Journal of Middle East Studies* 39, no. 1 (Feb 2007): 103–122.

Herberg, Will. *Protestant-Catholic-Jew: An Essay in American Religious Sociology*. Chicago, IL: University of Chicago Press, 1955.

Hodgson, Marshall G. S. *The Venture of Islam: Conscience and History in a World Civilization*. Vol. 1. Chicago, IL: University of Chicago Press, 1974.

Hodgson, Marshall G. S. *The Venture of Islam: The Gunpowder Empires and Modern Times*. Vol. 3. Chicago, IL: The University of Chicago Press, 1974.

Hofstadter, Richard. *Anti-intellectualism in American Life*. New York: Vintage Books, 1962.

Holbrook, Donald. "The Spread of Its Message: Studying the Prominence of al-Qaida Materials in UK Terrorism Investigations." *Perspectives on Terrorism* 11, no. 6 (December 2017): 89–100.

Holifield, E. Brooks. *The Gentlemen Theologians: American Theology in Southern Culture, 1795–1860*. Eugene, OR: Wipf and Stock, 1978.

Holifield, E. Brooks. *Theology in America: Christian Thought from the Age of the Puritans to the Civil War*. New Haven, CT: Yale University Press, 2003.

Holloway, David. *9/11 and the War on Terror*. Edinburgh: University of Edinburgh Press, 2008.

Hoover, Jon. *Ibn Taymiyya's Theodicy of Perpetual Optimism*. Boston, MA: Brill, 2007.

Hughes, Richard T. and C. Leonard Allen. *Illusions of Innocence: Protestant Primitivism in America, 1630–1875*. Chicago, IL: University of Chicago Press, 1988.

Hume, David. *An Enquiry Concerning Human Understanding*. Edited by Peter Millican. New York: Oxford University Press, 2007.

Hume, David. *A Treatise of Human Nature Being: A Critical Edition*. Oxford: Clarendon Press, 2007.

Huntington, Samuel P. "The Clash of Civilizations?" *Foreign Affairs* (Summer 1993): 22–49.

Huntington, Samuel P. *The Clash of Civilizations and the Remaking of the World Order*. New York: Simon & Schuster, 1996.

Ibn al-Jawzī. *Virtues of the Imām Aḥmad ibn Ḥanbal*. Vol. 1. Translated by Michael Cooperson. New York: New York University Press, 2013.

Ibn Taymiyya. *Ibn Taymiyyah Expounds on Islam: Selected Writings of Shaykh al-Islam Taqi ad-Din Ibn Taymiyyah on Islamic Faith, Life, and Society.* Translated and edited by Muhammad 'Abdul-Haqq Ansari. N.p. N.d. https://archive.org/details/IbnTaymiyyahExpoundsOnIslam-Alhamdulillah-library.blogspot.in.pdf.

Inge, Anabel. *The Making of a Salafi Muslim Woman: Paths to Conversion.* New York: Oxford University Press, 2017.

Institute for Social Policy and Understanding. "American Muslim Poll 2020." April 22, 2020: 12.

Islamic State in the Levant. "Kill the Imāms of Kufr in the West." *Dabiq* no. 14 (April–May 2016): 8–17.

Jackson, Sherman. "Ibn Taymiyyah on Trial in Damascus," *Journal of Semitic Studies* 39, no. 1 (Spring 1994): 41–85.

Johnson, Sylvester A. and Steven Weitzman, eds. *The FBI and Religion: Faith and National Security before and after 9/11.* Oakland: University of California Press, 2017.

Kant, Immanuel. *Prolegomena to Any Future Metaphysics with Selections from the Critique of Pure Reason.* Edited and translated by Gary Hatfield. Cambridge, UK: Cambridge University Press, 2004.

Kendall, Elisabeth and Ahmad Khan. *Reclaiming Islamic Tradition: Modern Interpretations of the Classical Heritage.* Edinburgh: Edinburgh University Press, 2016.

Kepel, Gilles. *Jihad: On the Trail of Political Islam.* Translated by Anthony F. Roberts. Cambridge, MA: Belknap Press, 2000.

Kidd, Thomas S. *The Great Awakening: The Roots of Evangelical Christianity in Colonial America.* New Haven, CT: Yale University Press, 2007.

Kidd, Thomas S. *Who Is an Evangelical? The History of a Movement in Crisis.* New Haven, CT: Yale University Press, 2019.

Knight, Michael Muhammad. *Why I Am a Salafi.* Berkeley, CA: Soft Skull Press, 2015.

Koopmans, Ruud. "Fundamentalism and Out-Group Hostility," *WZB Mitteilungen,* December 2013. www.wzb.eu/system/files/docs/sv/iuk/koopmans_englisch_ed.pdf.

Korb, Scott. *Light without Fire: The Making of America's First Muslim College.* Boston, MA: Beacon Press, 2012.

Kramer, Martin. "Coming to Terms: Fundamentalists or Islamists." *Middle East Quarterly* (Spring 2003): 65–77.

Krawietz, Birgit and Georges Tamer, eds. *Islamic Theology, Philosophy and Law.* Boston, MA: De Gruyter, 2013.

Kristof, Nicholas. "Jesus and Jihad." *New York Times*, July 17, 2004. www.nytimes .com/2004/07/17/opinion/jesus-and-jihad.html.

Kugle, Scott. *Rebel between Spirit and Law: Ahmad Zarruq, Sainthood, and Authority in Islam.* Bloomington: Indiana University Press, 2006.

Kundnani, Arun. *The Muslims Are Coming!: Islamophobia, Extremism, and the Domestic War on Terror.* New York: Verso, 2014.

Lacroix, Stéphane. "Al-Albani's Revolutionary Approach to Hadith." *Institute for the Study of Islam in the Modern World* 21 (Spring 2008): 6–7.

Lacroix, Stéphane. *Awakening Islam: The Politics of Religious Dissent in Contemporary Saudi Arabia.* Translated by George Holoch. Cambridge, MA: Harvard University Press, 2011.

Lal, Vinay. *Empire of Knowledge: Culture and Plurality in the Global Economy.* London: Pluto Press, 2002.

Lauzière, Henri. "The Construction of Salafiyya: Reconsidering Salafism from the Perspective of Conceptual History." *International Journal of Middle East Studies* 42 (2010): 369–389.

Lauzière, Henri. *The Making of Salafism: Islamic Reform in the Twentieth Century.* New York: Columbia University Press, 2016.

Lav, Daniel. *Radical Islam and the Revival of Medieval Theology.* New York: Cambridge University Press, 2012.

Ledwig, Marion. *Common Sense: Its History, Method, and Applicability.* New York: Peter Lang Publishing, 2007.

Lee, Umar. *The Rise and Fall of the Salafi Dawah in North America.* St. Louis: Self-published, 2014.

Lepore, Jill. *These Truths: A History of the United States.* New York: W. W. Norton & Company, 2018.

Lewis, Bernard. "The Roots of Muslim Rage." *The Atlantic* (Sept 1990). www.theatlantic.com/magazine/archive/1990/09/the-roots-of-muslim-rage/ 304643/.

Lewis, Donald M. and Richard V. Pierard. *Global Evangelicalism: Theology, History, and Culture in Regional Perspective.* Downers Grove, IL: InterVarsity Press, 2014.

Lonergan, Bernard. *Method in Theology.* New York: Herder and Herder, 1972.

Luhrmann, Tanya. *When God Talks Back: Understanding the American Evangelical Relationship with God.* New York: Vintage Books, 2012.

Madigan, Daniel A. "People of the Word: Reading John with a Muslim." *Review & Expositor* 104, no. 1 (2007): 81–95.

Mahmood, Saba. *Politics of Piety: The Islamist Revival and the Feminist Subject.* Princeton, NJ: Princeton University Press, 2005.

Malik, Jamal and John Hinnells, eds. *Sufism in the West.* (New York: Routledge, 2006).

Mandaville, Peter. *Global Political Islam.* New York: Routledge, 2007.

Marsden, George M. *Fundamentalism and American Culture.* 2nd ed. New York: Oxford University Press, 2006.

Marsden, George M. *Reforming Fundamentalism: Fuller Seminary and the New Evangelicalism.* Grand Rapids, MI: Eerdmans, 1987.

Marsden, George M. *The Evangelical Mind and the New School Presbyterian Experience: A Case Study of Thought and Theology in Nineteenth-Century America.* Eugene, OR: Wipf & Stock, 1970.

Marty, Martin E. "Fundamentalism Reborn: Faith and Fanaticism." *Saturday Review* (May 1980).

Marty, Martin E. and R. Scott Appleby. *Fundamentalisms Observed.* Chicago, IL: University of Chicago Press, 1991.

Mathiesen, Kasper. "Anglo-American 'Traditional Islam' and Its Discourse of Orthodoxy." *Journal of Arabic and Islamic Studies* 13 (2013): 191–219.

Mattu, Ayesha and Nura Maznavi, eds. *Love, InshAllah: The Secret Love Lives of American Muslim Women.* Berkeley, CA: Soft Skull Press, 2012.

May, Henry F. *The Enlightenment in America.* Oxford: Oxford University Press, 1976.

McCants, William and Jacob Olidort. "Is Quietist Salafism the Antidote to ISIS?" *Brookings Markaz.* March 13, 2015. www.brookings.edu/blog/markaz/2015/03/13/is-quietist-salafism-the-antidote-to-isis/.

McCracken, Brett. *Hipster Christianity: When Church and Cool Collide.* Grand Rapids, MI: Baker, 2010.

McDermott, Gerald R., ed. *The Oxford Handbook of Evangelical Theology.* New York: Oxford University Press, 2010.

McGhee Jr., George R. *Convergent Evolution: Limited Forms Most Beautiful.* Cambridge, MA: MIT Press, 2011.

Mead, Sidney E. *The Lively Experiment: The Shaping of Christianity in America.* New York: Harper & Row, 1963.

Mehanna, Tarek. "Tarek Mehanna's Sentencing Statement." *HistoryIsAWeapon. com.* April 12, 2012. www.historyisaweapon.com/defcon1/tarekmehannasen tencing ?statement.html.

Meijer, Roel, ed. *Global Salafism: Islam's New Religious Movement*. New York: Oxford University Press, 2009.

Meleagrou-Hitchens, Alexander. "As American as Apple Pie: How Anwar al-Awlaki Became the Face of Western Jihad." International Centre for the Study of Radicalisation and Political Violence (2011). https://icsr.info/wp-content/uploads/2011/09/ICSR-Report-As-American-As-Apple-Pie-How-Anwar-al-Awlaki-Became-the-Face-of-Western-Jihad.pdf.

Meleagrou-Hitchens, Alexander. *Incitement: Anwar al-Awlaki's Western Jihad*. Cambridge, MA: Harvard University Press, 2020.

Meleagrou-Hitchens, Alexander. "Salafism in America: History, Evolution, Radicalization." The George Washington University Program on Extremism, October 2018. https://extremism.gwu.edu/sites/g/files/zaxdzs2191/f/Salafism%20in%20America.pdf

Meyer, D.H. "The Uniqueness of the American Enlightenment." *American Quarterly* 28, no. 2 (Summer 1976): 165–186.

Miller, Perry, ed. *American Thought: Civil War to World War I*. New York: Holt, Rinehart and Winston, 1954.

Mills, Sara. *Discourse*. New York: Routledge, 1997.

Mohamed, Besheer. "New Estimates Show US Muslim Population Continues to Grow." *Pew Research Center*, January 3, 2018. www.pewresearch.org/fact-tank/2018/01/03/new-estimates-show-u-s-muslim-population-continues-to-grow/.

Mohamed, Yasien. *Fitrah: The Islamic Concept of Human Nature*. London: Ta Ha Publishers, 1996.

Mohler, R. Albert, Jr. ed. *God and the Gay Christian? A Response to Matthew Vines*. Kindle edition. Louisville, KY: SBTS Press, 2014.

Moll, Yasmin. "Islamic Televangelism: Religion, Media, and Visuality in Contemporary Egypt." *Arab Media and Society* 10 (Spring 2010), www.arabmediasociety.com/islamic-televangelism-religion-media-and-visuality-in-contemporary-egypt/.

Movsesian, Mark L. "*Fiqh* and Canons: Reflections on Islamic and Christian Jurisprudence," *Seton Hall Law Review* 40 (2010): 861–888.

Muneer, Imran, Mahin Islam, Murtadha Siddiqui, and Amir Saeed. "[BBUK] EP 39: The Beef with Yaqeen | Daniel Haqiqatjou." Interview by Dilly Hussain. *The Mad Mamluks podcast*. June 29, 2020. www.youtube.com/watch?v=JD5mt90_tyY.

Muneer, Imran, Mahin Islam, Murtadha Siddiqui, and Amir Saeed. "EP 027: The AlMaghrib Origin Story with Irtiza Hasan." *The Mad Mamluks* podcast.

September 11, 2016. https://themadmamluks.com/the-almaghrib-origin-story-irtiza-hasan/.

Muneer, Imran, Mahin Islam, Murtadha Siddiqui, and Amir Saeed. "EP 150: Supercharger Alma Mater with Muhammad AlShareef." *The Mad Mamluks* podcast. May 4, 2019. www.youtube.com/watch?v=mMg_JCaEZpg.

Muneer, Imran, Mahin Islam, Murtadha Siddiqui, and Amir Saeed. "EP 166: Salafis and Ibn Abd Al-Wahhab, Science and Miracles, Yajuj and Majuj." *The Mad Mamluks* podcast. October 4, 2019. https://themadmamluks.com/dryasir qadhi/.

Muneer, Imran, Mahin Islam, Murtadha Siddiqui, and Amir Saeed. "EP 195: The Failure of Establishing the Caliphate with Mazin Abdul Adhim." *The Mad Mamluks* podcast. August 2, 2020. https://themadmamluks.libsyn.com/ep-195-the-failure-of-establishing-the-caliphate-mazin-abdul-adhim.

Muneer, Imran, Mahin Islam, Murtadha Siddiqui, and Amir Saeed. "EP 198: Ali Timimi Freed, Peace with Israel, David Wood Eats Quran, Bilal Abdul Kareem Arrested!" *The Mad Mamluks* podcast. August 19, 2020. www.youtube.com/watch?v=dkdKTM3ffrc.

Murphy, Eamon. *The Making of Terrorism in Pakistan: Historical and Social Roots of Extremism*. New York: Routledge, 2013.

Nasser, Seyyed Hossein. *Traditional Islam in the Modern World*. New York: Kegan Paul International, 1987.

National Commission on Terrorist Attacks upon the United States. "The 9/11 Commission Report," July 22, 2004. www.9-11commission.gov/report/911Report.pdf.

Naylor, Brian. "Radical Islam or Radical Islamism? It Depends Whom You Ask." *NPR News*, June 14, 2016. www.npr.org/2016/06/14/482011041/radical-islam-or-radical-islamism-it-depends-who-you.ask.

Newport, Frank. "Who Are the Evangelicals? Estimates Vary Widely." *Gallup*. June 24, 2005. https://news.gallup.com/poll/17041/who-evangelicals.aspx.

Newport, Frank and Joseph Carroll. "Another Way to Look at Evangelicals in America Today." *Gallup*. December 2, 2005. www.gallup.com/poll/20242/another-look-evangelicals-america-today.aspx.

Nissinen, Martti. *Homoeroticism in the Biblical World: A Historical Perspective*. Translated by Kirsi Stjerna. Minneapolis, MN: Fortress Press, 1998.

Noll, Mark A. *America's God: From Jonathan Edwards to Abraham Lincoln*. New York: Oxford University Press, 2002.

Noll, Mark A. *Between Faith and Criticism: Evangelicals, Scholarship, and the Bible in America*. 2nd ed. Vancouver, BC: Regent College Publishing, 2004.

Noll, Mark A. "Common Sense Traditions and American Evangelical Thought." *American Quarterly* 37, no. 2 (Summer 1985): 216–238.

Noll, Mark A. *In the Beginning Was the Word: The Bible in American Public Life, 1492–1783*. New York: Oxford University Press, 2016.

Noll, Mark A. *The Civil War as a Theological Crisis*. Chapel Hill: University of North Carolina Press, 2006.

Oberman, Heiko. *Forerunners of the Reformation: The Shape of Late Medieval Thought*. Translated by Paul L. Nyhus. Cambridge, UK: James Clarke & Co, 2002.

Okoye, Ify. "Anwar al-Awlaki Jailed," *IfyOkoye.com* (blog). November 8, 2006. https://ifyokoye.com/2006/11/08/anwar-al-awlaki-jailed/.

Okoye, Ify. "Dar us Salaam Salafi? The Goal Is Not Isolation." *IfyOkoye.com* (blog). September 8, 2006. https://ifyokoye.com/2006/09/08/dar-us-salaam-salafi-%E2%80%93-the-goal-is-not-isolation/.

Okoye, Ify. "Pray in Accordance to the Sunnah: Muslim Women Protest against Marginalization." *Muslim Matters*. June 7, 2010. https://muslimmatters.org/2010/06/07/pray-in-accordance-to-the-sunnah-muslim-women-protest-against-marginalization/.

Okoye, Ify. "The Mormoms [sic] Helped Me Become Muslim." *IfyOkoye.com* (blog). June 6, 2009. https://ifyokoye.com/2009/06/06/mormons-witnesses-shahadah-twice-almaghrib/.

Okoye, Ify. "The Penalty Box: Muslim Women's Prayer Spaces." *Muslim Matters*. February 8, 2010. https://web.archive.org/web/20100212124810/https://muslimmatters.org/2010/02/08/the-penalty-box/.

Okoye, Ify. "Update: What's Up with Anwar al-Awlaki?" *IfyOkoye.com* (blog). November 10, 2009. https://ifyokoye.com/2009/11/10/whats-up-with-anwar-al-awlaki/.

Okoye, Ify. "Use Your Mind – You Don't Need a Fatwa for Everything." *IfyOkoye.com* (blog). January 19, 2011. https://ifyokoye.com/2011/01/19/use-your-mind-you-dont-need-a-fatwa-for-everything/.

Okoye, Ify. "Yes, I Am." *IfyOkoye.com* (blog). August 21, 2012. https://ifyokoye.com/2012/08/21/yes-i-am/.

Olidort, Jacob. "In Defense of Tradition: Muḥammad Nāṣir al-Dīn al-Albānī and the Salafi Method." PhD diss., Princeton University, 2015.

Olidort, Jacob. "The Politics of 'Quietist' Salafism." The Brookings Project on US Relations with the Islamic World. Analysis Paper no. 18 (February 2015).

Olsson, Susanne. *Contemporary Puritan Salafism: A Swedish Case Study*. Bristol, CT: Equinox Publishing, 2019.

Pall, Zoltan. *Salafism in Lebanon: Local and Transnational Movements.* Cambridge, UK: Cambridge University Press, 2018.

Patton, Kimberly C. and Benjamin C. Ray, eds. *A Magic Still Dwells: Comparative Religion in the Postmodern Age.* Berkeley: University of California Press, 2000.

Pew Research Center. "America's Changing Religious Landscape." May 12, 2015. www.pewforum.org/wp-content/uploads/sites/7/2015/05/RLS-08-26-full-report.pdf.

Pew Research Center. April 10, 2001. www.pewresearch.org/wp-content/uploads/sites/4/legacy-pdf/15.pdf.

Pew Research Center. "The Diminishing Divide… American Churches, American Politics." June 25, 1996. www.pewresearch.org/wp-content/uploads/sites/4/legacy-pdf/126.pdf.

Pew Research Center. "The Future of World Religions: Population Growth Projections, 2010–2050." April 2, 2015. www.pewforum.org/2015/04/02/religious-projections-2010-2050/.

Pew Research Center. "US Muslims Concerned about Their Place in Society, but Continue to Believe in the American Dream." July 16, 2017. www.pewresearch.org/religion/wp-content/uploads/sites/7/2017/07/U.S.-MUSLIMS-FULL-REPORT-with-population-update-v2.pdf.

Pew Research Center. "US Religious Landscape Survey." June 1, 2008. www.pewresearch.org/wp-content/uploads/sites/7/2008/06/report2-religious-landscape-study-full.pdf.

Pfennig, David and Karin Pfennig. *Evolution's Wedge: Competition and the Origins of Diversity.* Los Angeles: University of California Press, 2012.

Philpott, Daniel. "The Religious Roots of Modern International Relations." *World Politics* 52, no. 2 (Jan, 2000): 206–245.

Poston, Larry. *Islamic Da'wah in the West: Muslim Missionary Activity and the Dynamics of Conversion to Islam.* New York: Oxford University Press, 1992.

Prothero, Stephen. *American Jesus: How the Son of God Became a National Icon.* New York: Farrar, Straus, and Giroux, 2003.

PRRI Staff. "Competing Visions of America: An Evolving Identity or a Culture Under Attack? Findings from the 2021 American Values Survey." *Public Religion Research Institute.* November 2021. www.prri.org/research/competing-visions-of-america-an-evolving-identity-or-a-culture-under-attack/.

Qadhi, Yasir. "On Salafi Islam." *Muslim Matters.* April 22, 2014. http://muslimmatters.org/2014/04/22/on-salafi-islam-dr-yasir-qadhi/.

Qadhi, Yasir. "Rethinking Salafism: Shifting Trends and Changing Typologies Post Arab Spring." Prince Alwaleed bin Talal Center for Muslim-Christian

Understanding. Georgetown University. April 17, 2019. https://youtu.be/ hOTDNkHTEnU.

Qadhi, Yasir. "Salafi-Ashaʿrī Polemics of the 3rd & 4th Islamic Centuries." *The Muslim World* 106 (July 2016): 433–447.

Qadhi, Yasir. "Rethinking Salafism: Shifting Trends and Changing Typologies Post Arab Spring." "Salafism, a Growing Islamic Movement." Panel at American Academy of Religion. San Antonio, TX. November 2016.

Qadhi, Yasir (writing as Yasir Kazi). "Reconciling Reason and Revelation in the Writings of Ibn Taymiyya (d. 728/1328): An Analytical Study of Ibn Taymiyya's *Darʾ al-taʿāruḍ*." PhD diss., Yale University, 2013.

Quisay, Walaa and Thomas Parker. "On the Theology of Obedience: An Analysis of Shaykh Bin Bayyah and Shaykh Hamza Yusuf's Political Thought." *Maydan: Islamic Thought*. January 8, 2019. https://themaydan.com/2019/01/ theology-obedience-analysis-shaykh-bin-bayyah-shaykh-hamza-yusufs-polit ical-thought/.

Rabil, Robert G. *Salafism in Lebanon: From Apoliticism to Transnational Jihadism*. Washington, DC: Georgetown University Press, 2014.

Reid, Thomas. *An Inquiry into the Human Mind on the Principles of Common Sense*. Edinburgh: Anderson, MacDowall, and Robertson, 1818.

Renkema, Jan. *Introduction to Discourse Studies*. Philadelphia, PA: John Benjamins Publishing Company, 2004.

Riesebrodt, Martin. *The Promise of Salvation: A Theory of Religion*. Translated by Steven Rendell. Chicago, IL: University of Chicago Press, 2010.

Riley, Krista Melanie. "'You Don't Need a Fatwa': Muslim Feminist Blogging as Religious Interpretation." PhD diss., Concordia University, 2016.

Robinson, Daniel N. "The Scottish Enlightenment and the American Founding." *The Monist* 90, no. 2 (April 2007): 170–181.

Rock-Singer, Aaron. *In the Shade of the Sunna: Salafi Piety in the Twentieth-Century Middle East*. Oakland: University of California Press, 2022.

Rosenfeld, Sophia. *Common Sense: A Political History*. Cambridge, MA: Harvard University Press, 2011.

Rosenfeld, Sophia. "Tom Paine's Common Sense and Ours." *The William and Mary Quarterly* 65, no. 4 (October 2008): 633–668.

Roy, Olivier. *Globalised Islam: The Search for the New Ummah*. London: Hurst and Company, 2004.

Ryan, Michael W. S. *Decoding Al-Qaeda's Strategy: The Deep Battle against America*. New York: Columbia University Press, 2013.

Saad, Lydia. "Three in Four in US Still See the Bible as Word of God." *Gallup Politics*. June 4, 2014. www.gallup.com/poll/170834/three-four-bible-word-god.aspx.

Schultz, Kevin M. *Tri-faith America: How Catholics and Jews Held Postwar America to Its Protestant Promise*. New York: Oxford University Press, 2011.

Schulze, Reinhard. *A Modern History of the Islamic World*. New York: New York University Press, 2002.

Senate of Canada. "The Standing Committee on National Security and Defence." 41st Parliament 2nd Session. February 2, 2015. https://sencanada.ca/en/Content/Sen/committee/412/secd/51874-e.

Shane, Scott. "Anwar al-Awlaki, Yemen, and American Counterterrorism Policy." Brookings Institution. Washington, DC September 17, 2015. www.brookings .edu/wp-content/uploads/2015/08/20150917_awlaki_yemen_transcript.pdf.

Shane, Scott. *Objective Troy: A Terrorist, a President, and the Rise of the Drone*. New York: Crown Publishing Group, 2015.

Shane, Scott. "The Enduring Influence of Anwar al-Awlaki in the Age of the Islamic State." *Combating Terrorism Center Sentinel* 9, no. 7 (July 2016): 15–19. https://ctc.usma.edu/the-enduring-influence-of-anwar-al-awlaki-in-the-age-of-the-islamic-state/.

Silk, Mark. "Notes on the Judeo-Christian Tradition in America." *American Quarterly* 36, no. 1 (Spring 1984): 65–85.

Sinani, Besnik. "Post-Salafism: Religious Revisionism in Contemporary Saudi Arabia." *Religions* 13 (2022): 340–356.

Smith, Christian. *American Evangelicalism: Embattled and Thriving*. Chicago, IL: University of Chicago Press, 1998.

Smith, Christian. *The Bible Made Impossible: Why Biblicism Is Not a Truly Evangelical Reading of Scripture*. Grand Rapids, MI: Brazos Press, 2011.

Smith, Hannah Whitall. *Every-day Religion, or the Common-sense Teaching of the Bible*. London and Edinburgh: Fleming H. Revell, 1893.

Smith, Hannah Whitall. *The Unselfishness of God: A Spiritual Autobiography*. London and Edinburgh: Fleming H. Revell, 1903.

Smith, Jonathan Z. *Imagining Religion: From Babylon to Jonestown*, Chicago, IL: University of Chicago Press, 1982.

Smith, Wilfred Cantwell. *What Is Scripture? A Comparative Approach*. Minneapolis, MN: Fortress Press, 2005.

Steinfels, Peter. "Ideas and Trends; There's Nothing Monolithic about Evangelical Politics." *New York Times*, March 13, 1988.

Suleiman, Omar. "Faithful Activism: A Sunnah Framework." Yaqeen Institute. October 30, 2020. https://yaqeeninstitute.org/omar-suleiman/faithful-activism-a-sunnah-framework.

Sutton, Matthew Avery. *American Apocalypse: A History of Modern Evangelicalism*. Cambridge, MA: Harvard University Press, 2014.

Tamney, Joseph B. "American Views of Islam, Post 9/11." *Islamic Studies* 43, no. 4 (2004): 599–630.

Taylor, Matthew D. "A Cautionary Tale for Interreligious Studies from Comparative Fundamentalism: Who Is at the Table?" *The Journal of Interreligious Studies* 21 (October 2017). https://irstudies.org/index.php/jirs/article/view/279/259.

Taylor, Paul. "The Military-Civilian Gap: War and Sacrifice in the Post-9/11 Era." Pew Research Center. October 5, 2011. www.pewresearch.org/wp-content/uploads/sites/3/2011/10/veterans-report.pdf.

Thomas, Pradip Ninan and Philip Lee, eds. *Global and Local Televangelism*. New York: Palgrave Macmillan, 2012.

Thurston, Alexander. *Salafism in Nigeria: Islam, Preaching, and Politics*. New York: Cambridge University Press, 2016.

Topolski, Anya. "The Dangerous Discourse of the 'Judaeo-Christian' Myth: Masking the Race-Religion Constellation in Europe." *Patterns of Prejudice* 54, no. 1–2 (2020): 71–90.

Tucker, Glenn. *Dawn of Thunder: The Barbary Wars and the Birth of the US Navy*. [no place]: Bowsprit Books, 2018.

Tyler, Alice Felt. *Freedom's Ferment: Phases of American Social History to 1860*. Minneapolis: University of Minnesota Press, 1944.

US House Permanent Select Committee on Intelligence and US Senate Select Committee on Intelligence. "Report of the Joint Inquiry into the Terrorist Attacks of September 11, 2001." December 2002. www.intelligence.senate.gov/sites/default/files/documents/CRPT-107srpt351-5.pdf.

USC Center for Religion and Civic Culture. "The Varieties of American Evangelicalism." November 1, 2018. https://crcc.usc.edu/report/the-varieties-of-american-evangelicalism.

Varouxakis, Georgios and Mark Philp, eds. *Happiness and Utility: Essays Presented to Frederick Rosen*. London: University College London Press, 2019.

Vines, Matthew. *God and the Gay Christian*. New York: Convergent Books, 2014.

Vogel, Frank. *Islamic Law and Legal System: Studies of Saudi Arabia*. Boston, MA: Brill, 2000.

Voll, John. *Islam: Continuity and Change in the Modern World*. Syracuse, NY: Syracuse University Press, 1994.

Wagemakers, Joas. *Salafism in Jordan: Political Islam in a Quietist Community*. New York: Cambridge University Press, 2016.

Wagemakers, Joas. "Salafism's Historical Continuity: The Reception of 'Modernist' Salafis by 'Purist' Salafis in Jordan." *Journal of Islamic Studies* 30, no. 2 (2019): 205–231.

Webber, Robert E. *Common Roots: The Original Call to an Ancient-Future Faith.* Grand Rapids, MI: Zondervan, 1978.

Wellman Jr., James K., Katie E. Corcoran, and Kate J. Stockly. *High on God: How Megachurches Won the Heart of America.* New York: Oxford University Press, 2020.

Westrop, Sam. "Flexible Salafis: The Growing Political Power of 'Woke,' Modernist Islamism." *Middle East Forum.* May 9, 2020. www.meforum.org/60924/flexible-salafis.

White, James R. *What Every Christian Needs to Know about the Qur'an.* Bloomington, MI: Bethany House, 2013.

White, James R. and Jeffrey D. Niell. *The Same Sex Controversy: Defending and Clarifying the Bible's Message about Homosexuality.* Minneapolis, MN: Bethany House, 2002.

Wiktorowicz, Quintan. "A Genealogy of Radical Islam." *Studies in Conflict & Terrorism* 28 (2005): 75–97.

Wiktorowicz, Quintan. "Anatomy of the Salafi Movement." *Studies in Conflict & Terrorism* 29 (2006): 207–239.

Wiktorowicz, Quintan. *The Management of Islamic Activism: Salafis, the Muslim Brotherhood, and State Power in Jordan.* Albany: State University of New York Press, 2001.

Wilson, Peter H. "The Causes of the Thirty Years War 1618–1648." *The English Historical Review* 123, no. 502 (June 2008): 554–586.

Wolterstorff, Nicholas. *Thomas Reid and the Story of Epistemology.* New York: Cambridge University Press, 2001.

Wood, Graeme. *The Way of the Strangers: Encounters with the Islamic State.* New York: Random House, 2017.

Wood, Graeme. "What ISIS Really Wants." *The Atlantic,* March 2015. www.theatlantic.com/magazine/archive/2015/03/what-isis-really-wants/384980/.

Wright, Robin. *Sacred Rage: The Wrath of Militant Islam.* New York: Simon and Schuster, 2001.

Wuthnow, Robert. *Communities of Discourse: Ideology and Social Structure in the Reformation, the Enlightenment, and European Socialism.* Cambridge, MA: Harvard University Press, 1989.

Index

US House of Representatives, 235, 246
US war in Afghanistan, 130, 169, 173, 246, 256, 257
US war in Iraq, 130, 169, 173, 202, 257
ustadh / ustadha (teacher, professor), 133, 146, 180, 234, 251
Utaybi, Juhayman, 119–120

Valls, Manuel, 154
Vines, Matthew, 228–233, 236, 238, 251, 252, 259
voting, 163, 178, 179, 183, 184

Wahhabi / Wahhabism, 19, 20, 54–58, 59, 61, 62, 64, 71, 114, 117, 120, 147, 158, 255, 263, 279
    and governance in Saudi Arabia, 16, 57, 61, 107, 111, 143, 159
    relationship to Salafism, 4, 62, 111–112
Wahhaj, Siraj, 215
War on Terror, 18, 70, 152, 160, 168, 169, 173, 204, 256, 259
Webb, Suhaib, 215

Wesley, John, 33
Whitall Smith, Hannah, 214, 216
White, James R., 231, 232, 259–264
Whitefield, George, 33, 34
Wiktorowicz, Quintan, 155–156, 158, 186, 187, 272
woke, 246
World Assembly of Muslim Youth, 61
World Muslim League, 61
Wycliffe, John, 31

Yale University, 89, 193, 209, 212, 259
Yaqeen Institute, 244–249, 257
Yasir Qadhi, 2
Young Life, 215
Yusuf, Hamza, 125, 128–131, 135, 139, 140, 142, 143, 147–151, 153, 167, 247, 262, 294

ẓāhir (the literal, plain meaning of a text), 200, 292
Zaytuna College, 130–137, 138, 140, 146, 147–149, 150, 235, 244
Zwingli, Huldrych, 31